10,001
TIME
SAVING
IDEAS

READER'S DIGEST

10,001
TIME
SAVING
IDEAS

10,001 **TIMESAVING** IDEAS

Consultants and Contributors for Australia, New Zealand and South Africa Pamela Allardice, Edwin Barnard, Derek Barton, Georgina Bitcon, Linda Calabresi, Frank Gardner, Pat Kramer, Jennifer Stackhouse

Project Editor Liz Connolly

Senior Editor Samantha Kent

Project Designer Clare Forte

Senior Designer and Cover Design Donna Heldon

Design Concept Sue Rawkins

Publishing Assistant Filomena Pezzimenti

Translator Narelle Fletcher

Picture Researcher Jude Fowler-Smith

Photographer Ian Hoffstetter

Illustrators Jacqueline Caulet, Pierre Corade, Sylvie Guerraz, Christiane Soares

Proofreaders Kevin Diletti, Bronwyn Sweeney

Indexer Diane Harriman

Production Manager General Books Janelle Garside

READER'S DIGEST GENERAL BOOKS

Editorial Director Elaine Russell

Managing Editor Rosemary McDonald

Art Director Carole Orbell

10,001 Timesaving Ideas is published by
Reader's Digest (Australia) Pty Limited
80 Bay Street, Ultimo, NSW 2007
www.readersdigest.com.au; www.readersdigest.co.nz;
www.readersdigeststore.co.za

First published 2008
Copyright © Reader's Digest (Australia) Pty Limited 2008
Copyright © Reader's Digest Association Far East Limited 2008
Philippines Copyright © Reader's Digest Association Far East Limited 2008

This book was adapted from *Trucs et astuces pour gagner du temps* published by Reader's Digest, France, 2005

National Library of Australia Cataloguing-in-publication data:

  10,001 timesaving ideas.
  Includes index.
  ISBN 9781921344152 (hbk.).
  1. Time management. I. Reader's Digest (Australia).
  II. Title.

  640.43

Prepress by Sinnott Bros, Sydney
Printed and bound by CT Printing Limited, China

We are interested in receiving your comments on the content of this book. Write to: The Editor, General Books Editorial, Reader's Digest (Australia) Pty Limited, GPO Box 4353, Sydney, NSW 2001, or email us at bookeditors.au@readersdigest.com.

To order additional copies of *10,001 Timesaving Ideas* please contact us at:
www.readersdigest.com.au or phone 1300 300 030 (Australia),
www.readersdigest.co.nz or phone 0800 400 060 (New Zealand),
www.readersdigeststore.co.za or phone 0800 980 572 (South Africa) or email us at customerservice@readersdigest.com.

About this book

If you've always wondered how other people manage to fit so much into a day when they're juggling family and work commitments, caring for a home and garden, and organising holidays – not to mention staying fit and healthy – you'll find out how in *10,001 Timesaving Ideas*. This book is a one-stop reference for getting things done in the shortest time possible, and saving time with ingenious ideas and speedy solutions.

We all know that clever shortcuts can save hours of time wasted, but sometimes you need to take time to save time, and by this we mean that you'll save time in the long run if a job is done properly in the first place. As with many tasks, this takes a bit of know-how that not all of us have. In *10,001 Timesaving Ideas*, you'll find a wealth of hints and tips that cover both instant time savers and simple how-tos for helping you to save time in the 'stitch-in-time' sense, by avoiding time-wasting complications.

This clear and comprehensive volume shows you how to: renovate in the minimum time, avoiding common pitfalls; how to speed clean your home, both day-to-day and once-a-year spring cleaning; tips and tricks for staying in touch, organising your home office and preparing for retirement; easy ways to save time shopping, cooking and entertaining; and getting your garden looking good without spending hours on back-breaking work using tricky techniques or expensive equipment.

So read on and start enjoying the benefits of time saved on what you have to do, so that you'll have more time to spend doing what you really want to do!

The Editors

Contents

1 Organising your home

2 Family, work and wellbeing

3 Cooking and entertaining

4 Maintaining your home

5 Caring for your garden

1 Organising your home

The kitchen

The ins and outs of practical surfaces

Choosing surfaces that are shock-resistant, easy to maintain and that can withstand heat and moisture is an investment in time saved on cleaning.

▶ Marble and raw timber look beautiful, but they require a lot of time and effort to keep them that way. First decide how much maintenance you're prepared to do in your kitchen before choosing a surface material.

▶ Dark-coloured, glossy surfaces might make a stunning statement, but they're also hard to keep clean, which takes up extra time.

▶ Choose patterned or textured surfaces that reflect fewer spots or streaks.

▶ Splashbacks on the walls are essential for making cooking spills easy to clean up – traditional tiles have been joined by a variety of non-porous materials such as stainless steel, glass, stone and plastic laminate. Make sure the material used behind your stove is non-flammable. If you're planning to use tiles, make the gap between the benchtops and overhead cupboards a multiple of the tile width to save time cutting tiles to fit.

▶ There are two certainties about your benchtop: the first is you can never have too much of it, and the second is it's going to get a lot of wear and tear. Plan to have as much benchtop space as you can, particularly next to the fridge, stove and sink, and choose from natural or engineered stone, sealed timber, stainless steel, glass or laminates. Tiles aren't a great choice on benchtops as they tend to collect food and debris.

▶ There are various types of suitable flooring for kitchens, including tiles, slate, timber, cork and vinyl. Tiles should be non-slip and all floor surfaces should be sealed to cope with the inevitable spills. Softer surfaces such as sealed cork and vinyl are kinder on legs and feet.

Plan the work flow of your kitchen

The 'work triangle' refers to the triangle formed between the fridge, the stove and the sink, and represents the core work area of the kitchen. Here are some tips to help you work more efficiently in high-traffic areas.

▶ Try to design the layout of your kitchen so that traffic doesn't flow through the work triangle, which will decrease efficiency of movement.

▶ In a galley kitchen, allow at least 1200 mm between facing rows of cabinets to allow sufficient room to prepare food (or practise your salsa!).

▶ Leave at least 300 mm either side of the stovetop for hot saucepans to be put down, to minimise unnecessary movement.

▶ Allow 600 mm of benchtop space between the stovetop and the sink.

TIMELY TIP

Spare tiles

Keep extra tiles on hand in case you have to replace some that are damaged. Styles and colours go out of fashion and you can spend weeks chasing tiles that will match.

▶ Allow 600–800 mm in height between an electric stovetop and the exhaust fan above it, and 650–800 mm for gas. (Always check the manufacturer's instructions.)

▶ Locate the dishwasher next to the sink for ease of installation and so that you can pre-rinse dirty plates quickly before stacking them in the dishwasher.

▶ Set the oven at eye level, if at all possible, to save having to constantly bend down, and for safety reasons if you have small children around.

▶ Position a utensil drawer next to the stovetop so that all utensils are always handy.

▶ Make sure you have accessible storage areas built in to your kitchen. Drawers and slide-out units make a great alternative to fixed cupboards, maximising space and access.

▶ Consider installing overhead doors that lift to open cupboards, so that you have easier shelf access than with doors that open outwards.

TIMELY TIP

A point on power

Plan to install twice as many power points as you think you'll ever need – you will use them! Ask the electrician to set the kitchen up on a separate circuit from the rest of the house.

Good lighting for maximum efficiency

▶ Proper ceiling lighting is essential for doing almost any job in the kitchen, and it should be positioned so that it shines on what you are doing rather than on your back.

▶ If it's possible, provide natural light during daylight hours through large windows or skylights, and consider installing extra lights under wall units, over the sink, over the stovetop and over any preparation areas.

▶ Another option is to fit lights inside cupboards, which can be set to go on and off automatically when you open and close the doors.

Get the height right

Having benchtops and cupboards at the right height can mean the difference between working in a comfortable and uncomfortable kitchen. Standard base-unit heights range from 860–940 mm, but a benchtop should be designed for the person who uses the kitchen the most, which is probably not the person who's building it!

A good rule of thumb for working out the correct height is to stand with your arms at your sides and your palms lifted at right angles. This is a good height for the bottom of your sink. Add on the depth of the sink, and you'll have a good working-height measurement. Wall units should be positioned so that the bottom shelf is at, or slightly below, eye level.

TIMELY TIP

Quick access

Wall-mounted aluminium foil, plastic wrap and paper towel holders provide instant access, which saves time spent searching through kitchen drawers. Other handy items to think about having are a utensil caddy, a magnetic knife rack and a mug tree.

Essentials of efficient ventilation

Efficient kitchen design combines heating, light and ventilation into a clear work-flow pattern. Here are some tips for maximum ventilation.

▶ Reduce the amount of time spent keeping your kitchen aired and free of bad smells by installing an effective extraction fan, so that the whole house doesn't become overrun with steam, smoke or smells.

▶ Open windows and doors whenever and wherever possible, for natural ventilation. There are some easy-to-install bifold doors available that open up fully, to quickly and efficiently ventilate your kitchen.

▶ The addition of ceiling fans in an open-plan kitchen helps to disperse odours quickly, and whirlybird extraction systems fitted to the roof can speed up the removal of hot air from the ceiling cavity.

Well-organised storage and work spaces

Consistent use of materials and integrating as many appliances as possible – as well as keeping clutter to a minimum – creates a well-organised kitchen that looks good and feels spacious, without sacrificing function.

▶ Reserve enough benchtop space to lay out cookbooks, ingredients and utensils. Your stove doesn't need to be complex, but it should have adequate bench space on either side of the hotplate, with necessary equipment close to hand.

▶ Extra storage can be made by attaching racks or hanging rails beneath overhead cupboards (e.g. wine glass racks) and inside lower cupboard doors (e.g. a kitchen garbage bin).

Alarms

● **Save time and wastage** Choose those appliances that have built-in warning signals for, say, a power failure; a fridge door left open, causing a rise in temperature; or overloading a washing machine.

● **Save lives** Install smoke alarms, which are a requirement in all residential properties, as per Australian Standards (AS: 3786). However, under current Australian legislation, heat alarms can be used in kitchens as well as other areas where there may be dust, smoke or steam.

Keep a stash handy

Always have a stock of light bulbs for your fridge and oven on hand. They fail at the most inconvenient times.

▶ Conceal everyday appliances in a benchtop appliance cupboard.

▶ Install a shallow drawer for spices. It will keep your benchtop clear and you'll see each bottle at a glance, cutting down on time spent searching.

A hard-working sink

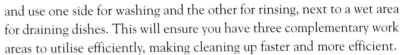

▶ Take advantage of natural light in your kitchen by installing the sink near a window (and enjoy the view while you're working).

▶ Overhead lighting will give you better visibility, too, meaning you'll be washing dishes properly the first time around.

▶ Choose a double-sink model, and use one side for washing and the other for rinsing, next to a wet area for draining dishes. This will ensure you have three complementary work areas to utilise efficiently, making cleaning up faster and more efficient.

▶ Choose a stainless steel sink. They're hygienic and clean up well after just a few wipes with a damp sponge.

▶ Choose a practical, one-touch kitchen tap with good nozzle reach over a deep sink and a wet area for draining. A chopping board that sits over the wet area increases your work space.

▶ Install your dishwasher next to the sink so that dishes can be pre-rinsed quickly, if necessary, before loading into the dishwasher. This will ensure they're washed properly after a shorter, water-saving cycle.

Create a people-friendly kitchen

Avoid spending time in a kitchen that's not connected to the living areas. Try to plan your kitchen so you can maintain contact with your family and friends while you're preparing meals or cleaning up.

▶ One way to achieve this is to include a servery that's open to the dining area. Sliding panels allow you to hide the mess or to see your guests.

▶ A bench with bar stools in your kitchen allows guests to sit and chat with you while you cook. And it also doubles as a convenient breakfast bar for speedy, early-morning departures, or lunch for one, or a place to catch up and enjoy an after-school snack with younger children.

▶ If you have enough space, try to include a small eating area or breakfast nook. This could consist of transformable furniture such as a half-moon table, a folding table attached to the wall or the work surface, and a folding table and chairs, or be as complex as a built-in corner bench and table unit with storage under the seats.

Labour-saving devices

There are many jobs that need doing in the kitchen that you can buy a machine to do for you. This usually results in time saved, but it can also mean more cleaning and storage problems, so choose wisely.

▶ Choose machines where the programs correspond to your needs. It's useless to spend hours learning all the functions in the instruction manual if you are only going to use two or three of them.

▶ Buy appliances you can program to operate while you're away or while you're sleeping. Make sure they are quiet: this means they can run at any time without disturbing other family members or neighbours. So when you're shopping, don't just look at appliances – listen, too.

▶ Check that appliances are easy to clean. Setting up a juicer for a glass of orange juice can mean 15 minutes spent dismantling and washing up a number of components, which isn't time saving at all.

▶ Built-in appliances will be used more often than ones stored at the back of a cupboard. Consider the convenience of cold-water and ice dispensers in refrigerators and benchtop espresso machines, not to mention the everyday must-haves such as dishwashers, fridge-freezers, automatic stove-oven combos, microwave ovens, toasters and kettles.

▶▶ ▶ FIND OUT MORE

• You'll find plenty of amazing design and storage solutions and ideas on the Internet. The web sites listed below include links offering clever storage hints and tips. Ikea and Howards Storage World products are currently not available to customers in New Zealand or South Africa. If you're looking to buy products listed in online catalogues, search the web for design and storage outlets that deliver to your area.
www.ikea.com.au
www.hsw.com.au

Clever kitchen storage

If cupboards and pantries are too deep, you'll waste time looking for things. To maximise time efficiency and accessibility, install a carousel or pull-out shelving. And use drawers rather than cupboards in a small kitchen as they offer a better use of space and save a lot of back strain. The other advantage is that benches can be deeper without sacrificing accessibility. There are hundreds of handy storage solutions available (*see* 'Find out more' at left), but for timesaving efficiency try these:

● Self-closing, full-extension drawers
● Short and tall pull-out pantries
● Pull-out baskets
● Glass-fronted units
● Open shelving
● Hanging rails
● Swing-open rubbish bins on the cupboard door under the sink
● Hideaway chopping boards or those that fit into the sink to increase bench space
● See-through containers

The ideal fridge

Here are some timesaving tips to help you get the most out of your fridge while you also anticipate futuristic advances in its design and function.

▶ Buy a fridge with an adequate capacity and adjustable shelving so that you can organise its contents properly, and clear bench space alongside it.

▶ Choose a fridge-freezer with the freezer section at the bottom of the unit or at the side. This means you won't have to bend over to open the fridge, which is the most frequently used of the two sections.

▶ Choose a model where the air is circulated, or opt for a frost-free fridge, which will guarantee a uniform temperature.

▶ Don't overfill your fridge, as air needs to circulate. Packing the fridge without overfilling also saves time because things are easier to find.

▶ Place paper towels in the bottom of the crisper drawers each week. They make it quicker to clean and they absorb excess moisture.

▶ Many refrigerators have specially designed compartments for fresh produce, cheese or meats. The air circulation and temperature settings have been regulated, and so are perfect for those particular products.

▶ Newer models being developed boast amazing timesaving features: watch out for those that keep track of the contents' inventory and ordering, along with models boasting separate temperature controls for each internal area. There's even one that connects to your computer to automatically place food orders over the Internet.

(*See also* 'The fridge' and 'The freezer', starting on pages 223 and 227.)

An intelligent oven

▶ Install your oven with the grill positioned at eye level so you can frequently check the progress of cooking. The grill pan should have a support and stops to prevent it from being pulled out too far.

▶ Look for a smokeless grill tray that traps fat and grease below it, rather than a wire rack – important for ovens with an internal grill, as spattering and smoking fat can be messy; why create more cleaning?

▶ Choose an oven with a catalytic liner or a pyrolytic cycle. Pyrolysis uses a high heat to incinerate grime, leaving a powdery ash to be wiped up. Catalytic ovens operate on a continuous-clean basis but major spills must be wiped up immediately, before they become baked on.

▶ Consider buying a model that has automatic cooking programs for a variety of food types, ranging from biscuits to roast chicken. You select the type of food and specify the weight, and the oven sets the time, temperature and oven functions needed to cook it.

▶ Light-speed ovens use halogen lamps and claim to cook up to 70 per cent faster than a regular conventional oven.

TIMELY TIP

Self-cleaning ovens

If you have a self-cleaning oven with pyrolysis, or one with a catalytic liner, all you need to do is give it a quick wipe over with a sponge, using a mixture of equal parts white vinegar and water. This will help prevent grease build-up on the inside walls.

TIMELY TIP

You rang?

Most stoves have a built-in timer –
program the timer and you won't
have to keep checking your watch
or looking to see if dinner is cooked.
Some digital timers have a remote
beeper that will alert you up to
30 metres away.

The microwave oven – a champion time saver

There's nothing like a microwave oven for defrosting, reheating and
cooking food in record time. You can reheat or prepare meals in minutes.

▶ Many of the latest appliances on offer
are combination microwave-convection
models, which means that you can both
cook food and brown it on the top, too.

▶ Electronic programming and memory
keys are fairly standard in most models
and save time with meal preparation.

▶ Some have an automatic defrosting

function, which saves time when you're preparing frozen food for cooking.
(*See also* 'Getting the most from your microwave', on page 247.)

Opt for fast conduction

There are three types of stovetop available: gas, electric and induction.

▶ The fastest option is gas, which responds immediately. Using LPG or
natural gas, these stovetops provide you with instant and precise
temperature control. You'll save money on energy bills, too.

▶ Electric stoves are more energy efficient than gas, as no heat is lost
into the air, but they are often slower to respond and harder to control.

▶ Ceramic radiant stovetops provide a smooth, flat surface with electric heating coils under ceramic glass. They heat up quickly and retain
heat after being turned off. Reasonably energy efficient, they incorporate
a heat-warning light, indicating whether the surface is still hot.

▶ Induction stovetops, while not as common, are becoming increasingly
accepted as a useful, energy-efficient way to prepare food. The heating
power is practically instantaneous and because of the way they work,
they don't get as dirty. It's the saucepan itself – not the stovetop – that heats
up and cooks the food, so once the pan is removed from the stove, the
energy transfer stops. And parents won't have to worry about children

▶ CAUTION!

Microwave no-noes

It might seem as though you're saving time by reheating takeaway leftovers
in those aluminium containers, but you're not. Never put metal or aluminium
foil containers in your microwave oven: metallic surfaces cause electric arcs
inside the oven, which can seriously damage the appliance. Instead, scrape
the leftovers into a microwave-safe container before reheating.

touching a hot burner because the stovetop surface remains cool. Changing cooking temperatures is achieved quickly because there's no waiting time for the stovetop to heat up, only the pan.

The indispensable dishwasher

Look for a highly efficient dishwasher so that dishes go straight from the machine into your kitchen cupboards without any fuss.

▶ The majority of energy used in a dishwasher is for water heating, so choose an energy-efficient model and you'll save both energy and water. Check the energy-efficiency rating of various brands before buying a new dishwasher. (*See* 'Compare energy-efficiency ratings', on page 66).

▶ When you buy a new dishwasher, read the manual carefully and visit the company web site to find out how to get the most out of the appliance. This includes researching the most efficient water temperature and cycle for your needs. A shorter cycle might be all that's needed.

▶ Let the dishwasher finish its cycle, because drying by condensation prevents the water from becoming stagnant (e.g. on the stems of glasses).

▶ If you can set the water temperature on your dishwasher don't make it too high, as very hot water makes crystal become opaque over time.

The bathroom

Easy-to-clean from floor to ceiling

▶ For bathroom walls, choose tiles that are shock- and humidity-resistant, and that can be cleaned quickly and easily.

▶ Ensure the area to be tiled has been waterproofed to meet national standards, and that the tiles go high enough to offer proper protection against water – 1.8 metres is recommended near the shower, although the current trend is floor-to-ceiling tiling.

▶ For the ceiling and the upper part of the walls, choose acrylic paint that is suitable for wet areas so it can be wiped clean in a flash.

▶ When choosing flooring, opt for materials that are non-slip and suitable for wet areas. Look for tiles with an R12 slip resistance. (The 'R' scale is used to classify slipperyness, where R9 is the most slippery and R13 is the least slippery.)

Keep it fresh and dry

Without adequate ventilation, a bathroom becomes, smelly, mouldy and unhygienic, requiring constant maintenance to keep it clean.

▶ Good airflow and efficient extraction of steam are the key to keeping your bathroom fresh and reducing the time spent cleaning.

▶ Ideally, bathrooms should have a large (opaque, if necessary) opening window, though an alternative is a louvred window with panels that open separately. This allows the top panels to be opened to release steam while the lower ones remain closed for privacy.

▶ If you have only a small window in your bathroom, or none at all, consider installing an opening skylight for both light and ventilation.

▶ An electric exhaust fan ducted to an external vent can be mounted in either the ceiling or on the wall. Three-in-one units incorporate an exhaust fan, heater and light as a single unit, which saves on space and installation costs, and also saves on cleaning time.

Bath basics

▶ If you can, choose a bath that's big enough for you to stretch out in. There are some available with arm and head rests, and even with small side shelves where you can place everything you need.

▶ For safety reasons, think about installing side handles that allow you to get into and out of the bath easily. You should also ensure that

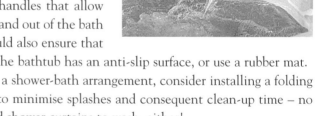

the bottom of the bathtub has an anti-slip surface, or use a rubber mat.

▶ If you have a shower-bath arrangement, consider installing a folding shower screen to minimise splashes and consequent clean-up time – no mouldy-rimmed shower curtains to wash, either!

▶ Consider a spa bath – an affordable option for soothing away the stresses of the day at any time, without having to leave your home.

TIMELY TIP

Heated towel rails

Apart from a pleasant ambient warmth, towel-drying rails offer warm towels on demand. No more humid, semi-dry bath towels that smell unpleasant and need to be washed more often.

TIMELY TIP

Mould-free grout

If bathroom tiles are sealed with mould-resistant grout they'll stay clean, as long as you don't use ammonia-based products such as bleach. Clean occasionally with just warm water with a little white vinegar added.

Multi-service taps

▶ Choose mixer taps that can be operated with the touch of one hand. They offer water at the preselected temperature… and make sure it stays there! Some water-saving taps have been designed to delay the supply of water until it has reached the desired temperature.

▶ Attach an adjustable hand-held shower nozzle on the bath spout, for washing hair (great for washing children's hair) and quick rinsing.

▶ For shower-baths, select a single mixer tap with a dual function that can direct water to either the shower or the bath at the flick of a button.

▶ For the shower, choose a multi-function column fitted with a high, adjustable shower rose for shampooing and a hand-held shower attachment with jets of varying intensities.

▶ Install water-saving shower heads and flow-control nozzles in taps.

▶ Taps that turn off automatically are a great choice if you have children.

▶ Help to save time (and water) by installing a timer in the shower, which will deter all those family members that may feel tempted to break into an aria! It will save you money, too.

TIMELY TIP

Check the shape

Corner baths are great for filling a small space, but can be more awkward to clean than rectangular ones, as you may have to climb into the bath itself to reach the back ledges.

A place for everything

Organise your bathroom storage so that there's room for all the items you need for bathing and grooming, and you'll instantly save time.

▶ Opt for a vanity unit with plenty of drawers and cupboard space or shelving to store towels, soaps, toothpaste and other toiletries.

▶ Install a shallow, mirrored cupboard on the wall for additional storage so that you're not taking up unnecessary space in the vanity unit.

▶ Position towel rails and hooks close to the shower cubicle, the bathtub and hand basins for easy access.

▶ Consider installing a modular shower unit, many of which have moulded shelving to keep everyday items close at hand.

▶ Hang a shower caddy over the shower head. Some come with refillable pumps for shower gel, shampoo and conditioner, a shelf for soap and shavers, as well as hanging rails and hooks for face washers and loofahs.

▶ Make use of the space over the toilet cistern by installing narrow shelving or a shallow, lock-up cabinet for medicines.

TIMELY TIP

Put an end to queuing

Choose a unit with a double basin rather than one large one. This allows two people to use it at the same time, saving time when you're in a hurry.

Lighten things up

▶ Wherever possible, make sure you have a good supply of natural light coming into your bathroom, via opaque windows, glass bricks or skylights.

▶ Position the switch that operates general lighting near the entrance to the bathroom, for easy access. Light the room using a central light or low-voltage halogen lights installed in the ceiling.

▶ Choose other sources of light to specifically illuminate storage units and the mirror above the basin – where you need clear, strong light for shaving, styling hair or applying make-up. Install a large, luminous strip above the mirror, encased in a bulkhead or framed with symmetrical strips or wall lights to avoid any areas of shadow.

▶ Buy a mirror surrounded by small bulbs, reminiscent of the mirrors in actors' dressing rooms, so that you can get ready quickly and efficiently.

Mirror, mirror on the wall

Mirrors increase the amount of light in a room and give the impression of space.

▶ Two mirrors positioned opposite each other create the illusion of an endless room, and allow you to see yourself from the side and the back.

▶ Consider attaching an illuminated enlarging mirror to the wall to make close-up jobs such as make-up application much easier.

▶ A mirrored shaving cabinet is perfect for storing medicines and keeping toiletries handy.

Clever bathroom accessories

Making wise choices when it comes to the appliances and devices you use several times a day means you'll save time on cleaning and tidying.

● Keep your hair dryer somewhere handy ready for use, rather than storing it in a cupboard where it can take time to find.

● A wall-mounted dispenser for cotton buds and make-up remover pads is more quickly accessed than one stored in a drawer and it frees up cupboard storage space for larger items.

● A laundry basket with a tilting lid, or a basket on wheels, is a smarter timesaving choice than one with a cover, which encourages dampness.

● Choose a liquid soap dispenser over a cake of soap, which is messier.

● Talking scales, which immediately tell you your weight, are better than those where you spend ages peering down, trying to read the numbers.

The bedrooms

Get off to a good start

A bed isn't just a piece of bedroom furniture: a good night's sleep ensures that you're ready to go from the moment you wake up, so choose wisely.

▶ Only research good-quality bedding before you buy, and just accept that you'll have to change it after about 10 years.

▶ Buy a thick mattress that has a high density of foam, latex or springs, because it will provide you with the required level of comfort and support. You can also buy mattress pads that add a layer of thickness.

▶ Use a fitted sheet and a Doona (duvet) on your bed, without a flat top sheet, so that you only need to take a few seconds to make your bed in the morning, and washing will be kept to a minimum each week.

Wardrobe basics

▶ A walk-in wardrobe and dressing room, with everything on display and a full-length mirror, is the ideal timesaving solution for busy people.

▶ A built-in wardrobe system organises everything for easy access, and there are some great DIY solutions available that are quick and easy to install (go online and look at ikea.com.au). Use mirrored doors to give an illusion of space and an instant reflection of your style.

▶ Store items that are only used occasionally (blankets, suitcases, travel bags, etc.) on the upper shelves, leaving room for the clothing and accessories you use regularly within easy reach.

▶ Personalise wardrobe storage with hanging space that is adjustable vertically and horizontally, with numerous movable sliding baskets or drawers. This will organise the storage of your clothes to suit your needs.

TIMELY TIP

Mattress basics

Choose a bed base that's suited to your mattress so that the mattress doesn't become worn faster than it should. For example, an innerspring mattress should be matched with an innerspring base, whereas a foam or latex mattress should be used with a slat bed. Choose slats that are close together (offering better support), and a lined surface to prevent the mattress from slipping, which will ensure comfort and stability.

TIMELY TIP

Spotlight on clothes

To avoid wasting time searching for clothes first thing in the morning or late at night, think about installing low-voltage lights in the top of your wardrobe.

▶ Group like items together to avoid wasting time searching through your entire wardrobe to find a particular piece of clothing. And rearrange your wardrobe twice a year, packing away out-of-season clothes until needed.

▶ Use a shoe rack for quick-and-easy matching up of pairs.

▶ De-clutter regularly to avoid overcrowding – it'll limit choices and make decision making faster.

▶ A valet chair is a great way to neatly store clothes that you need instant access to the next day, such as coats, ties, belts and shoes.

Measure it up!

● Wardrobe hanging space for storing trousers, men's suits, and women's suits and dresses should ideally measure between 550–600 mm in depth.

● The hanging space for storing jackets, waistcoats, shirts and blouses should be 950 mm high.

● Wardrobe shelving should be 350 mm wide and drawers should be around 120 mm high.

Keeping everything together

▶ A chest of drawers with two or three rows of drawers allows you to store a whole range of items that would be hard to find in a larger storage area. Use smaller drawers to store jewellery, either in small boxes or a larger case, and clothing that will not crease, such as underwear, socks and scarves. Invest in drawer dividers to organise within each drawer.

▶ Consider storing smallish items in a larger area using see-through storage containers so that you can identify the contents at a glance.

▶ Choose a bedside table fitted with one or more drawers and keep one on each side of the bed. Use them to hold everything from books, magazines and reading glasses to medication, tissues, a clock and earplugs.

▶ If you don't have a dedicated linen cupboard and space in your clothes cupboard is tight, think about utilising under-bed pull-out drawers on castors. For this to work, you'll need to first find out if there's enough clearance for them to fit between your bed base and the floor.

CAUTION!

Fire hazard

Avoid placing any bedside light – either traditional or halogen – next to anything covered in netting, to prevent accidental fire. Halogen lighting in particular generates very intense heat, so be wary of touching metal light fittings with halogen bulbs in them, as it could result in serious burns. For that reason, don't install halogen bedside lights in children's rooms.

TIMELY TIP

Train them early

Encourage children, no matter how young, to tidy their own rooms before you vacuum or clean, so that you don't spend needless time putting things back where they belong before you start cleaning.

Smart lighting in the bedroom

▶ Install a general light switch at the entrance to your bedroom so you can find your way around as soon as you are in the doorway.

▶ If you like to read in bed, choose bedside lighting that's high enough to project a direct light on the reading area, in addition to ceiling spotlights or wall lighting with dimmer switches that create a soft, relaxing atmosphere.

Easy-to-clean children's rooms

▶ Make sure that the walls in children's rooms are washable, regardless of whether they are painted or wallpapered, so that any marks can be wiped off easily in the wink of an eye.

▶ Paint one wall with magnetic blackboard paint, or attach a white board to one wall and keep a box of magnetised letters and numbers or felt pens handy, so that budding artists are free to express themselves without ruining the walls. Don't offer chalk – it creates more mess.

▶ Opt for timber flooring with colourful synthetic rugs, or consider putting down tiles (synthetic carpet or vinyl), which can be replaced easily if one of the tiles gets damaged or stained.

▶ Make life easier for everyone by choosing furniture that can be wiped down or is covered with machine-washable fabric.

Handy storage container
Reuse an old baby wipes container for storing little bits and pieces that children love to play with, but that often end up lost under the bed or in the car. It may save you having to dismantle the vacuum cleaner if a tiny toy or game piece gets stuck.

Great storage ideas for kids

▶ Unless you want to redecorate from time to time, design children's rooms so that they evolve as the children get older.

▶ Children's storage requirements change over time, so install wardrobes where the hanging space can be extended and shelves where they can be easily moved.

▶ Invest in some stackable boxes that can be stored one on top of the other, or baskets on shelves, so children can put their own belongings away.

▶ Place a fabric shoe holder with several pockets on the inside of cupboard doors, for storing all sorts of different items such as combs, elastics, hair clips, sunglasses, belts and ribbons.

▶ Provide plenty of hooks at a suitable height for hanging hats, coats and bags. Look for painted ones to suit the child's age.

▶ Toy boxes can be padded to double as seats or bedside tables, and soft toys can be stored in hanging baskets attached to walls with suction cups.

▶ Be inventive with storage. For instance, a dirty linen basket hanging on the back of a bedroom door beneath a basketball hoop might have a greater chance of being filled than one on the floor. (And you'll save time on wash days searching for dirty clothes strewn around the room.)

Quick-and-easy bedding solutions

▶ If two of your children sleep in a small room, or if they often have friends sleeping over, opt for double bunks to save space or trundle beds mounted on wheels, so that they can be quickly pulled out and put away.

▶ A sleeping bag, which is quicker than making up a bed, is another great solution for kids sleeping over.

▶ If there's enough room, keep a sofa bed, futon or a daybed in children's bedrooms, so that it can double as seating when not in use. Store the linen for that bed in the same room so that you can make it up in a flash.

▶ Folding beds are quick and easy to use, and you can save time by leaving the sheets in place. They're very handy for occasional use and don't take up a lot of space, but if enclosed storage for larger items is a problem in your home, then it may not be a practical solution for you.

▶ Buy a self-inflating mattress, which can be easily deflated and packed away to store.

The dining room

Protect your dining room table

▶ If it's possible, store all your table linen in the dining room itself. Store individual tablecloths together with their matching serviettes, to avoid wasting time searching frantically for matching sets a few minutes before you sit down to the table.

▶ Save time on washing and ironing by buying polyester tablecloths.

▶ Use good-quality paper serviettes to match the table setting, instead of linen or fabric ones. Some of them are incredibly strong and look almost as good as their woven equivalents.

▶ If you have young children, the best solution is to use plastic-coated tablecloths. Water collects on them in droplets and they can be easily cleaned with a quick wipe over using a sponge.

▶ The quickest and easiest way to set a table is by using placemats. These are available in a variety of colours and styles, from wipe-over plastic to bamboo and high-quality linen.

Handy stand-by furniture

▶ So as not to clutter your dining room unnecessarily, choose a table with several extensions, which will allow you to adapt the size to your needs at the time. Some extensions fold in under the table itself, which means you don't need to find a place to store the spare leaf.

▶ Choose chairs that are easy to maintain (no regular oiling required or meticulous dusting, as is the case with some cane and wickerwork seating), or cover them with machine-washable covers or drop-in seats.

▶ Consider using a service trolley, to limit trips to and from the kitchen. After a meal you simply load it up and cart the dirty dishes back to the kitchen in one go.

▶ Keep a few folding tables and chairs handy if you have storage space. They're perfect for those times when you have a few more guests to seat for dinner than chairs at the table.

Quick service

If your dining room shares a wall with the kitchen, consider installing a servery. It allows you to keep in contact with dinner guests and speeds up the business of serving and clearing away crockery.

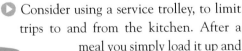

TIMELY TIP

SWAP 'n' GO

Many petrol stations and some other outlets in Australia have a system in place called SWAP 'n' GO, where you can swap your empty barbecue gas bottle for a full one without waiting. The easiest way to find the nearest outlet to you is by typing 'swap n go' into your computer's search engine.

A place for everything

▶ If the size of your dining room allows, choose a buffet or a dresser with adjustable shelves. Depending on its size, it can hold most of your crockery or can be kept for one particular set of crockery and cutlery.

▶ Stack different-sized plates together so that you can reach them easily. And store table accessories that don't go in the dishwasher – salt-and-pepper shakers, placemats or coasters, knife rests, serviette rings, dish warmers or champagne buckets – in a dining room dresser, too.

▶ Consider a wine storage refrigerator or bar fridge for convenience.

Barbecue bistro

Long summer days are perfect for firing up the barbecue and dining outdoors. Follow these simple tips and you'll spend more time enjoying al fresco dining than you will cleaning your indoor kitchen.

● Choose from the huge range of hooded barbecues and outdoor kitchens available that allow for gourmet cooking – beyond sausages – with a minimum of work. You'll save time on cleaning, too.

● Buy a barbecue with a closed-in storage area underneath so all the necessary equipment and tools are always close to hand. And make sure you always have a full spare gas bottle handy.

● Choose an outdoor table setting that is low maintenance and weather resistant so that you don't spend a lot of time looking after it.

● Install a sink in the benchtop alongside the barbecue, to make cleaning up quicker and easier.

The living room

Sofas, armchairs and seating

Chances are, the type of seating you choose for your home will depend largely on your needs, and not just because of efficient use of space.

▶ If possible, choose furniture with removable covers that are machine washable, and make sure you dry washed covers in the shade.

▶ Protect soft furnishings with throws or covers that can be removed easily, especially if you share your home with small children or pets.

▶ Many manufacturers offer fabric protection such as Scotchguarding, but you'll need to have it redone each time furniture is professionally cleaned. Or, buy a can of Scotchguard and do it yourself.

▶ If you buy a leather sofa and armchairs, they can be wiped down and only need to be treated from time to time to keep them in top condition. Only use cleaning products recommended by the manufacturer.

Dust-free displays and accessible books

▶ Choose adjustable cabinets that can be adapted as necessary. This means you can have a display cabinet for trinkets; change the shelves to suit the size of your books; store your files, photo albums, cassettes, CDs and DVDs; and, if required, install a sound system or television. Add doors and the whole unit can be hidden away when not in use.

▶ Install glass doors on display cabinets to avoid dust collecting and include in-cabinet lighting to show off your treasures.

▶ If your living room has an unusual shape, think about having a bookcase made to measure, which can then be adapted to the slope of the ceiling or designed to serve as a divider.

▶ Browsing in a bookshop is a great way to spend time, but at home you're less likely to be in browsing mode. Save on time spent searching for a particular book by having a logical storing system for your books: according to theme, author, publisher or by collection.

TIMELY TIP

Double-up on books
If you're short on space but have a passion for books, think about installing a sliding bookcase, which offers double storage space along the length of a wall.

TIMELY TIP

More than a bar

If you have a small bar in the living area, include a fridge, a sink and power points. Add tea- and coffee-making facilities and you can cater for everything from tea breaks to supper.

At-home entertainment

▶ Choose an integrated home entertainment system that includes television, DVD player/recorder (and VCR if you still use one), and a sound system.

▶ Look for a digital programmable system that will record your favourite show while you watch another or are away, and reminds you when your favourite show is about to start on another channel (most pay-TV companies offer this function).

▶ Think about investing in a DVD recorder that has a hard drive, which can record and store hundreds of television programs without the need for discs, making stored programs available at the click of a button.

▶ Instead of wasting time looking for one remote control among many, incorporate them all into one universal remote.

▶ Having your own home theatre gives you that big-screen experience instantly, without having to travel to your local cinema.

The office

Computer comfort

Having ergonomic furniture is important in work places to prevent time lost as a result of repetitive strain injury and associated health problems.

▶ Choose a comfortable desk seat, with adjustable height and that has been fitted with armrests to release the muscle tension in your arms. Work with your back pressed up against the back of the chair and ensure that your elbows and knees are at right angles.

▶ Position the top of the computer screen at eye level, around 50 cm from your face, and if it's a flat screen, tilt it slightly backwards.

▶ Adjust the height of your keyboard to ensure it is a direct extension of your hands and wrists. When you type, make sure your forearms form a right angle with your upper arms and place the mouse as close as possible to the keyboard.

▶ Use a wrist rest for support, if necessary.

Professional storage

If you don't have adequate
storage space in your office and
the volume of records just keeps
on growing, opt for one of these
space-saving solutions:

● A tall filing cabinet with
multiple drawers positioned
one on top of the other

● A small, two-drawer filing
cabinet on castors, that can
be stowed under a desk

● A trolley on wheels, which
has been specially designed for
keeping hanging files together

Effective filing

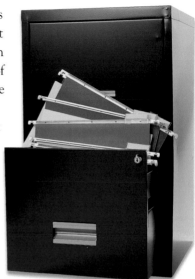

▶ Use an office chair with wheels
so that a simple push in the right
direction will move you quickly in
front of the filing cabinet or row of
shelves where your archives, reference
books, binders and files are stored.

▶ Use a multi-drawer filing cabinet
and allocate each drawer to a
different collection of files rather
than filing everything alphabetically (e.g. household bills,
investments, tax and work).

▶ Choose different-coloured
files, with each one corresponding
to a theme, in order to identify the
file you need as quickly as possible.

▶ Label each file specifically so that they are easily identifiable.

▶ Organise files in chronological order so you can find them in a flash.
(*See also* 'Papers, bills and documents', starting on page 176.)

Keep abreast of everything

▶ Note your appointments as you make them, in a
diary next to the telephone. If necessary, transfer
them immediately to your personal diary or a wall
planner containing your complete schedule.

▶ If you prefer a more mobile solution, buy yourself
a personal organiser, either electronic or paper, to
manage your schedule and your address book.

▶ Choose a multifunction printer, copier and fax
with memory and photo printing capabilities.

▶ Keep a supply of correct paper and ink cartridges handy for refilling.

The entrance area

Neat storage for outdoor gear

▶ A traditional hallstand is ideal for keeping hats, umbrellas and visitors' coats near the front door, which saves you hunting for them before you head out the door. Many hallstands have a small mirror on them so you can quickly check for 'hat hair', too.

▶ A lift-up bench doubles as storage and a seat for removal of shoes.

▶ If you live in a flat or unit and space is at a premium, the easiest solution might be to attach a line of hooks – one for each family member – on the wall leading up to the door, for immediately accessible storage.

▶ If your entrance area is relatively small, opt for a traditional coat rack or a hatstand with multiple heads, such as those found in cafes and restaurants. They're usually strong enough to hold a few coats.

Phone messages and mail

Dispense with the business side of coming home first up and then you can move on to relaxing in the living or family room.

▶ You'll save time the minute you come in the front door if your keys, the mail you've just brought in and the telephone answering machine are all kept in the same spot, such as a hall table.

▶ Think about rigging up some sort of mail holder near your front door so that you won't forget to post urgent letters, and where you can store mail as you come in the door. That way, bills and important letters don't get lost in your bag or stuck under a pile of clutter on the kitchen or dining room table.

▶ Keep all your regular phone numbers in a Rolodex, an index file or a separate book in alphabetical order, on a hallstand or hall table so you can access them quickly. Keep the index, your phone books and a pen and paper beside the telephone to record phone messages.

▶ Put your phone near the front entrance and connect an answering machine so you can check your messages as you come in. An answering machine allows you to screen calls while you're home, or have callers leave messages while you're out and about or on holidays.

If your home is large or more than two stories high, consider installing a phone system with multiple handsets and an intercom, so you have instant access to the telephone from all over the house.

Make your front door secure

▶ Choose a front door made of solid, weatherproof materials.

▶ If you have glass panelling, consider security grates or a security screen door for peace of mind.

▶ Install a peephole as a quick-and-easy way to identify callers (and encourage children to use it before opening the door).

▶ Minimise cleaning time by providing mats and installing weather strips, which will reduce the amount of dirt and plant matter that blows under the door and into the entrance.

▶ Keyless entry systems save the time spent searching for keys (*see* 'Find out more', below), as well as providing a much higher level of security for you and your family.

▶ Alarm master key pads and automatic garage opening controls should be located just inside the front door for easy access. Many automatic garages have remote controls (*see* 'Home automation', starting on page 35).

(*see* 'Home automation', starting on page 35)

TIMELY TIP

Anticipate short circuits

The electricity meter is often near the front of the house, which is where you'll be heading if you have tripped a circuit-breaker, leaving you suddenly in the dark. Store a torch right next to or nearby the meter so you'll be able to restore the current as quickly as possible.

▶▶ **FIND OUT MORE**

• Identify callers before answering your front door by installing an intercom. Some come with a video camera, so you can decide if you are going to be at home or not, while others allow you to unlock the door remotely. The Valet web site, below, showcases a number of time-efficient solutions, from video intercoms and security systems to ducted vacuum systems and intercom and music systems.
www.valet.com.au
• Check the web site below for examples of keyless entry systems.
www.lockweb.com.au/nexion, www.clipsal.co.za

Using the roof space

TIMELY TIP

Quick access

If you plan to use your attic space frequently, a staircase will need to be installed. However, a quick solution is a pull-down or foldaway attic ladder if the area is used mainly for storage. These come in a variety of sizes and styles, and for rooms that are not used often or if space for a staircase is limited, they are the best solution. (Remember that they will limit the size of objects and furniture you'll be able to move into the attic.)

Creating an attic

Wasted space under the roof can be converted to an attic and used for storage or as an extra living area, depending on how much room you have.
▶ Use your attic space to store items that are seldom used, and free up your more immediate storage space in other parts of the house.
▶ Before deciding to create an attic you'll need to work out the floor–space ratio to see that it conforms to council regulations and that the house footings are strong enough to carry the extra weight. Consult your relevant building code for compliance figures before starting out.

Letting in the light

If you're using your attic for basic storage you may not need to install windows in the roof, but adequate ventilation and lighting is essential.
▶ Consider installing a whirlybird system in the roof and have an electrician put in light fittings that are adequate for the space.
▶ Dormer windows are usually framed into a steep-sloping roof.
▶ Install roof windows that can be mounted low for a view, opened for ventilation, or tinted or double-glazed to help with temperature control.
▶ A handy alternative is to install a skylight in a pitched roof to allow natural light to diffuse through the room.

Timesaving checklist

Don't even waste time thinking about attic storage solutions unless you can tick all of the following points. You will need:

● About 2.4 m of height over 60 per cent of the floor space for a habitable room (check your local council requirements first)

● A roof with at least a 30-degree pitch (most old terraced houses have a 30–35-degree pitch)

● Room for stairs. The higher the ceiling, the more steps you'll need to access attic storage

Use all your available space

The key to maximising roof space is to use built-in joinery at the edges, where headspace is lacking.

▶ There are many storage options available, such as lift-up, slide-out and up-the-wall built-in storage units.

▶ You can make use of awkward corners or areas where access is diminished, and where the rafters meet the floor, simply by installing a triangular storage compartment with lift-up doors or angled shelves on castors that roll away under the eaves when not in use.

▶ Open shelves allow you to see everything at a glance in a limited space, and can be stepped to follow the line of the roof.

▶ Another great time saver is to have a collection of clear storage boxes on castors so that the contents can be clearly seen. And they usually stack easily, thereby maximising a small space.

Home automation

The ultimate luxury

By making your home 'smart' you'll save both time and energy.

▶ Computerisation removes the need to actually flick a switch or turn a knob to make something work, and allows elements of your home to be controlled remotely, or to respond automatically, at your command. You don't even have to be at home – your house can be programmed to meet your needs via remote control to be ready for your arrival.

▶ When you retire at night, you can automate your system to allow your bedroom and ensuite lights to remain on long enough for you to prepare for bed, while the house automatically begins to shut down, ready for the night. This means you don't have to check the lights around the house to make sure they have all been turned off.

▶ Consider the convenience of an integrated system, such as those available from www.beconnected.com.au. As you approach home you

TIMELY TIP

Intercom convenience

An intercom at your gate or front door saves time and adds security. Choose one with a camera and connect it to your security system so doors can be locked or unlocked remotely.

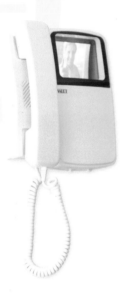

simply press your remote key-chain button to open the garage door; your smart home then starts to make decisions. Firstly, it turns the security alarm off and activates the 'welcome home mode'. The system adjusts room lighting automatically, blinds and louvres may open (depending on the time of day or night) and airconditioning turns on automatically.

▶ Save time by choosing appliances that can be pre-programmed to be ready when you get up in the morning. From the automatic clock radio that wakes you to blinds and electric window shutters that open at a set time, and from airconditioners or heaters that control the desired room temperature to ready-made coffee in your automatic drip-filter coffee machine and freshly made bread in your automatic bread maker. The list of gadgets and options is becoming longer every year!

TIMELY TIP

Keeping it alive

One of the most basic and timesaving ways to automate your home is to install an automatic watering system. Drip irrigation units comply with current water restrictions, and you can safely go on holidays knowing that your garden will still flourish without you having to lift a finger.

▶▶ HOME AUTOMATION SERVICES

- **A touchpad that operates with a digital code**, or a key on the gate and the garage door, will enable you to open the garage even if you've lost your remote control. But if you have an e-key, then lost keys, cards and forgotten codes will become a distant memory. An Australian company called iQhome offers top-quality home automation services, including wireless lighting control and e-keys, to Australian consumers. Check the web site, below, for a variety of services on offer, or search the Internet for services in your area. www.iqhome.com.au
- **External blinds and shutters** can be opened automatically, and the simplest solution is to buy motorised units. You can convert pre-existing units to automatic without having to change them, by linking them to a remote control or an integrated automated system. Smarthome are a US-based company, but ship to anywhere in the world. Check out the selection of automated blinds and shutters on the Smarthome web site – an electronic home-improvement and automation superstore – below. www.smarthome.com
- **A complete louvre roofing system**, such as Vergola, can be adjusted to let the light in, keep the sun out or protect outdoor entertaining areas from rain with the flick of a switch. Rain sensors close a Vergola automatically during wet weather. The web site, below left, explains all the ins and outs of Vergola louvre roofing systems. Check the New Zealand web site, below right, for Vergola agents in New Zealand. www.vergolawa.com.au, www.vergola.com/contact_newzealand.htm

Let automation do the work for you

▶ Why disturb a good night's sleep to check out every noise made by a stray cat? Install external lights with sensors that will automatically turn on, scaring off whatever woke you up in the first place, and without the need for you to be falling over a skateboard or bike left in the way.

▶ When you leave your house, a smart home can shut itself down. Lighting turns off throughout the house; airconditioning systems shut down, saving you time and energy costs; and louvres and blinds (if fitted) close without you having to do it manually.

▶ While you're away on holiday, an automated home system can turn your lighting and watering systems on and off as necessary, and open and close automatic blinds and shutters, thereby giving your empty home that lived-in appearance. It's a good way to fool any would-be intruders into thinking someone is home.

Self management

A self-managing blind is fitted with a wind detector and will retract automatically, which means it won't be ripped or damaged. And to keep the inside of your home cool, there's nothing better than an automatic sun detector, which lowers the blind automatically.

Sensitive lighting indoors

If a fully integrated automated system is not feasible for you, try these tips.

▶ For transit areas such as the hallway and stairs, there are two main solutions: the two-way switch and a timer. A two-way switch allows you to control the lighting from two different places, but installing a timer is even better, as lights are turned off automatically.

▶ Install movement detectors so that you no longer have to worry about finding light switches in the dark. The lights turn on when you go into a room and turn off a few seconds later, when you go out.

▶ To control the lights in all the internal rooms in your house, the best solution is centralised lighting. You control all the lights from one location, using either a remote, a touchpad or a touch screen. As you leave the house, you can turn off any lights you choose, and when you come back, you can turn the lights on in one or two rooms at will.

Three smart solutions for outdoor lighting

If you live in a poorly lit area and have to negotiate outdoor steps or a perilous garden setting in the dark before you get to your front door, it can become a dangerous journey. Luckily, there are a number of quick and easy-to-use lighting solutions available to you.

● Regular lighting around garden paths, a pool or a terrace, along with decorative lighting effects, can be activated by remote control or set to a timer so that specified areas are well-lit when required

● Sensors can be installed to turn lights on and off as you pass by them, so you won't have to fumble for a light switch in the dark

● Solar lights save considerable amounts of energy and activate automatically at dusk, then turn off again at dawn

Fast heating options

▶ Dual-cycle airconditioning provides all the advantages of gas central heating, along with the luxury of ducted split-refrigerated cooling. It is made up of three main components – the indoor gas central-heating unit, the cooling and outdoor condensing unit, and a centrally located thermostat that controls the entire system with the flick of a switch. The system will heat or cool your home to your ideal temperature year round.

▶ For the ultimate in winter comfort, fully ducted gas central heating is the perfect solution. This flexible system enables you to heat your entire house or just selected areas, depending on your needs. You have control over the heat distribution, temperature and timing with this option and, as a bonus, you might save some money on energy bills.

▶ Stay warm underfoot in winter with slab heating, which is an electric heating option whereby a central heating system heats a concrete slab floor using electric cables embedded in the floor. It's great for tiled areas of the house that take a long time to heat up using regular heaters.

▶ For a quick warm-up, install heat pads under carpeting (great for the spot your feet land on when you get out of bed!), or use portable heat mats near chairs to warm your feet.

Control from your phone

TIMELY TIP
All the automatic systems you have fitted in your house will be even more effective as a means of saving time if you can manage them from work, while you're shopping or from your car on return from a weekend away. Some automated home security systems and equipment can be controlled remotely by landline or mobile phone using a telephone interface system, either by SMS, numeric keypad controls or voice commands.

Clearing out clutter

Get into the de-cluttering habit

Constantly negotiating the clutter in your home wastes an enormous amount of time, so make time to de-clutter and enjoy the many benefits.

▶ De-cluttering allows you to make space for the things that you do need to keep; it makes it easier to tidy up, because there's less mess and everything has a place; it's quicker, easier and more effective to clean in a tidy house; and it's much quicker to find what you're looking for.

▶ Identify your clutter problem areas and deal with them one by one.

▶ Don't get overwhelmed: go into one room and identify a problem area, then work on that, or even just a section of that. If the whole wardrobe needs sorting, start with the sock drawer. If the kitchen looks like carnival night at the tip, clear one drawer or cupboard at a time. Set a stopwatch or timer and time yourself – devote an hour or so per session to the task, until it's done.

▶ When in doubt, ask yourself: Do I really want or need it? Is it in good order? Could I replace it easily if I needed to? Have I used it recently? Will I really miss it?

▶ Be ruthless – haven't worn that skirt for 12 months? Give it away! Have you used any of the gift wrap you've been carefully saving? Put it in the recycling bin! Do you hate the Eiffel Tower doorstop your aunt gave you for Christmas? Take it to the op-shop or charity shop today!

Dealing with clutter 'hot spots'

Clutter has a way of sneaking up on you, especially in certain parts of the house or with particular items that tend to accumulate very quickly – one folded newspaper in the corner quickly becomes ten.

▶ If paperwork is your weakness, get a filing system and create a separate folder for bills due, bills paid, banking, tax documents, receipts and appliance instructions etc., and file them each day.

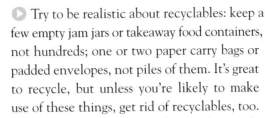

In the know

Keep a file labelled 'Instructions' in your filing system and save all the instructions that come with various items, appliances, toys and games. You can then quickly and easily find how to change the battery in your smoke alarm, reset the clock on the oven or rebuild a Lego pirate ship.

▶ Try to be realistic about recyclables: keep a few empty jam jars or takeaway food containers, not hundreds; one or two paper carry bags or padded envelopes, not piles of them. It's great to recycle, but unless you're likely to make use of these things, get rid of recyclables, too.

▶ Not all clutter is immediately obvious. It can be hidden in garages, wardrobes, kitchen drawers – even in the freezer! Recognise clutter 'hot spots' and given them regular attention.

▶ If you're an incorrigible hoarder, get seriously organised about your storage and display systems, so that what you do keep is efficiently stored and is not cluttering up your living space.

▶ Once you've got your clutter reduced, stay on top of it. All you need to do is spend a few minutes every day returning things to their proper place – this is now simple tidying, rather than de-cluttering – and you'll find that it's easier to keep your home clean, too.

Sort, store and toss!

Sort a cluttered area quickly into a series of empty cardboard boxes, with the boxes labelled as follows:

- **Box 1** Everyday things that need to be put back in their place.
- **Box 2** Things to be given away or recycled.
- **Box 3** Items that you don't need every day, but need to store.
- **Box 4** Anything that can be categorised as 'absolute rubbish'.
- **Box 5** Items you simply can't decide what to do with.

Put everything in box 1 back where it belongs, take box 2 to the op-shop or charity shop, label and decide where to store box 3 and dispose of the contents of box 4. Now go back to the contents of box 5 with a new-found zeal and make a decision!

Fast frozen

Having tossed out all the ancient and unidentified objects in your freezer, attach a magnetised list of its contents to the front, and update it as you use or add items. This saves rummaging through the freezer and makes compiling a weekly menu or a shopping list considerably quicker and easier.

Day-to-day cleaning

Getting organised

Some cleaning jobs need to be done on a daily basis, others need doing once a week and still others are a once or twice a year job.

▶ Neglecting daily cleaning tasks means that the whole job becomes more difficult and time consuming, so the key to staying on top of cleaning – doing it as efficiently and quickly as possible – is to develop a system, and then stick to it.

▶ Write down the jobs that you need to do every day.

▶ For the weekly tasks, you can either devote a couple of hours to them at one time, or simply add 15 to 20 minutes per day onto your day-to-day schedule and complete the job – such as vacuuming the whole house – over the course of the week.

▶ Choose whichever method fits in best with your available time.

TIMELY TIP

Many hands...

For each member of the family, draw up individual schedules that include personal tasks as well as one or two of the general household ones. Even small children can help by putting their toys on the shelf and helping to stack the dishwasher.

Day-to-day cleaning schedule

By drawing up a schedule and sticking to it, you get on top of cleaning. And because your house never gets really dirty, you save time.

Every day
- Make the bed (children can make their own)
- Store dirty clothes in the dirty laundry basket
- Put away clothes that don't need washing
- Wipe down the kitchen sink, benchtops and bathroom benches
- Wash dirty dishes or put them in the dishwasher
- Wipe over the stovetop
- Sweep the kitchen floor
- Wipe down the shower recess and/or bath
- Use the toilet brush before you go to bed
- Put away toys and games (a daily rule for children)
- Put recyclables in recycling bins
- File bills and paperwork

Once a week
- Remove cobwebs
- Dust and polish
- Sweep and/or vacuum hard floors and carpet
- Vacuum upholstery

TIMELY TIP

Stop dirt in its tracks

Stop dirt and grime before it gets trampled inside – by putting a good quality doormat at every entrance, and train the family to use them!

Your basic cleaning kit

To do your housework quickly, it's vital to have the appropriate materials to hand and ready to use. Have a bucket or caddy that can be carried about with you, to store items you use in multiple areas. And store specialised products in the room where they'll be used, such as toilet cleaner in the bathroom.

- **Bucket** This is in addition to your caddy bucket – necessary if you need to wash floors.

- **Small brush and dustpan** Choose a combination that allows you to have them immediately to hand.

- **Rubber gloves** Even the mildest products can irritate your skin.

- **Duster** Feather and lamb's wool dusters have been supplanted by microfibre versions that can reach absolutely everywhere, speeding up all your dusting chores.

- **Dust cloths** While these have traditionally been made from cotton, the timesaving choice is to use microfibre cloths and mitts.

- **Chamois leather** Ideal for polishing metal.

- **Floor cloths** These can be washable rags, microfibre cloths or disposable towelettes that fit over the end of a mop.

- **Floor cleaner** Choose one that's appropriate for your type of floor.

- **Scrubbing brush** Choose a nylon brush, as it dries more quickly. A brush/squeegee combination is great for shower recesses.

- **Paper towels** Useful for dealing with quick spills.

- **Dishwashing liquid** Buy it in bulk or in concentrated 500-ml doses.

- **Multi-use cleaner** Choose one cleaner so you don't accumulate useless products.

- **Bicarbonate of soda** An indispensable multi-purpose cleaning agent.

- **White vinegar** A multi-purpose cleaning agent that's almost indispensable.

- **Furniture polish** For light cleaning, you can use cloths impregnated with wax.

- **Garbage bags** For emptying wastebaskets.

- **Mop** For hard floors, such as vinyl, timber and stone.

- **Vacuum cleaner** Choose one that's appropriate for your floor types.

Choosing the right vacuum cleaner

As well as a basic cleaning kit, the one piece of equipment you can't do without is a vacuum cleaner. Take the time to choose one that suits your particular needs and you'll save valuable time later on.

▶ Don't get bamboozled by the choices on offer. The differences between canister and upright vacuum cleaners have been blurred. It used to be as simple as upright for carpets, canister for bare floors. Now it's more a matter of personal preference.

▶ The most important things to consider are: the size of your house, the amount of use the machine will get and the type of surfaces to be vacuumed. Price is an important consideration, too.

▶ With an enormous range of models available at hugely varying prices, write a list of what you're looking for, including the power of the unit (the higher the power in watts, the more efficient the dust-removing capacity), the range of accessories, the capacity of the dust collector, the type of filtration system, whether or not it can vacuum liquids, and so on.

▶ If you have a lot of carpeting opt for an upright cleaner: they're faster and more efficient. And because they are taller and often self-propelled, you won't have to stoop or manhandle the unit as much, which is a great timesaving feature. They are also generally easy to store.

▶ If you or someone in your family has asthma or allergies, look for a model with a HEPA filter so that fewer dust particles are expelled.

▶ Look for a cleaner with manual pile adjustment, not only for better dirt retrieval when vacuuming carpets, but also for better carpet protection, since the 'standard' setting on many beater bars can destroy a carpet's fibres and wear out the vacuum cleaner's motor.

TIMELY TIP

Hand-held vacuum cleaners

For quick jobs, you can't beat the rechargeable mini vacuum cleaner, which also comes in a wet/dry option. Keeping it constantly recharged and ready to use means that you don't need to get out your regular vacuum cleaner to clean small spills and surfaces in a flash.

▶ If your house has a mixture of carpet and bare floors, or if you have lots of curtains, upholstery, mattresses and window blinds to vacuum, canister vacuum cleaners are usually the better choice.

▶ Canister models have a built-in hose plus attachments, often including a turbo-powered nozzle with a beater bar for carpeting. They're easy to carry around the house and up the stairs, although they are typically more difficult to store, since they take up more floor space than uprights.

▶ If you want to clean areas outside the house as well as inside, consider a wet/dry vacuum. These are powerful machines that will clean carpet and floorboards, but will also vacuum liquids and can cope with gravel, dead leaves and a range of other materials.

▶ Whichever type of vacuum cleaner you decide on, be sure to choose one that has a gauge to show when the dust collector is full. No vacuum cleaner works efficiently when it is more than half full of dust.

▶ Billed as the vacuum cleaner of the twenty-first century, the small robotic vacuum cleaner cleans your floors all by itself while you busy yourself with something else – the ultimate time saver! However, these machines are still prohibitively expensive, and they are not yet as effective at cleaning carpet as a traditional vacuum cleaner.

The right tool for the job

Not all of the accessories listed below are included in the price of the vacuum cleaner, but if you can order them as extras, they'll help you to clean quickly and efficiently. Some models have on-board storage.

● **Flexible hose with nozzle** Allows you to reach easily into corners or behind household appliances.

● **Turbo-brush** Brushes against the pile in the carpet and releases embedded matter.

● **Special parquet brush** This tool vacuums and polishes.

● **Special brush for hard floors** Use this to avoid the risk of scratching timber, tile and vinyl flooring.

● **Flat, extra-long suction nozzle** Great for vacuuming in the narrowest gaps.

● **Combined suction fitting and furniture brush** This will remove the need to change the accessory. It fits onto the flexible hose or the telescopic tube.

● **Special suction fitting for upholstery and mattresses** This tool is equipped with an end that is specially designed for vacuuming hair.

● **Kit for pets** No pet hair can resist it.

● **Anti-dust mite sachet** Tip contents into the vacuum bag.

TIMELY TIP

Mop and toss

These lightweight, swivel-headed mops come with dry or pre-moistened disposable pads or wipes for quick and easy floor cleaning. When the towelette is soiled, simply replace it with a new one.

Magic mop

▶ To clean hard floors, the best tools are a broom and a mop.

▶ The new generation of microfibre mops, which can be used wet or dry, allow you to do it all – from sweeping and dusting to damp-mopping and washing. They're made of microscopic synthetic fibres that act as hooks to latch onto dust, dirt and grime, and they can hold several times their weight in water. The fibres are lint-free and non-abrasive and can be used on all floor types, including timber.

▶ On a really dirty, non-timber hard floor, such as tiles or vinyl, a squeeze-style cellulose sponge mop and bucket is probably the fastest and most effective choice of all. These mops need to be changed or washed out and replaced when they get very dirty.

Clean and fresh

Worn-out cleaning tools, such as sponges, mops and squeegees, are a waste of time. They make you work harder to get the job done. Dirty cleaning tools are worse, because they're actually counterproductive – they smear grime and germs all over the things you're trying to clean.

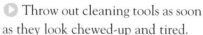

▶ Throw out cleaning tools as soon as they look chewed-up and tired.

▶ Wash cleaning cloths and cotton rags regularly, in your washing machine, using detergent, hot water and ½ cup of white vinegar. Do not use any sort of rinse additive when washing microfibre cloths as it will interfere with their ability to clean effectively.

▶ Wash cellulose sponges in the washing machine or even in the top rack of the dishwasher (rinse them out beforehand).

▶ Unless you have a bagless system, replace your vacuum cleaner bag at least once a month – more often if you have pets that shed. Vacuum bags need air inside to suck properly, so make sure you change them when they're two-thirds full. Keep vacuum brushes clean, too.

CAUTION!

Spraying wisely

When you use a spray cleaning product, spray it onto the cloth rather than the surface you want to clean so that the product can be applied evenly. This will also prevent you from accidentally spraying something precious, or a plant. It's also a good idea to protect your hands, eyes and lungs when using cleaning products, by wearing rubber gloves, goggles and a dust mask, too, if necessary.

TIMELY TIP

No more rinsing

To make floor cleaning faster, choose products that don't require rinsing. There are plenty to choose from in the cleaning section of all major supermarkets.

Bedroom cleaning schedule

Every day	• Make the bed • Put dirty clothes in dirty laundry basket • Hang up clean clothes • Put shoes, jewellery and accessories away
Once a week	• Change bed linen • Dust, wipe and polish (if required) • Sweep and/or vacuum hard floors and carpet • Vacuum upholstery • Clean mirrors
Once a month	• Flip the mattress over and vacuum it. You should also reverse the direction of the mattress

Bed-making made easy

Doonas (duvets) make bed-making a breeze – a few shakes and you're done. If you still use sheets and blankets, maybe it's time to swap to a Doona.

▶ Each day, fold back the bedclothes or the Doona towards the foot of the bed, open the bedroom window (if you have one) and air the bedroom while you are showering, dressing and having breakfast.

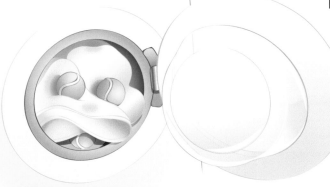

▶ Give your pillows and the Doona a good shake before you start making the bed.

▶ If your washing machine is large enough and your Doona is machine washable, wash it regularly instead of taking it to the drycleaners. Place three tennis balls in the drum to prevent the filling in the Doona from accumulating in clumps. Dry the Doona thoroughly outside or in a dryer, again adding the tennis balls, along with a sheet of fabric softener.

TIMELY TIP

The magic of microfibre

In the kitchen, microfibre cloths absorb particles, water and dirt, and eliminate stains on all types of surfaces. In the bathroom, they dry damp surfaces, eliminate soap residue and clean and polish stainless steel and mirrors. They are also great for removing the most stubborn stains on glass tables. They are lint-free, don't leave any marks and eliminate the need for harsh chemicals and cleaners. The perfect tool for speed cleaning!

Living/family room cleaning schedule	
Every day	● Tidy away things that don't belong in that room
	● Wipe down areas where food has been consumed
Once a week	● Dust, wipe and polish (if required)
	● Sweep and/or vacuum hard floors and carpet
	● Vacuum upholstery

Speedy solutions for carpet and furniture stains

Stains must be cleaned as quickly as possible, otherwise you run the risk of them becoming ingrained and it will take much longer to clean them.

▶ If stains have been caused by a thick substance, such as chocolate, jam or vomit, start by scraping up the residue with a spoon or a spatula before applying any product to clean off the stain left behind.

▶ Blot up as much liquid as possible with paper towels or a clean white cloth, working from the outside to the inside so as not to spread it. Only then should you use a cleaning product, but don't pour it directly onto the stained area, except in the case of powder or spray products.

▶ Dab the stain repeatedly to avoid the risk of ending up with ring marks, do not over-wet the area, and use several cleaning cloths (or old, clean towels), changing to an unused area of the cloth with each dab.

▶ Rinse sparingly, blot with a large colour-fast towel, then dry as quickly as possible using a hair dryer, but do not use heat until you have completely removed the stain.

TIMELY TIP

Gone like magic!

Magic Erasers are chemical- and detergent-free sponge blocks (available from supermarkets) that remove marks and stains from all types of hard surfaces (benchtops, window panes, coffee mugs, televisions, floors, walls, etc.). Simply dampen and rub gently.

Stains on carpet and upholstery

STAIN	CARPET	COTTON UPHOLSTERY
Biro	● Wool and synthetics: Clean with a cotton bud soaked in dry-cleaning fluid, then dab with mild detergent and water; rinse and blot	Dab with a mixture of equal parts white vinegar and methylated spirits
Blood	● Wool: Dab with cold water mixed with a small amount of ammonia ● Synthetics: Clean with cold water	Dab with cold water mixed with salt or ammonia
Chocolate	● Wool and synthetics: Dab with cold water and pure soap	Dab with cold water and pure soap
Coffee, tea, chocolate drink	● Wool: Blot, then dab with glycerine, or a mixture of one part water to three parts methylated spirits; then dab with washing powder and water and rinse ● Synthetics: Absorb the stain, dab with lukewarm water and white vinegar	Dab with a solution of water, methylated spirits and vinegar
Fruit	● Wool and synthetics: Sponge with mild detergent and with a solution of 1 part white vinegar to 2 parts water; rinse and blot	Dab with water, mixed with a little methylated spirits and white vinegar
Grass	● Wool: Clean with a cotton bud soaked in dry-cleaning fluid or methylated spirits, then sponge with detergent and water ● Synthetics: dab with water mixed with vinegar	Dab with water mixed with ammonia
Grease and oil	● Wool: Dab with a solvent (such as eucalyptus oil), then clean with detergent suds and a little water	Dab with a solvent (such as eucalyptus oil), then clean with detergent suds and a little water
Ice-cream	● Wool and synthetics: Dab with lukewarm water mixed with methylated spirits	Dab with a mixture of cold water and liquid detergent
Jam	● Wool: Dab with a mixture of methylated spirits and water ● Synthetics: Blot with soda water	Dab with white vinegar
Red wine	● Wool: Blot, then sponge with a cloth dipped in a mixture of water and white vinegar ● Synthetics: Clean with soda water	Dab with white vinegar, then clean water
Urine	● Wool: Dab with water mixed with ammonia ● Synthetics: Dab with water mixed with white vinegar	Dab with white vinegar
Vomit	● Wool: Dab with water mixed with ammonia ● Synthetics: Dab with soda water or water mixed with white vinegar	Dab with lukewarm water mixed with ammonia

TIMELY TIP

A silver lining

If you often use the drip tray in your oven or griller, protect it with several layers of aluminium foil to avoid having to wash it repeatedly. You can also use aluminium foil to line the walls of an oven that isn't self-cleaning.

CAUTION!

Stick to the instructions

If you have a catalytic self-cleaning oven, follow the manufacturer's instructions for keeping it clean, and don't use any cleaning product – commercial or homemade – unless the manual says it's safe to do so. Not only will you not be covered by the manufacturer's warranty, you could also damage the walls of your oven.

Kitchen cleaning schedule

Every day
- Wipe down the work surfaces and the stovetop
- Wipe over the sink and taps
- Wash the dishes progressively or put them into the dishwasher as you go along
- Wipe the kitchen table
- Sweep the floor
- Quickly wipe over the floor with a sponge mop or a special floor wipe, if necessary
- Empty the garbage bin
- Rinse out kitchen cloths and sponges, then sprinkle them with vinegar or eucalyptus oil

Once a week
- Put bicarbonate of soda and white vinegar in the sink and drain, to clean and disinfect
- Wash the floor thoroughly
- If your oven is not self-cleaning, wipe it over while it is still hot
- Clean your microwave oven. Put the ceramic or glass turntable in the dishwasher
- Clean the kitchen bin with a small amount of detergent or white vinegar
- Change the tea towels and kitchen cloths
- Empty the crumbs from the toaster
- Wipe over the fronts of the cupboard doors
- Wipe over all kitchen appliances to remove grime and finger marks

Once a month
- Clean the inside surface of the glass in the kitchen windows. Of all the windows in the house, these are the ones that become dirty the fastest. To make the job an easy one (and to avoid streaking), buy disposable towelettes that have been impregnated with window-cleaning solution
- Wipe the cupboard shelves with a damp sponge
- Wipe over the inside of the fridge with a damp cloth and a solution of bicarbonate of soda and water with a few drops of vanilla added
- Soak the burners of your stove in detergent overnight, if necessary. Rinse and dry them
- Clean the oven, if necessary (taking all the precautions to protect yourself)
- Clean light fittings

How to keep your kitchen clean

Long-term dirt and grime can take days to clean up, whereas just a few minutes' cleaning every day will save you an enormous amount of time, not to mention elbow grease, in the long run. This is how to do it:

▶ Wipe over your sink and kitchen benches every day. Use a sponge with a spray-and-wipe type of cleaning product or a disposable wipe (available from supermarkets).

▶ Both porcelain and fibreglass sinks can be washed quickly using hot water mixed with a few drops of vinegar.

▶ Clean stainless steel sinks using only dishwashing liquid or a special product for stainless steel.

▶ Wipe spills and spatter from the hotplates, burners, range hood and surrounds of your stove as soon as you have used it – and while it's still warm – to avoid having to struggle with dry, burnt residue that's difficult to remove.

▶ When you're using a spray product to clean up grease spills in the kitchen, give it a few minutes to work before wiping it off. It's faster and easier.

▶ Sweep the kitchen floor every day, and damp-mop it if there have been spills, or if the contents of your pet's bowl leaves a mess behind.

TIMELY TIP

Strike while it's hot

Wipe out your oven and microwave after every use, while they're still warm. Dirt is easy to remove, does not get baked on and you save yourself a horrible cleaning job further down the track. And remember always to cover food in the microwave to cut down on spills and splatters in the first place. A sheet of paper towel will do the trick.

Don't forget the barbecue

Barbecued food is delicious, and barbecuing is a great timesaving way to cook, but it also precludes a whole lot of dirty, greasy saucepans.

▶ Don't let your barbecue get so dirty that it becomes unhygienic and inefficient to cook with. Clean it as you go to save a bigger cleaning job.

TIMELY TIP

SOS burnt saucepan

If you have burned the bottom of a saucepan, quickly fill it with water and add detergent or washing soda. Let it soak for several hours then bring it to the boil. The black deposits will come off easily, without the need for scraping or rubbing.

Line the drip tray with a double thickness of aluminium foil and a layer of commercially available barbecue soak or clay-type kitty litter. When it becomes completely fat-soaked, simply wrap the litter in the foil and dispose of it, before re-lining the tray.

When you've finished cooking on the grill, allow the flames to burn on *High* for another 5 minutes or so, to allow any fat and stuck-on residue to burn and carbonise. Anything remaining is then very simple to scrape off.

Using a metal brush, scrape down the hotplate after every use. You can remove any accumulated fat and debris with paper towels.

If your barbecue has an oven hood, wipe it down while it's still warm, using bicarbonate of soda and vinegar.

Wipe the outside of the barbecue and spray the grill and hotplate with a light coating of cooking oil to keep it lubricated and rust-free.

Don't leave dirty dishes lying around

Besides cluttering up the kitchen, dirty pots and dishes are unhygienic and will attract flies and cockroaches into your home.

Put dirty dishes into the dishwasher as soon as possible, but only start the program when the dishwasher is full, to save time and energy.

If it takes you more than two or three meals worth of cutlery and crockery to fill the dishwasher, do a quick pre-wash or rinse cycle between washes so that the dirty dishes don't dry out in the machine.

When stacking the dishwasher, do it systematically, with like items together, so that when you're unloading and putting things away you can pick up all the bowls in one go, or all the forks and spoons.

TIMELY TIP

The big guns

If you've let your barbecue grill get thickly coated with fat and food residue, place it in a heavy-duty garbage bag and spray liberally with oven cleaner. Seal the bag with a twist tie and leave overnight. The next day, open the bag very carefully, keeping your face away from the fumes. The burned-on gunk should now be easy to remove.

TIMELY TIP

Starting at the top

Cut pieces of thick paper or newspaper to fit on the tops of high cupboards, where grease from cooking settles and gathers dust. Change the paper twice annually and you won't need to clean up there.

▶ Clean the filters and spray arms regularly, to keep the machine running at maximum efficiency. While the dishwasher is running, wash up the items that must be washed by hand, such as sharp knives.

▶ If you don't have a dishwasher, rinse and stack the dishes and wash them as soon as you can, to discourage pests (see below).

A clear winner

Blocked drains are a time-wasting nuisance. Keep them clear with a few simple measures.

▶ Catch food debris with a sink strainer and put tea leaves and coffee grounds into the compost or garden.

▶ Don't put fat and oil down the drain. Scrape or pour it into an old milk carton, freeze, then throw in the garbage bin on garbage night. By freezing it, you avoid all the nasty odours brewing in your home.

▶ Clean the drain periodically by pouring in 1 cup bicarbonate of soda, followed by 1 cup vinegar. When the fizzing stops, follow up with boiling water. Use a plunger if the drainage is sluggish.

Banish kitchen pests

Cockroaches and pantry moths (weevils) gather in the kitchen because it's warm and has a plentiful food supply. It's almost impossible to keep them completely at bay, but a serious infestation is much more time consuming to deal with than taking some simple, preventive steps to keep numbers under control. It's an issue that needs constant attention.

▶ Keep kitchen benches spotless and train your family to clean up after themselves so that you don't encourage a pest problem in the first place.

▶ Don't leave dirty dishes or uncovered food (including pet food, which has a very strong odour), lying around.

▶ Block the gaps in walls, around pipes and between skirting boards and flooring to prevent cockroaches from getting in and breeding.

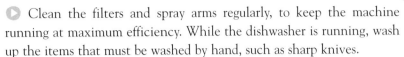

A sticky end

TIMELY TIP Make an environmentally safe cockroach bait by mixing equal parts of borax and jam or icing sugar, and placing in jam lids near where cockroaches congregate. Keep this mixture away from small children and pets, as it is poisonous if ingested in large enough quantities.

▶ Fix leaking kitchen taps and pipes promptly – cockroaches love to gather in damp, dark, warm places.

▶ De-clutter the cupboard under the sink.

▶ Keep your kitchen garbage bin firmly covered, and empty it frequently, to avoid cockroaches collecting there.

▶ If you use commercial cockroach baits, replace them regularly: write the date on your calendar to remind you when they need replacing.

▶ Transfer everything in your pantry into pest-proof storage containers. Throw out anything that shows signs of weevil infestation.

▶ Wipe up shelf spills when they happen and regularly clean cupboards, washing them out with detergent. Try adding a few drops of pest-repelling oil of cloves to the washing water, to discourage infestation.

▶ To deter weevils, scatter bay leaves or cloves on cupboard shelves and tape them inside container lids. Opt for non-toxic sticky traps that catch adult moths and are safe to use near food.

TIMELY TIP

The night shift

Instead of removing the shower head and spending ages scrubbing it to lift off built-up soap scum and scale (especially in a hard-water area), pour about 8 cm of ordinary white vinegar into a sandwich bag and then secure the bag over the shower head, using masking tape, so that the shower head is submerged in the vinegar. Leave it overnight and in the morning it'll rinse clean without any scrubbing.

Bathroom cleaning schedule	
Every day	● Air the room after you have had a shower or bath
	● Wipe the basin, the bathtub and the shower walls
	● Wipe up traces of water on the vanity and floor
	● Empty the bathroom bin
	● Use the toilet brush
Once a week	● Vacuum
	● Clean the bathroom fittings and towel rails
	● Clean around the taps and the shower recess, and if you have a hard-water problem, wipe with a scale-removing product or white vinegar
	● Wash the toothbrush glasses
	● Empty the water lying in the soap holder
	● Change the towels, hand towels, face washers and bath mats
	● If you have one, wash the shower curtain in the washing machine
	● Clean and disinfect the toilet
	● Spray an anti-mould product on the grout and joins in the shower recess (or wipe with oil of cloves)
	● Wash the floor, using a product that does not require rinsing
	● Soak your brushes and combs in warm water containing a little detergent and a few drops of eucalyptus oil. Rinse well and allow to dry

TIMELY TIP

Anti-mist

Regardless of whether you are taking a bath or a shower, don't begin by running the hot water. Instead, run the cold water first; this will avoid mist forming on the mirrors, thereby saving you extra cleaning time.

Bathrooms: the basic kit

Keep a basic bathroom kit in the bathroom cupboard so it's always on hand for a quick clean. To do the job properly, you'll need a microfibre cloth or sponge, a glass cleaner, all-purpose cleaner, a toilet cleaner and toilet brush. If you have a serious mould problem, you might need bleach as well, but try to use it sparingly (*see* 'Caution!', below left).

Quick tips for a sparkling bathroom

▶ To keep your enamel bathtub looking shiny, clean it with a non-abrasive product so that you don't permanently dull the surface.

▶ For fibreglass bathtubs, simply use a mixture of warm water and dishwashing detergent, rather than a product that is too abrasive. The same mixture is also effective for the bathroom basin.

▶ To ensure the toilet bowl is completely clean, brush it as often as possible and use a toilet cleaner (proprietary or homemade) once or twice a week. If you disinfect it regularly with bleach, make sure that you don't use it in large quantities. It is environmentally toxic and can damage the porcelain finish if it is in contact for too long.

▶ Clean the toilet seat, cistern and the outside of the bowl with a detergent-and-water mix, then rinse thoroughly.

Leave without a trace

▶ When the whole family has finished using the bathroom, wipe down the bath, the shower walls and the basin to prevent soap scum building up, and keep things looking sparkling.

▶ Wipe bathroom surfaces while you're brushing your teeth. You'll avoid a more arduous cleaning task later on. Use a large microfibre cloth that can then be simply rinsed and hung out to dry.

▶ Train family members to wipe out the bath or shower after using.

CAUTION!

Take necessary precautions

When you're using bleach or ammonia-based cleansers in your bathroom, make sure there is adequate ventilation, to prevent breathing in noxious fumes. And wear rubber gloves and some form of eye protection, to prevent splashes damaging your skin or eyes. If any type of cleaning product is ingested or causes an adverse reaction on the skin or in the eyes, seek medical attention immediately.

TIMELY TIP

The self-cleaning toilet

Add toilet cleaner – commercial or homemade – to the bowl of the toilet before you go to bed at night. In the morning, give it a quick brush, flush and it's clean!

Spring cleaning

Getting organised

Spring cleaning doesn't have to be done in the spring of course, although there's something about the end of winter that seems to signal a need to get the doors and windows open and freshen everything up.

▶ It makes good sense to clean twice a year instead of leaving everything for one overwhelming clean-up, so schedule a second cleaning session six months or so after your spring clean.

▶ Even if it takes you a few days, undertaking major cleaning twice a year is time saving because your house will remain cleaner and more organised for longer, and easier to maintain with just a light daily touch-up. Do it in spring, when it's time to open up the house after winter (but before the Christmas season when you're getting ready to welcome family and friends), and also during autumn, when it's cooler and there's less incentive to spend your days outdoors.

▶ Plan the operation to avoid finishing only part of the work. If you can't do it over several consecutive days, draw up a schedule for each room and follow it rigorously as soon as time allows.

▶ Before you begin, make sure you have all the necessary materials and that they are in good condition. And check that you have enough garbage bags to get rid of all those things that are useless or beyond repair.

Perfect linen

Whether your linen press is a dedicated cupboard for all the family's linen needs or a camphorwood chest, you need to clear it out a couple of times a year, re-sort the contents and clean the interior.

 Keeping your linen press neat and tidy means you can avoid insect damage (moths breed in dust and dirt), and you'll always find what you're looking for immediately, which is a definite time saver.

▶ Remove the contents of your linen press and check the items for signs of wear, tear and insect damage. Re-fold and replace only those items that pass the test, and repair or bin those that don't.

Spring cleaning schedule

IN THE BEDROOM
Twice a year

- Empty the wardrobe and drawers, sort and discard unwanted clothes
- Vacuum all interiors before replacing items
- Dust/vacuum the tops of cupboards
- Move the bed and vacuum thoroughly underneath
- Clean curtains, blinds, rugs and upholstery
- Clean lamps and light fittings
- Replace moth-repellent sachets if you use them
- Wash pillows made from synthetic fibre in the washing machine, two at a time, selecting a short cycle and placing tennis balls in the drum. Dry-clean feather down pillows
- Treat bed linen with an anti-dust mite product if there are allergy sufferers to consider

Once a year

- Air Doonas (duvets) and pillows outside (not in direct sunlight), and clean the covers, too

IN LIVING AREAS
Twice a year

- Clean curtains, blinds, rugs and upholstery, and wash the windows
- Clean lamps and light fittings
- Clean out and sort bookshelves; sort, cull and re-arrange videos, DVDs and CDs
- Move furniture that you don't normally move and vacuum thoroughly

IN THE KITCHEN
Twice a year

- Wash the grid of the exhaust fan and replace the filter
- Clean and disinfect the dishwasher by operating it when it's empty, using an appropriate product, or bicarbonate of soda in the detergent tray and vinegar in the rinse additive holder
- Empty out cupboards and drawers; vacuum the drawers and wipe out the cupboards
- Get rid of cracked glasses, badly chipped plates, kitchen implements you never use, threadbare or torn tea towels and ancient kitchen sponges
- Renew washing-up brushes and scourers
- Thoroughly clean the splashback and wall tiles
- Clean and defrost the freezer, discarding any UFOs (unidentified frozen objects)
- Take everything out of the fridge, cull the half-empty jars and anything past its use-by date, thoroughly clean the fridge – inside (including shelves and crispers), outside, underneath and at the back. Wipe over the door seals with bicarbonate of soda and vinegar and a few drops of oil of cloves to inhibit mould
- Remove the contents of the pantry, throw out anything infested with weevils or past its use-by date, and wipe over the shelves
- Clean the eating area or kitchen table thoroughly
- In hard-water areas, de-scale coffee machines and the kettle using water and vinegar
- Clean curtains and blinds
- Wash all the windows

IN THE BATHROOM
Twice a year

- Remove the contents of your medicine cabinet, discard out-of-date medicines and prescription drugs and wash the shelves
- Remove the contents of the vanity unit, discard old make-up, used razor blades, half-used hair products etc., and clean the unit thoroughly

▶ Instead of storing different items on different shelves, store complete sets together: a tablecloth with its matching napkins, or a complete set of bed linen. It's quicker to grab what you want in one go. Or store all the double sets on one shelf and the single sets on another.

▶ If you have children, put their bath towels on a shelf that they can reach without having to pull everything down and make a mess.

▶ Store unwrapped cakes of soap in the linen press – the soap scents the linen and, at the same time, hardens to become longer lasting.

▶ Tie dried lavender, rosemary or whole cloves in small squares of muslin and keep them in the linen press to deter moths.

Growing longer arms

▶ Clean your walls and ceilings regularly and you'll avoid having to paint or wallpaper more often. You'll be amazed at how removing a few cobwebs and fly specks makes it look as though you've just repainted.

▶ Use a broom and attach a clean cloth to the end, or use a special telescopic, long-handled cobweb broom made from microfibre, which is ideal for getting into corners.

▶ Clean walls and ceilings with your vacuum cleaner and a telescopic tube with an attachment for textiles. This attachment is ideal for dusting walls, whether they are painted or covered with fabric or wallpaper.

▶ Remove the accumulated dust from the tops of doors and architraves using a microfibre duster with an extension handle or a clean broom.

Simply sparkling windows

Everything looks suddenly lighter and brighter with clean windows. If you've only got time for one job before visitors arrive, do the windows.

▶ You can use a commercial spray or window cleaner, or a homemade cleaner (see 'Clean and green', on page 64). Wipe with newspaper

TIMELY TIP

A good sort

Don't hoard old newspapers that you won't read any more, or books, DVDs and CDs that you have forgotten to give back. Make the most of your major cleaning to throw them out or give them back to their owner. They are dust catchers and the beginning of a new clutter problem.

Banish damp

TIMELY TIP

Tie 12 pieces of ordinary blackboard chalk together in a bunch and hang them inside a damp cupboard. The chalk will absorb the moisture from the air.

scrunched into a ball. Don't work in direct sunlight, as this causes the product to dry too quickly, leaving streaks behind.

▶ There's nothing like good old elbow grease, but give yourself a boost with a microfibre cloth specially designed for windows: with thick soft fibres, it cleans and polishes windows in the twinkling of an eye.

▶ To clean a lot of windows, the fastest solution is to hire a steam cleaner or an electrical steam window cleaner fitted with a long enough handle to reach high windows.

Clean blinds and curtains easily

▶ Blinds need to be cleaned at least once a year. Dust venetian blinds by running your hands – encased in cotton gloves – along the slats. Clean dirty spots with a damp cloth and a little detergent.

▶ Vacuum roller blinds with the upholstery attachment or dusting tool. If the blinds are spongeable, wipe them with a solution of dishwashing liquid and then rinse with a damp cloth. Applying a fabric-protection spray will help to keep them clean. (Apply the spray outdoors.)

▶ You can wash curtains in the machine if they are colour-fast or if the accompanying care instructions clearly indicate this is possible. Wash large curtains in the bath, because they are very heavy and may cause damage to your washing machine.

▶ Professionally dry-clean lined curtains, even if they are washable – the fabrics may shrink at varying rates if you wash them yourself.

White light

▶ Wash sheer or lace curtains in the washing machine about twice a year. If they seem very dirty or yellowed, soak them first in an oxygenated powder soaker (do not use chlorine bleach).

▶ Borax also has a whitening effect. Dissolve 4 tablespoons of borax in a bucket of very hot water. Soak the curtains until yellowing disappears, then rinse well and dry flat, in the shade. If they have a few creases when you hang them up again, spray lightly with cold water.

TIMELY TIP

Clever coathanger

To avoid giving yourself extra work, if the curtains aren't dirty when you're about to clean the windows, don't take them down. Instead, slip them out of the way onto a coathanger or wedge them behind the back of a chair. Use a wooden coathanger, to avoid leaving any marks on the fabric.

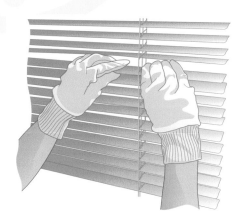

TIMELY TIP

Marking the spot

When removing curtain hooks, mark their positions with an indelible felt pen or a dab of nail polish. This way, you will not have to spend time guessing the correct spacing when replacing the hooks.

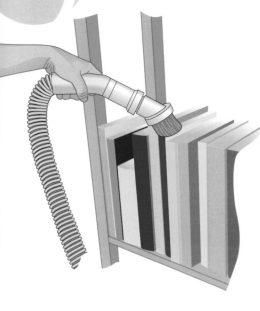

Shelf life

▶ Once a year, clean all the books in your bookcase by vacuuming them using the soft brush attachment on your vacuum cleaner, (and, at the same time, take the opportunity to cull the ones you don't want).

▶ Open individual books, tap off excess dust and then carefully wipe them. Put them back on the shelves in some sort of logical order so you'll be able to find them again quickly.

▶ Clean old leather-bound books using a special wax (available from antiquarian booksellers) to protect them from dust. Allow them to dry for an hour then polish gently using a soft cloth.

Comfort zone

Armchairs and sofas need to be thoroughly cleaned at least once a year. This major cleaning will keep them looking good longer and will shorten the amount of time you need to spend on a regular vacuuming job.

▶ Remove slipcovers and wash them according to the fabric instructions. While the covers are still damp, put them back on the furniture and press with a cool iron. If you have any doubts about the type of material, have them dry-cleaned.

▶ Wash or dry-clean the covers of scatter cushions.

▶ Use an upholstery shampoo on non-removable covers (or call in professionals). Take care not to overwet the furniture.

▶ Wipe dirty leather with a damp cloth wrung out in a soap-flake or leather-soap solution (do not overwet or rinse). Allow to dry naturally, then polish with a clean, dry cloth and apply leather conditioner.

▶ Once or twice a year, wax your old furniture using beeswax or a specialist product for antiques. Polish in the direction of the wood grain, using clean, old woollen socks to do the job, ensuring the product gets into all the recesses. Allow to dry and then polish with a dry cloth.

TIMELY TIP

Clean leather

To keep your leather armchairs and sofa looking good, rub them over every six months with a white cloth lightly dampened with water and Sunlight or Marseille laundry soap.

Yellow keys

If the keys on your piano have become yellow, rub them with a cloth wrung out in 10 per cent hydrogen peroxide if they are made of ivory, and in lemon juice if they are plastic. Take great care not to overwet.

TIMELY TIP

Taking care of accessories

▶ If dust has accumulated on a lampshade, going over it with a mini vacuum cleaner or an adhesive roller will clean it up in no time.

▶ If you have bronze objects that have been stained with verdigris, simply soak them in white vinegar, then rinse well.

▶ To ensure that your silver accessories remain shiny, rub them with a chamois leather after cleaning.

▶ Place a camphor ball next to your silver cutlery to prevent it from becoming tarnished too quickly.

▶ Spray a fine layer of hair spray on objects made from copper and brass – it will protect them from dust and stains until the next major cleaning.

▶ To eliminate deposits on a vase, without rubbing, fill it with water and vinegar, and in some cases add a little sand. Shake the vase well, then rinse.

Don't wait for spring in the garden

▶ Brush down teak garden furniture twice a year and paint with a commercial product that's designed to nourish it and restore its satiny appearance. This makes it much easier to clean away day-to-day spills.

▶ Remove dust from your cane furniture by blowing it away with a hair dryer, then clean the furniture with a brush dipped in soapy water.

▶ If you live in a very cold area, carefully wash your balcony furniture and cover it in clear plastic before winter comes. This will ensure it's in good condition when you uncover it again in spring.

A cleaner's friend

▶ Don't overlook humble methylated spirits during spring cleaning. It's cheap and effective for cleaning a wide range of items such as mirrors, windows, switches, light bulbs, power sockets, glass or crystal lights, television screens, computer keyboards and screens, and most plastic surfaces. It also has the advantage of drying almost immediately.

One, two, three... shine

If a sealed wooden floor is regularly vacuumed and damp-mopped, it doesn't require much serious maintenance because its grain is protected against the infiltration of dust and water. From time to time, make it shiny again by applying a liquid floor polish.

Oiled parquet or floorboards must be sanded once or twice a year and covered with a new, thin layer of oil to maintain them in top condition.

Traditional waxed parquet requires much more meticulous care. When you're doing your spring clean, go over stained areas with steel wool and polish the whole surface using beeswax or another solid-paste polish. Using an electric polisher fitted with brushes that wax, polish and shine the floor evenly will help to speed up the process.

Do-it-yourself carpet cleaning

If you have a lot of carpet, cleaning it using a machine, rather than doing it by hand, will get the job done faster. Once or twice a year, depending on how dirty it is, hire a shampooer and buy the appropriate products (check with the manufacturer before shampooing wool). Always work from front to back, starting with the part that is the furthest away from the door, to avoid walking on damp carpet.

If you don't have time to do more than one room at a time, use dry shampoo as a temporary measure. Sprinkle your carpet with bicarbonate of soda, let it dry for about 15 minutes, then vacuum it up.

If you have very high quality carpet, call in a professional carpet cleaner every 2–3 years for a really thorough job.

TIMELY TIP

Lightning-fast waxing

If you only have a small floor area, tie a duster around a soft broom and use this instead of an electric polisher to apply and buff wax polish on a wooden floor. Always clean floors thoroughly before applying polish for the first time.

TIMELY TIP

Carpet: spot recovery

When you move a piece of heavy furniture and it leaves indented marks on the carpet, place an ice cube on the mark and allow it to melt. Continue with your cleaning and vacuum as soon as the carpet is dry; the marks will disappear completely.

Fresh air

Sprinkle a few drops of your favourite essential oil on a cotton wool ball and drop it into the bag or canister of your vacuum cleaner for a lovely fresh smell as you clean. A small saucer of vinegar left in any room of the house will also keep the room smelling fresh, even if it has been closed up for a while.

Quick tips for your rugs

▶ Take the opportunity during your spring cleaning to change the direction of your rugs. Beat them outdoors with a carpet beater or an old tennis racquet. If they still seem a little dull, dampen them with soda water, let them dry and then brush them gently to revive the pile.

▶ To prevent rugs from sliding on hard floor surfaces, stick strips of heavy-duty, double-sided tape around the edges. Use self-adhesive Velcro to prevent rugs from creeping on carpet.

On the tiles

If you take care of your tiles on a daily basis, they will stay in good condition and the little facelift you'll need to give them every once in a while won't take very much effort or time.

▶ If your sandstone floor looks a little dull, revive its colour once or twice a year by rubbing it with a cloth soaked in white vinegar. If the joints contain ingrained dirt, rub them using a hard brush and a mixture of water and vinegar and rinse thoroughly.

▶ If your floor tiles are porous, take care to protect them once a year using a product that will seal them against spills and grease.

▶ If you have marble floors, get them professionally sealed and buffed as regularly as the manufacturer recommends. This will make them shiny again, as well as giving them excellent protection.

Easy-care floors

Vinyl and linoleum floors are tough, and so easy to care for, but a little everyday attention will help to prolong their life and make spring cleaning much easier for you. Revive their shine twice a year by using products that are quick and easy to apply.

▶ Clean and protect vinyl floors with a layer of liquid floor wax.

▶ Protect linoleum from stains with a wax polish. Spread it over the floor's surface using a waxing machine or a soft cloth.

Clean and green

Cleaning quickly and efficiently doesn't mean you have to arm yourself with a load of toxic commercial products that can harm both you and the environment. Natural cleaning products clean just as effectively – and just as fast – as their chemical-laden counterparts, and often end up costing considerably less. Keep a stock of the basics under your sink: a spray bottle of white vinegar and a shaker jar of bicarbonate of soda – you'll be amazed at how much you can clean with just these two things.

All-purpose spray cleaner
A safe and natural alternative to commercial sprays, for using on any surface that needs wiping down.

1 teaspoon bicarbonate of soda
1 teaspoon pure soap flakes
dash of white vinegar
1 cup warm water

● Mix all the ingredients together in a spray bottle and shake until soap has dissolved. Spray and wipe with a kitchen sponge.

Degreasing vinegar spray
Ideal for use on stainless-steel sinks, tiled and wooden surfaces, plastic finishes and telephones.

2 cups white vinegar
1 cup water
25 drops eucalyptus oil

● Combine all ingredients in a spray bottle. Shake well before use. Spray and wipe. No need to rinse.

Scouring paste
An easy-to-make paste that's safe for use on sinks, oven doors, stovetops and inside stained mugs.

4 tablespoons bicarbonate of soda
1 tablespoon water

● Mix ingredients to a stiff paste and apply with a damp sponge. Buff residue with a dry cloth.

Microwave oven cleaner
● Add the juice and skin of a lemon to a bowl of water and place inside the microwave. Run on *High* for 2 to 5 minutes. Remove the bowl and wipe the interior of the oven clean.

Oven cleaner
To avoid having to clean your oven too often, get into the habit of wiping it out while it's still warm after every use. Remember to protect your hands.

bicarbonate of soda
water
white vinegar, in a spray bottle

● Make a stiff paste from bicarbonate of soda and water. Damp the walls of the oven and apply the paste.
● Spray with vinegar (the bicarb soda will fizz up). Shut the oven door and leave for 10 minutes.
● If the oven is dirty all over, scrub with a nylon brush, then wipe out the gunk and rinse clean with water.

Toilet cleaner
This effective cleaner and disinfectant is cheaper and safer to use than bleach.

1 cup borax powder
¼ cup white vinegar

● Sprinkle the toilet bowl with borax, then spray with the vinegar. Let it sit for an hour or two (or overnight), then scrub with a toilet brush and flush.

Shower cleaner
This will disinfect the shower recess and help prevent mould on grout.

¼ cup borax
2 cups very hot water
¼ teaspoon tea-tree oil or oil of cloves

● Shake ingredients in a spray bottle until borax dissolves. Spray on surfaces, leave overnight and rinse.

Soap-scum remover
Spray this on your shower screen daily.

½ cup methylated spirits
½ cup white vinegar
1 cup water

● Combine the ingredients in a spray bottle. Spray onto the shower screen and rub off with a soft cloth.

Disinfectant and air freshener
Great for the kitchen or bathroom. (Lavender makes a lovely linen spray.)

25 drops clove, pine, tea-tree, lavender, eucalyptus or peppermint essential oil
2 tablespoons methylated spirits or vodka
500 ml distilled water

● Add oil to alcohol in a clean, dry bottle and let stand for 24 hours.
● Add water and decant into a spray bottle. Shake thoroughly before use.
● For air freshener, use a fine mist.

Window cleaner
Use this cleaner with a microfibre cloth.

½ teaspoon liquid detergent
3 tablespoons vinegar
2 cups water

● Mix all the ingredients together in a spray bottle. Spray on glass and wipe off with a cloth. Really dirty windows might need rinsing and wiping as well.

Fabric softener

You can add a few drops of your favourite essential oil, too.

1 cup white vinegar
1 cup bicarbonate of soda
2 cups water

● Combine ingredients slowly and carefully over the sink (they fizz up).
● Pour into a plastic bottle and replace the lid. Use ¼ cup in the final rinse or in your washing machine's softener dispenser.

Pre-wash stain remover

Ammonia is very strong, with fumes that can irritate, but it quickly breaks down in the environment and is safer than many commercial products.

125 ml water
125 ml liquid laundry or dishwashing detergent
125 ml non-cloudy ammonia (cloudy will do at a pinch)

● Combine all ingredients in a spray bottle and spray onto stains, then wash immediately. (Leaving clothes lying unwashed when sprayed with this solution can result in bleaching.) DO NOT USE WITH CHLORINE BLEACH.

All-purpose laundry 'powder'

Use this 'powder' in the washing machine or for hand washing.

½ cup washing soda
1 cup finely grated pure soap (such as Sunlight)
½ cup salt
½ cup borax
½ cup bicarbonate of soda

● Put the washing soda crystals in a plastic bag and crush them finely with a rolling pin. Mix the crushed washing soda with the rest of the ingredients and store in an airtight container.
● Use 1 tablespoon for a small washing load, 1½ for a medium load and 2 tablespoons for a large load.

● Dissolve the 'powder' in a jug of hot water before adding to a top-loading machine. For a front-loading machine, dissolve it in a small amount of hot water and add to the dispenser.
● If using this laundry 'powder' for hand washing, wear rubber gloves to protect your skin.

Wool wash

This traditional recipe is ideal for blankets, quilts and pillows.

2 cups soap flakes (such as Lux)
½ cup methylated spirits
25 ml eucalyptus oil

● Empty all the ingredients into a wide-mouthed jar and shake well until combined.
● Use 2 tablespoons of wool wash per litre of warm water. There's no need to rinse unless garments are being stored for a long period.

Carpet stain foam

Use this stain foam to clean your carpets and upholstery.

2 cups pure soap flakes (such as Lux)
½ cup methylated spirits
25 ml eucalyptus oil

● Shake the ingredients together in a large jar until combined.
● Add a little hot water if the mixture is too hard to mix (it should be quite thick, though). Store in a sealed jar.
● To use it, mix 2–3 tablespoons of mixture into 1 litre of very hot water and whisk vigorously until suds form.
● Rub just the foam (no liquid) over the carpet stain and let it sit for about 10 minutes. Wipe away the foam with a damp sponge dipped in white vinegar (this step neutralises the alkalinity left by the foam).
● Blot thoroughly with a clean pad. For extra-tough stains, add ¼ cup washing soda to the hot water with the foam mix and whisk until all the soda crystals have dissolved.

Strong cleaner for hard floors

This recipe contains washing soda, which can damage your skin, so wear rubber gloves. Note: this cleaner is not intended for use on timber floors.

1 tablespoon liquid soap
¼ cup white vinegar
¼ cup washing soda
3 litres hot water

● Mix all the ingredients together in a bucket. Rinse thoroughly with clean water after use.

Furniture polish

This simple homemade polish leaves wooden furniture smelling wonderful.

125 g beeswax, grated
500 ml raw linseed oil (for dark wood) or olive oil (for pale wood)
1 teaspoon lavender or rosemary essential oil

● Melt the wax in a heat-proof bowl over a saucepan of simmering water. Carefully add the oil and stir over heat for 3 minutes.
● Remove from the heat and stir in the essential oil. Transfer to a clean jar and allow to set.
● Using a soft cloth, rub sparingly into the wooden surface, leave for 30 minutes, then polish off.

Quick-and-easy silver cleaner

This cleaner works like magic.

2 sheets aluminium foil
1 tablespoon salt
1 tablespoon bicarbonate of soda

● Line the bottom of a non-metal bucket or large bowl with foil. Add the salt and bicarb soda to the bowl and fill with boiling water.
● Immerse your washable silver items (sterling or plated) in the solution and allow them to soak for an hour or two (the foil will get darker).
● Remove the silverware, rinse, then dry thoroughly to restore its shine.

Washing

Wash by weight

If you're doing multiple loads of washing, wash the heaviest items first to give them the longest time to dry. And try to divide your whites according to how heavily soiled they are, instead of having one load where they are all mixed in together. You'll avoid the less soiled items taking up grease or oil from heavily soiled ones, making them appear off-white.

Choose your washing machine carefully

Like death and taxes, clothes washing is an unavoidable fact of life. And since you're going to spend time keeping your laundry clean, it's worth doing all you can to make things as speedy and efficient as possible.

▶ The single most important investment is a washing machine, so do some research before you buy.

▶ Limit the time you spend washing, in a family of more than four people, by choosing a machine with a capacity of at least 6 kg. Singles and couples should look for a model that has an automatic variable capacity.

▶ Choose a front-loader (minimum 60 cm wide) if you have the space. It uses half the water of a top-loader and gives you a larger work surface.

▶ Some new washing machines come with a dryer function as well, which is space- and cost-saving, but if you do multiple loads, you won't be able to wash and dry at the same time, which may not save time.

▶ ▶ **COMPARE ENERGY-EFFICIENCY RATINGS**

• **In Australia and New Zealand,** consumers can check energy rating labels (label shown at left, top) which outline the different efficiency criteria of appliances, before making their final decision on which one to buy. Every new washing machine should display a sticker giving its energy and (in Australia) water-conservation rating. The government web site, below, allows you to compare the energy ratings of a number of well-known brand washing machines available in both Australia and New Zealand. Look for the appliance with the highest number of stars.
www.energyrating.gov.au

• **In South Africa,** appliance labelling is voluntary, but is likely to become mandatory in the not-too-distant future. Current energy labelling is modelled after that of European Union member states, with appliances carrying a rating from A to G, with A being the most energy efficient (label shown at left, bottom). Look for the Department of Minerals and Energy's energy star symbol and choose the most energy-efficient washing machine. The web site, below, explains the system of appliance labelling for current standards in South Africa.
www.dme.gov.za/energy/app_faq.stm

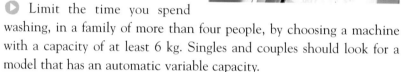

TIMELY TIP

Fancy footwear

You can wash canvas and other fabric shoes, such as nylon runners, in a pillowcase in the washing machine. Dry them outside in the sun, not in the dryer, to prevent damage.

Timesaving features on washing machines

● **Fast-wash program** Reduces the washing time by 40 per cent.

● **Anti-crease or easy-ironing program** Eliminates the thermal shock suffered by the washing load during rinsing (it is less creased and therefore easier to iron).

● **High-speed spin-drying (minimum of 1200 revolutions per minute)** Allows the washing (especially cotton) to dry more quickly.

● **Removable product holders** These are much faster to clean.

● **Collapsible wheels** These sorts of wheels make it easier to clean beneath and around your washing machine.

● **Wide opening doors and lids** Having these two simple features will help speed up the loading and unloading of the washing.

● **Woollen or 'like dry-cleaning'** This machine function removes the need for hand-washing programs.

● **Delayed start or end function** Allows the time for starting or ending the washing to be programmed.

Establish a routine

You probably don't have a whole day to devote to the washing, as perhaps your mother or grandmother did. Thankfully, automated machines mean you don't have to, either. But you can still save time with a washing routine that fits in with your lifestyle.

▶ Make sure your family understands when washing is scheduled to be done (specifically, what day and what time of day). If their dirty clothes are not in the laundry by that time, they don't get washed.

▶ It might suit you to do a dark wash on one day and a white wash on another. Or put the washing on before you go to bed (if the noise doesn't disturb anyone), ready for pegging out first thing in the morning, or vice versa. Simply choose the routine that suits you best.

⮕ CAUTION!

Weigh up the cost

In these days of global warming, you might find yourself torn between a highly energy-efficient washing machine and one that does the job a little quicker by using more energy. Don't justify those few extra minutes you gain against the health of the planet, go for the machine that is most energy efficient (*see* 'Compare energy-efficiency ratings', at left).

TIMELY TIP

And two make a pair

To avoid collecting a lot of unmatched socks, buy identical socks for all the adult members of your family. This will save you time matching pairs.

One step ahead of the repairman

A little easy maintenance will help keep your washing machine in tiptop condition for longer.

▶ To clean your washing machine, do an empty wash once a year. Set the machine on the hottest program and replace your normal washing product with bicarbonate of soda. Add white vinegar to the rinse cycle.

▶ If the water in your area is very hard, use a scale-removing product regularly. This will protect your washing machine from quickly becoming worn, because nothing damages the mechanisms more than scale. Check the manufacturer's instructions to find out which product is safest and best to use on your particular machine.

▶ Regularly clean out your machine's lint filter. The washer will function more efficiently and drain correctly. To prevent bad smells from appearing, leave the door of the washing machine open after use.

Sort and win

▶ It might be asking the impossible, but see if you can get your family to sort their own washing into light and dark, by providing a divided hamper, or two separate baskets or bags. It'll save time on washday.

▶ Sort according to colour rather than according to material. To save time, you can wash whites and light-coloured clothing together, but do separate washes for bright and dark-coloured clothing.

▶ For black and dark clothes, you can buy a special laundry detergent that protects fabric against fading.

▶CAUTION!

Check for colour runs

If you're washing a new item of clothing for the first time, test it to ensure that the colour does not run. Wet a section of the material with hot water and press a white handkerchief against it. If there are traces of colour on the handkerchief, wash the garment separately. You can also place a towelette, specially designed to solve this problem, in the bottom of the drum (it attracts the colour that is not fast, which then does not stain the other light-coloured clothing). However, certain dark-coloured items, such as jeans and large towels, should always be washed separately.

Better safe than sorry

▶ Empty all the pockets of the clothes you are preparing to wash. Forgotten keys or pins could seriously damage the drum and the pump. And don't forget to remove tissues, otherwise you'll be spending time brushing an endless stream of white fluff off your clothes.

▶ Remove certain metal accessories from items before washing, such as buckles, the hooks on overalls or curtain rings.

▶ Remember to close press-studs and to remove loose buttons. These could break free and block your washing machine's drainage pump.

▶ Close zips, to protect them, and also close Velcro fastenings to avoid pulling threads on clothes that may catch on the Velcro.

▶ Check that the sleeves on shirts are not rolled up.

The dos and don'ts of stain removal

▶ Don't panic: The good news is that about 90 per cent of common stains disappear if they are treated immediately.

▶ Do try to deal with a spill that is likely to cause staining as soon as it happens so that it doesn't become ingrained or dried, which would make it more difficult to remove later on.

▶ Do dab stains gently with absorbent paper or a clean white cloth, starting from the edges and moving towards the centre. Do not rub.

▶ Don't wet a stain with hot water or you will make it fast.

▶ Do rinse the stain in cold water. If it resists, leave the garment or item to soak in water mixed with well-dissolved washing detergent, unless it's a garment or item made of silk or wool.

▶ Don't put an untreated stained garment directly in the washing machine; in most cases, the stain must be treated first.

▶ Do pour or spray stain remover on the soiled section, before placing the garment in the machine.

▶ Do use a more specific stain-removal treatment (see pages 70–72) if you suspect that the stain is not going to respond to a simple pre-wash spray. In this case, wait until the stain has been completely removed before washing the garment in the machine.

⮫CAUTION!

Expiry date

If you are a committed bleach user, be aware that it is an unstable product that loses its efficacy as it ages. Always discard any bleach past its use-by date. Never use bleach on silk, wool or viscose. And never mix bleach with ammonia – the fumes are highly toxic.

A quick stain-removal kit

- **A roll of paper towel**

- **Clean white towels or rags**

- **Marseille or Sunlight soap** Pure, gentle soaps that can be used on most fabrics.

- **Washing detergent with enzymes** Use these stain removers to dissolve stains at a low temperature, especially stains of organic origin (urine, vomit, blood). Do not use them on wool or silk.

- **Oxygenated powder soaker** (e.g. Napisan Oxyaction Max) Useful for a wide variety of stains, including proteins and fats.

- **Pre-wash stain remover** Available commercially in aerosol form or the more environmentally acceptable trigger spray, or you can make your own (*see* 'Clean and Green', on page 65).

- **White vinegar** An acidic cleaner that neutralises stains. Used for ink, rust and wine stains, but also revives and makes colours fast.

- **Bicarbonate of soda** A wonder substance that's useful on stains in powdered form as well as in solution with water or vinegar.

- **Borax** This useful stain and grease remover also acts as a bleach and disinfectant. It is considered environmentally safe, but is poisonous if ingested, so handle with care.

- **Cloudy ammonia** Acts as a strong alkaline cleaner, mild bleach and a grease solvent. Use strongly diluted (10 per cent) and in a well-ventilated space. Do not use on wool or silk.

- **Hydrogen peroxide** An oxidising bleach that breaks down quickly into water and oxygen. Sold diluted as a 3 or 10 per cent solution. Use it to remove wine, coffee and ink stains, among others, instead of bleaches that contain chlorine. Do not use on wool or silk.

- **Glycerine** This colourless and non-toxic liquid is good for loosening stains that have set or dried.

- **Methylated spirits** In particular it dissolves ink and grass stains. It is usually used diluted; it can cause damage if used undiluted on synthetic fabrics.

- **Eucalyptus oil** An antiseptic, water-soluble oil that is invaluable on a variety of stains, especially glue residue and grease.

- **Dry-cleaning fluid** Also known as white spirit, a powerful solvent that's useful for removing grease and oil stains, especially on non-washable fabrics.

- **Talcum powder or cornflour** Highly absorbent and useful for spreading on grease stains to help absorb grease and oil.

Stain removal at a glance

STAINS	WASHABLE TEXTILES	NON-WASHABLE TEXTILES
Beer	● Dab with a solution of 50 ml cloudy ammonia in 1 litre warm water	Sponge with methylated spirits then rub in a little hard soap. Leave to dry, then brush out the soap
Biro	● Dab with methylated spirits or eucalyptus oil	Dab with dry-cleaning fluid or eucalyptus oil
Blood (new)	● Soak as quickly as possible in cold soapy water or in a mixture of water and ammonia	Mix cornflour with cold water to a thick paste, spread over the stain, allow to dry, then brush off. You may need to repeat
Blood (old)	● Dab with glycerine to soften, then treat as for new blood	Dab with glycerine to soften, then treat as for new blood
Chocolate	● Dab with, or soak in, a solution of 2 tablespoons borax per 500 ml cold water, then warm launder	Dab with water mixed with vinegar or methylated spirits
Coffee, tea, chocolate drink, soft drink	● Dab with, or soak in, a solution of 2 tablespoons borax per 500 ml cold water, then warm launder	Dab with a mixture of white vinegar and methylated spirits
Fruit, fruit juice, egg	● Dab with, or soak in, a solution of 2 tablespoons borax per 500 ml cold water, then warm launder	Dab with cold water followed by glycerine. Leave for an hour, then sponge with lemon juice and wipe off with a damp cloth
Grass	● Dab with dry-cleaning fluid or eucalyptus oil before laundering as usual	Dab with a mixture of white vinegar and methylated spirits
Grease	● White or colour-fast cotton: apply dishwashing liquid. Leave it to act ● Colours: Dab with water mixed with ammonia	Dab with dry-cleaning fluid and cover with talc. Leave it to dry then brush away the residue
Ice-cream	● Soak in water mixed with washing detergent or oxygenated soaker	Dab with methylated spirits, then sponge with water
Jam	● Dab with, or soak in, a solution of 2 tablespoons borax per 500 ml warm water, then launder	Dab with a solution of one part water to three parts methylated spirits or ammonia
Lipstick	● Dab with dry-cleaning fluid, then launder	Dab with dry-cleaning fluid
Perspiration stains	● Apply a thick paste of oxygenated soaker and water, leave for 20 minutes before washing. Repeat if necessary	Have garment professionally dry-cleaned

(Continued overleaf)

Stain removal at a glance (continued)

STAINS	WASHABLE TEXTILES	NON-WASHABLE TEXTILES
Red wine	● Contrary to common thinking, do not pour salt on the stain; on table linen, pour on white wine or vinegar. Dab with a damp cloth soaked in vinegar, or soak in water mixed with borax	Dab with a mixture of one part white vinegar, one part methylated spirits and two parts water
Urine	● White or colour-fast cotton: rinse thoroughly. If necessary, dab with water mixed with hydrogen peroxide ● Colours: Dab with water mixed with ammonia	Dab with diluted white vinegar
Vomit	● White or colour-fast cotton: soak in washing detergent with enzymes, or dab with 10 per cent hydrogen peroxide ● Colours: leave to soak in washing detergent with enzymes. Dab with a mixture of water and ammonia	Dab with a solution of one part water to three parts methylated spirits or water and white vinegar

Keep that new look longer

By taking a few precautions before washing your clothes in an automatic washing machine, you'll keep everything looking cleaner and brighter, and your clothes will be longer lasting as a result.

▶ Turn jeans, trousers and velvet clothing inside out. For the first wash, pre-soak jeans and dark clothes in a mixture of two-thirds water and one-third white vinegar. This will ensure they remain colour-fast and retain the vibrancy of the colour for a longer time.

▶ To prevent shrinkage, wash delicate cotton blouses at a low temperature, with the buttons done up and turned inside out. In the case of a very special blouse or one with pearly buttons, place it in a closed pillowcase. Use this same procedure for underwear and stockings, or use a small bag made of synthetic mesh. Even larger items will have a longer life if they're washed in a mesh bag.

TIMELY TIP

Miracle wipes
Keep a packet of individually wrapped stain-removing wipes on hand. They are very useful for removing or alleviating various stains on clothing.

TIMELY TIP

Baby clothes

A newborn baby's skin is fragile, so wash baby clothes using a special hypoallergenic baby product, or pure mild laundry soap, such as Sunlight or Lux flakes. This will avoid a lot of irritation. Take care to dissolve the soap in very hot water before washing the clothes.

Label washing tips

To keep your clothes in optimum condition, always follow the washing, drying and ironing instructions on the label of a garment.

   This means a garment is machine washable on normal cycles, provided you don't exceed the temperature indicated in the tub symbol

 This symbol indicates a permanent press or wrinkle-resistant garment, which should be washed on a permanent-press cycle (wash at a reduced speed and rinse at a lower temperature with reduced spin-drying)

 A gentle/delicate machine wash is called for. Use the delicate cycle (wash at a greatly reduced speed and rinse at a lower temperature with very reduced spin-drying)

 Hand wash only

 Do not wash at all, even by hand

Maximum load in a machine with a 5-kg capacity

When you're loading up your washing machine, don't cram the washing in, as doing that won't save you any time. The end result will be badly washed clothes that need to go through yet another cycle to get them clean. Use these tips as a guide for what constitutes a maximum load.

▶ As much as 5 kg of cotton that is not very dirty, or 4 kg of very dirty cotton, will make up a full-capacity load.

▶ For very dirty washing, 2.5 kg is the maximum.

▶ Limit synthetics to 2–3 kg (1 kg of nylon panti-hose takes up more room that 1 kg of tea towels).

▶ For woollens, 1–1.5 kg is the maximum load (each item of clothing needs a large space to avoid rubbing, which leads to pilling).

▶ Just 1 kg of delicate washing or silk is a full load.

Average dry weight

Bath towel	250 g
Fitted double sheet	600 g
Flat double sheet	1.3 kg
Pillowcase	200 g
Towelling bath robe	1.4 kg
Shirt	300 g
Man's T-shirt	200 g
Synthetic nightdress	180 g
Child's pyjamas	200 g
Underpants	120 g
Pair of woollen socks	75 g

Skip the pre-wash cycle

Only use the pre-wash cycle for very dirty clothing. Instead, get into the habit of spraying stain remover onto your clothes before washing them.

TIMELY TIP

TIMELY TIP

False time saving

Some machines are fitted with programs for half loads, designed for small quantities of laundry. If you really want to save time, wait until you have enough laundry to do a full wash load.

The right dose

▶ Choose concentrated washing detergents (in packaging that does not take up a lot of space). These detergents are efficient, even at low temperatures.

▶ Adapt the amount of washing detergent to the load of laundry and how dirty it is. It's preferable to use a smaller quantity of detergent rather than waste time having to do extra rinsing. Even if the laundry is heavily soiled, do not overdose on the product: you will not obtain a better result.

▶ Don't use too much fabric softener, either. If you use too large a dose, your washing will not be softer. Instead, it risks becoming stained. And don't forget that fabric softeners can cause allergic reactions.

Smart machine washing

▶ As often as possible, choose low temperature washing cycles (40°C maximum) to reduce the duration of your washes.

▶ If you're really pressed for time, use the ecological program judiciously: although it does allow you to save water and electricity, it increases the washing time because the laundry is moved around for a longer time.

▶ Use the quick wash program only for items that are not particularly dirty. It will not do a satisfactory job on heavily soiled clothes and you'll just have to repeat the process, taking up more time and energy.

CAUTION!

Delicate materials

Never spin-dry clothes made from silk, acetate, rayon or viscose – they may well lose their shape.

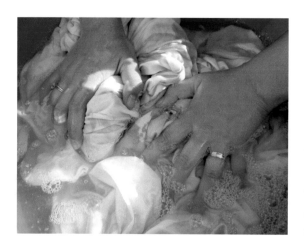

Hand washing know-how

▶ Fragile woollen and silk items – and some synthetic fabrics – must be washed by hand. The fastest solution is to use a gel washing product.

▶ If you run out of detergent or soap, use a regular hair shampoo, and use hair conditioner as a fabric softener. You'll be surprised by the quality of the result.

▶ If you've been too generous with the detergent and your washing is covered in foam, take a piece of laundry soap and swish it in the water. The suds will dissipate almost instantaneously.

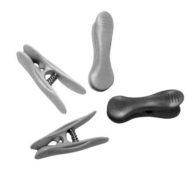

Drying

For starters

▶ Like the washing machine, the automatic dryer has made life much easier for modern families. Dryers mean dry clothes in winter, on rainy days and in dwellings where outdoor line space is at a premium. They dry clothes quickly, remove creases and soften fabrics.

▶ It's easier to put wet washing into the dryer and forget it, rather than peg it out, but line-drying has some distinct advantages: it's considerably more environmentally sound, it costs nothing, it's kinder to your clothes and sunlight is a great natural antibacterial agent. So try to make time to peg out your washing and save your dryer for emergencies only.

Spin-drying equals faster line-drying

▶ Spin-dry your washing as much as possible to reduce drying time. However, if the washing load is made up of different fabrics, such as cotton and synthetics, adapt the spin speed to the most fragile material.

▶ Remove washing from the machine as quickly as possible and then immediately peg it out to dry so that it doesn't crease. This will save you valuable time when it comes to ironing.

Putting it on the line

▶ To avoid the time-wasting task of removing stains from your clean wash, set up your clothes line as far as possible from fruit trees or hedges that may attract birds.

▶ Ensure your washing line is solid, rot-proof and stainless. And give it a regular clean using a damp cloth.

▶ Have an adequate supply of wooden or plastic clothes pegs without any metal parts that could leave traces of rust. And keep the pegs in a covered container so they don't become sodden and leave stains on clean laundry.

Spinning time

Spin-dry your washing at the highest speed possible to reduce the time it takes to dry it on a clothes line (on a sunny day with a light breeze). Adapt the spinning speed to the most fragile material.

SPIN-DRYING SPEED	DRYING TIME
1000 rpm	3 hours
800 rpm	5 hours
400 rpm	8 hours

▶ To ensure that large items dry quickly, do not drape them evenly over one clothes line. Hang them up by their two ends, with the fold hanging down, and then add extra pegs in the centre. This method allows for a good circulation of air and your tablecloths and sheets will dry in the blink of an eye. They'll be easier to fold, too.

▶ Reduce the time you spend ironing by getting into the habit of putting T-shirts on a hanger and smoothing them out with the flat of your hand, then fold them and put them away when dry.

▶ The same method applies to shirts and blouses made from synthetic fibres. As soon as they are dry, you can hang them up directly in the cupboard without ironing.

▶ Most of your clothes won't need ironing if you smooth and neatly fold everything as you take it down from the washing line.

The inside story

Even inside your home or under cover you can dry your washing easily without a clothes dryer if you hang it up in a room with a window or in one that is well ventilated and heated. There are several options that are both practical and fast. Here are a few examples:

▶ The wall dryer, made up of cords that retract into a box after use, has the advantage of taking up very little space, and can be installed in a garage or carport, or even in the bathroom.

▶ Folding drying racks are also convenient to use, provided you have enough space for them once they are unfolded. As with the clothes line, make sure the drying rack is clean, to avoid leaving marks on clothing.

▶ Less common but just as effective, ceiling dryers can be installed over a claw-foot bath and raised and lowered in just a few seconds. The downside is that they can become heavy when loaded up with wet washing.

In good shape

To ensure that your woollen jumpers continue to look new for as long as possible, hand wash them unless the label specifically says they are machine washable. Remove excess water by squeezing them in a towel, without wringing, and dry them flat on a bath towel or on mesh for drying jumpers, which is placed over the bathtub. Above all, don't hang your woollen jumpers up, or they may lose their shape.

COMPARE ENERGY-EFFICIENCY RATINGS

• **In Australia and New Zealand,** consumers can check energy rating labels (*see* page 66) before making their final decision on which appliance to buy. Every new clothes dryer should display a sticker giving its energy rating. The government web site, below, allows you to compare the energy ratings of a number of well-known brand clothes dryers available in both Australia and New Zealand. Look for the appliance with the highest number of stars and you'll save both energy and money. www.energyrating.gov.au

• **In South Africa,** appliance labelling is voluntary, but is likely to become mandatory in the not-too-distant future. The labelling system currently in use is modelled after that of European Union member states, with appliances carrying a rating from A to G, with A being the most energy efficient (*see* page 66). Choose the most energy-efficient clothes dryer for long-term savings. The web site, below, explains the system of appliance labelling for energy standards in South Africa. www.dme.gov.za/energy/app_faq.stm

TIMELY TIP

Clever anti-creasing

In the new generation of dryers, if you don't immediately remove your washing from the dryer when it's dry, the anti-creasing function will make the machine start again. The drum will continue to turn to prevent your clothes from piling up and becoming creased, which will save you ironing.

Choosing a clothes dryer

▶ If you have enough room, choose a separate clothes dryer rather than a combined washing machine and tumble-dryer. This will allow you to dry a lot more laundry at the same time as you wash.

▶ One of the best choices is a front-loading machine with a large drum.

▶ If you live in a freestanding house, choose a tumble-dryer that has the option of ducting the wet air outside, which is a faster system than the condensation system of many other dryers.

▶ Choose a model that's fitted with an electronic auto-sensing program, rather than a simple timer. The machine senses when the clothes are dry and turns itself off, rather than running for a pre-set period, which can be a waste of both time and energy.

▶ If you intend to mount your new clothes dryer on a wall or shelf, first check that the wall can support the dryer's weight.

Smart drying

▶ Check clothes for stains before tumble-drying, as heat might set a stain permanently. If you find a stain, treat it, then re-wash the item.

▶ Shake damp items before drying, to loosen them. This will also help to dry them faster, which saves both time and energy.

▶ Don't overload your tumble-dryer. If the clothes don't have enough room, they will take longer to dry, and the weight will stress the machine's motor, which could end in unnecessary damage.

▶ Don't underload the dryer, either. Besides wasting energy, a nearly empty dryer doesn't work as well as one that is fuller, because the tumbling effect is reduced, resulting in a longer drying time.

CAUTION!

Heat is their enemy

Never dry the following in a dryer: wool, silk, oilskin or linen. They risk being seriously damaged and you will spend fruitless time trying to repair them.

TIMELY TIP

Not a mark

Invest in a set of special drip-dry pegs (available from selected supermarkets and department stores) that don't leave any marks on your clothes – drip-dry and nothing to iron!

Label drying tips

To keep your clothes in optimum condition, always follow the washing, drying and ironing instructions on the label of a garment.

 You can tumble-dry the clothes without any temperature restrictions

 You can tumble-dry the clothes at a moderate temperature

 You can tumble-dry the clothes on low

 Do not tumble-dry

▶ To reduce the risk of creases and shrinkage in your clothing, use the right setting for the fabric you're tumble-drying.

▶ Avoid overdrying: leaving clothes in the tumble-dryer for too long causes shrinkage, static build-up and wrinkling. Ironically, overdrying actually sets wrinkles into fabric, making them difficult to remove during ironing.

▶ Use a mesh laundry bag for drying nylon hosiery and small, delicate items.

▶ Clean the lint filter after each use: this not only improves airflow, which means a more efficient machine and quicker drying time, but it also reduces the risk of fire. (Hold the lint filter at arm's length, to avoid breathing in dust.)

▶ With a condensation machine, empty the collection tray each time you use the dryer and clean the water condenser once a month.

▶ To perfume your washing, reduce static and make it easier to iron, put a fabric-softener sheet (a sort of tissue impregnated with fabric softener; available from selected supermarkets) in your machine. You can also replace this with a face washer that has been soaked in water mixed with fabric softener and wrung out.

On a roll

Roll silk scarves around cardboard tubes from aluminium foil or plastic wrap. This will prevent the scarves from creasing when they're stored in drawers or on shelves, which will save you having to iron them.

Ironing

Pressing matters

The goal for most of us is to do as little ironing as possible, but still look neatly turned out and not as though we've slept in our clothes. Despite the wonderful advances in permanent press and crush-resistant fabrics, sometimes you just have to iron your clothes, but there are tips and tricks to make that job quicker and easier. And taking a little care to wash and dry correctly means you'll cut your ironing time down considerably.

▶ Keep your equipment in a dedicated and easily accessible spot. Don't pile washing baskets and brooms in front of your ironing board or leave the electrical cord of your iron in a tangle.

▶ As soon as your washing is dry (make sure it's properly dry, to avoid clothes becoming musty and smelly), firstly put away everything that doesn't need to be ironed, then make piles according to fabric types.

▶ If your cotton or linen clothes are very dry, moisten them and roll them into a ball for a few minutes. This will allow you to iron them more easily. You can also put them back in the washing machine with a wet towel for a short time. Set the washing machine on the spin-dry cycle and let it run until the cycle has finished.

▶ While the washing machine is moistening some of your ironing pile, start to iron the clothes that require an iron at moderate temperature, and finish up with those that require a higher temperature.

▶ To save time, fold large items in two. Firstly, iron on one side, then fold again and iron on the two other sides.

Label ironing tips

To keep your clothes in optimum condition, always follow the washing, drying and ironing instructions on the label of a garment.

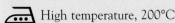 High temperature, 200°C

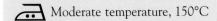 Moderate temperature, 150°C

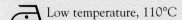 Low temperature, 110°C

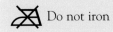 Do not iron

TIMELY TIP

Hold that crease

When you're in a hurry, there is nothing more irritating that having to fight with the creases in a garment. To speed up the task, iron trousers using a damp cloth moistened with water and vinegar. For skirts, use clothes pegs to hold the creases in place at the hem.

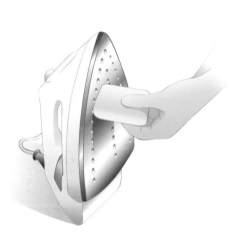

▶ If you prefer ironed sheets, leave a sheet folded in two or in four on the ironing board and iron the other items on top of it. When you have finished your ironing, the sheet itself will be practically ironed.

▶ You can make things go even faster by spraying cotton items with a mixture of 1 litre of water and 2 capfuls of fabric softener.

▶ To keep your silk and velvet clothes or an embroidered shirt looking new longer, iron them on the wrong side, on a towel, using a damp cloth between the garment and the iron. This will also prevent thick material such as wool and rayon from becoming prematurely shiny.

▶ Never iron over a stain – this will heat-set it permanently.

Full-steam ironing

▶ If your household contains at least five people, think about buying a professional steam iron. Because of its large flow of steam, this type of iron halves your ironing time. Choose a model that offers a large range of settings adapted to the different qualities of fabrics and a function that allows you to steam-press clothing on the hanger – this will save you a few trips to the drycleaner.

Silky smooth

To ensure that your iron slides quickly over the washing, its sole plate (base) must be kept perfectly clean at all times.

▶ Rub Marseille laundry soap or toothpaste over the lukewarm base of your iron, then wipe it with a clean, dry cloth.

▶ Do not use anything abrasive on a non-stick iron. Instead, clean the sole plate with a sponge dipped in a detergent and warm water solution, or use methylated spirits on a clean cloth.

▶ **CAUTION!**

Safety first

If you are constantly being interrupted while ironing, choose an iron equipped with a safety cut-off switch that will turn the iron off after 8 minutes if it is unmoved in a vertical position, and after 30 seconds in a horizontal position. (Note that these irons take longer to heat up than a traditional iron, and can be heavier.) If you prefer a classic steam iron, choose a model that is equipped with an integrated self-cleaning and anti-scale system, as well as with a non-stick base so that it slides perfectly.

▶ If the sole plate is marked with brown spots (which can happen, for instance, if you iron starched tablecloths, or an acrylic fibre at too high a temperature), clean it with a specialised product or with a slightly abrasive sponge. You can also turn the iron to hot and iron over a piece of blotting paper until the gunk comes off the sole plate.

The right board

▶ Choose an ironing board where the height can be adjusted to avoid getting a sore back and having to stop ironing frequently.

▶ With a traditional or professional steam iron, choose an ironing board that has an open metal plate so that the humidity can escape and the clothes won't remain damp.

▶ An ironing board should also be fitted with a thick protective cover to lay over an open metal plate and provide an absolutely smooth work surface. Check that the space provided for the iron to rest on is suited to the board you have, especially if it is a professional steam iron.

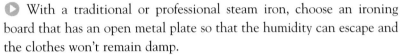

TIMELY TIP

Steam press
Avoid ironing some woollen clothes, such as tailored suits, by hanging them in the bathroom while you're showering. Any creases will drop out in the steam.

Caring for your clothes

TIMELY TIP

The long and short of it
Prevent a long evening dress from trailing in the wardrobe by sewing loops at waist level inside the dress. Turn the bodice inside out and hang the loops from a hanger.

Ready to wear

To ensure that your clothes are always perfect when they come out of the wardrobe, sort them properly when you take them off.

▶ Put dirty clothes into the dirty laundry basket immediately.

▶ Brush, fold or hang up the other clothes that don't require washing. Avoid squashing them together or piling them up on a chair.

▶ If your clothes smell of tobacco, leave them outside overnight on a coathanger in the garden or on a balcony.

▶ Use the right hanger for the job: skirts on skirt hangers with clips, trousers on wooden trouser hangers, curved coathangers for jackets, thick hangers padded at the ends for woollen clothing, a tie rack for ties.

▶ Hang light-coloured dresses inside out.

Give your clothes a good brush

There's no end of clothes brushes available from supermarkets and department stores. Choose one best suited to your clothing's needs.

▶ Use adhesive rollers for lifting human hair, pet fur and fluff off clothes in a flash. Always keep a spare roller handy.

▶ Pill removers are perfect for keeping woollen garments or fleece-type jackets looking good longer. You can buy battery-operated ones that use small razors to cut off woollen pills very quickly.

▶ Pivoting-head clothes brushes that work against their fabric's nap are fast and easy to use (and clean).

Revive colours in the blink of an eye

▶ Some tired-looking clothes can be quickly and inexpensively revived. For example, put your cotton or mixed-fibre jackets and trousers in the washing machine with a washing-machine dye, a fixer and – depending on the type of material – fine salt or white vinegar. Once the cycle has finished, program the appropriate washing cycle and then dry. In a few spins of the drum, you will have a new piece of clothing.

TIMELY TIP

Non-slip coathangers

Ever found an item of clothing you want to wear crumpled in a heap at the bottom of the wardrobe? Wrap several large rubber bands around each end of the coathanger – these will prevent garments from slipping off, especially those made in a super-slippery fabric, such as satin.

TIMELY TIP

No more shine

Areas that get a lot of wear on a woollen suit, such as the knees and elbows, often become shiny. Sponge those areas with 20 ml cloudy ammonia diluted in 300 ml water to remove the shine.

The button war

Buttons will not come off easily if you dab the threads of the buttons on new garments (along with buttons you're re-sewing) with clear nail polish.

Fast care of swimwear

You won't need to race off to buy a new swimming costume every time you go on holiday if you take a little care with the ones you've already got.

▶ To ensure that swimming costumes stay looking new, don't bring them into contact with sunblock, which can affect their elasticity.

▶ Don't leave swimming costumes lying around, wet and rolled up in a ball, when you come back from the beach or the swimming pool.

▶ Always rinse swimming costumes out in cold soapy water, then rinse them thoroughly.

▶ Dry them away from direct sunlight.

Always on the right foot

Keep your shoes looking good from year to year by giving them a little loving care occasionally. They don't require a huge investment in terms of time, but looking after leather shoes means they'll last you for years.

▶ Never dry leather shoes or boots near a heat source as they will become as stiff as cardboard.

▶ Leather shoes need regular cleaning and polishing.

▶ Keep leather shoes on shoe-trees or in a shoe holder and they won't lose their shape.

▶ Roll up a magazine and put it inside knee-length boots so that they keep their shape until the beginning of winter.

Up to the mark

Sponging a small area of a garment often leaves behind a water mark. Hold the stained area in the steam of a boiling kettle until the mark disappears.

TIMELY TIP

Coming unstuck

Rub the lead in a pencil, a bit of dry soap or even the end of a candle along a difficult zip and it will finally give in.

A stitch in time...

▶ Keep a simple sewing kit on hand for mending as quickly as possible. It should include a supply of needles, buttons, different coloured thread, pins and safety pins, as well as scissors, a thimble and a tape measure.

▶ Having trouble threading a needle? Always cut the thread at an angle – a slight point is easier to thread through the eye of the needle.

▶ Always thread the needle before cutting the thread from the spool. This keeps the thread pulling in the right direction of the twist and avoids the time wasted undoing knots.

▶ Keep a scrap of felt or a needlecase with a few needles pre-threaded in basic colours, such as black and white. This makes it much faster to do a quick repair when you're in a hurry.

▶ Keep clear monofilament thread handy – it will match any fabric.

▶ Store matching sets of buttons or those of a similar colour on a length of dental floss or threaded onto a large safety pin. It'll save you having to rummage around for the button you need.

Simple quick fixes

▶ If you want to put up a hem quickly, buy heat-adhesive, double-sided hemming tape, which can be applied in seconds using an iron.

▶ To remove the hemline mark when you're letting down cotton, woollen or denim clothes, wring out a cloth in a solution of 1 cup water, ½ teaspoon white vinegar and ½ teaspoon borax. Place the cloth on the wrong side of the hemline and press with a hot iron.

▶ For a super-strong hold, sew on buttons using dental floss.

▶ When you're sewing on a press-stud, sew on one half, then rub it with dressmaker's chalk. Press against the opposing fabric and it will mark the exact spot for the corresponding side of the fastener.

▶ When sewing on a button, thread your needle with doubled thread so that you're sewing with four strands. You'll need fewer stitches – and less time – to secure your button.

▶ If the pull tab on a zipper comes off, replace it with a small paper clip. If there's time, wind thread or fine yarn around the clip in a colour to match the garment fabric and you'll be good to go.

A sticky situation

Use strips of gaffer (duct) tape to hold a temporary hem on jeans or other firm fabric. It will even last through a couple of washes if you need to buy some extra time!

TIMELY TIP

Preparing to move

Organise the removalist early on

▶ When you have a date for the big move, make a list of all the things that need to be done beforehand, so that you'll be organised when the day of the move arrives (*see* 'Moving house – the countdown', on page 86).

▶ Get quotations from a professional removalist as soon as you can; they book up quite quickly. You can find a removalist using the Internet or the Yellow Pages phone directory, but make sure you compare prices, time frames and services offered for each company, to make the job as simple as possible. Draw up a table so you can compare them at a glance.

▶ Email digital photos of big items to the removalist, to make it easier to estimate the volume of goods needing to be moved. Emailing digital photos is fast and easy, and could be just the insurance you need in the unlikely event of a dispute arising concerning goods being moved.

▶ If you want to take care of part or all of the removals yourself, find out about the rental costs of trucks and vans, and contact people who may be able to help you on the day of the big move.

▶ If the removalist doesn't supply boxes, or you're moving everything yourself, start collecting boxes from your local supermarket. And don't forget to buy all necessary supplies, such as packing tape, bubble wrap and marker pens.

▶ Give some thought to what you're going to do with the furniture you don't take with you. Will you give it away, throw it away or sell it? Make these decisions as early as possible. (*See also* 'Clearing out clutter', starting on page 40.)

Think ahead and don't waste a minute!

▶ If you want repair or renovation work done on the new house or apartment before you move in, have it done as soon as possible to avoid delaying your move. Repair jobs often take longer than expected.

▶ Ask for quotations before you're in possession of the keys so that work can begin immediately and no time is wasted (and just in case an unforeseen problem arises with the repairs or renovations).

▶ Organise additional furniture for storage in your new home as quickly as possible (go online to browse catalogues from companies such as Ikea or Howards Storage World, or Mak-Rak in South Africa), so that your order can be delivered in good time.

Moving house – the countdown

Having a few tips and tricks up your sleeve can save a lot of heartache, not to mention wasted time, when a big house move is looming. All it takes is a bit of forward planning and clear thinking. Follow this checklist as a general guideline.

2–3 months before the move

● If you're renting, send a letter via Express Post or registered post, or an email, to the owner or estate agent agreeing on the date of the move.

● If you're buying, inform your solicitor and the real estate agent of the date you plan to move. The date you can occupy a property will normally be around six weeks from the date of sale. Everyone must then agree on the date and time of a move. (The period may be shorter or longer, depending on circumstances, but both buyer and seller – and their solicitors or conveyancers – must agree on the date).

● Ask for quotations for the move from removalist.

● Inform your employer and ask for time off to move.

● Draw up a standard letter that you can send to official bodies: send by email or standard mail advising them of the details of your anticipated change of address.

● Order new furniture, new carpets, etc.

● If necessary, look for a parking space to rent.

● If you have children start to discuss the move with them and try to engage them in the process rather than exclude them. Remember that change can cause anxieties that may need to be managed.

● Enrol your children in their new school and establish when they can start. At the appropriate time, ensure they are removed from the roll in the schools they are currently attending.

The month before

● Ask your insurance company to cancel your current policy and to issue a policy to insure your new home – taking into account any new furniture you have acquired.

● Change your bank branch, if necessary.

● Cancel or change any direct debits you currently pay, and advise utilities service providers of the move (electricity and gas, cable TV, taxation department, telephone service, Internet provider, the local council if you pay rates, etc.), and give them details of your new address. Make arrangements to have your meters read (electricity, water and gas).

● Notify your local post office and arrange to have your mail redirected. They will redirect mail free for a short period but it may be worth paying for a longer period to ensure that nothing goes astray.

● Ask for your address to be changed on official documents such as tax office notices, rate notices from your local council, the body corporate in an apartment block and the rental bond board, if applicable (you can download many of the relevant forms from the Internet).

● Use the Internet or a local supplier to order any extra boxes you think you'll need for moving.

● Confirm a date with the removal company and, if necessary, pay a deposit to make sure they stick to the specified moving date.

● Start sorting your things out and pack them into boxes supplied by the removalist, or by you.

● Organise your children's timetables for the day of the move and the following day.

● Make an appointment to do a property inspection report on the home you're leaving or notify the body corporate so that strata fees are no longer payable.

● Sort out home office files.

A few days before

● Dismantle any kit furniture you have, and if you haven't kept the assembly instructions, number the different pieces in the order in which they should be reassembled. Make sure you know where the tools are (e.g. an Allen key) to reassemble the furniture.

● Find a specific place for storing your valuables, or give them to someone else for safekeeping.

● Pack the last boxes.

● Have extra house keys cut for the new home.

● Attach keys to the doors of furniture (in small plastic bags so that they don't leave scratches) on the pieces of furniture themselves, using sticky tape.

● Start loading up your car and, if possible, make a few trips to unload some of your basic things, including food if you plan to have an evening meal in the new home – though it would be a lot quicker and easier to have a takeaway meal.

● Disconnect your electrical appliances and pack them with their respective cables attached, wrapped together in paper or plastic bags.

● Empty your fridge and freezer.

● Give your family pet to a friend or relative to mind for a few days while the move takes place.

● Make sure you charge up your mobile phone and keep the charger handy.

Packing up

Well-planned packing

▶ Start packing a few weeks ahead and pack several boxes a day, if you can, remembering to only pack items you won't need in the interim.

▶ Firstly, pack the objects you rarely use (a formal dinner service, books, trinkets, clothing that's out of season), and two days before you leave, pack all the things you'll need on a day-to-day basis into suitcases.

▶ Number each box and note its exact contents as well as the room it's destined for in your new home (kitchen, main bedroom, etc.). Make a full list of the numbers and contents of the boxes, which will allow you to quickly check that everything has arrived safely.

▶ De-clutter while you pack. It's preferable to give things away or throw them out before you move – take the opportunity to give away clothes you're not likely to wear again. And consider throwing out anything you haven't worn for more than a year.

TIMELY TIP

Specialised boxes

To save transport and packing time, don't hesitate to ask your removalist for specially designed boxes to suit different types of objects (you may have to pay extra for them). There are boxes for crockery and books, portable wardrobes for hanging clothes, and sturdy boxes for computer hardware, etc. Or you can buy or rent them from suppliers found on the Internet.

The art of packing boxes

Packing boxes might seem like a straightforward job, but there's an art to it. Take the time to do it properly and you'll save an awful lot of time on unpacking.

▶ Put a strip of packing tape in a crisscross pattern on the top and bottom of each box.

▶ Protect fragile objects by first putting a 3-cm layer of bubble wrap and soft material in the bottom of the box, then put all the heavier items in the bottom of the box before filling it up and sealing it properly. Separate objects from each other using extra layers of padding and pack up all the empty spaces.

▶ Use white butcher's paper, not newspaper, to wrap items: the print comes off on everything and you'll have to wash all your things after you unpack them.

▶ Protect crockery and ceramic items by wrapping them in old, clean tea towels or worn bath towels.

▶ Mark the top and bottom of each box clearly, so that the removalist knows which way is up (and so will you when you come to unpack everything).

▶ Don't overfill packing boxes, as it's better to move more boxes that are easy to handle, than to struggle with a few that are too heavy and risk unnecessary breakages.

Moving interstate or overseas

Making the move to another state or territory

Most of the rules for moving within a city also apply to interstate moves, but here are a few specific tips to save you time.

▶ Find out when removalists are at their busiest and book in as early as possible, or save time and extra stress by moving house at less busy times of the year (usually spring, autumn and winter).

▶ Planning the move in detail as far ahead as you can will save time when you arrive at your destination.

You'll be faced with a mountain of boxes at your destination, so use detailed descriptions on each box to make sorting them out a quick-and-easy job. A box labelled 'clothes' isn't much help, but 'Lucy's clothes' will quickly arrive at the right bedroom.

Consider having a combined garage sale and party to farewell your friends and neighbours. It's also a great way to ensure you pack only those things that you really need, and to get rid of excess clutter.

If you're driving interstate, have the car checked beforehand. Breakdowns cause significant delays that may end up creating problems for the removalist if you don't reach your destination in time.

Relocating overseas

Choose a removal company with strong partnerships and full freight and luggage tracking in the country you are moving to, as well as quarantine and customs-clearance facilities.

Moving overseas can be expensive and complicated, so think about using a free Internet service, such as OneEntry, to compare moving companies and to help you pick the best option.

Ask your removalist to provide you with a list of agents they use for locating pre-schools, child care or kindergartens, as well as local doctors and dentists if you don't already have your own list.

Keep all your important documents with you and make sure they are kept safe. Identity documents such as birth and marriage certificates, passports (and visas if you need them), as well as driver's licence and

---

▶▶ ONLINE INFORMATION FOR FOREIGN NATIONALS

• **Australians** can find out who to contact if they need help while they're overseas, along with other important information, on the Smartraveller web page, which is accessed through a link on the Australian Government's Department of Foreign Affairs and Trade web site, below. www.dfat.gov.au

• **New Zealanders** can visit the web site of the Ministry of Foreign Affairs and Trade, which includes a link to

Safetravel, a site that supplies important information for New Zealanders living and travelling abroad, including specific travel advisories for particular areas overseas. www.mfat.govt.nz

• **South African nationals** can check the Government Services web site, below, for useful information before they begin travelling outside South Africa. www.services.gov.za

Extra luggage

It's a good idea to pack a few extras, such as bed linen and towels, into your regular luggage when you're moving overseas. It could be a life-saver if your boxed and freighted possessions don't arrive on time.

travel insurance, are the most important. Make sure you leave copies with family members, your lawyer or a financial institution in case something gets lost along the way.

▶ Don't forget school and medical records for the whole family, as well as books and games to keep children entertained on your journey.

▶ Use the Internet to research contact details of utility companies.

▶ Take recent insurance and telecommunications bills (phone, Internet Service Provider [ISP]) with you – local companies will accept them as proof of a good record in starting up new services.

▶ If you're taking pets with you, remember to also take proof of their vaccinations and ID chip, if they have one.

▶ Make sure you know where electrical adaptors are for any essential appliances (and chargers for mobile phones and laptops), so that you don't waste time searching for them when you first arrive.

Moving in

Make it quick and painless

▶ Form two teams. One team will supervise or undertake loading up. The other team will unload everything and start to unpack.

▶ Unload the toolbox and the torch first. You will need to have these handy all day on the first day of the move and the following days as well.

▶ Quickly hang up all the clothes in the cupboard or wardrobes on the coat hangers that you have sensibly left them on.

▶ Slide lightly packed drawers, which can be transported as they are, straight back into place (having only removed fragile objects).

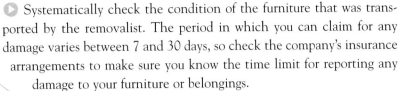

Systematically check the condition of the furniture that was transported by the removalist. The period in which you can claim for any damage varies between 7 and 30 days, so check the company's insurance arrangements to make sure you know the time limit for reporting any damage to your furniture or belongings.

Check that the number of boxes unloaded corresponds to the number on your list, and that you haven't left anything behind in your old home. If any boxes are missing, alert the moving company.

Don't try to unpack everything on the day you move. Take time to work out the best position for favourite decorations in their new setting, because this will help everyone to think of the new place as home.

The final formalities

In the days after the move, make sure you change your electoral details to include the new address.

Change the address on your driver's licence and car registration papers, and let your car insurance company know about the new address.

When redirected mail comes to your new home, alert each sender to your new address, so that you notify everyone of the move.

Advise your local council or rates authority office and your household insurance company of your new home address.

If you haven't already done so, get to know your new neighbours and introduce them to everyone in your family, including your pets. New neighbours can also help out by lending things you need and haven't unpacked yet, or save you a trip to the shops.

Make a list from day one of all the things you need to buy or replace, then do one big shopping trip instead of wasting time going back and forth to the shops.

CAUTION!

Unpack carefully

Check that you have completely emptied each box. When you unpack, you may risk throwing away small items of crockery, such as lids or saucers, or small fragile items as you throw away their protective wrapping.

TIMELY TIP

Finish the finishing touches

Plan to move in only when varnished floors and any new paintwork is finished and dried, so that you won't have to wait weeks before you can unpack.

2 Family, work and wellbeing

Pregnancy and parenting

 ▶▶ **FIND OUT MORE**

- If you're seeking access to government services such as subsidies for pre-school and out-of-school care, get up-to-date information from the Family Assistance Office web site, below. **www.familyassist.gov.au**
- The Working for Families web site, below, details government services available to all New Zealanders, irrespective of marital or employment status. **www.workingforfamilies.govt.nz**
- Check the New Zealand Ministry of Social Development's Work and Income web site, below, to see if you're eligible for the Family Tax Credit and the Childcare Subsidy. **www.winz.govt.nz**

What financial services are available?

▶ Before your baby is born, find out what level of government financial support is available to you, and have the necessary paperwork organised (*see* 'Find out more', at left). Investing in a trip to the appropriate social security office – in Australia, it's Medicare or Centrelink – while you're still pregnant can save you considerable time and money in the long run. Always call ahead first, to make an appointment or an enquiry, to avoid wasting time, as government offices are notoriously busy.

▶ If you're in paid employment, find out the details of your maternity leave entitlements – and for some fathers, paternity leave – and supply all the necessary details to make the most of these entitlements.

▶ If you're paying off a home loan, and taking time off to have a baby is going to put you under considerable financial strain, discuss repayment options with your bank or lender as soon as possible. You might be able to pay more off while you're still working in order to reduce the payments when you're on maternity leave, or rework the conditions of repayment temporarily. A quick check early on could save a lot of hassle.

▶ In Australia, benefits such as the one-off maternity payment need to be applied for after the baby is born. Family tax benefits and childcare benefits are also usually applicable, but vary depending on individual circumstances. Phone Centrelink to find out which forms need to be filled in before you front up to the customer services' centre in your area.

Consider your childcare options

▶ Start researching child care before your baby is due, to take advantage of all the available options. If you're planning to put your child into care when they're under one year of age, or if your child has special needs, your choices may be more limited, so booking in early is essential.

▶ Before deciding what sort of care is best for you, ask yourself four questions: What are my family's needs? What are my lifestyle restrictions? How far am I prepared to travel for child care? and What is my budget?

▶ Take advantage of information and tips from other parents when it comes to making

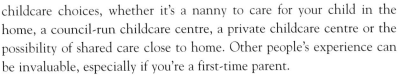

childcare choices, whether it's a nanny to care for your child in the home, a council-run childcare centre, a private childcare centre or the possibility of shared care close to home. Other people's experience can be invaluable, especially if you're a first-time parent.

▶ Find out what the options are in your area. Finding a government-accredited childcare centre in your area can be as easy as contacting your local council after checking the available information online.

▶ Web sites such as careforKids.com.au not only provide data on childcare vacancies for Australians in various localities, but also help to streamline waiting-list applications. Do a bit of online research while you're pregnant, as the more popular centres tend to book up quickly.

TIMELY TIP

'Special' care

If you're looking for special conditions in a childcare facility, such as one that's centred around a particular religion, your choices are going to be more limited, so ask around for recommendations as soon as possible.

Top 10 questions for childcare providers

Before making your final decision about child care, based on your research and discussion with other parents, find out what the policy of childcare providers is so that you can feel completely confident you're making the best possible decision for your family.

● **What is the childcare and development policy?**

● **Is there a discipline policy?** Find out how staff discipline children so that you can feel confident your child is being thoughtfully guided and not harmed by harsh punishment or lax attitudes that encourage bad behaviour. It's best to talk to the centre's coordinator about this.

● **What safety and security measures are in place?**

● **What is the rate of staff turnover?** A rapid turnover of staff, or too many casual staff, can be very unsettling for some children.

● **What sort of food is offered?** If your child has an allergy, or you want to make sure that only healthy food and snacks are supplied, you need to make enquiries and ask whether the staff are trained to cater for special needs or treatment in relation to allergies.

● **Is there a sickness policy?** What sort of conditions are children sent home for, and how sick do they have to be to stay at home?

● **Is there an option for 'sick care'?** For some parents, having an option for those times when their child is not seriously sick can be a great time and job saver.

● **Do I have to pay for days that my child is absent?**

● **Is there a late fee if I don't pick up my child on time?** If it's possible that you'll be held up at work or in traffic occasionally, you might need to arrange for someone to pick up your child at those times, to avoid incurring late fees.

● **Can I stay with or visit my child at any time?** Some children benefit from having a parent stay for a while at drop-off time, until they settle in, but not all childcare centres encourage it, so check first.

TIMELY TIP

Minimise stretch marks

Whether or not you develop stretch marks is largely genetic – if your mother had them, chances are you'll have them, too. Try to minimise them by moisturising sensitive areas (thighs, stomach, hips) regularly from the third month of pregnancy onwards. It'll also reduce the itchiness that often occurs during pregnancy. Any moisturising cream or oil will do, but particularly one containing vitamin E.

Understand your birth options

Being organised long before your baby is born will ensure that you're not hampered by limited options and unnecessary disappointment.

▶ Think about where you want to give birth (in a hospital labour ward, a hospital birth centre or at home as part of an assisted home birth with a midwife, a GP or an obstetrician), and make your decision, along with the necessary bookings, as soon as possible.

▶ If you're privately insured and have chosen an obstetrician, book an appointment as soon as your pregnancy is confirmed. You'll need a referral from your GP before attending the actual visit, but you don't need a referral to make the booking. If you leave it until later you might literally spend hours on the phone trying to find an obstetrician. If you are not sure about who to go to or what to do, visit your GP or ring your local hospital's maternity section and ask for advice.

▶ Find out your antenatal care options. The public health system in Australia, New Zealand and South Africa has antenatal clinics in major public hospitals, and some offer programs of midwife antenatal care, where, after regular visits, a midwife manages your delivery. Usually, this is only available for 'low-risk' pregnancies. Your doctor or local hospital will be able to tell you whether this service is available to you.

▶ Consider a shared-care arrangement, where both your GP (if they're certified) and the hospital share your antenatal care. To do this in Australia, you have to be considered 'low risk'.

▶ While your first priority is your own and your baby's health, if numerous types of care are suitable for you and you feel a bit confused by all the options, look at factors such as waiting times and locations for your antenatal visits – it could save you many hours of waiting around.

▶ Always ring before turning up for antenatal visits, to check the waiting time. This is especially important if you're seeing a private obstetrician, as it's not uncommon for them to be called out for an urgent delivery during consulting times, which can play havoc with their appointment schedule – not to mention yours!

Take care of your body

It's vitally important to prepare yourself for all the body changes during pregnancy, and act before problems arise. You'll save time by avoiding the unpleasant difficulties that inevitably come with complications.

▶ If you don't want to be incapacitated by morning sickness in the first few months, ask your doctor to prescribe treatment as soon as the first signs appear. Or try a few home remedies that are safe for use during pregnancy, after you have consulted your doctor.

▶ If you have any problems with acne, heartburn, cramps and dizziness, and symptoms persist, make sure you get treatment instead of suffering.

▶ If you're prone to backache ask about appropriate strengthening and pain-relieving exercises and start doing them early on in the pregnancy. As the saying goes, an ounce of prevention is worth a pound of cure.

▶ Start wearing support pantihose if your legs begin to ache or your ankles swell, or if you have a family history of varicose veins. This can prevent a lot of disabling leg pain later on. Specially designed support hose are available from pharmacies.

▶ Try to schedule in a 10-minute rest in the early afternoon during the second and third trimester, if possible. Keep your legs raised higher than your heart while resting and generally regroup in readiness for the afternoon and evening. This will improve your endurance throughout the day.

Invest in suitable clothing

TIMELY TIP

Go Internet shopping

The number of shops specialising in maternity wear is small, so it's faster and easier to buy maternity clothes online or by mail order. Another quick option is to buy regular clothing in a larger size, in a style that's flattering to an expanding waistline.

Depending on what you wear, chances are you'll be able to fit into your regular clothes up until the fifth month of pregnancy. After that, you'll need to expand your wardrobe to match your expanding girth.

▶ Your choice of clothing during pregnancy is important, not least because it can have a very positive effect on the way you feel about yourself. The trick is to choose carefully and keep it simple. You don't need to go out and spend hours shopping for expensive items, just write down a list of basics.

▶ First things first: invest in good-quality maternity underwear. Wearing bras and underpants that are too tight is both uncomfortable and breast tissue could be compromised at a time when your breasts are undergoing enormous change.

▶ During the first few months, a sports bra is the best option (because it's designed to offer maximum support), before moving on to a proper maternity bra or a breastfeeding bra. It's essential to be properly measured before buying a maternity bra.

▶ Choose at least one pair of pants and a skirt with an adjustable waist or those made from material that can expand over your stomach.

TIMELY TIP

Read all about it

Browse online and buy one good general reference book on pregnancy and the early years of childhood. *Baby Love* by Robin Barker and *The New Contented Little Baby Book* by Gina Ford are two well-known and respected reference books. Grandparents often find reference books useful, too.

▶ Opt for loose tops and jackets or cardigans.

▶ Leggings, if suitable for your body shape, can work well with a short dress or under a long shirt, and they're very comfortable in the later months of pregnancy when your legs may ache at the end of the day.

▶ Have one 'formal' outfit on hand so that you can look and feel good on special occasions, even in the last few months.

▶ Try to stick to a colour scheme so you can mix and match your maternity pieces to maximise the wear you get out of them.

▶ Buy clothes that are low maintenance – suitable for the washing machine, not dry-clean only. Anything that doesn't require ironing is also a great time saver.

▶ Borrow whatever you need from a friend. It's possibly the quickest and easiest way to acquire a complete wardrobe without lifting a finger!

Pregnancy timetable

Under 10 weeks
● Confirm pregnancy and discuss options of care with your GP
● Consider a dating ultrasound if applicable (about 8 weeks)
● Blood tests
● Genetic counselling for women 37 years and older
● Discuss prenatal screening options with your doctor
● Referral to hospital antenatal clinic or private obstetrician

10 weeks
● Routine visit (antenatal clinic or private obstetrician)

11–13 weeks
● Ultrasound scan – screening for Down's syndrome, including blood tests

16 weeks
● Routine visit. Organise birth classes through the hospital or a private midwife

18–19 weeks
● Ultrasound scan – check dates as well as growth, organs and (if desired) sex of baby

20 weeks
● Routine visit

24 weeks
● Routine visit and blood tests

28 weeks
● Routine visit (anti-D given if the mother is Rh negative)

32 weeks
● Routine visit

34 weeks
● Routine visit

36 weeks
● Routine visit (anti-D given if the mother is Rh negative)

37–40 weeks
● Weekly routine visits

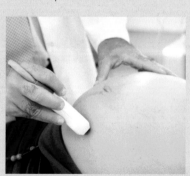

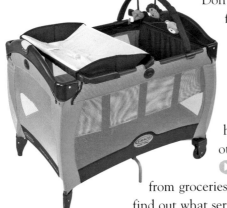

Get ready in good time

Don't leave everything to the last minute. The tiredness you feel before the birth is minimal compared to how you'll feel with a newborn to care for.

▶ Fill your freezer with food in advance so you spend less time in the kitchen (or ask family to do it for you).

▶ Do as much house cleaning as you can before your due date, or pay professional cleaners to give your home a thorough going over while you're busy getting other things organised.

▶ See what you can possibly have home delivered – from groceries to a mobile car service and car wash. Surf the net to find out what services are available online and, if you can, try them out beforehand. Not having to go supermarket shopping every week when you have a new baby at home is a great saving in time.

▶ Prepare the baby's room, wash and put away the baby clothes and store the baby-care products and nappies.

▶ Organise the pram, change table, cot or bassinette, and have the baby capsule fitted into the car. If you're organised and invest just a little bit of time researching online, you'll find most of what you need and can arrange to have it delivered to your home. And don't forget to check eBay auctions for fast bargains.

▶ Say yes to any friends who want to pass on baby clothes, and sort out what they give you as soon as possible. With a good supply of singlets and all-in-one bodysuits you'll save plenty of time on washing, which is a huge help.

TIMELY TIP

It's a... baby!

Put a list of emergency phone numbers next to the phone, and prepare a list of the people to call after the birth. Or organise a group email list so that when the baby is born one message can be sent – and a digital photo – with the push of a button. Similarly, you can send out a group SMS with the push of a button.

Make the most of your stay in hospital

▶ Have everything you need ready to go. If you're expecting your first child, make sure you have everything that's written on the list you'll be given by the hospital, even if some items seem unnecessary. It may be complicated to get some things afterwards if you need them.

▶ At least for the first few weeks, choose bodysuits rather than cross-over clothing for your baby because they're easier to put on.

▶ Don't be shy about asking friends not to visit while you're in hospital, and let phone calls on your mobile go to your message bank. You'll need all the time you have to bond with and feed your baby, and get as much rest as possible before going home, where help may not be on hand. Some hospitals have a nursery so that new mums can have a break.

TIMELY TIP

Declaration of birth

You have to register your baby's birth with the Registry of Births, Deaths and Marriages in both Australia (in your state or territory) and New Zealand. In Australia this needs to be done within 60 days of the baby's birth. Usually, the form is given to new parents in the hospital but it is also available from the Registry office or any post office.

▶▶ **FIND OUT MORE**

• For any questions concerning breastfeeding, contact the Australian Breastfeeding Association's web site, below.
www.breastfeeding.asn.au
• The La Leche League web site, below, has a lot of useful information and support for breastfeeding mothers.
www.lalecheleague.org.nz
www.llli.org/SouthAfrica.html

▶ Some of the larger public hospitals offer free post-natal classes to help you with everything from bathing your baby to doing pelvic floor exercises. Try and attend as many of these as you can.

▶ Ask nurses all the questions that come into your mind, and note down anything you may need to refer to later on. This will save precious time looking for answers when you're back home and feeling flustered.

▶ Larger hospitals often employ a lactation consultant to help new mothers who are experiencing breastfeeding difficulties. Midwives are also a great source of general information on baby health.

▶ Many of the problems associated with breastfeeding can be avoided by establishing good technique early on, so take advantage of the help and advice that is readily available in hospital.

Breastfeeding

Opt for breastfeeding wherever possible. Not only will it save you a lot of time during the first four months of your baby's life, it's the best whole food for newborns.

▶ You won't have to prepare, heat and clean bottles, or take them with you when you go out.

▶ Your milk will always be at the right temperature, it will usually be a sufficient quantity, it will be sterilised and of optimal quality.

▶ Breastfeeding gives the new-born baby natural immunity to most infections and also triggers the uterine contractions in the mother, which are essential to enable the uterus to go back to its previous size.

▶ For some women, breastfeeding also allows them to easily lose the extra kilos they put on during pregnancy.

Make breastfeeding as easy as possible

Often, the advice and help you receive at the beginning is the key to successful and happy breastfeeding (*see* 'Find out more', at left).

▶ Inform the midwives at the hospital or birth centre, or a visiting consultant midwife that visits your home, that you have chosen to breastfeed, and ask them to help you put your baby on the breast soon after birth or offer support and advice if you're having difficulties.

TIMELY TIP

Express bottles

To save time on preparation, fill all the sterilised bottles you'll use during the day with the right amount of water. Then all you have to do is add the baby formula powder and give the bottle a good shake before warming.

▶ Most Australian and New Zealand major public hospitals have a policy of newborns 'rooming-in' with mothers, which means that you can feed on demand from day one. Ask for help whenever you need it.

▶ Avoid many of the common breastfeeding problems by asking the lactation consultant or midwife to explain everything to you, from how often to feed to the positions associated with breastfeeding.

▶ Wear clothing that opens at the front to make it easier to breastfeed.

▶ If you have trouble breastfeeding when you go home, call your local doctor or the hospital and ask for someone to do a home visit, or go along to a lactation clinic so that you can receive support and help.

Pump it!

Many women who breastfeed also choose to express breast milk so that their baby can be fed breast milk via a bottle. A great way to save time and hassle is to use the breast pump days, or even weeks, prior to when it's needed, then freeze the milk.

Breast milk stays fresh for up to 24 hours in the fridge and three months in the freezer. This is especially useful for those times when the milk is going to be fed to your baby by your partner if you need to sleep, or by a babysitter if you go out.

An electric breast pump is generally easier to handle than a manual one (you can hire pumps from many pharmacies or the Australian Breastfeeding Association). With a little experience and skill, you'll soon be able to pump your milk from one breast while you are feeding your baby with the other, which is a great timesaving solution.

Keep bottle feeding simple

Some babies feed via a bottle from day one, while others move on to bottle feeding after weening, especially when the baby is less than six months old. In any case, get organised to save time preparing feeds.

▶ As a general rule of thumb, you'll need six to eight bottles each day for full bottle feeding, otherwise you'll have to sterilise bottles more than once a day, which takes up a lot of extra time.

▶ Buy bottles of the same brand so you don't waste any time trying to match up teats and rings.

▶ Rinse each bottle and teat straight after use to make cleaning and sterilising fast and efficient.

TIMELY TIP

Control the flow

Different teats suit different babies, and research has so far failed to show that 'orthodontic' teats are any better than regular ones. Most brands have teats with different flow rates: slow (0–3 months), medium (3–6 months), or fast for older babies.

▶ Options for sterilising bottles include boiling, using a chemical sterilant or using a steam steriliser. An electric express steam steriliser takes about 8 minutes, while a device that you place in the microwave oven usually takes around 10 minutes. Try to always have bottles sterilised in advance so you can just grab one and fill it with boiled water if you need to go out unexpectedly.

▶ You don't need to sterilise bottles after your baby is four months old. Simply rinse used bottles, then put them through a dishwasher cycle.

▶ Most toddlers can safely drink either cow's milk or soy milk after one year of age. If your child has a reaction to cow's milk, see your GP.

Try your hand at multi-tasking

▶ You may not want to make a habit of it, but making phone calls while you're breastfeeding or bottle feeding can really help to get things done. And the sound of your voice is music to your baby's ears.

▶ Buy a cordless telephone so you can phone at the same time as you take the washing out of the machine, prepare the dinner, do the ironing, etc.

▶ Make the most of the time you're in your baby's room, and he or she is still in their cot, to tidy up and do some light cleaning. You can still talk and hum songs while you're working so that they can listen to your voice and see you. And it teaches your baby to spend some awake time in the cot.

▶ A sling or baby backpack is a godsend for the multi-tasking mother, especially when the baby is having trouble going off to sleep or is having a crying spell and grocery shopping still needs to be done, along with setting the table or hanging out some washing.

▶ Slings and strollers or prams are also great for achieving two things at once: you can exercise by going for a brisk walk or jog (if you have the correct sort of stroller) while your baby sleeps.

TIMELY TIP

Fuss-free sterilisation

The fastest and least complicated way to sterilise babies' bottles and dummies is with a steam sterilising unit, such as the Avent steriliser.

Establish a routine

Try to establish a routine for specific times of the day. All mothers will tell you that this helps you to save precious time, which is especially true of sleep. Every minute spent in training is 10 minutes saved later on.

▶ Establish a set routine – dinner, bath, story time, bed – so you lead up to bedtime in the same way each day. Routine is comforting for babies.

▶ Teach your child from an early age to go to sleep by him- or herself. It's a real gift, both for the baby and the rest of the household. It's not always easy at first, but there are methods that work successfully without inflicting trauma on the parents or the baby.

▶ To find the right method for you and your baby, read one of the many books on the subject while you're feeding. Save time by checking titles online, then simply order one from Amazon.com or another big book seller. Or phone your local bookshop and ask them to order it in for you.

The dos and don'ts of baby attire

▶ Don't dress your baby in fancy outfits every day. It's incredibly tempting to dress up a baby to show them off, but many outfits aren't practical, and you can waste time just getting them on and off for nappy changes.

▶ Do keep the little fancy outfits and accessories for big occasions or for photo sessions, avoiding anything with stiff lace or creased fabric that may hurt the baby's delicate skin.

▶ Do use practical clothes that can be washed at 30–60°C, because in the first few years you'll be doing a lot of washing – probably on a daily basis.

▶ Do choose clothes with press-stud closings instead of buttons, and do make sure all the clothes fit the baby properly. Overly tight clothing is constricting whereas overly loose clothing can present a choking hazard.

▶ Don't waste time ironing baby clothes, especially terry-towelling bodysuits and jumpsuits; simply fold them as they come off the clothes line or out of the tumble-dryer.

▶ Don't buy booties that continually fall off and don't worry about putting shoes on your baby until he or she has been walking for at least six weeks (no matter how tempting it might be!). Instead, buy well-fitting socks with non-skid material on the soles.

Average clothing sizes	
SIZE	AGE OF BABY
0000	Newborns under 4 kg (approx birth to 3 months)
000	Babies under 6 kg (approx 3–6 months)
00	Babies between 6–8 kg (approx 6–9 months)
0	Babies more than 8 kg (approx 9–12 months)
1	Babies above 10 kg (approx 12–24 months)

TIMELY TIP

Blending baby food

To prepare babies' meals faster, buy a hand-held blender designed for soups and sauces. All you have to do is blend a batch of cooked food and it's ready to eat. Freeze leftovers in small containers and you've got food to go, too.

Eat as a family

▶ As a general rule, train small children to eat what everyone else is eating, to save having to prepare multiple meals. A good example is a roast dinner: adults eat it with a knife and fork, toddlers feed themselves after it has been cut up into small dice, and babies are fed roast meat, vegetables and gravy that has been blended.

▶ As much as possible, only use the little jars of baby food, soups and other dishes as a back-up when you don't have time to cook or you're out and about.

▶ Try to encourage a wide range of tastes as soon as possible, instead of offering pasta with a bland sauce every night.

▶ Check current recommendations with your GP, but six months is usually the time to start babies on pureed foods, which can be mixed with a little boiled water, baby formula or breast milk. Pureed potato, pumpkin, carrot, apple or banana are ideal.

▶ When your baby can sit up unaided, it's a good time to introduce a selection of appropriate finger foods, such as toast, rusks, cheddar cheese or pieces of soft fruit. While it can be messy, getting them used to a variety of textures may discourage fussy eating later on.

CAUTION!

Say 'no' to honey

Do not feed honey to babies under 12 months of age – on its own, mixed into other foods or in processed foods containing honey. The spore of the bacteria *Clostridium botulinum* can be found in honey, and in children under 12 months of age the spores can release a toxin that causes botulism, which can result in prolonged and serious illness.

TIMELY TIP

Freeze the excess

Prepare your purees, compotes and soups in larger quantities and freeze the excess in small plastic bags (after first freezing them in ice-cube trays). That way, you will always have homemade food on hand.

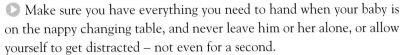
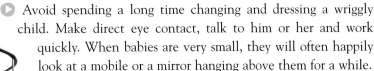

Safe changing saves time – and disaster

▶ Make sure you have everything you need to hand when your baby is on the nappy changing table, and never leave him or her alone, or allow yourself to get distracted – not even for a second.

▶ Avoid spending a long time changing and dressing a wriggly child. Make direct eye contact, talk to him or her and work quickly. When babies are very small, they will often happily look at a mobile or a mirror hanging above them for a while.

▶ For older babies and toddlers, fill a basket with small objects that you can give them each time. Change the contents of the basket regularly, to keep interest levels up.

▶ If your baby still starts to cry or move too much, do everything you can to attract their attention: sing, dance, pull faces, play a music box, tell a story, etc. Chances are they'll quickly become absorbed in what you're doing and stay still for another few seconds. Luckily, the more nappies you change, the faster you get!

▶ Start changing nappies on the floor or the bed when your baby is old enough to fight a nappy change, or if they keep flipping over while you're wrestling with them and the nappy at the same time.

▶ Some toddlers will tolerate having their nappy changed while they're standing up, but do it in the bathroom, both to save on cleaning up if there's a spill, and to signal to them that this is where toilet business is usually conducted. And encourage them to dress themselves afterwards.

Keep special items handy

To avoid spending hours looking for a lost dummy or security blanket, follow a few golden rules.

▶ Get yourself a large supply of dummies so you always have one on hand: a spare in your handbag, one in the car glovebox and one in the pram, etc.

▶ Scatter two or three dummies in the cot near a toddler's head. This way they'll be able to find one

and won't wake you up in the middle of the night to replace the one that's fallen out of their mouth, which is a common scenario.

▶ Buy dummy clips so you can attach a dummy to the top sheet or to your baby's pyjamas. You can also sew one on to the safety blanket.

▶ As soon as your child starts to show a distinct fondness for a security blanket, go and buy one or two extras, just in case. If you ever need a replacement in a hurry, you'll save time and unbelievable hassle!

▶ Rotate security blankets so they all have more or less the same smell and the same degree of wear to avoid time-wasting tantrums.

TIMELY TIP

Home hairdresser

If you want to cut your child's hair but he or she won't stop moving, choose a calm moment (after meals, perhaps). Then put them into the high chair with a special toy or a snack that will keep them quiet long enough for you to finish cutting their hair.

Early training

Encourage toddlers to be independent as early on as possible.

▶ Encourage small children to dress themselves by laying out their clothes on the bed and letting them do as much as they can on their own, only helping when it's necessary (and don't forget to praise them).

▶ Buy a toy box so that small children can put their toys away easily.

▶ Build good habits. Encourage small children to help you do the housework and put away the shopping (within reason). Consider buying a toy broom, a wooden spoon and bowl, or a garden tool set so they work with you. It may take them a little longer to get their 'tasks' done, but, in the meantime, you'll be able to complete your own.

▶ Make the most of your trips to the supermarket to educate small children about food. It will help to keep them involved if you talk about the products you're buying (comment on their shape, colour, taste, etc.), or ask them to pick up items you know they'll recognise ('Can you please find a can of sweet corn for me?') as you go along the aisles.

Act fast with minor injuries

▶ As soon as your child starts to move around by themselves, always have a tube of arnica, some antiseptic and a few Band-aids on hand so you can act quickly.

▶ Be prepared for bronchial infections, which are unavoidable once your child starts socialising.

▶ Wash your hands often. Many infections are transmitted from hand to mouth, so get everyone in

your family to wash their hands properly and frequently. And teach young children good hygiene habits from early on to keep illness at bay.

▶ During cold and flu season, rinse your child's nose with normal saline (0.9 per cent salt water), to help keep the nasal mucosa moist and to flush out germs. You can buy saline spray packs from most pharmacies.

▶ To help small children swallow medication without added traumas, try a few tricks, such as buying fruit-flavoured medication, mixing the medicine with a little cordial and water, or having a sweet biscuit and a glass of water on hand as soon as the medicine's gone down. Never mix medicines with honey (*see* 'Caution!', on page 104), as honey forms a coating on tooth enamel, encouraging the formation of dental caries. (*See also* 'Caring for your health', starting on page 122.)

School years

Ease back into the routine

Getting children ready to go to school, at any age, is a simple equation: the better prepared you are, the fewer surprises you'll have and the less time you'll waste on last-minute details.

▶ Plan to return from holidays at least two days before school resumes, because children need a few days to readapt to their environment and the change of rhythm that the school term brings.

▶ During the last two weeks of holiday, slowly get your children back into their usual bedtime routine and avoid late nights so that they wake up in time.

▶ Use the day or two before school resumes to take your children to the dentist for a check-up, or to get their hair cut.

▶ Make a list of what needs to be done before school resumes and check items off as you go, as well as noting anything outstanding.

▶ Buy iron-on name labels instead of sewing cloth labels onto school uniforms. You can order them online at www.mynamelabel.com.

▶ Buy lace-up school shoes, not sports shoes, for everyday school wear. Joggers and sneakers tend to make feet sweat excessively and don't provide enough ankle support.

▶ Opt for school trousers with enough length to have a generous hem on them so that you can let them down as necessary and not have to go shopping for a new pair. Use iron-on hemming tape for super-fast hemming. (*See also* 'Simple quick fixes', on page 84.)

▶ Consider buying clothing and accessories – that don't need to be tried on – from mail-order companies, or shop online and place an Internet order, then simply wait for your goods to be delivered.

TIMELY TIP

Beat the crush

Avoid the usual back-to-school crush and queues by buying school clothes and shoes well ahead of time (not too far ahead, though, or you may have to replace those clothes and shoes sooner than is necessary!).

➡ CAUTION!

Comfort versus style

Before giving in and buying the backpack or school bag your child is begging for, check that the straps are wide enough and that it isn't too heavy (when it's full, it shouldn't exceed 10 per cent of your child's weight). This will also save you having to go and buy a more appropriate model, which may be harder to find once the school year has begun.

TIMELY TIP

Zip it up!
Put a charm, a small key ring or a ribbon through the hole at the end of the zipper on a small child's jacket. This will allow them to use the zip much more easily.

Keep on top of supplies

▶ To avoid the rush at the end of the holidays, buy all the necessary items (paper, pens, pencils and rubbers, notebooks, folders, diary, homework diary, etc.) well ahead of time.
▶ Take advantage of any second-hand book sales organised in your children's school. And don't forget that you can buy second-hand books on the Internet, along with stationery supplies, saving you both time and money.

Get with the program

Being involved in your child's school life isn't a timesaving exercise, but make the time you do have to offer as useful and practical as possible, and you'll reap the rewards and avoid wasting time.
▶ Set aside time to volunteer help in your child's school, even if it's only once or twice a year. While it's important to foster a growing level of independence in children, being present occasionally at school is a way of staying in touch with what's happening in the school community and with your child and the families of their friends.

▶ For the first year or two at least, drop your child off at his or her classroom, and pick them up there as often as possible. This encourages a feeling of security, which pays off in time saved when they're older, and it also gives you the chance to meet and talk to other parents or the class teacher.
▶ Invest in an hour or so at parent-and-teacher meetings and open days held at the school, and you'll save time ringing around to find out what's going on in the school community.

> **CAUTION!**

Get the sizing right
If you're going to buy school clothes without your children present, make sure you note their current clothes size, or take their measurements beforehand. It'll save you having to return, exchange or alter clothing.

▶▶ **PRINTABLE FORMS ONLINE**

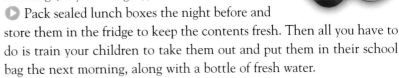

• **Visit web sites devoted to helping you get organised** and simplify your life. It's all there waiting for you, from a form listing the phone numbers for your preferred takeaway restaurants – with a list of favourite dishes so that you're ready to order in a flash – to emergency contacts and birthday party planners. Take advantage and download printable forms that will help you to save valuable time. Here are two examples of these sorts of web sites.
www.realsimple.com/organizingforms
www.organizedhome.com/printable

TIMELY TIP

Keep it cold, keep it fresh

A quick-and-easy way to keep your child's lunch fresh during the hot summer months is to freeze small tetra packs of fruit juice and then pack them into the lunch box to act as an ice brick. The food will stay fresh for hours and the fruit juice will melt to become a refreshing drink.

Avoid morning madness

Whatever can be done the night before school saves time getting ready in the morning. Remember, putting away should be as easy as getting out.

▶ Encourage children to empty out their school bag at the end of the day, put their lunch box and drink bottle in the kitchen, hand over notes or permission slips, put dirty clothes in the laundry and organise their homework to avoid having to do it all in the morning (or you doing it), when time is short.

▶ Pack sealed lunch boxes the night before and store them in the fridge to keep the contents fresh. Then all you have to do is train your children to take them out and put them in their school bag the next morning, along with a bottle of fresh water.

▶ Think about buying bread rolls in bulk, buttering and filling them, then freezing them in zip-lock bags. Then all you have to do is pull one out of the freezer in the morning, pack it into a lunch box and it'll be thawed and ready to eat by lunchtime. You can organise up to a month's lunches in advance, if you have room in your freezer.

▶ Get school clothes ready the night before to save time in the morning. There's nothing worse than a uniform crisis first thing!

▶ Help smaller children prepare their school bag and sports bag so that they don't end up carrying around unnecessary extras.

▶ Print out an easy-to-read roster for the whole family and assign jobs for each person. For example, one child cleans all the school shoes while another empties out the lunch boxes or puts away sports equipment. This will go a long way to help avoiding a serious case of morning madness!

Don't overload the timetable

▶ Avoid arranging too many after-school activities, such as music lessons or team sports, especially if they're located a long way from home. Balance the activities and locations so that you don't waste time ferrying your children to one lesson or activity after another.

▶ If other children in your area belong to the same sporting team as your child, try to arrange for other parents to take your child to practice sessions after school, or set up a roster system to save time.

▶ Investigate the activities offered at school. Many schools have a vast range of sporting and cultural activities in the grounds, either during school (chess club, dancing and drama, sport) or after school (school band or string ensemble, choir, debating). If you're time-poor, encourage your children to engage in structured after-school activities offered on the school grounds.

▶ Save time by printing out month-by-month planners from the Internet, so that your children can see, at a glance, what's on each day and organise themselves and any equipment they need (*see* 'Printable forms online', on page 109).

▶ Encourage your children to use a monthly or term planner, or a school diary. Look for one that's easy to use and that is durable. Sturdy plastic covers, snap-on page finders and flat-fold spiral bindings help children make the most of these time-management tools.

▶ Keep track of regular homework and projects by listing due dates on a large family calendar in the study area or kitchen. Encourage your children to look at the calendar and check due dates regularly. (*See also* 'Staying in touch', starting on page 112.)

What are my babysitting options?

Family support can be invaluable when it comes to babysitting, but it's not an option for everyone. Luckily, there are other choices open to you.

▶ Contact agencies specialising in child minding. The Yellow Pages telephone directory has listings to help you find an agency in your area.

▶ Think about enrolling your children in before- or after-school care if your children are school age, you work outside the home and babysitting just isn't an option. After-school care is offered by most schools (both public and private), but there are others run by some local councils. Enquire what the carer–pupil ratio is and the level of staff training.

▶ CAUTION!

Check them out

Before leaving your child with a babysitter, especially one from an agency, make sure the babysitter has a basic knowledge of first aid, knows what to do in the event of an emergency and, most importantly, knows your mobile phone number. If you ever feel uncomfortable leaving your child with a particular person – don't. Trust your instincts.

Babysitting 101

Need a short course in how to prepare for the babysitter? Follow these simple tips and you'll save yourself time and unnecessary worry.

● Plan and organise any meals before the babysitter arrives and keep the preparation simple so that you don't waste time on it.

● Think about making a list of favourite meals (and recipes) if the babysitter is cooking, along with the sorts of snack foods that are allowed and those that are not, and phone numbers for favourite takeaway restaurants (*see* 'Printable forms online', on page 109).

● If there's a special trick for getting your children to eat their greens, let the babysitter in on it. The same goes for bedtime: the babysitter needs to know what works and what doesn't.

● Alert the babysitter to any known food allergies. For younger children, the list needs to be as detailed as possible. The babysitter also needs to know what to do in the case of an allergic reaction (e.g. how to administer adrenaline via an EpiPen).

● Always supply a list of emergency contact numbers, both yours and at least two other numbers of reliable friends or family that can stand in for you if you are not contactable.

▶ Keep the school and after-care phone numbers in your mobile phone's phone book, along with the names and numbers of your child's friends' parents, so that you can arrange for someone to pick up your child if you're running late or in the case of an emergency.

▶ Make enquiries at your child's school and check the noticeboard or school newsletter to find out if there are any people offering babysitting services out of school hours. Always interview prospective babysitters.

▶ If you have older children (13 years and over) who are capable of going home to an empty house after school or during the holidays, make sure they stay in touch by phoning to let you know when they have arrived home, and if they're going out again and with whom.

Help each other out

Set up a reciprocal care system with other parents to give yourself some free time and your child more play time. Just make sure you know the parents well enough before entrusting your child to their care.

▶ Within the same area, organise a roster system where one parent drops off or collects the children from school.

▶ Take turns having your child's friends over for a sleepover – you can enjoy some spare time when the favour is returned. It's a great way to encourage independence in children and to build healthy relationships with other families in the school community.

Staying in touch

Be methodical

Avoid constantly getting your communication wires crossed and you'll instantly save a lot of time. All that is required for managing family life well and without time-wasting hassles is a high level of communication and organisation, a mind that's both creative and rational, and a good memory – or at least a good reminder system.

▶ Put up a large calendar for the whole family, in a place where everyone can see it, and update it as often as necessary.

▶ Buy a ring-bound diary with sufficient space to write down all your appointments – for both home and work – as well as reminder notes.

Up the technology with a PDA

▶ A Personal Digital Assistant (PDA) is a fantastic timesaving option. At the lower end of the scale, basic electronic organisers store and retrieve names, addresses and phone numbers, as well as appointments and other diary-type entries. Some also come with a calculator.

▶ A step up from a basic organiser are devices such as the BlackBerry and Palm Pilot. They're pricey, but have extra functions, such as phone, email, SMS, web browser (meaning you can do a quick Google search), and an integrated address book, calendar, memo pad and task list.

▶ Always have your diary or PDA handy to avoid double bookings, or to make alternative arrangements in advance when something unexpected crops up before an important meeting or appointment.

▶ Update your mobile phone or PDA address book as often as necessary, and keep a backup copy on your computer's hard drive or on a CD or DVD in case the phone or PDA is lost or stolen. Finding everyone's contact details from scratch can literally waste hours of your time.

▶ Always keep your diary or PDA in the same place, just as you would your house or car keys, to avoid misplacing it. Keep it on a hall table next to the phone at home, or in a zippered compartment in your handbag.

TIMELY TIP

Plan tasks

Draw up a schedule of the tasks shared by different members of the family. This means you'll avoid disputes and no one will forget what they have to do. At the beginning of the week, note down whose turn it is to buy bread or put out the bin and walk the dog, for example.

Tips for managing family timetables

Get organised by being fully aware of everyone's timetable.

▶ As soon as school resumes after summer holidays, draw up the class timetable for each of your children, along with their extra-curricular activities and a list of what accessories are needed for those days, so that both you and they can get organised in advance.

▶ Nothing calms timetabling chaos like a calendar. Invest in a large paper calendar for the whole family and put it up where everyone can see it at a glance. Use a highlighter pen to distinguish special events.

▶ Make the family calendar do double-duty by noting all the usual things – school events, birthdays, appointments – as well as listing what's for dinner up to a week ahead. It will make shopping lists quicker and easier to compile and you can avoid shopping more than is necessary.

▶ Use the family calendar to record your children's long-term school assignments, so that you also know when work is due and you can help to avoid any last-minute dramas that will waste your time as well as theirs.

▶ Make a note on the family calendar, and in your diary or PDA, of school holiday dates, so you can organise holiday lettings, tickets and pet care well in advance. It may save you time researching alternative options.

▶ Keep older children on top of your timetable (especially if you work outside of the home) by putting up a noticeboard in the kitchen, and update notes as necessary. For instance, if you're going to be home late after a meeting, leave a note telling the children to call you when they're home and that dinner is in the fridge and only needs reheating.

▶ Using text messaging, or SMSing, is a fast-and-easy way to alert family members to a change of timetabling. Without having to actually call and interrupt each other, you can instantaneously communicate a change of plan, which saves both time and inconvenience.

(*See also* 'Don't overload the timetable', on page 110.)

Keep a copy of contact details

Always keep a list of important numbers on you and another one at home. To ensure that your mobile phone or PDA address book is practical, organise it according to categories – doctor, school, parents, work, etc. And to enable you to use the numbers more quickly, store them in the telephone's memory, just as you do on your home phone. Think to include the numbers of your repairmen and other tradesmen, too, so you can call on them quickly if there's a problem.

Write it down so you don't forget

▶ Put a magnetic white board on the fridge and get everyone to write down shopping items as they're used up, or have a list or a set system so that you don't forget anything, and you'll save time.

▶ Make sure phone messages get passed on by placing packets of Post-its next to each telephone in the house. Then all you have to do is stick the message on the person's bedroom door to make sure they get it.

Timesaving features on your home phone

▶ Invest in a cordless phone so that you can do two things at once: load the washing machine or make dinner while you're talking on the phone.

▶ Use the hands-free option, if it's available, so that you can chat on the telephone without using a handset. It's perfect for busy parents.

▶ If you have one telephone line, activate the 'call waiting' option, if it's available. That way, when you're talking on the telephone, a small insistent beep alerts you that someone else is trying to call, so you can put the first caller on hold while you speak to the second caller.

▶ Read the manual. Get to know what all of those short-cut buttons on your home phone are for and you'll save time on redialling, recalling, etc.

▶ Program the most commonly used numbers into your home phone's memory, so that you only have to push one button to make a call. Most telephones have at least six automatic-dial buttons.

Don't forget to recharge

If you're a frequent mobile phone user, save yourself time and extra hassle by getting into the habit of recharging every night or two. That way you'll have a fully charged battery to get you through the day, and save the time wasted looking for a pay phone (it can be difficult to find one!).

SMS language in one lesson

Using Short Message Service, or SMS (otherwise known as 'texting' or 'txt talk'), on your mobile phone can save a lot of time when you're in a hurry or you don't have time to make a phone call. Follow these basic tricks and you'll be SMSing in no time.

ENGLISH	SMS	ENGLISH	SMS
Are	r	Great	gr8
You	u	Before	b4
See	c	You are	ur
Be	b	Later	l8r
Why	y	Text	txt
Ate	8	Please	plz
For	4	Talk to you later	ttyl
To or too	2	Laugh out loud	lol
Mate	m8	I don't know	idk

Get the most out of your mobile

Ever wondered if your mobile phone was more trouble than it was worth? Try putting these tips into action and you'll put an end to the wasted time associated with mobile phone usage.

▶ If your mobile phone is also a camera, take a photo of frequent callers and attach it to their phone number so that when the phone rings you see a picture of them (not all phones have this option). It saves time when the name coming up on screen is too small to read quickly, and gives you the option of taking the call or letting it go to message bank.

▶ Don't fumble through your bag to find your mobile when it rings during an important meeting or in the cinema. Turn off the ring tone and switch to vibrate, so that you can be reached if necessary, but you can also quickly decide whether to step out and take the call or ignore it, without disturbing others.

▶ Look out for new-generation mobile phones: the technology is constantly being improved and refined with amazing time-saving features, such as touch screens, being introduced.

What to do if your mobile phone is stolen

Mobile-phone theft is a growing problem everywhere. Don't wait until you see a dramatic increase in your phone bill before you react.

▶ Call your mobile phone company immediately to suspend your service, then organise to have your phone blocked before the SIM card has been changed, by providing the 15 digits of your International Mobile Equipment Identity number (IMEI). (Find out what your IMEI number is – before your mobile is lost or stolen – by dialling *#06# then pressing call or send.) This allows the exchange of blocking and unblocking information between carriers.

▶ Make a statement at the police station and provide the phone's IMEI number. The primary responsibility for enforcing criminal law in Australia and New Zealand rests with police (state and territory).

▶ Send a copy of the police statement to your mobile phone company.

▶ If you have insurance, send a declaration of theft to your insurer.

Instant messaging equals instant communication

Stay in touch in real time using instant messaging. If you have teenagers in your family, it's essential to learn how to use instant messaging.

▶ Using instant messaging systems such as MSN Messenger and Yahoo! Messenger makes staying in touch quick and simple. No more waiting on the end of a telephone line.

Messaging etiquette

Instant messaging is a fast-and-easy way to stay in touch, but don't forget your manners – there is such a thing as cyber etiquette – because you're in touch with a real person, not a computer screen. For starters, always introduce yourself (minus personal details), ask recipients if they have time to chat, avoid using too much jargon, don't forget 'please' and 'thank you', and don't SHOUT (type your message in capital letters).

▶ MSN Web Messenger (also called Windows Live Messenger) is one of the best known and used. Using free software (called 'freeware') that can be downloaded from the Internet – or a web browser such as Microsoft Internet Explorer, Mozilla or Netscape if you're on a shared computer at work or a friend's house – you can 'chat' online in real time with friends and family, anywhere in the world.

▶ To use MSN Messenger, all you need to get started is a relatively fast broadband connection and Microsoft Windows to support the latest version of MSN Messenger software.

(*See also* 'Better use of your computer', on page 168.)

Webcam – the next best thing to being there

You may have heard of webcams (web cameras) for live video link-ups at home, but finding out how they work can be time consuming. Here's a simple explanation to help you decide if it's an option worth investigating further.

▶ Not only can you talk in real time with anyone, anywhere in the world, you can also see them with a webcam. It's a great way to take advantage of free Internet communication, and the images are delivered at around 30 frames per second, which means you get quite a good-quality picture.

▶ All you need to get started is a computer with a fast broadband connection, the webcam sensor, a built-in microphone or a high-performance headset with a boom microphone attached, and whatever software is necessary for running the webcam.

▶ Most webcams simply connect to your computer via a USB port or FireWire connection (Mac computers), and the sensor can be positioned anywhere. There is no other installation required and they are very easy to use once you're set up and ready to go. If you have any problems with your webcam, search online for troubleshooting tips.

▶ Don't use your computer monitor as a light source with a webcam – it results in poor picture quality. Turn on a desk lamp to lighten the foreground and even a cheap webcam will send a reasonable-looking image.

The family pet

Do your homework

There's nothing inherently time saving about owning a pet. Quite the reverse, in fact, so despite the amount of love and joy a pet can bring into your life, the first thing you need to decide is whether you and your family actually have the time to take proper care of one.

▶ Find out how much feeding, grooming, training, exercising – and boarding when you go on holidays – is required, and realistically assess whether all of those things are going to fit into your daily schedule. Animal shelters are full of unwanted pets whose owners underestimated the level of commitment required to look after them properly.

▶ Don't buy a pet on a whim from a pet shop.

▶ Think carefully about the sort of animal that would suit your needs: Have you got the time and patience to groom a long-haired cat or dog? Do you have the time and inclination to exercise a very energetic dog every day? Will you be able to clean up after a puppy for the first six months? Have you got the time to train a young dog? Are you away from home all day? Are the kids responsible enough to keep the guinea pig clean and fed? Ask yourself all these questions before buying a pet.

▶ Read up on the animals and breeds that interest you, and ask your local vet for advice before you start approaching breeders.

▶ Go to your local park and ask dog owners about their particular breed's attributes – both positive and negative.

Trouble-free animals

You've decided to get a pet, you've thought about how much time you can devote to it, and the whole family can't wait to get it. But how do you go about getting one? That's a job that can eat up masses of your spare time, making what should be a pleasure an absolute chore, so cut to the chase and follow these tips.

▶ Before buying a cat or a dog from a pet shop, drop in and check how clean the premises are and how well the animals are kept.

▶ If you're choosing an animal from a shelter, take time to watch how it interacts with both humans and other animals before taking it home.

▶ An animal who shares his or her existence with the owners (breeders or individual owners) is much more likely to be sociable, so the chances of it fitting in with your family will be higher.

▶ Make sure the breeder you choose is registered and ask to see the animal's vaccination certificate and microchip certificate.

▶ If you're adopting a puppy or kitten, wait until the animal is at least 3 months old. He or she will be sociable and weaned. And don't forget to ask for the animal's veterinary documents.

▶ If you're looking to acquire a bird as the family pet, make sure you buy one from a reputable breeder.

▶ Not sure what breed of cat or dog to buy? Do some Internet research or simply ask the local vet which breed would best suit your physical surroundings and family requirements.

Fast, practical pet care

▶ If you have a long-haired dog or cat but don't have time to take it to be washed and/or groomed, make an appointment with a mobile grooming service. That way you can take full advantage of timesaving home visits.

▶ Cats are in the habit of eating grass, which allows them to regurgitate any fur they have swallowed as they clean themselves. If you live in a flat or unit, buy fast-growing grass and sow the seeds in a pot once a month.

▶ To change a cat litter tray in record time, line the bottom of the tray with a special plastic cover (available from pet shops and supermarkets), or simply fashion a litter tray liner from a recycled plastic bag from the supermarket. Then all you have to do is remove the bag or liner, tie a knot in it and throw the whole lot in the garbage bin.

▶ Take a handtowel or large face washer with you on rainy walks and wipe your dog before it tracks moisture and mud into your home.

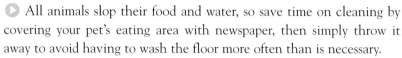

TIMELY TIP

Time for a walk

If you're too busy to take your dog for a regular walk, engage a professional dog walker to do the job every day. It's not hugely expensive, the dog will love it and the walker can also feed your pet if you're going to be late.

▶ All animals slop their food and water, so save time on cleaning by covering your pet's eating area with newspaper, then simply throw it away to avoid having to wash the floor more often than is necessary.

▶ Pick up pet hair from upholstery and rugs by rubbing the hair while you're wearing a damp rubber glove. It's incredibly fast and efficient!

▶ If your pet doesn't mind – and many actually enjoy it – run over its coat with the vacuum cleaner using the upholstery attachment. It's great for removing loose hair and skin. Otherwise, try brushing your cat or dog while you're watching television, so that you don't have to devote separate time to the task, or encourage your children to do it.

Emergency vet services

If your animal is sick or has suffered an accident outside normal vet's hours or on a public holiday, who should you call?

▶ Keep a list of your own vet's number, along with any emergency vet

numbers, by your phone. It's a vital waste of time to be looking for a number during an emergency.

▶ If you don't have emergency numbers, then call your regular vet. The answering machine will supply an emergency number or the details of the nearest open veterinary clinic.

▶ If you don't live far from a university vet school, take your animal there. They'll have all the necessary infrastructure required for domestic animal surgery.

▶ If you live in a big city, call on an emergency veterinary service that makes home visits.

Animal taxi

If your pet is unwell over the weekend and you don't drive, call on a specialised taxi or an animal ambulance to transport you and them to the nearest veterinary hospital. You can find the relevant contact details in the Yellow Pages or on the Internet. Or check if your regular vet provides a pick-up service.

TIMELY TIP

Carefree holidays

▶ Withhold food from your pet for 2 or 3 hours before travelling, to avoid any unpleasant accidents, such as vomiting, that require cleaning up.

▶ Before leaving, check that your pet's vaccinations are up to date.

▶ Check well in advance if animals are allowed in the hotel or rental accommodation you'll be staying in, so that you can organise boarding.

▶ Take your pet's bedding with you – an animal will settle in much faster in a familiar bed. If possible, wash it first, or at least give it a brush.

▶ If your pet disappears while you're on holiday, notify the national dog or cat register and supply the microchip number (record it in your diary).

Report your missing pet at the police station, and check with the pound and animal shelters and the nearest vets.

▶ Think about boarding your pet or having it minded. Your vet will often have details of boarding kennels, catteries and local animal minders, and some vets board.

▶ If your pet only needs to be visited during the day, ask a neighbour to drop by and feed it while you're away.

How to encourage good behaviour

▶ Set the rules and don't break them. Remember, your pet has to fit in with the family routine, not vice versa, so make it clear who's boss.

▶ If your pet behaves inappropriately in certain situations (e.g. children's parties), then limit their exposure to those situations whenever possible.

▶ Stick to set meal times (for your pet) and discourage begging at the family table or jumping up on benchtops where meals are prepared.

▶ Encourage good behaviour with praise, attention and rewards.

▶ Never punish your pet physically or with undue force: this may only lead to aggression or further bad behaviour.

▶ Expose a new pet to other family members (including other pets) as soon as possible, in the environment you want them to live in.

▶ Seek help for major behavioural problems before they seriously disrupt family life. Retraining is possible with most behavioural problems; ask your vet for advice, or research pet behaviour on the Internet.

TIMELY TIP

Decorate the whole tree

Save having to redecorate your family Christmas tree more than once a year, by also decorating the trunk and base with pet-friendly items such as pine cones. Cats (and some dogs) often see the tree as a climbing post, with potentially disastrous effects!

Instant identification

TIMELY TIP

If you take your pet to the same holiday home each year, get a collar tag made with that address and phone number on it. Even if your pet is microchipped, the details will relate to your regular home address.

Caring for your health

Keep on top of medication

▶ Keep your medication in a cool dry place – not in the bathroom if it's likely to be exposed to heat and steam. And store all medications out of reach of children.

▶ Do a quick check for expired products in your medicine cabinet from time to time. Return them to your local pharmacy at the same time you fill a new prescription.

▶ If you take regular prescribed medication, always keep repeat prescriptions in the same place. A lost script means a return trip to the doctor, which is an annoying time waster.

▶ Note when it's time to renew prescriptions, to avoid an unnecessary and inconvenient panic appointment when you only have a few tablets left.

▶ Always complete a prescribed course of antibiotics, even if your symptoms have improved. Otherwise you risk having a relapse.

▶ Keep a list of your medication names and dosages on you when you travel so that correct medication can be replaced easily and complications will be avoided.

Act fast to treat a nosebleed

▶ Sit with your head bent forward over a receptacle. Avoid sitting with your head back, as this could lead to swallowing blood and vomiting.

▶ Blow your nose, then pinch it very firmly for at least 5 minutes without removing the pressure. At the same time, place an ice cube wrapped in a face washer on the top part of your nose.

▶ If a nose bleed persists, seek medical help immediately.

Treat burns quickly

▶ Place the affected part under cold running water immediately and continuously for at least 15 minutes to reduce pain and limit tissue damage.

▶ Protect the burn area with a sterile gauze compress. Don't apply any greasy substances because they will only make the burn worse.

▶ Apply antiseptic to avoid infection.

▶ If the burn is serious, go to your nearest accident and emergency centre immediately, or call an ambulance.

TIMELY TIP

Contain the infection

Cover your mouth when you sneeze or cough, and make sure everybody – including yourself – washes their hands frequently and thoroughly during cold and flu season. And avoid sharing drinking glasses, cutlery or even towels if you have an upper-respiratory tract infection.

 SELF-EDUCATION

• **Stay well by being informed.** Good medical care is vital to the health of individuals and the community, but don't underestimate the importance of health self-education. Visit the web site for your country, below, to find out about specific health issues, and consult your GP if you have any queries.

www.aihw.gov.au

www.everybody.co.nz

www.health-e.org.za

Essentials for the medicine cabinet

● **Sterile adhesive dressings** Band-aids are fine for small injuries. Use larger, pre-cut adhesive dressings for bigger wounds, as they're quick and easy to apply and have a built-in sterile pad.

● **Sterile compresses** Use them to clean or dress a simple wound.

● **Gauze strip** Use gauze strips tied all the way around a limb or appendage to keep a dressing in place (instead of tape).

● **A crepe bandage** These are useful for sprains as well as keeping dressings in place.

● **Round-ended scissors** These are essential for cutting compresses and trimming dressings safely.

● **Tweezers** Useful for removing splinters.

● **Thermometer** There are various types available: glass, rectal, digital and one with a sensor that fits into the outer ear.

● **Antiseptic solution** For cleaning and disinfecting a wound.

● **Analgesics** Use aspirin, ibuprofen or paracetamol for lowering fever and reducing pain. Use only special paediatric preparations for children under 12 years of age.

● **Burn cream** This is handy for treating superficial burns only.

● **Insect-bite treatment** There are a number of preparations available, such as Stingose, to calm skin irritations.

Emergency numbers at your fingertips

Take the time to prepare ahead for emergency situations and you'll save wasting time when it matters the most – in a life-or-death situation.

▶ Keep an updated list of all the emergency numbers you may need, including your local poisons information line (*see* 'Printable forms online', on page 109). Make sure that everyone in your family is aware of the list and keep it next to the phone so that it can be referred to at a glance, or have it laminated and attach it to the wall above the phone.

▶ Update the emergency numbers for your local doctor, pharmacist and hospital in your mobile phone or PDA address book. And if your children have mobile phones, add them to their address books, too.

▶ Make sure your children are aware of general emergency numbers so that they know which numbers to dial when time is of the essence (*see* 'What to do in a medical emergency', on page 124).

Damage control for diarrhoea

There's no time to waste if someone in your family has diarrhoea. For mild cases, follow the tips here, but see your doctor if symptoms persist, or if the diarrhoea is accompanied by vomiting, especially in children.

▶ Drink, drink, drink, then drink some more. It doesn't matter if it's water, flat lemonade, clear soup or herbal tea, just make sure you take in as much fluid as you can. Steer clear of carbonated and caffeinated drinks.

▶ Make up for the loss of water and mineral salts by drinking rehydration fluids such as Gastrolyte or Hydralyte (available from pharmacies). They'll help to restore the electrolyte balance that was affected by fluid loss and make you feel better sooner.

TIMELY TIP

Take it slowly

It can be difficult to get small children to replace larger volumes of fluid at any one time after a bout of diarrhoea or vomiting, so try offering small sips of water every 10 to 15 minutes. And start back on solids slowly, using dry toast as a starter.

What to do in a medical emergency

● **Call for help** In Australia, call 000; in New Zealand, call 111; and in South Africa, call 10177 (for police or fire services in South Africa, call 10111). The international emergency number for GSM mobile networks is 112, and operates in most countries, including Australia, New Zealand and South Africa.

● **Follow the DRABC rule before commencing resuscitation**
D = Danger – check the person is not at any risk of further injury, from power lines or in the line of traffic. Make sure they are safe.
R = Response – check if the person is conscious or unconscious.
A = Airway – check the person's airway is clear. Look in their mouth and clear away any obstructions.
B = Breathing – check if the person is breathing.
C = Check – can you feel a pulse, either at the wrist, near the thumb or in the neck?

● **Commence resuscitation** If the person isn't breathing and doesn't have a pulse, commence cardiopulmonary resuscitation. If you're by yourself, you need to do 30 chest compressions fairly quickly, followed by two quick breaths. It there are two people doing the resuscitation, do 15 compressions to one breath. Repeat until an ambulance arrives.

● **Position the patient and wait for help**
If the person is breathing and has a pulse, but is unconscious, place them on their side in the coma position until help arrives. Check for any bracelets or necklets that might alert you to an underlying condition, such as diabetes or epilepsy, that could account for the collapse. Stay with the person until help arrives.

To avoid becoming dehydrated (and possibly disorientated), elderly people need to drink at least 2 litres of water a day for 48 hours after the diarrhoea has stopped, to make up for the loss of fluid.

Give high-fibre foods a miss for a while if you want to reduce the length of time you have a bout of diarrhoea. Also avoid fatty foods and dairy foods. Instead, eat foods that make stools firmer, such as rice, pasta, bananas, white bread, potatoes (without the skin) and chicken, fish or beef.

For the same reason, change an infant's diet for five days after a bout of diarrhoea. Give him or her breast milk if you're breastfeeding, or lactose-free milk, apple puree, water and mashed banana.

Apart from paying special attention to your diet, also look after the skin around your anus by wiping with unscented baby wipes, or toilet paper and sorbolene cream, to avoid dragging or damaging the anal skin, which could result in painful and time-consuming complications.

Rest up. Losing a lot of fluid in a short space of time plays havoc with your electrolyte balance, and you'll feel very tired and worn out, so take it easy for a few days and you'll get better faster.

Reduce a fever

Until a child has reached the age of five, a fever above 38.5°C may cause convulsions, so take all the necessary precautions.

Administer an analgesic recommended by your doctor or a pharmacist (syrup or drops). Double-check the dosage before administering.

Take off the child's clothes and leave him or her in their underwear, and try to keep the temperature in his or her room at a constant 19°C.

Put the child in a lukewarm bath for around 15 minutes, making sure that they don't start shivering in a cold bath. Shivering is the body's response for raising the core body temperature.

Give the child a sponge bath using lukewarm water, and have a fan going in their room to keep the air cool and create a gentle breeze.

Don't hesitate to repeat the procedure if necessary. If a fever doesn't respond to these measures, or if your child requires more than four doses of analgesia in 24 hours, seek medical help immediately.

TIMELY TIP

Ready for hospital
Avoid being held up with formalities on admission by taking your Medicare or health-care card with you along with details of your health-insurance. If you are currently taking medication, take that with you, too, along with any prescriptions.

TIMELY TIP

Get an accurate reading fast
To get an accurate temperature reading in a baby or small child, first remove wraps or heavy clothing, then use a thermometer with a sensor (they fit into the outer ear). They're fast, non-intrusive, safe and efficient.

Massage the blues away

Colicky babies inevitably spend a lot of time screaming in discomfort and pain, which means their parents spend a lot of time holding them, pacing and trying to soothe a sore tummy. Instead, try baby massage. You may find that it soothes the colicky blues away long enough for you to have time to do something more pleasurable – such as sleep!

Start by removing the baby's clothing, including the nappy, and place the baby on its back. Rub a few drops of sweet almond oil into the palms of your hands and gently stroke the baby's tummy in clockwise circles around the belly button, with one hand following the other. (A good tip is to try to relax the baby a little before the massage by giving him or her a warm bath.)

CAUTION!

Minimise exposure

If you're pregnant and don't have immunity to rubella, stay away from small children whenever possible: infection can lead to serious deformities in an unborn child. Rubella can be identified by a fine, red rash, swollen glands and fever.

Identify childhood illnesses a.s.a.p

Despite widespread immunisation in many countries, some of the more serious infectious diseases still occur occasionally. Identifying these illnesses as soon as their first symptoms appear is vital, not only for the child but also for adults, who can be seriously affected, too. Here are some of the most common ones to look out for.

▶ If you're not immune to chickenpox and come into contact with someone who has it, see your doctor immediately – vaccination against the disease might at the very least minimise its course if you catch it. Adults who have chickenpox can develop serious complications, such as pneumonia. In Australia, New Zealand and South Africa, children aged 9 months to 2 years are eligible for chickenpox immunisation.

▶ Quickly recognise the classic symptom of mumps – swelling in the lower part of the face. In men, this infection can lead to sterility.

▶ Glandular fever (also called 'infectious mononucleosis' or the 'kissing disease') is usually associated with a very sore throat and swollen glands, and it can take many weeks to recover. There is no immunisation available.

▶ Parvovirus (also called 'slapped-cheek syndrome') is characterised by a mild fever and bright red cheeks, and usually causes little if any problem in children, but it has been associated with early miscarriage in pregnant women.

▶ Impetigo (also called 'school sores'), which are yellow, crusty lesions that often develop near a child's mouth, are most often caused by a staph bacteria that can be contagious. It is treated with regular cleansing followed by topical antibiotics.

Help at hand

Always having a first-aid kit handy on outings is a definite time saver, especially when time is of the essence.

▶ Put your own simple first-aid kit together or buy one from a pharmacy or hiking supplies shop. There's usually a choice of kits for different purposes. Consider buying one for the car, one for camping or hiking holidays, and another purse-sized one for your handbag or backpack.

▶ Pack a few paracetamol tablets or capsules, a Band-aid or two and a bottle of Stingose for outings. It can mean the difference between a lazy Sunday picnic and a frustrating hunt for a pharmacy that's open.

▶ If you take your children out for a walk, a bicycle ride or roller-blading, take a kit comprised of antiseptic solution, sterile compresses and bandages in case of any little accidents.

No more blisters

The best advice is to wear in new shoes gradually, to prevent a blister forming, but if you do have a blister and it's large, it should be treated.

▶ If a blister bursts of its own accord, clean the area with an antiseptic solution and protect the exposed skin with a light non-adhesive dressing.

▶ Burst the blister (if it hasn't already). Do this by heating a needle in a flame then allowing it to cool before using it, or use a sterile needle.

▶ Disinfect the skin surrounding the blister, then pierce it and press on it gently to extract the liquid, wiping it away with a sterile compress. Don't peel off the white protective skin – leave the affected area exposed to air overnight, and the next day apply a hydrocolloid bandage (available from pharmacies) to protect the area from rubbing.

Don't wait to treat a bee sting

While in 99 per cent of cases they are simply painful, bee stings can occasionally have serious consequences. And as long as the sting remains in place, it will continue to release its venom.

▶ Remove the sting quickly by scratching it with a blunt object, such as a blunted knife blade or the edge of a credit card.

▶ Apply ice to the sting site immediately, to reduce swelling and redness.

▶ If a sting reaction includes facial swelling or difficulty breathing, go straight to the nearest hospital accident and emergency department, or call an ambulance (*see* 'What to do in a medical emergency', on page 124).

▶ In the case of a bee sting in the mouth or throat, suck on an ice cube to reduce the swelling, and consult your GP or go to the nearest hospital accident and emergency department as soon as possible.

TIMELY TIP

A prick in time...

Any person who is at risk of having an anaphylactic reaction to bee or wasp stings should always carry an adrenaline injection (EpiPen). Use it at the first sign of a reaction – this will not only save time but could also save a life.

CAUTION!

Don't use cotton wool

Avoid using cotton wool to disinfect or clean an open wound, because fibres risk becoming attached to the wound. Instead, use sterile compresses.

TIMELY TIP

Bluebottle stings

Forget about ice, vinegar and other remedies. Get rid of the pain caused by a bluebottle sting by removing any blue tentacles (taking care not to get stung again), and then immerse the sting site in hot water – as hot as you can tolerate – for at least 10 minutes. If necessary, get into a hot shower.

Dress a wound quickly and efficiently

Knowing what to do after an accident can save precious minutes that add up to time saved on wound healing. Wound healing time is greatly increased if an infection develops, so do what you can to avoid it.

▶ If a wound is bleeding, apply pressure to stem the flow. Use any clean cloth you have on hand, but apply pressure continuously for at least 5 minutes. If the bleeding is profuse, appears to spurt or does not stop, seek medical help immediately.

▶ Inspect the wound to see if it needs stitching before it's dressed. Generally, wounds heal better and faster if the edges are stitched or glued (superficial, simple wounds only) together. Deep or long cuts need to be stitched up by a doctor using sterile equipment.

▶ If the wound is on your leg and it's bleeding a little, raise the limb higher than the heart while you're dressing it, to stem the bleeding.

▶ If there's a foreign body lodged in the wound, seek medical attention immediately (unless it's a simple splinter, in which case a clean needle or a pair of tweezers may do the trick).

▶ If the wound is a graze that has dirt or gravel particles in it, place the wound under cold running water to flush away as much dirt as possible before applying antiseptic and a self-adhesive dressing.

What to do after a fall

Act fast if you are the first person on the scene of an accident involving a fall. It could mean the difference between a long and a short recovery time. But before taking action, make sure you fully understand the extent of the person's injury, to avoid making it worse.

▶ Make sure the person who has fallen is conscious and alert. Ask them if they know what happened and if any part of their body is hurting, then inspect their head and limbs for signs of obvious injury.

▶ If the person who has fallen has trouble getting up, check whether the painful limb is out of shape – it might be fractured.

▶ If difficulty getting up and around is an obvious problem, even in the absence of any visible signs of injury, don't persist, otherwise you may further damage an affected limb or soft-tissue injury.

▶ If the person can't get up but doesn't complain of any neck pain, place a rolled towel or folded clothing under their head. Cover them with a light blanket, then call for a doctor or ambulance and wait until it arrives, and do not offer food or fluids.

Preventive medication

If you suffer from motion sickness and are planning a boat trip or long car trip, take preventive medication beforehand – don't wait until the nausea starts to come on.

Similarly, if you take regular medication to prevent a condition such as asthma, then remember to take it. It may sound simple, but so many people forget about their health when they feel well and end up having to endure sick days because of unnecessary flare-ups of a particular health issue.

TIMELY TIP

Improve your chances

Regular visits to a dentist or dental hygienist will save you time (and money) in the long run. Apart from general cleaning, these visits are useful for preventive treatment – identifying issues before problems with your teeth and gums arise.

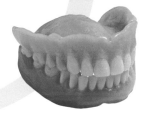

Prevention is always the best cure

Take the necessary steps to maintain good health and you'll spend less time visiting your doctor or dentist. An ounce of prevention is worth a pound of cure, which also translates to time not spent being sick!

▶ Watch your diet and steer clear of fatty foods. If you maintain a healthy weight you're much less likely to suffer from associated health complications such as gout, high blood pressure and diabetes.

▶ Stay active throughout all the stages of your life. Find out what sort of physical activity suits you and make time (as little as 30 minutes a day) to do it, and you'll save time in the long run. You'll increase your chances of having clean arteries and good lung function. Anything that gets you moving is also likely to be a stress buster, too.

▶ If you smoke, quit now. Not only does smoking itself rob you of time, it also robs you of good health, and often results in unnecessary health complications. So quit the habit and enjoy time spent on something more positive (and enjoy the money saved, too).

▶ Keep your alcohol intake to a minimum. Diseases associated with consistent or excessive alcohol intake are some of the most wasteful in terms of time, not to mention all the other obvious reasons.

CAUTION!

A risky bite

If you've been bitten by a dog, immediately wash the wound with soap and water and disinfect it before you go to your GP – dog saliva is loaded with germs. Your doctor will give you a tetanus injection if necessary. Depending on the wound, you may also be prescribed a course of antibiotics.

TIMELY TIP

Keep up the good work

Remember to floss regularly – just a few minutes spent flossing every day can save hours spent in a periodontist's chair later on (not to mention the unnecessary pain and added cost).

A healthy lifestyle

TIMELY TIP

Pack in the fibre

An easy way to reach your daily quota of dietary fibre – two servings of fruit and five of vegetables – is to have fruit with your breakfast, fruit or vegetable sticks at morning tea, mixed vegetable soup or a salad sandwich for lunch, fruit or vegetable sticks for afternoon tea, and stir-fried vegetables with meat or fish protein for dinner.

CAUTION!

Avoid the blockage

With all the fibre you need to consume each day for optimum health, it's easy to become constipated if you don't drink enough water to help the bulk move through your large bowel. Aim to have at least eight 250-ml glasses of water a day.

Get moving to stay well

Improving your fitness makes you more effective in your daily life. If you don't have time to attend a gym regularly, think seriously about adopting a few healthy habits – for life!

▶ Regular physical exercise prevents or delays the appearance of certain problems, such as cardiovascular disease, diabetes or osteoporosis. If you already have one of these diseases, the good news is that exercise will be an important management tool.

▶ Take the stairs at work, and walk for at least 15 minutes during your lunch break.

▶ Do two things at once: walk to the shops with a pull-along trolley and you'll get some exercise while you stock up on pantry supplies at the same time.

▶ Get off the bus or the train one stop early and walk to where you work. It's a quick-and-easy way to get a short burst of exercise. Do the same thing on the way home.

▶ Include physical activity in your leisure time: play a sport, do some heavy gardening or sign up for a dance class.

Rewards for your efforts

Here's a list of how many kilojoules you burn after 1 hour of specific physical activity. If you're not burning enough, think about changing your chosen sport, or pick up another one in addition to what you're already doing. (These readings are based on a 67-kg person. Lighter people burn fewer kilojoules, while heavier people burn more.)

After one hour of...	You burn (in kJ)
● Volleyball (casual)	855
● Kayaking/canoeing	1430
● Gardening	1430
● Golfing (walking)	1570
● Ice skating/rollerblading	1715
● Hiking	1715
● Tennis	2000
● Scuba diving	2000
● Swimming	2285
● Cycling	2285

Exercise when and how you want to

Finding the time to exercise can be a real problem, so here's how you can make the most of the time you do have or factor it into your work day.

▶ To make the most of your free time and boost your performance, set up equipment in your home to build your muscles and improve cardio-vascular function. Depending on your muscle structure and the effort you want to – or are able to – make (and the storage in your home), choose a home trainer or an exercise bike; a rowing machine to work your shoulders, abdominal muscles and back; a treadmill; a cross-trainer to train for cross-country skiing; a step machine to simulate stairs; a mat equipped with a head rest so you can do your abdominal exercises in the right position; or a skipping rope.

▶ If you work impossible hours and don't want any extra travelling time, think about having structured exercise classes during lunch break with a gym instructor, either alone or with a small group of friends (to make it affordable), and at a time that suits you. It's a timesaving and efficient solution.

▶ If you need structure and motivation when you exercise alone, make enquiries about a personal trainer who can draw up a training program for you, give you advice and monitor your progress.

You are what you eat

Save time reading up on the latest diet by following these five simple tips.

▶ Lessen health risks and keep in shape by paying close attention to the quality of the food you eat. It's not necessarily about buying organic produce, rather choosing fresh fruit, vegetables and lean meat over salty, fatty takeaway meals and sugary, processed or highly refined foods.

▶ Stay healthy by burning up a percentage of the energy you eat, to avoid it being stored as excess fat. It's a simple equation: burn the same number of kilojoules you take in to maintain a healthy weight, or eat less and burn more kilojoules if you want to lose weight.

▶ Pay attention to the size of your meals and steer clear of food that is too rich – buttery or saucy foods in particular.

▶ Aim to adapt the number of kilojoules you take in to your age, your sex and your level of physical activity. Adult men require between 8900–15,800 kilojoules per day, whereas women require in the range of 7300–12,500 kilojoules per day. Discuss your target with a dietitian.

▶ Your everyday water needs will vary greatly depending on your level of activity and the climate you live in, but try to drink at least 2 litres per day to maintain a good physiological balance.

TIMELY TIP

Build on your assets

The easiest way to build up your level of physical activity to your target time, and not get discouraged, is to do it gradually. Factor in a brisk walk for as little as 5 or 10 minutes the first day, then do a few extra minutes each day after that.

TIMELY TIP

Energy boost

Instead of reaching for a cup of coffee when your energy levels are low, try controlled breathing, which is thought to both energise the body and lower blood pressure. It takes as little as 2 minutes, and can help you to manage the afternoon slump. Close your eyes and be mindful of each breath as it goes slowly in and out.

Maintaining balance for optimum energy

Eating may not sound like a time-saving exercise, but it is, in effect. Being healthy means having more energy, which means you can do all you have to do in a day and still have time for leisure.

▶ Aim to eat well. For a healthy, balanced diet, 15–20 per cent of energy from food should come from proteins, 50–55 per cent from carbohydrates and 30 per cent from lipids (fats). Aim to have a balance of them in each meal.

▶ Find out which foods are going to give you all the vitamins you need to stay well. Without taking in all the necessary vitamins and minerals, the proteins, carbohydrates and lipids would be ineffective.

▶ Don't forget about mineral salts, which are also important for good health and wellbeing. They play a vital role in bone regeneration, as well as ensuring that muscle and nerve cells function correctly.

How much of each type of food do I need?

CARBOHYDRATES

About a gram of carbohydrates provides the body with 16 kJ. Unless otherwise indicated, you should consume about 250 g per day of a mixture of fast sugars (F) and slow sugars (S).

Average percentage in 100 g

- Fresh fruit (F + S)   5–20
- Potatoes, pasta, rice (S) 20
- Prunes (F)   40
- Wholemeal bread (S)   55
- Dried dates (F)   75
- Honey (F)   75
- Breakfast cereals (S)   80
- Sweets (F)   98
- Sugar (F)   100

FATS

About a gram of fat provides the body with 37 kJ. Unless otherwise indicated, you should consume approximately 50 g of fat per day.

Average percentage in 100 g

- Wholemeal bread   1
- Sausages   41
- Small goods   15–55
- Peanuts   55
- Mayonnaise   78
- Butter, margarine   84
- Oil   100

PROTEINS

One gram of protein provides the body with 17 kJ. You should consume about 60 g per day (adolescents, 75 g; men with non-sedentary jobs, 90 g; women more physically active, 75 g).

Average percentage in 100 g

- Wholemeal bread   8
- Soft-boiled egg   12
- Steak   24
- Gruyere   29
- Tuna   30
- Parmesan cheese   36

Counting kilojoules in a flash

Use this table as a quick ready reckoner. The energy value of food is calculated in kilojoules (kJ) per serve, unless otherwise indicated.

Fats	kJ
Butter (1 tsp)	150
Margarine (1 tsp)	150

Meat	
Bacon (1 rasher)	230
Skinless chicken breast	605
Lean beef mince (100 g)	710
Sausages (80 g)	875
T-bone steak (medium)	960
Beef mince (100 g)	1230

Eggs	
Boiled or poached (1)	290
Fried (1)	417

Fish	
Barramundi (100 g)	360
Rainbow trout (100 g)	500
Salmon (50 g)	500

Starches	
White rice (½ cup, cooked)	430
Brown rice (½ cup, cooked)	450
Pasta (1 cup, cooked)	835

Bread	
Wholemeal bread (1 slice)	260
White bread (1 slice)	275

Dairy products	kJ
Cottage cheese (2 tbsp)	155
Brie cheese (30 g)	375
Blue vein cheese (30 g)	395
Feta cheese (30 g)	400
Skim milk (250 ml)	460
Cheddar cheese (30 g)	500
Natural yogurt (200 g)	670
Full-cream milk (250 ml)	700
Fruit yogurt (200 g)	965

Drinks	
Water, coffee or tea	0
1 can light beer	260
White wine (120 ml)	315
Red wine (120 ml)	335
Sparkling wine (120 ml)	395
Orange juice (250 ml)	400
1 glass cola	460
Pineapple juice	530
1 can beer	585

Fruit and vegetables	
Lettuce (1 cup)	10
Broccoli (2 florets)	45
Peas (½ cup, cooked)	85
Strawberries (1 cup)	125
Carrot	135
Mandarin	145
Kiwifruit	150
Peach	167
Apple	270
Potatoes (100 g cooked)	280
Orange	335
Sweet corn (1 cob)	392
Mango	425

Desserts and snacks	
Ice-cream (1 scoop vanilla)	375
Milk chocolate (1 bar)	840
Potato crisps (1 packet)	1045
Jam doughnut	1360

Looking good

TIMELY TIP

When you run out...
Bicarbonate of soda is a fantastic quick fix, and not just for blocked drains and smelly sneakers. You can also use it to brush your teeth when you run out of toothpaste, apply it as a paste to a pimple to help dry it out overnight, massage it through dampened hair to remove product build-up and you can use it as an exfoliant on your face or roughened elbows, knees and feet.

First things first

You can shave dozens of valuable minutes off your morning routine by being better organised. Think of it this way: if you spend 10 minutes every morning hunting for make-up or toiletries that aren't in the right place, you'll waste more than 60 hours a year!

▶ Keep all your cosmetics and hairstyling preparations together. If you do your hair and make-up in the bedroom, keep all your cosmetics and grooming aids near the mirror or in your wardrobe or dressing table, wherever you will be getting dressed.

▶ Be neat. If you usually get yourself ready in the bathroom, utilise walls to hang extra shelves, or buy wicker or mesh stackable baskets or trays for handtowels, tissues, soap and bath essences. Under-sink wheeled trolleys are an option for even the smallest bathroom. (*See also* 'Personal-care clutter-busters', opposite.)

▶ Install enough towel rails for everyone's towel. A heated towel rail is a wonderful luxury on a chilly morning. It also helps towels dry more quickly and reduces damp, musty smells.

▶ Throw out any medicines that have exceeded their expiry date. Store all drugs and medical supplies in a medicine cabinet or a lockable first-aid box (*see* 'Keep a first-aid kit handy', on page 137).

▶ Discard old toiletries and fragrances, especially if they're over a year old. Unopened fragrant products such as aftershave and cologne should last about two years, but if they've been opened and/or exposed to light, the formula oxidises and breaks down.

▶ Watch out for signs of decay: rancid odour, oil separation, flaking and discolouration. The shelf life of moisturisers, sunscreen, toothpaste and shampoo is usually between two and three years, but it's less once they've been opened. Cosmetics with less water in them (e.g. lipstick) last longer

TIMELY TIP

Plan ahead
Save time and unnecessary stress by getting into the habit of noticing how much of something is left over – especially often-used beauty and personal-care items such as toilet paper, toothpaste, dental floss, soap or shampoo – and put it on your shopping list before you run out, to avoid extra trips to the supermarket.

than those with more (e.g. body lotions). Items mixed with saliva, such as mouthwashes or eye cosmetics, go off fastest of all.

▶ Group like items (hair-care products or bath items) together. Take into account what order you use different items in, and how often. For instance, if you only style your hair every two or three days, store hair gels and sprays behind the frequently used items, such as moisturisers, toothbrushes and toothpaste.

▶ Organising your beauty products and toiletries, and also culling them occasionally, can save you the aggravation of hauling out half a dozen bottles or jars that you don't need, not to mention the time you save by being able to put your hand on exactly what you need when you need it, use it and then return it to where it belongs.

Personal-care clutter-busters

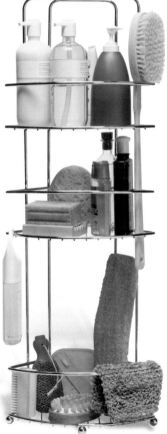

Clearing away clutter is like putting your bedroom or bathroom on a diet. Here are some of the best and inexpensive time- and space-saving gadgets you can buy for organising cosmetics and personal-care products.

▶ Tiered shelves come in different levels and widths so that you can see the bottle or aerosol can behind the ones in front without having to rummage – fantastic for a dark or poky bathroom cupboard.

▶ A spice rack is not just for spices. The narrow shelves, which are just the right height and depth of so many little bottles, tubes and pump-spray packs, take up next to no room at all and can be easily attached inside an eye-level mirrored bathroom cupboard.

▶ In addition to the standard cutlery trays available, there is now a wide variety of drawer organisers you can buy. Use them in the top drawer of your dressing table and in any drawers in the bathroom to make sense of all the small jars, tubes, boxes and awkwardly shaped bits and pieces, such as eyelash curlers, nail files and hair clips.

▶ Hang a shower caddy over the shower head to organise shampoos, conditioners, loofahs, nail brushes, soaps, shower gels and razors, which otherwise clutter up the floor of the shower or topple over and leak out.

▶ Install a magnifying shaving mirror on a retractable arm on the best-lit side of the shower recess. Shaving in the shower saves time and eliminates, once and for all, the mess of whiskers and shaving gel in the bathroom sink.

▶ Put a hook on the inside of the bedroom door for a dressing gown you use every day, for example, or on the back of the bathroom door for your shower cap.

Give your handbag a hand

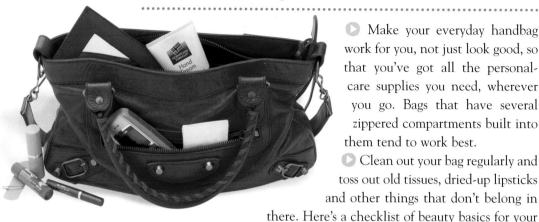

▶ Make your everyday handbag work for you, not just look good, so that you've got all the personal-care supplies you need, wherever you go. Bags that have several zippered compartments built into them tend to work best.

▶ Clean out your bag regularly and toss out old tissues, dried-up lipsticks and other things that don't belong in there. Here's a checklist of beauty basics for your handbag: lip balm, lipstick, hand cream, mini-fragrance roll-on or stick, mirror or powder compact, tissues, tampons or a sanitary pad in a sealed pouch, a safety pin and a Band-aid.

▶ Buy miniature sizes of beauty products to save space – you'll be prepared for touching up your make-up during the day with a mini-stick of foundation or tinted moisturiser, and a cover stick for blemishes.

Taking it on the road

Whether you're a regular business traveller, or just go away on the odd weekend with family and friends, being a savvy bag packer can save time, reduce stress and go a long way towards keeping you looking well groomed and relaxed on your trip.

▶ Buy travel-size bottles of favourite toiletries. Keep them in a bag separate from your regular supplies so you won't be tempted to use them.

▶ Leave beauty and personal-care essentials in your suitcase or overnight bag (e.g. underwear, travel hair dryer, emergency medical kit and zip-lock plastic bags for holding miscellaneous things such as leaky shampoo bottles). That way, you can pack and go at a moment's notice.

TIMELY TIP

Fast and easy oil control

For centuries, many Asian women have used tissue-thin pieces of rice paper to smooth skin and to even out an oily complexion. You can still buy tiny packets of rice-paper squares in Asian supermarkets and some beauty salons. Slip one into your handbag and use the sheets for 2-second touch-ups to your make-up on hot or humid days.

TIMELY TIP

Control the bleeding – fast!

Pick up an alum pencil (also known as a styptic pencil) from a pharmacy, or buy one online at Pharmacy Online (www.pharmacyonline.com.au), and keep it in your medicine cabinet or first-aid kit. This handy little pencil is haemostatic and highly astringent, meaning you can apply it to small cuts, such as razor nicks or a popped pimple, and it stops the bleeding immediately.

Keep a first-aid kit handy

Every home should have at least two first-aid kits for common, everyday health and beauty emergencies: one in the house and one in the car. Either buy a first-aid kit from a pharmacy, or assemble your own. If you have small children, the kit must be stored well out of their reach. Check your kit every few months and replace any missing or expired items. Here's a selection of what you need:

- **First-aid manual**
- **Fever and/or pain relievers** Aspirin, paracetamol, etc.
- **Antibiotic cream** For cuts and scrapes.
- **Disinfectant liquid** For cleaning wounds.
- **Decongestants and cough syrup** Include lozenges, too.
- **Indigestion tablets**
- **Adhesive bandages** Have several sizes and shapes.
- **Tweezers**
- **Thermometer**
- **Cotton balls, sterile gauze pads and rolls of gauze**
- **Scissors**
- **Elastic bandage**
- **Safety pins and a length of calico** For making a sling.
- **Saline eye-drops and an eyebath**
- **Medicine measuring glass and/or dropper**
- **Icepack** Keep one handy in the freezer.

Putting on the war paint

In the morning, there often isn't a lot of time for applying make-up. The solution? Choose products that work as both a beauty treatment and cosmetic at the same time, and adopt the 'less-is-more' approach.

▶ Instead of a complicated beauty routine of foundation, cover stick, powder and blush, opt for a quick once-over with an all-in-one tinted moisturiser and sunscreen product, followed by a quick application of mascara and lipstick. You'll be done in 5 minutes.

▶ If your skin is oily, choose a foundation product with a built-in toner and/or powder that absorbs excess sebum and gives your skin a long-lasting matt finish: you'll avoid having to powder your nose constantly.

▶ Try one of the new light-reflecting foundation/powder creams or gels. These products literally scatter light over the surface of your skin, blurring flaws and evening out skin tone, giving your skin a healthy sheen in a few seconds flat. After cleansing and moisturising your face, smooth on one of these all-in-one optical illusion foundations.

▶▶▶ SHOP FROM HOME AND BUY IN BULK

• **Shopping online** makes easy work of all those jobs that just have to be done, such as buying cosmetics and personal-care items. It's also much faster – no more driving around looking for parking spots or wandering aimlessly through shopping centres – and you may even save some money into the bargain. The five web sites below are just some of the large number of professional suppliers of cosmetics and perfumes available in Australia, New Zealand and South Africa. www.strawberrynet.com, www.aussiecosmetics.com.au, www.fragrancesandcosmetics.com.au, www.beautynet.co.za, www.ascotdirect.co.za

• **Browse online catalogues** to view a wide variety of beauty-care products. Avon, Mary Kay and Nutrimetics sell their beauty products via online and printed catalogue, so you can shop whenever you like. Visit their web sites to contact a consultant with your order, or organise to have a catalogue delivered to your home. www.avon.com.au, www.avon.co.nz, www.marykay.com.au, www.nutrimetics.com.au

• **Browse online, then buy in bulk** at discount pharmaceutical warehouses such as Priceline, and you won't have to make as many shopping trips. www.priceline.com.au

▶ Other multi-tasking cosmetics include lipsticks with a built-in gloss; brow mascara, where you groom and colour the brows at the same time; tinted cream shadows that can double up as a blush, eye shadow or lip colour; and wet-and-dry eyeliner pencils, which can be used to create either a soft, smudged effect or a sharply defined line.

▶ Choose cosmetic colours that coordinate with each other (e.g. shades of pink or brown), rather than cluttering up your make-up box or bag with eye shadows and lipsticks that only go with one particular outfit.

Fake good looks

If you think the only way to look 10 years younger is to go under the knife, think again. Smart cosmetic choices and quick-and-easy tricks of the beauty trade will do the job for a lot less time and trouble.

▶ The first step to lifting droopy eyelids is to gently tweeze your eyebrows, as having more of the brow bone showing gives the illusion of lifted lids. And use a neutral-coloured eye shadow – an ivory or a pale pink – rather than a dark colour, which can make your eyes look heavy.

TIMELY TIP

Perfect lashes in a flash

An ordinary eyelash curler can make you look more alert straight away. Heat the curler with a hair dryer for a few seconds before using it on your eyelashes, being careful to test the curler to make sure it's not too hot.

TIMELY TIP

Two birds, one stone
While you're at the beauty salon, why not lash out and get your eyebrows and eyelashes tinted as well? It only takes 15 to 20 minutes, and the results last for around six weeks. And there'll be no more accidentally jabbing a mascara brush in your eye when you're in a hurry. An eyelash and eyebrow tint is also a must-do before going on holiday if you don't want to wear make-up while you're away.

▶ If you are one of those people with a propensity towards dark under-eye circles, look for an opaque concealer a shade lighter than your regular foundation. Blend in the concealer using your ring finger, very gently, then set the concealer with a thin layer of translucent powder, and it will stay in place all day.

▶ Those fine lines collecting around your mouth are permanent, but you can at least keep your lipstick from bleeding into them, which accentuates them. Once a week, exfoliate your lips by massaging them briskly with a warm face washer, then moisturise as usual.

▶ Dab foundation onto the lines around your lips and blend with a sponge, then use a tissue lightly dusted with loose powder to blot the area and prevent your lipstick colour from feathering. This trick also makes lipstick stay on longer. Choose a light-coloured lipstick or sheer lip gloss: darker colours make your lips look thinner.

Fast and efficient hair removal

▶ Getting your legs, underarms and bikini line waxed by a professional beautician in a salon saves time and is certainly safer – no more painful nicks on your knees and ankles caused by a razor slipping when you're in a hurry, or unsuccessful home waxing.

▶ Waxing is a small, affordable luxury. Experts suggest that you exfoliate your skin before a waxing treatment to reduce the likelihood of ingrown hairs. After waxing, rub in natural aloe vera gel and you'll save time by moisturising and disinfecting your skin, all in one go.

▶ If you do get ingrown hairs along your bikini line, get rid of them fast with gentle exfoliation and an acne cream.

▶ Depilatory creams are a practical and safe do-it-yourself option – setting aside, say, half an hour on a weekend every month can actually save time in the long run, as you reduce your morning routine.

TIMELY TIP

Weigh up the cost
Use a calculator when buying the more expensive personal-care items, such as moisturisers, self-tanners and sunscreens, as they're very handy for comparing prices on a gram-for-gram basis.

Look better in a hurry

Diet, exercise, sleep and other long-term healthy habits are the foundations of looking good. But sometimes you just need a super-quick fix to look better straight away. Try this timesaving trick: dull, dry skin magnifies fine lines, so spritz on this recipe whenever skin feels tight.

In a spray bottle, combine 1 cup still mineral water, ¼ cup witch hazel, ¼ cup rosewater and 3 drops chamomile essential oil (available from a health food shop, or buy online at www.perfectpotion.com.au). When stored in a cool dry place, this blend will keep indefinitely.

TIMELY TIP

Banish under-eye bags

The secret weapon of make-up artists is... a cold teaspoon. Place two in the freezer for a few minutes, then hold over puffy eyes. The spoons' bowls fit the contours of the eyes perfectly and, unlike cucumber slices, the metal stays cold long enough to do the trick.

Quicker make-up removal

When you're dead tired at the end of a frantic day, it's all too easy to flop into bed without first removing make-up and grime. This is not good for your skin, or for the state of your pillowcases. Speed up your bedtime routine with these snappy solutions.

▶ Use eye make-up remover pads to ease off mascara in one quick swipe.

▶ One of the most effective new beauty inventions of recent times is the pre-moistened disposable wipe. These are light, strong, fine-textured tissues that have been impregnated with different ingredients for different purposes. The most popular are probably the facial cleansing wipes, which remove make-up and dirt in one quick-and-easy wipe (and, seeing as you don't have to rinse, they're perfect for taking on an aeroplane or a camping trip).

▶ Also in the disposable wipe category are specialised treatment wipes, patches and pads (e.g. pads containing mild bleaching agents for age spots and others with styptic and astringent ingredients that help reduce under-eye puffiness, and still others with antiseptic and disinfectant abilities to provide on-the-spot attention for pimples, blackheads or acne).

▶ Give anti-ageing contoured 'patches' a try. Impregnated with wrinkle-fighting ingredients such as hyaluronic acid and collagen, these patches are shaped to fit particular areas, such as under the eyes, the forehead and the lines running between the nose and mouth, and are designed to be left on overnight as a treatment.

▶ Try a two-in-one cleanser/moisturiser combination. These products gently lift and remove dirt and debris, leaving a protective moisturising film behind on your skin. There are also cleanser/toner combination products that contain ingredients such as witch hazel to rebalance your skin's pH level after cleansing, and so do away with the need for a separate toning lotion or skin freshener.

Get your beauty sleep

Don't kid yourself that you can save time by cutting back on sleep. If you want your life to run smoothly and efficiently you need to get enough rest. Here are some tips on how you can do that.

▶ Change your bedroom. A dark, cool room helps you fall asleep faster when you go to bed. Cut down on noise with wall-to-wall carpeting, hanging tapestries, curtains and earplugs, if necessary. Eliminate televisions, phones and computers – all of which are associated with activity, and are sources of obvious distraction that will stop you from nodding off and getting that all-important sleep.

▶ Establish comforting bedtime habits. If you pay bills just before going to bed, you won't drop off to sleep easily. Instead, taking a few minutes to stretch, meditate or read will help you wind down faster.

▶ Keep sleep stress-free. For many people, bedtime is the first quiet time they've had all day. Schedule 30 minutes of 'worry time' sometime during the day, well before bedtime. Make a list of the things you're anxious about, and how you're going to cope with them. Then promise yourself you'll think about them tomorrow.

▶ Calm your brain. Protein foods contain tryptophan, which the body converts into sleep-inducing chemicals. The best bedtime snack is a mixture of protein (like milk), complex carbohydrates (to dispel amino acids other than tryptophan) and calcium (to help the brain use the tryptophan). Quickest and easiest of all? A plain biscuit and a glass of milk.

▶ Try a relaxation trick: get comfortable, then take eight very slow, deep breaths, noticing how your stomach expands and contracts as you breathe. Consciously centre your focus on your breathing.

TIMELY TIP

Call it a night...
Go to bed half an hour earlier. If you're just sitting around at night, killing time until you feel tired, go to bed. Chances are you'll go straight to sleep, and the extra rest will give you more energy the next day.

Schedule some 'me' time

▶ Put beauty therapy sessions in your diary, the same way you would a doctor's appointment. Whether it's a hair cut, a facial or simply relaxing with a fashion magazine, make quality time for yourself. Most of us are better time managers than we realise. These mini-sessions are great, as they allow you to recharge your batteries as you go along.

▶ Don't wait until you're tense. To avoid tension build-up, follow this rule: for every 50 minutes you work, take a 5-minute relaxation break. And don't feel guilty. Taking quick time-outs has been proven to increase overall productivity, thereby saving you time in the long run.

▶ Meditation offers a gentle way to slow yourself down during a hectic day. Even if you can't see yourself sitting cross-legged and saying 'Om', you can still learn to relax – which is the real essence of meditating, and a big bonus when it comes to maintaining your looks as well as your health. Sit comfortably in a place where you will not be disturbed. Close your eyes or keep them open and softly focused on something in front of you. Practise this exercise for about 15 minutes every day.

TIMELY TIP

Leisure time well spent

Plan a weekend of complete beauty indulgence and well-deserved R 'n' R. Plan ahead and find a weekend that is free in your diary, then draw a line through it and plan to wake up on the Saturday morning and do whatever you feel like doing for fun, or start pampering yourself.

Three ways to look and feel better – immediately

Got a minute? We've timed these three simple tips so that you can see how fast and easy it is to make your life a little healthier and happier every day. Give them a go and you'll be amazed at how well they work.

5 seconds	● Stand up straight and you'll look better instantly. If you stoop, you look old and tired. Poor posture can result from even just slinging your handbag or briefcase over the same shoulder every day.
30 seconds	● Add cucumber slices to a jug of water and put it on your desk. This spa-inspired beauty trick makes drinking water even more palatable and beneficial, as studies have found that cucumber's fresh scent and taste reduce anxiety, and drinking at least eight 250-ml glasses of water a day will help to keep your skin hydrated and smooth. It's essential in an airconditioned office.
1 minute	● Sit quietly by yourself for 1 minute with your eyes closed. Gently bring to mind a happy memory of a friend, a parent or a child. Breathe in deeply through your nose for a count of four, then exhale through your mouth for a count of eight. Happy, positive thoughts give you a glow from the inside out.

Natural therapies that really work

These pick-me-ups only take a few seconds to organise or do, and can make all the difference to how you look and feel.

▶ Try do-it-yourself reflexology. If you're relaxed you look better, and stimulating the pressure points on your feet reduces stress. Press your thumb into your solar plexus point, located just below the ball of your foot. Hold and repeat on your other foot.

▶ Banish the bloat. Retaining water can make you look and feel heavier. Diuretic herbs such as horsetail (*Equisetum arvense*) or dandelion (*Taraxacum officinale*) can help. However, don't exceed the recommended dose or you could lose essential minerals.

▶ Try a course of Siberian ginseng (*Eleutherococcus senticosus*). The energy you feel from taking this herb is sustained, rather than a quick jolt.

CAUTION!

Avoid unnecessary risk

When taking herbal supplements, use the dosages recommended by the manufacturer on the packaging, but check with your doctor beforehand, as some seemingly 'natural' substances are contraindicated for use with specific prescription medications.

Pamper yourself – in 15 minutes or less

Pick your favourite do-it-yourself beauty treatments, or better yet try them all! These fast treatments won't cost you the earth, either.

▶ Scrub up. Mix together 1 cup oatmeal with 2 teaspoons each of honey, olive oil and powdered milk, ½ cup water and 3 tablespoons finely ground sea salt. Before you step into the shower, briskly massage the mixture into your skin, paying particular attention to elbows and knees, and avoiding sensitive areas around the nipples. Rinse off in the shower and then smooth on a thick body lotion.

▶ Get glowing. A self-tanning lotion, cream or spray is a quick and safe way to get a gorgeous glow without spending time in the sun.

▶ Steam your face. Boil 4 cups of water, then pour into a heat-resistant bowl and add 3–5 drops of a calming essential oil, such as rose or ylang ylang. Create a steam tent by covering your head with a towel and let the steam envelop your face for 10 minutes.

▶ Beat bad hair. After shampooing, quickly rinse with a 50:50 mixture of warm water and apple cider vinegar. It reduces frizz and also removes dirt, mineral deposits and soapy residue.

Rushing out the door?

Most busy people would agree that getting everyone up and out the door in the morning looking clean and respectable is, at best, a challenge. Even the most hectic days work out better than expected if they start well. These timesaving ideas will help.

▶ Put a mirror and shelf in the hallway for last-minute checks, to avoid going out with lipstick on your teeth, a half-baked hairstyle or a popped button, and being the last one to find out. Put a lidded jar on the shelf and use it to keep a couple of safety pins and a comb handy for when you check yourself at the door.

▶ Set your alarm clock 15 minutes earlier every morning and get up when it goes off, rather than waiting. Even if you don't need those extra 15 minutes for a last-minute beauty or wardrobe emergency, it makes you much more relaxed to know that they're there.

▶ Make an effort to move and talk in a more relaxed manner in the mornings. Drive within the speed limit, pause before you reply to a question or just let the telephone ring a few times before you answer it. Set out to work or dropping the children off 10 minutes early instead of waiting until the last possible moment. As a result, you won't have to rush and you'll be less stressed, which means you'll look fresher.

Reclaim your fitness

If you're reasonably fit you can function well physically, and you look and feel better for it. However, if you're not in good shape, you'll find it even more difficult to get through what needs to be done in a day. No time, you say? Keep these time-savvy ideas in mind.

▶ Use stairs, not escalators or lifts. It's nearly always only a flight or two.

▶ Do two things at once. Try doing some leg lifts or knee bends while you're brushing your teeth. If you have a cordless telephone, stretch or walk around while you talk.

▶ Play with children. Get out there and ride a bike or have a go on the swings. When you go to watch children play football or netball, walk up and down the sidelines for a bit of incidental exercise, which is exactly what experts are telling us we're not getting enough of.

▶ Walk wherever possible. Always put a little distance between yourself and your destination. Walk up the street to get milk or bread. Park and then walk to the theatre, school or office. (Apart from the exercise, it saves time otherwise spent trying to get the best parking spot.)

▶ Try Eastern-style exercise. Even the most die-hard couch potatoes can enjoy graceful practices such as yoga and tai chi, which enhance physical and spiritual wellbeing.

▶ Buy a stationary bike, treadmill or mini-trampoline so you can grab small snatches of exercise at home, at any time of the day.

▶ Dance while you dust. Cleaning your house can be a good aerobic work-out if you put on dance music while you work.

Get instant energy

Your body creates energy from nutrients, oxygen and invigorating stimuli, such as fragrance. Natural mood, beauty and body boosters such as these suit our increasingly busy lives because they provide an instant lift and are so simple to do each day.

▶ Massage your ears. According to traditional Chinese medicine, stimulating acupressure points on your ears increases blood circulation, and thus energy. Vigorously rub your ears all over for about a minute. They should start to feel hot and, almost immediately, you should feel more alert. Start at the lobe and massage up to the top of the ear.

▶ Take a power shower. Sprinkle eucalyptus oil on the floor of your shower before stepping in. Stand under steaming hot water and rub your body with a loofah. The eucalyptus scent stimulates your brain, while the hot water and the rub-down increase blood flow, sending oxygen to your cells where it's transformed into energy.

▶ Wake up with a break. Your body can only handle about 45 minutes of sitting without becoming fatigued. Get up and march around briskly for 3 to 5 minutes, or do some quick stretches or squats.

▶ Make a splash. Dip a face washer in cold water and wet both the front and back of your neck. Then gargle with cold water for a couple of seconds. Your neck and throat are rich with sensitive nerves, and by stimulating them with the cold water you shock them into the 'fight-or-flight' reaction, which temporarily shifts more blood towards your brain.

TIMELY TIP

Breathe fire!
Sitting for long periods causes carbon dioxide to build up in your blood, which in turn makes you sleepy. The 'breath of fire' is a traditional yoga exercise that helps clear the lungs completely. First, breathe in deeply through your nose, then exhale using 15–20 short, sharp bursts, clenching your stomach muscles to really push out each burst. Repeat three times.

Feed your face

Eating simple carbohydrates such as cakes and biscuits when you're strapped for time ends in a brief spurt of energy, usually followed by a crash.

▶ The best beauty snacks provide a mix of protein, complex carbohydrates and fat, because the body metabolises these slowly, and they help to nourish and sustain skin and hair health from within.

▶ Quick snack choices that provide long-term energy include apple slices with peanut butter, multigrain toast with hummus or low-fat cheese, porridge with dried fruit and honey, or plain low-fat yogurt with a handful of chopped fresh or dried fruit added to it.

▶ Many people feel tired because they're dehydrated. If you don't drink enough water, body fluids become thicker and move more sluggishly, making circulation slow, impairing the chemical reactions in cells that produce energy, and making skin feel dry and taut.

▶ The strong, head-clearing scent and cool taste of a breath mint makes you feel and look more bright-eyed and alert.

Hair care in a hurry

You can save a considerable amount of time when it comes to grooming your hair by simply selecting the right hair-care products.

▶ If your hair isn't too dry or oily and isn't permed or coloured, a combined shampoo and conditioner provides a quick, tangle-free result.

▶ If you have dry hair, choosing products with extra-nourishing and moisturising properties will save time when it comes to drying and styling (take care, though, not to apply too much). The same principle applies if you have greasy hair or dandruff – choosing a product tailor-made to your needs will save time and effort in the long run.

▶ Rather than work your way through a complex routine of hair mousse or gel, styling lotion and hair spray, experiment with one of the newer texturising pastes or waxes. These versatile products can be used on wet or dry hair, and also double up as a styling aid if you want to blow-dry your hair. They are available from supermarkets and hair salons.

Be shampoo savvy

We nearly always use too much shampoo and conditioner – a habit encouraged by manufacturers who want you to use the product up sooner.

▶ Using unnecessarily large amounts of product on your hair wastes time and water as well as money, because it takes longer to rinse out.

Make a conscious effort to only use enough shampoo or conditioner – about the size of a large coin – and you'll find it will still do the job well.

▶ Ignore the label instructions that say you should shampoo twice. Unless your hair is extremely dirty or excessively oily, shampooing twice only takes up time and wastes more product.

▶ Tame hair tangles by combing conditioner through your hair before you rinse it out. Not only will you avoid the pain and time wasted spent combing out tangles and knots, you'll also save time on styling.

Dry on the fly

▶ Pick up one of the new super-absorbent microfibre towels or turbans from sporting goods suppliers, discount department stores or online (www.bodmop.com). These towels absorb moisture twice as fast as a normal bathroom towel and halve the time it takes to dry your hair. And they're easy to pack into a gym bag.

▶ For short, fine hair, work a small amount of styling mousse or gel into the roots, tip your head over and dry your hair upside down for a spiky, trendy new look. You'll create more volume in half the time it would take to blow-dry it with a styling brush. Just make sure you don't put in too much product.

▶ Be careful not to have your hair dryer on too hot a setting. You may think that you are saving time, but you're actually creating two problems that will waste time in the long run. For one thing, your hair will become oily more quickly, meaning you'll probably have to wash it more often, and secondly, you increase the risk of damaging your hair, making it more difficult to style and manage.

Go, go gadget

Hairstyling aids can go a long way towards saving time and effort in maintaining your tresses, especially when they are used properly.

▶ If you don't have time for regular haircuts, buy a razor comb from a pharmacy or a discount pharmaceutical supplier such as Priceline. For a small outlay, you can easily touch up a haircut yourself. This is also a great time- and money-saving option for children's haircuts.

TIMELY TIP

Quick-dry your nails

As soon as you apply nail polish, dip your fingertips into iced water. This will make the polish dry much more quickly, and save the time wasted reapplying smudged nail polish. Another quick-dry option is to spray on a light coating of olive-oil cooking spray. It's a great moisturiser, too.

TIMELY TIP

Keep it simple

Get a simple, well-cut hairstyle that is easy to maintain and that, preferably, can dry naturally, rather than one requiring a full blow-dry every morning.

TIMELY TIP

Do-it-yourself hair spray

This simple hair spray takes seconds to make, costs just a few cents and it really works. It lasts about a fortnight if you store it in the fridge. Put 2 lemons into a saucepan with 2 cups of water and simmer for 1 hour, or until liquid is reduced to about ⅔ cup. Strain and pour into a pump-spray bottle.

A heated styling brush is a two-in-one appliance that can be used to smooth and dry hair in half the time it would take to use a hair dryer and a straightening iron. For variety, choose one with an optional spiral head that you can use to create curls if you fancy a different look.

Heated styling brushes are a great idea for either very unruly, springy hair or very soft or fly-away hair, as they impose maximum control in the minimum amount of time. There is a wide range of styling brushes and other hair-care gadgets at Beauty Heaven (www.beautyheaven.com.au), where you'll be able to compare models and different features.

If you fancy having curly hair, but don't have time for a full set and blow-dry, buy a packet of heated twist-and-snap sticks (available from discount shops or specialty beauty and accessory outlets). Simply wind a strand of wet hair around the heated stick, twist in a knot and snap to secure in place. Repeat all over your head. When the sticks are cool and your hair is dry, simply pop them open and shake your head, and you'll instantly have loose, thick curls.

Smile!

Looking after your teeth is probably the one area where you can't skimp on the amount of time you should take. Experts suggest that, in order to thoroughly clean your teeth, you should spend at least 3 – and preferably 5 – minutes twice a day, gently and methodically working your way around the entire surface of every single tooth. To reach all parts of your teeth and mouth effectively, choose an electric toothbrush, and use dental floss at least once a day.

When the bristles on a toothbrush start to spread and fray, it is no longer efficient and may actually scratch your gums. Change your toothbrush every month.

Feel good to look good, all year round

Highlight the positive as often as you can. Instead of focusing on what you want to change about your looks, make a list of your good qualities and all the things you are thankful for.

Pamper yourself. Once a week, do something just for you: take a herbal bath, give yourself a pedicure, meditate or rent a favourite movie.

Try yoga. Quiet and invigorating, yoga is a perfect anytime, anywhere exercise. And if you work at a computer, check out Keyboard Yoga at www.ivillage.com/fitness/yoga/index.htm for yoga poses, such as the 'third-eye massage', that you can do from your chair.

Get a close shave in minutes

To soften beard hair and so speed up shaving, wash your face first with hot water. Apply a mousse or gel product that is suitable for your type of beard and leave it on for a few minutes while you do something else.

▶ Shave in the direction of the hair growth, using a multi-blade razor with a pivoting head to avoid going over the same area several times. Rinse the blade often in hot water. Remove the remaining shaving cream with cold water and apply a specialty aftershave cream, which is more effective than ordinary skin lotion for calming irritation and helping to heal nicks.

▶ Don't splash cologne on shaving nicks as this will only make them sting and irritate your skin even more. Opt for a spray-on disinfectant or an alum pencil, available from pharmacies.

▶ If you don't mind sprinkling your suit with the odd bristle, and if you have a relatively light beard, you can make the most of your commute by shaving while stopped at traffic lights. To make it an efficient process, choose an electric razor fitted with several rotating heads that dispense a moisturising gel. Recharge it regularly so that it's always ready to go.

TIMELY TIP

Shaving time

Since the average man spends some 3350 hours of his life shaving, it makes good sense to save time by shaving in the shower. Not only will you accomplish two jobs at the same time, the hot water and steam will soften beard hair fast, making the job easier, faster and safer.

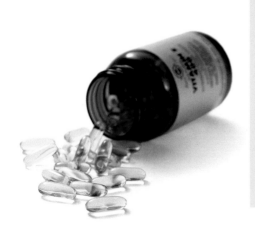

Three quick fixes

● **Brush up** Teeth have a tough time staying white. Food, wine and coffee all seep into and stain the protective enamel, which also thins naturally as we age, allowing the yellowish dentin to show through.

Instead of spending an hour or more in the dentist's chair for a lengthy whitening treatment, try brushing your teeth once a month with a mixture of 1 tablespoon bicarbonate of soda, 1 teaspoon fine sea salt and just enough hydrogen peroxide to make a paste. Make sure you rinse thoroughly after this treatment.

● **Easy mouthwash** Stop bleeding gums by rinsing your mouth twice a day with a strong solution of salt. Antiseptic and astringent, this mixture will relieve inflamed gums and also tighten gum tissue.

● **Nice nails in no time at all** Pierce a vitamin E capsule and massage the liquid into your nails. This oil softens cuticles, strengthens nails and helps heal minor cuts and dry or cracked skin, all in one go.

TIMELY TIP

Roadside assistance

If you do a lot of driving it's worth joining a vehicle-recovery scheme operated by insurance companies and motoring associations. Make sure the cover you take out is appropriate to your driving pattern: some member-ship levels don't cover you for country travel and some don't include towing above a certain distance. (*See* 'Find out more', below.)

▶▶ FIND OUT MORE

• The big motoring organisations – NRMA, RACV, RACQ in Australia; AANZ in New Zealand; and AASA in South Africa – all have useful information posted on their web sites, listed below, and some issue magazines with road-test results and second-hand car values for quick comparison.

www.racq.com.au

www.mynrma.com.au

www.racv.com.au

www.raa.com.au

www.aa.co.nz

www.aasa.co.za

Getting around

Consider your options before buying

▶ If you buy a car through a dealer, get them to register it, and try to have it included in the price. Most dealerships do this automatically, but check first to make sure that the quote includes this service.

▶ If you need to change your car in a hurry, don't order a new one a few weeks before going on holiday (in case an unexpected fault needs urgent attention), and don't opt for a model that has only just been released, in case there are any new-model teething problems.

▶ If you have a car primarily for business use, save time maintaining it by taking a long-term lease or rental option instead of buying.

▶ Servicing can be included in rental and lease vehicles, and you don't have to organise insurance yourself. If there's a problem you receive a replacement car, and at the end of the contract term you get a new car as a replacement or the option of buying the old one at a reduced price.

▶ Think about car sharing. A few programs operate in Australia's bigger cities, where, as a member, you use a car that's parked locally for as long as you need it.

Used cars – too good to pass up?

▶ Check newspapers, motoring magazines or the Internet (*see* 'Find out more', at left). Motoring organisations can tell you what to look for in the model you've chosen, and offer vehicle inspections and advice.

▶ If you're buying from an individual rather than a car dealership, make sure you know which documents are required for transferring the car's registration. Is a safety inspection certificate required?

▶ After transferral, car registration can be renewed online in all the states and territories of Australia, in New Zealand and in South Africa.

▶ In Australia, be wary of buying a car registered in another state, as regulations may vary as to roadworthiness.

▶ When buying a second-hand car, set up a time to test drive it with the vendor, and always phone ahead to make sure the car is still for sale. (*See also* 'The benefits of car insurance', on page 188.)

TIMELY TIP

Don't get caught

It might seem like a good idea when you're in a hurry, but parking in spaces that have been reserved for disabled drivers is a definite no-no. Not only do you risk getting a hefty fine, but you also waste another person's time – someone who has fewer parking options open to them.

Practical parking

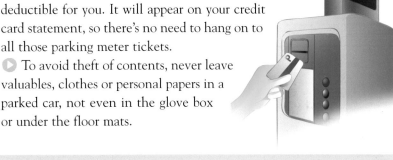

▶ In most big cities, choosing a parking station over metered parking is the fastest and easiest option. Apart from wasting time driving around looking for a metered spot on the street, meters can cost almost as much as some parking stations. And parking fines are yet another example of expensive, infuriating time wasters.

▶ In case you don't have the option of a parking station, make sure you always carry loose change with you or be prepared to use your credit card to clock up time on a parking meter.

▶ Using a credit card on parking meters is a quick and handy way to have a record of the parking fee if it's tax deductible for you. It will appear on your credit card statement, so there's no need to hang on to all those parking meter tickets.

▶ To avoid theft of contents, never leave valuables, clothes or personal papers in a parked car, not even in the glove box or under the floor mats.

Essentials to keep in your car

Always keep your car registration, Compulsory Third Party (CTP) green slip, pink slip, comprehensive insurance and the car manual in the glove box. As well as these things, it's also a good idea to carry the following:

- **Spare windscreen wipers**
- **Engine oil**
- **Spare bulbs** In case you blow a headlight or indicator bulb on longer trips.
- **Blanket, cleaning cloths and wet wipes**
- **Fire extinguisher**
- **Fuses**
- **Protective gloves**

- **Empty jerry can** On long-distance country journeys, always carry extra water and fuel. Keep a jerry can in the boot for this job. For travel in remote areas you may also need extra spare tyres, spades and winching gear, depending on the state of the roads.
- **Engine coolant** For times you're away and you find that your engine is low on coolant and you have a long drive ahead of you.
- **Maps** Street maps and country road maps are essential, wherever you're driving to.
- **Spare tyre** Make sure your spare tyre is inflated to the correct pressure and is in good condition. Don't wait until you have a flat before checking your spare tyre.

- **Wooden wedges and a jack**
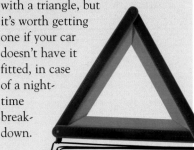
  - **Torch** Make sure the batteries are checked every six months and replace if necessary.
- **Tool kit** Most cars come complete with a small tool kit. Check that your car has one.
- **Emergency triangle** A few models come complete with a triangle, but it's worth getting one if your car doesn't have it fitted, in case of a night-time break-down.

How to change a car tyre

Knowing in advance how to change a tyre will save you time when you most need it – when you have a flat tyre. Follow these tips and you won't go wrong.

● Park on a hard, flat surface (away from traffic, if possible) and turn on the hazard lights.

● Put on the handbrake and leave the car in gear (manual) or put it into *Drive* (automatic).

● Remove the hub cap to expose the wheel bolts.

● Loosen the bolts on the wheel by turning them anti-clockwise half a turn.

● Place the jack under the jacking point (check the correct location in your car manual).

● Put a wedge in front of and behind the wheel on diagonally opposite edges.

● Turn the handle of the jack in a clockwise direction to raise the car.

● Undo the bolts fully and remove the wheel.

● Put on the spare tyre and tighten the wheel bolts in a star pattern – after tightening the first bolt, tighten the one located diagonally opposite to it.

● Once all the wheel bolts have been tightened, lower the jack completely and remove it.

● Tighten the bolts again and replace the hub cap.

Emergency solutions for a flat tyre

▷ Got a puncture? Many modern cars carry only a pressure pack or a 'temporary-use spare tyre' (also known as a space-saver spare). A puncture repair pressure pack will give you a temporary repair so you won't have to double park or stop on the side of a busy road for an extended time. It should get you on your way again quickly, without having to wait for roadside assistance, but it's not a permanent solution.

▷ Try tyre puncture first aid: park your car, remove the nail (if that's the problem), screw the end of a rubber mousse spray can (available from automotive outlets) onto the valve and inject the mousse – you may need two cans for a big car. The hole will be sealed and the tyre reinflated.

▷ If you use rubber mousse, start driving again as soon as you can so that the mousse is evenly spread. However, be aware that you can only drive for about 30 km and the maximum recommended speed is 80 km per hour.

▷ Whatever emergency measures you use, head for the nearest garage or tyre repair specialist and have the necessary repairs made as soon as possible. Emergency measures are temporary fixes only.

◁ CAUTION!

Don't rely on it!

A puncture repair pressure pack is of no use if your car tyre has been torn or lacerated. In these situations, replace the damaged tyre with a suitable spare tyre.

Maximise an automatic car wash

▶ Even if an automatic car wash isn't the most meticulous type of wash, it is fast. To make an automatic car wash more effective, pre-treat difficult stains on the car's body beforehand.

▶ An increasingly popular option is the car-wash cafe, which allows you to make use of the time your car is in the car wash – you can sit at a table where you can work, read or make calls on your mobile phone while your car is being cleaned.

Do-it-yourself car washing

▶ If you've got dead insects stuck to the car bonnet, avoid scratching your car's paintwork by removing the insects quickly and easily – before you wash the car – by dipping a pair of old pantihose in a bucket of suds and gently wiping the hardened insects off.

▶ Don't be tempted to pick or scrape off tar deposits on your car's paintwork before washing – it won't work. Buy a tar-removal product and the deposits will come off in a flash, or try using a bit of linseed oil. Washing the car afterwards will remove any oily residue left behind.

▶ Remove tar deposits thrown onto the wheels or hub caps of your car using a bit of white spirit on a clean cloth.

▶ Toothpaste is a fast and powerful cleaning agent for removing rust stains on alloy wheels, or try a commercial product.

▶ Current water restrictions in Australia prevent car owners from using a hose to clean their cars, but you can use a bucket. Wet the car first, starting from the roof and working downwards, then mix non-detergent

TIMELY TIP

Use water wisely

Current Australian water restrictions allow you to use a bucket to wash your car at home, but use that water wisely, too, by washing your car on the grass, not the pavement.

> **CAUTION!**
>
> **Go easy on the washing**
>
> Don't take your car to an automatic car wash too often, and check the condition of the wash equipment – if the brushes are worn and contain grains of sand they can cause micro-scratches on the bodywork of your car, which are difficult and expensive to repair.

TIMELY TIP

Watch the birdie

Don't wait to wash bird droppings off your car, because they can etch into the paintwork. Use a mist-and-wipe car detailing product (available from automotive outlets and some super-markets). Just spray it on and wipe it off. The added benefit is that you won't have to wax as often, which will save time.

car cleaner with water in a second bucket. Wash with a mitt or soft rag, in small areas at a time, making sure you clean, rinse and dry as you go, to avoid sections of the car air-drying and leaving marks. Rinse out the mitt from time to time, to avoid scratching the car's paintwork.

Clean the inside effectively

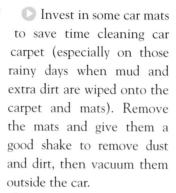

▶ Invest in some car mats to save time cleaning car carpet (especially on those rainy days when mud and extra dirt are wiped onto the carpet and mats). Remove the mats and give them a good shake to remove dust and dirt, then vacuum them outside the car.

▶ Buy inexpensive car mats and replace them each year.

▶ Give the inside of your car a quick vacuum regularly to avoid it becoming a huge job later on. And if you give the carpet a quick swipe with a stiff brush first, it will make the vacuuming job that much faster, easier and more efficient.

▶ Clean off spots and stains inside your car with a foaming cleaner (available from some supermarkets and automotive outlets). Spray it directly onto the stain, leave it to work for 5 to 10 minutes, then wipe it off with a clean cloth. If stubborn stains persist, repeat the process.

▶ Use a moisturising soap to clean leather car seats. Simply wipe the soap bar over a moistened cloth and then clean the leather. No need to rinse, just buff the leather with a clean cloth until it's dry.

▶ Clean the dashboard in no time using a clean, soft paintbrush. It will dislodge dust and particles in vents and all of those hard-to-get-at spots.

▶ Clean the inside of car windows with window cleaner or methylated spirits, spraying the solution onto a clean cloth not the window itself, to avoid inadvertently spraying anything else.

Pick the right polish

Never use shoe polish to clean leather car seats. It might appear to bring up the colour and shine, but it will ruin your clothes permanently.

TIMELY TIP

TIMELY TIP

Locating a stolen car

Many GPS receivers, in combination with a tracking system, can help to locate a stolen car quickly. Some GPS units can also be used to set off the car alarm and hazard lights by remote control, and some immobilise the car's engine.

▶ Eliminate persistent tobacco smells by placing anti-tobacco granules (available from larger department stores and automotive outlets) in the ashtray. As they come into contact with hot ash they neutralise odours. Replace the granules as soon as smells become more noticeable.

▶ Keep a packet of cleaning wipes in the glove box to polish plastic surfaces when you're stuck in a traffic jam. Or use a dry microfibre cleaning cloth – they're fast and efficient. If you use vinyl cleaner on plastic surfaces such as the dashboard, you must keep using them regularly, to avoid the plastic drying and cracking.

Use a GPS unit to find your way around

There are four main types of Global Positioning System (GPS): the car navigation system, the marine system, a portable outdoor unit and a PDA-GPS hybrid. Having a GPS unit fitted to your car can save you both time and money by getting you to your destination via the most direct route.

▶ GPS technology uses a satellite and computer link, a sender-receiver equipped with a screen, a power supply, a system for attaching it to the car and software on CD-ROM.

▶ If you have a poor sense of direction, having your car fitted with a GPS unit means you'll get directions as you go so you won't have to stop your car to check a printed street directory. And it will advise you when a direction change is needed.

▶ Firstly, decide what functions you want the GPS unit to perform. For example, if you're trying to find your way from point A to point B, then spoken instructions are considered to be essential. Otherwise you have to stop and check the screen.

▶ A GPS unit can provide the locations of hotels, restaurants, service stations, caravan parks, boat ramps and tourist sites.

▶ GPS units give a detailed street map of town centres, but tall buildings can interfere with the unit's accuracy, so be aware of this.

▶ While GPS units are readily available from electronics specialists and the major department stores, they are still quite expensive. Weigh up whether the cost is worth it for you, depending on your needs. If you can wait a while, the price may drop considerably.

▶ In Australia, New Zealand and South Africa, there are still gaps in the maps' accuracy outside major cities, so make sure the system is going to do the job you want it to before you buy one.

▶ **CAUTION!**

Good reception

If your car is fitted with a heat-deflecting windscreen that reduces the quality of the GPS reception, consider having an external antenna installed.

E-tags – fast and easy does it

An E-tag allows drivers who have subscribed to an electronic payment system to save time on toll roads, tunnels and bridges. (In New Zealand and South Africa, cash is needed to use toll roads and bridges, although E-tags are currently under consideration.)

▶ Using the designated E-tag lanes means you avoid lengthy queues at cash booths and don't have to stop to pay tolls – the tag you attach to your windscreen activates the fee mechanism automatically.

▶ You can sign up online at home in just a few minutes using the Internet. Use your computer search engine or ask around to find out which company suits you best.

▶ Most companies direct debit your credit card whenever the credit on your E-tag has been used up, then email you a record of debits so that you can keep a check on how much money you're paying on tolls. This also saves time if you need a record of tolls paid for business purposes.

▶ In Australia, many tags can be used on toll roads in several states, including New South Wales, Victoria and Queensland, but others can only be used on specific toll roads. Make sure the tag you buy works on the roads you intend to use.

TIMELY TIP

Oops! I didn't pay

Most tollway systems allow you pay the toll after you have used a tollway (if you don't have an E-tag, for example). But to avoid heavy penalties, you should call as soon as possible after you have used a tollway without an E-tag. The phone numbers to call are usually clearly displayed, or you can check the operator's web site.

A checklist for motorcyclists

Breakdowns are a major cause of wasted time and delays. In order to avoid this issue, attention to basic maintenance is essential, and it doesn't have to cost much. Delays in maintaining your motorcycle properly may end up costing you more in the long run.

- Check that your tyres are in good condition and are correctly inflated, and that the rims are not damaged. This will ensure satisfactory steering and minimise punctures.
- Make sure you're using the correct fuel mix and engine oil.
- Check that the drive chain is clean and correctly adjusted.
- Make sure the brake cables, drums, discs and pads are all in good working order.
- Check the battery is in good condition and is fully charged.
- Have the steering head bearings checked to make sure they are in good condition and are correctly adjusted.

Always wear a full helmet

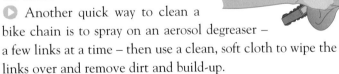

Buy a motorbike or scooter helmet quickly and painlessly, by following these few simple tips.

▶ Measure the circumference of your head to find the right size. Don't choose a helmet that's too big: the mousse padding will soften after just a few weeks. When you turn your head quickly, the helmet shouldn't move around on your head. Wear it for about 10 minutes, to make sure it's comfortable, before you decide to buy.

▶ If you wear glasses, make sure you can put them on and take them off easily while you're wearing the helmet.

▶ The ideal model to have is an adjustable full helmet with an anti-scratch visor. This sort of helmet will prevent you from getting too hot riding around in the city, or being deafened by road noise.

Bike-riding essentials

▶ To clean your bicycle chain quickly and well, buy a chain cleaner. This is a device fitted with small rotating brushes impregnated with degreasing and lubricating products, which allows you to clean the chain while it's on the bike.

▶ Another quick way to clean a bike chain is to spray on an aerosol degreaser – a few links at a time – then use a clean, soft cloth to wipe the links over and remove dirt and build-up.

▶ Clean non-moving bike parts with water and detergent, then rinse.

▶ If you mostly ride your bike in the city, fit the wheels with a self-sealing air chamber to ensure you won't be stopped by a puncture. This is a device filled with gel that is released at the smallest puncture. It seals the hole by hardening when it comes into contact with air.

TIMELY TIP

Remove adhesive labels

To remove an adhesive label from your motorcycle, use a hair dryer to warm up and soften the glue, so the label comes off easily. To leave a perfect finish, remove any final traces of glue using methylated spirits or white spirit.

The basic bicycle tool kit

Don't be caught short – these simple tools will allow you to carry out the most common bicycle repairs.

● Bolts and screws
● Scraps of cloth
● Scrubbing brush
● Toothbrush
● Adjustable wrench
● Bottlebrush
● Set of Allen keys
● Anti-puncture kit
● Insulating tape
● Screwdriver

Give rust marks the heave-ho!

If there are any rust marks on your bicycle's metal parts, you can quickly and easily remove them using a cloth soaked in lemon juice mixed with a lot of salt.

TIMELY TIP

Make the most of public transport

If you're a regular public transport user, there are some crafty ways to save time getting around. And if you only use public transport when you're travelling away from home, following these tips may mean the difference between a successful trip and a major disaster.

▶ The key to saving time when using public transport is to know the relevant timetables. Not only will you avoid long waits in bus shelters and on train platforms, you'll also be able to coordinate transport links more efficiently. Search the Internet and print out a timetable or contact the relevant transport authority and request a pre-printed version.

▶ Don't stand in queues. Buy a weekly, monthly or an annual bus, train or ferry ticket – it'll save you time and money.

▶ Many cities have interchangeable tickets for buses, trains and trams. A lot of this sort of information is available on the Internet and in guide books for specific destinations.

▶ Check transport web sites for ticket prices, routes and special fares.

▶ Check the details of your journey online and use a journey planner to link different forms of public transport. You'll find the best route to travel to your destination, and any suggested alternatives in case of delays.

▶ In some cities you can register your mobile telephone number so that updates on service delays or cancellations will be sent to you by SMS or email, which can save a lot of headaches.

▶ If you're using a taxi service to take you from a bus or rail station to your final destination, phone ahead and book on your mobile phone, rather than relying on hailing a cab or waiting in a long queue, which can result in unscheduled delays and time wasted.

Going to special events

Plan your cultural year

There's no doubt that advance planning can result in considerable cost and time savings when it comes to organising your leisure activities. There's usually no shortage of distractions available, but what is missing is the time to see them all, so up your chances with clever planning.

▶ Manage your time well by planning evenings out in advance. Make a note of all activities in your diary or PDA, to avoid double booking.

▶ Reserve theatre, concert, opera and ballet tickets as soon as the programs are announced, and take out subscriptions that run for the

TIMELY TIP

Avoid the queues

Avoid the queues at many famous galleries, such as the Uffizi in Florence, the Louvre in Paris or a major gallery closer to home, by booking overseas or interstate accommodation, with museum and gallery tickets included, ahead of time using the Internet. Major venues are set up for these bookings and usually offer package deals.

whole year. Not only is this a cheaper way to see a number of varied performances, it's much quicker than organising single tickets.

If you like singers, comedy, jazz and musical comedies, buy tickets several months before a show using specialised Internet booking sites that alert members to upcoming events. In some cases, you can choose your seats by consulting a plan of the theatre. This means you don't have to go in person to book, or wait on the telephone.

If you only give in to last-minute temptations, reserve your seats online through the venue itself or with a booking agency, and pick the tickets up at the box office on the night of the performance.

Web sites such as MyTickets and Ticketek are great for browsing to see what's on, then simply buy tickets online and have them posted to your home. Ticketek takes phone bookings if you'd prefer. MyTickets has a listing of major museums and galleries in Australia, and allows you to see, at a glance, what's free and what you need to book for.

The big picture

A growing number of mainstream cinemas offer the possibility of reserving tickets on the Internet, having already browsed to see what's on. Take your 'print-at-home' ticket along and there's no waiting in a long queue or seeing the last free seats snapped up before your eyes.

Some cinema chains offer the option of buying a subscription online or in person, which allows you discounted visits to the cinema over a set period of time, or buy a book of tickets so you don't have to wait in queues.

Join a cinema club to receive discounts and member-only benefits.

On exhibition

If you only have a short amount of time to satisfy your taste for painting, decorative arts or photography, there are a few solutions open to you.

Some museums, galleries and arts' festivals offer online ticketing, which gives you access to an event on a particular day within a specified time frame. (Many special festivals, such as film and writers' festivals, do this so that you can book tickets to multiple sessions.)

When you're on holiday overseas, buy a pass that's valid for several days in a number of museums. This usually represents a considerable cost saving and allows you immediate entry, with no time spent queuing.

At the beginning of the year, become a member of an association of friends of a major museum or gallery. You'll have the benefit of permanent priority access and you'll be able to attend private presentations of certain exhibitions and special events.

> Take advantage of guided tours wherever possible, because they allow you to look at a small number of works in detail.

> If you're a fan of specialised exhibitions, such as motor shows, boat shows, home shows, craft fairs and aeronautical shows, buy tickets online and subscribe to email lists for advance notice of special deals.

Check out online newspapers

Online newspapers are a handy one-stop shop for entertainment needs.

> Get on to the Internet and browse the online version of newspapers in major cities, both at home and abroad. They list everything from opera, ballet and concerts to fringe theatre, jazz, club cabaret and more. (*See* 'Find out more', at left.)

> Stay on top of what's on with email, SMS alerts and 'web feeds'. Subscribe to an online newspaper, choose the sort of updates you want (arts, sport, politics) and they'll be sent to you via email, PDA, mobile phone or Really Simple Syndication (RSS) – 'web feeds' that comprise a summary of content from the newspaper's regular web site.

> Click on links for theatre or entertainment and you'll find what's on, reviews, your ticketing options and more. For instance, if you're visiting New York, go to *The New York Times*'s home page and click on 'Arts', then 'Theatre'. You'll find listings for mainstream and 'Off Broadway' productions, along with reader reviews and critics' picks. *The New York Times* also has an integrated ticketing system, which means you can choose a show and book tickets on the same web site.

> *The New York Times* offers a service called TicketWatch, which is a free email service alerting you to the best offers and ticket deals for theatre and the performing arts. Go to www.nytimes.com/ticketwatch and become a subscriber, so you can book tickets before you travel.

> If you're travelling to the UK, subscribe online to the Times Online's 'The Knowledge' – entertainment listings for London that are sent to your mobile phone. Simply subscribe before you go to take advantage of this service and then unsubscribe when you return home.

▶▶ **FIND OUT MORE**

• Use online newspapers to find out what's on, read reviews and buy tickets, whether you're close to home or travelling abroad.
www.smh.com.au (Sydney)
www.theage.com.au (Melbourne)
www.nzherald.co.nz (Auckland)
www.press.co.nz (Christchurch)
www.iol.co.za (South Africa)
www.nytimes.com (New York)
www.timesonline.co.uk (London)

TIMELY TIP

Get tickets for 'sold out' events
If the tickets you want are sold out, do a Google search of the event itself and click on links to find ticketing agents or brokers who are eager to help, or, if money is no barrier, try an eBay online auction. And don't forget that many venues reserve 'stand by' tickets to sell just an hour or two before the event.

Too much sport is never enough

▶ Go online and find package deals that include air fares, transfers and accommodation as well as seats to the special sporting event you're dying to see and you'll save time and money. This applies to most major sporting events – in Australia, New Zealand and other countries – and an advantage is often that special-deal seats are still available when single seats to the event have long since sold out. It's certainly worth a try.

▶ Sign up for SMS sports alerts on your mobile phone, via an online newspaper. Most major newspapers offer this service, so go browsing to find out which one is best for you (*see* 'Find out more', opposite).

Holidays and weekends away

Make the most of a weekend away

▶ Avoid traffic jams by heading out before 3 pm on Friday and set off on Sunday while it's still light.

▶ Eat dinner before travelling at night, and delay your departure on Sunday until very late at night, or first thing on Monday morning.

▶ To minimise potential stress after a weekend away, have your meals prepared for Monday in the fridge or freezer. This means you can take your time, enjoy the trip home and arrive late on Sunday.

▶ Consult roads and traffic information centres (using the Internet or by phone) that give you details on the state of the traffic in real time.

▶ When circumstances demand it, take secondary roads. If your car isn't fitted with a GPS unit (*see* page 155), be sure to take adequate road maps and consult them frequently – before you get lost!

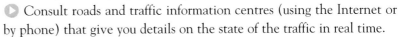

Travel pack

Instead of always having to pack up your toiletries when you're going away, keep a special travel pack permanently ready with all the things you need: toothbrush, toothpaste, shampoo and soap, etc. Saves forgetting things and it's always ready to go!

Don't be disappointed

If you're going on a camping holiday in December or January, or at other school holiday times, reserve your camping site well in advance to avoid missing out during peak times. There are Internet sites to help you with your research, with photos and detailed information to help you make your choice faster.

Tips for a safe and happy car trip

▷ Fill up your car's tank with petrol and check the oil and tyres the day before you leave so that you're not dealing with unnecessary hold-ups.

▷ Preferably leave on Sunday: a lot of holiday-makers will have already arrived at their destination and there will be fewer trucks on the road.

▷ If you're travelling on tollways, make sure you have an E-tag so you don't have to wait at the toll booths.

▷ Pack a picnic and a supply of drinks so you don't have to queue in a cafeteria or road house. If you're travelling with kids, find rest areas where they can play, and that have baby-change facilities, if necessary.

▷ Place any baby-care items that you may need during the trip in a separate bag that is easily accessible.

▷ Stop, revive, survive. No matter how quickly you might want to arrive at your destination, stop every 2 hours to stretch your legs.

Think before you jump in the car

▷ If you're planning to spend time with family or friends over a long weekend, take a train if possible. At times when roads are especially busy, you're more likely to shorten your travel time and avoid all the stress and potential road rage that delays often result in. Reserve your seat by phone or over the Internet a long time in advance, then sit back and enjoy the journey.

▷ If, on the other hand, there is no convenient rail connection and you need to drive, consider taking holidays outside peak times and school holidays. The journey will be quicker and easier, there is more accommodation to choose from and many destinations offer off-season discounts.

Guidebooks at your service

If you're an individual and hate large hotel complexes, preferring to do your own thing on holidays, invest in a couple of well-written, detailed tourist guides before you leave. These can make all the difference to the success of your stay. Find recommendations online or in a bookshop.

Resourceful camping

Practise setting up a new tent in the garden a few weeks before you leave. It'll make it much easier and quicker to set up after travelling all day. As soon as you return home, wash the tent with soapy water, rinse it with a hose and dry it in the fresh air before packing it away, ready for next time.

▶ Use guidebooks to find the contact details for charming little hotels or bed and breakfasts, the main areas of interest in your chosen region, the best places to eat and how to get around, along with cost comparisons for all of these aspects. Doing just a little bit of homework before the holiday will save time as well as add a great deal to your enjoyment.

▶ Go online and visit the web site of the accommodation you've chosen – before you make a reservation – to have a good look at the photos of the rooms and the details of the different services offered, to avoid any unpleasant surprises.

Make the most of rental accommodation

Seasonal rentals are especially suited to families with children. You can find flats and holiday houses to rent over summer well ahead of time, but in popular areas you may need to book up to 12 months in advance.

▶ Quickly familiarise yourself with existing offers by consulting newspaper advertisements and specialist magazines or by browsing web sites. Some owners give you the address of their personal web site, which is where you'll find photos and practical information.

▶ If you don't have access to the owner's web site, ask for photos of the house and garden and check the distances given on a map, for example between the house and the beach, or the nearest town.

▶ If you haven't been tempted by any offer, browse the web sites of real estate agents in the area you're going to, or place an advertisement yourself in the local paper, clearly specifying your requirements.

▶ If you return to the same location year after year, check out possible rentals for next time while you're there on holiday. That way, you'll know the exact location of the best houses. Keep a list of your 'possibles' and pre-book for the following year, if you can.

Fun in the snow

If you're going to spend a week in the snow, you don't want to waste precious time on your holiday organising equipment. The timesaving answer is, as always, be prepared!

▶ Limit the time you spend hiring skis by booking and paying for them over the Internet. When you arrive at your snowy holiday destination, all you have to do is pick your equipment up. Rent boots, helmets, ski clothes and snowboards in the same way.

TIMELY TIP

Get an inventory

Before packing your bags, ask the holiday-home owner or agent to send you a copy of the inventory. This means you can take essential items that aren't on the list and not waste time packing then travelling with a lot of stuff that's already there. And remember, 'sleeps six' might mean three double beds or six singles, so make sure you check before going.

FIND OUT MORE

• Visit a government travel advice web site to obtain a wealth of useful information, including whether your destination is a safe place to be going to. The web sites below contain valuable advice for Australians, New Zealanders and South Africans travelling abroad.

www.smartraveller.gov.au
www.safetravel.govt.nz
www.dfa.gov.za/consular/
 travel_advice.htm

▶ Try pre-ordering and paying for your ski pass over the Internet, before you go, which can save you both time and money.

▶ If you're travelling to the snowfields by car, make sure you listen to daily snow reports, or check on the Internet before you head out, so that you know of road closures and whether you will need to carry chains or not.

When you're travelling overseas...

If you're planning an overseas holiday, don't leave everything to the last minute. Advance planning pays in more ways than just time saved.

▶ Two to three months before your departure, check the expiry date on your passport. Many countries require you to have at least 6 months' validity remaining on your passport, so allow enough time for renewal if necessary (*see* 'Find out more', on page 177).

▶ Check if you need a visa and any other paperwork – and factor in a bit of extra time, as the process can sometimes be very slow.

▶ Find out in good time about recommended vaccinations – some need to be administered 6–12 weeks before departure. And don't forget to take your vaccination certificate with you on your trip.

▶ Consider taking out a comprehensive medical insurance policy, as overseas medical costs can be horrifyingly expensive.

▶ Talk to your GP about any prescription drugs you might need to take with you in case of emergency, and check that they won't contravene the drug laws of your destination country.

▶ Buy traveller's cheques or ensure that you have a credit card that's valid for your destination, and that can be used at ATMs.
(*See also* 'Check out online newspapers', on page 160.)

Personalise your luggage

Your suitcase is navy blue or black, with a solid shell and wheels. It's easy to handle and practical – in short, it's perfect for long plane journeys. To avoid your luggage looking the same as everyone else's, put on a sticker or a ribbon so it's easy to identify, and you'll have no trouble recognising it.

TIMELY TIP

Computer basics

Don't think it can't happen to you

Computers undoubtedly save us all a lot of time, but they can waste a lot of time, too. All it takes is for your hard drive to crash or a particularly destructive virus to attack your files, and weeks, or even months, of work can disappear in a second.

▶ Backing up is the only answer to avoiding having to painstakingly recreate missing documents, or you can give your computer to a specialist to try and salvage the damaged files. Either way, the result is always going to be a considerable loss of time.

▶ To protect your data, make it an inflexible rule that you always keep two copies of all important documents. Keep one copy on your computer's hard drive and another copy on an entirely independent storage device, such as a compact disc (CD) or digital video disc (DVD).

How to choose the best backup tools

▶ You can save time when backing up files by choosing the most appropriate storage medium. USB Flash Drives, also called ThumbDrives, are the quickest and easiest devices to use, provided you don't have too many files to back up. Use CDs for larger volumes of data – the recordable variety (CD-R) for material you want to back up permanently, such as completed work or photos, and the rewritable variety (CD-RW) to back up files that are constantly changing.

▶ If the quantity of data you need to back up calls for too many CDs – which can be time consuming to burn – use DVDs instead. One DVD can store the equivalent of six CDs' worth of data. As is the case with CDs, you can buy DVDs that are both recordable (DVD-R) as well as those that can be erased and rewritten many times (DVD-RW).

▶ If your computer doesn't have a built-in CD or DVD burner, you can always have one installed without breaking the bank. Alternatively, you can buy an external burner that plugs into the USB port of your computer. Do some research before you buy to make sure that the burner you purchase is capable of handling rewritable disks.

An external hard drive for major backing up

It's vital to back up important documents, but the process can become unnecessarily time consuming if you don't go about it in the right way.

▶ If you have large amounts of data to back up, or if you need to back up often, the task of burning dozens of CDs or DVDs can become onerous, and consequently tends to get put off. The danger here is that one day it may be too late. To prevent this from happening, buy an external hard drive, which is similar to the one inside your PC, but located in a separate case that plugs into the USB port on your computer.

▶ To make the job of copying important data from your internal hard drive to an external drive quick and easy, buy software that does it automatically. Once the files to be backed up have been copied to the external drive, the software will regularly compare the original files with the backup copies and resave only those that have changed.

▶ Automatic backing up is done very quickly, which enables you to keep a backup copy of everything on your internal hard drive. This will ensure a quick recovery from a major computer breakdown.

Don't let email become your Trojan horse

Few computer disasters waste more time than infection by a virus.

▶ Antivirus software is essential, but because these programs recognise viruses by comparing the files arriving on your computer with a database of known viruses, it is imperative that you keep the software up-to-date.

▶ To further minimise the chance of a computer disaster caused by infection, make sure your antivirus software is set to check all new material arriving on your computer, especially emails, which are the most common route used for spreading viruses.

▶ Be particularly wary of emails from senders you don't know, especially if they have an attachment. If there is a virus in an email, this is where it will be. Simply delete emails from senders you don't recognise and never open unusual attachments, however intriguing they may appear to be.

▶ It is also useful to know that files with certain extensions (*see* 'A quick guide to file extensions', opposite above) are more likely to contain viruses than others. Watch out for any files that end in the extensions .exe, .bat, .com, .pif and .scr. Windows normally hides file extensions, but you can set it to display them.

> ◗ **CAUTION!**
>
> ### Antivirus protection
>
> Having an antivirus program is just plain common sense, but to ensure it is really efficient, you should update its virus definitions regularly (at least once a week). If you are using one of the major antivirus packages this won't involve any extra work, since you should be able to instruct the software to carry out the task automatically.

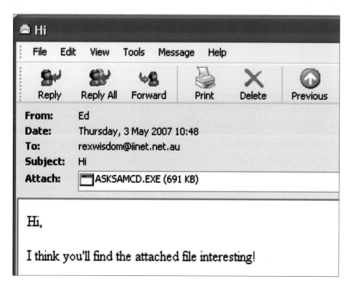

Back up emails in a flash

With Microsoft Outlook and Outlook Express, all you have to do to save copies of your most important emails is to select them in your email list and move them to a backup file. The email will be saved as a file with the same name as the initial email.

A quick guide to file extensions

An extension is a small label made up of two, three or four letters placed at the end of a file name, after a dot. For example, in the name 'file.doc', the extension 'doc' indicates that the file is a Word document, while 'file.xls' is an Excel document. This allows the type of file to be identified along with the program(s) that can open it. Here is a list of some of the most common extensions:

- **Text files** .asc, .doc, .htm, .html, .msg, .txt, .wpd
- **Picture files** .bmp, .eps, .gif, .ipg, .pict, .png, .tif
- **Sound files** .au, .mid, .ra, .snd, .wav
- **Video files** .avi, .mov, .mpg, .qt
- **Compressed files** .arc, .arj, .gz, .hqx, .sit, .tar, .zip

How to view file extensions

▶ File extensions are hidden by default in Windows, but you can speed up the process of identifying file types by having Windows display any extension automatically. In any Explorer window go to the **Tools** menu and click on **Folder Options**. Select the **View** tab to see options within the 'Advanced settings' box. Uncheck the box next to 'Hide extensions for known file types' and finally click **OK**.

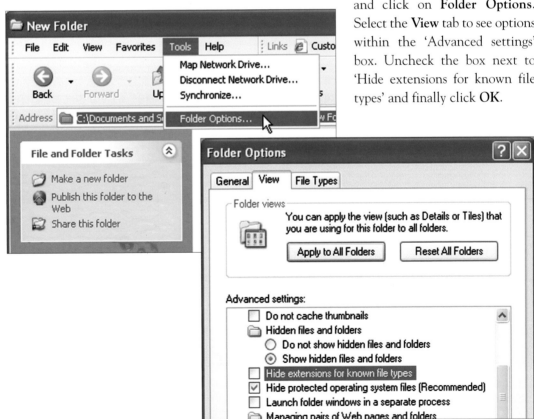

Better use of your computer

Keyboard shortcuts save time

Keyboard shortcuts can save a lot of time, so if you use a computer regularly it's worth memorising at least the basic ones.

▶ You use a shortcut by pressing two or three keys together, rather than by clicking on the screen with the mouse to carry out an action. Most shortcuts can be done with one hand, while the other directs the mouse.

▶ Shortcuts are particularly useful for all of those repetitive actions you do on a laptop, where the built-in pointing device can be much slower to use than a conventional computer mouse.

▶ Certain shortcuts are practically universal and will work for a whole range of software programs, especially those from a single manufacturer, whereas others are unique to one type of software only.

▶ Look for a list of unique shortcuts in the web-based instruction manual connected to some software, or in the program's help menu.

▶ Most shortcuts are accessed using the Alt, Control and/or Shift keys in combination with a single letter. So, for example, the shortcut Alt + E is done by pressing the Alt key and, while holding it down, pressing the E key. In the window below, in the word Find, the letter F is underlined. By pressing the Control and F keys, you can find a section of text without using the mouse. Similarly, you can replace some text using Control + H and go to a particular page or line, using Control + G.

TIMELY TIP

Shortcuts on a Mac

Many of the shortcuts that can be used on a PC will also work on an Apple Macintosh (Mac). All you need to do is use the Command (Apple) key instead of the Control (Ctrl) key.

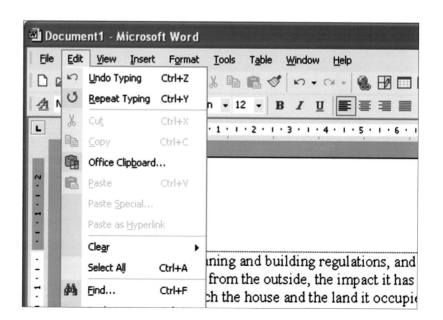

TIMELY TIP

Using a PC mouse on a Mac

To obtain many PC functions on a Macintosh, replace the original mouse with a PC mouse that plugs into the USB port on your computer. You will then have access to two buttons and a scroll wheel. All the big-brand PC mice (Microsoft, Logitech) are fully recognised by a Macintosh computer.

Basic keyboard shortcuts that work with most programs

Keys	Functions
Alt + F	Opens the file menu
Alt + E	Opens the edit menu
Alt + Z	Undoes the last keyboard action
Ctrl + S	Saves the file you are working on
Ctrl + X	Cuts the selected items
Ctrl + C	Copies the selected items
Ctrl + V	Pastes a copied item (or items)
Home	Takes you to the beginning of the current line
End	Takes you to the end of the current line
Ctrl + Home	Takes you to the beginning of a document
Ctrl + End	Takes you to the end of a document
Shift + Home	Highlights from the current position to the beginning of the line
Shift + End	Highlights from the current position to the end of the line
Ctrl + Left arrow	Moves one word at a time to the left
Ctrl + Right arrow	Moves one word at a time to the right

Don't neglect the right button on your mouse

The right button on a PC mouse gives you access to shortcut menus, which offer most of the useful options for any item you select with the mouse. They're faster than using the standard menus and toolbars.

▶ When you're processing text, for example, with one click you can access a list of synonyms to choose from, a choice of font or formatting controls.

▶ When using the Internet, the shortcut menu offers a range of useful options, such as opening a link in a new window without closing the previous window.

▶ By opening a new window you can start from a page showing a selection of interesting sites, and then follow several chains of links independently, without losing track of where you are.

Using the Internet

Broadband – the speedy, efficient choice

The term 'broadband' describes any high-speed Internet connection, and there are four main options: ADSL, cable, wireless and satellite. Using broadband means you have constant access to the Internet, there are no initial dial-up costs and you can still use the phone while surfing the Net.

▶ Still one of the most popular choices, ADSL uses telephone cable, but the signals move up to 20 times faster than a dial-up connection.

▶ Broadband cable can deliver up to 350 times faster than dial-up. It uses coaxial cable (similar to cable TV), but is not available everywhere.

▶ Wireless broadband is accessed via a radio signal, not a telephone line, and allows you to access the Internet on your laptop at home, when you are on the move (using 'hot spots') and in some public places if you subscribe to a wireless broadband provider. It's fast and easy to install.

▶ Satellite is a great option for broadband Internet access if you live in a remote area where other options are not available, but can be expensive.

▶ If you have several computers at home you can share the connection and have access to the Internet at the same time by using a piece of hardware called a router. Sharing can be wireless or via cable, although to establish a wireless network you may have to buy additional equipment.

Put a stop to those annoying pop-up ads

▶ Advertising can really slow down your Internet browsing speed. To stop advertising windows, or pop-ups, from opening, Microsoft has updated Internet Explorer with an 'anti-pop-up' filter (which you can deactivate).

▶ This update only works with the Windows XP operating system. For older operating systems, there is other third-party software available that does more or less the same thing, such as the Google Toolbar, which is available on the search engine site (http://toolbar.google.com/T4/?rd=f).

TIMELY TIP

Help when you need it

When choosing an Internet Service Provider (ISP), ask around to find out which ones offer the most efficient phone support. Help lines that seem to be permanently engaged, or that result in never-ending telephone queues, are both frustrating and time wasting.

Pre-set your contact details into email messages

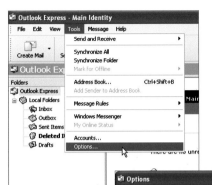

▶ If you use email for work or business, save time by inserting contact details (consisting of your name, address, telephone number and email address) automatically at the end of messages, using Outlook Express. You won't have to retype the same information time and time again.

▶ To compose a signature, go to the **Tools** menu in Outlook Express, choose **Options**, go to the **Signatures** tab and click on **New**. Type the text of your signature in the window provided. If you wish to add it automatically to all your messages, click the box 'Add signatures to all outgoing messages' and finally click **OK**.

▶ By highlighting your details in coloured type you'll make them just that much clearer for the person receiving the email message.

Quick tips for a successful Internet search

The Internet is a wonderful research tool, but it can also be a great time waster. The key is to be disciplined with your searches.

▶ Have a clear idea of what you are looking for and focus your search, ignoring all the distractions that inevitably present themselves.

▶ Stick to simple search words (preferably nouns) and put quotation marks around phrases. This will limit results to only those that contain all the words in your search and in the order you typed them, instead of the possible millions of others that contain any of your search words.

▶ Use special characters to narrow your search. For instance, if you put a plus sign (+) before a word, it will be included in the search; if you put a minus (-) in front of a word, then that word will not be included.

▶ Advanced searches can also improve your results and save time.

▶ Bookmark interesting sites and go back to them when you have time, remembering to organise them logically to make it easy to find them again.

CAUTION!

Keeping the baddies at bay

Having a broadband connection increases the chances that your computer may fall prey to outside attack. To minimise this risk, make sure your Windows Firewall is turned on. To do this, click **Start,** then **Control Panel**, then **Network and Internet Connections**. When the Network and Internet Connections window appears, click on the **Windows Firewall** icon and when that opens, check that **On** is selected. If it is not, select it and click **OK** for the change to take effect.

Organising digital photos

Catalogue your photos automatically

▶ Cataloguing and renaming all your digital photos before storing them in your computer will make it so much quicker and easier to find the individual shot you're after, especially when it's labelled 'Summer 2007 Bali 005' instead of something unhelpful, such as 'PIC00456'.

▶ When you connect a digital camera or a memory card reader to a computer equipped with Windows XP, a window is displayed offering several options. Choose **Scanner and Camera Wizard** from the list. The Wizard will guide you through the process of choosing, downloading and storing your images. When you are asked to provide the picture name and destination information, give the group of pictures you have chosen a memorable name (make it as specific as possible, if you choose a vague title such as 'holiday pics' you will soon forget whether that referred to 2006 in India or 2007 in Bali). Finally, check and, if necessary, choose a new destination file before clicking **Next**. The Wizard automatically copies the pictures onto your hard drive and offers to carry out any additional tasks. If there is no other task that you want or need to do, click **Next** to exit the Wizard. Your photos are now copied and properly filed, with sensible names that you can recognise quickly and easily.

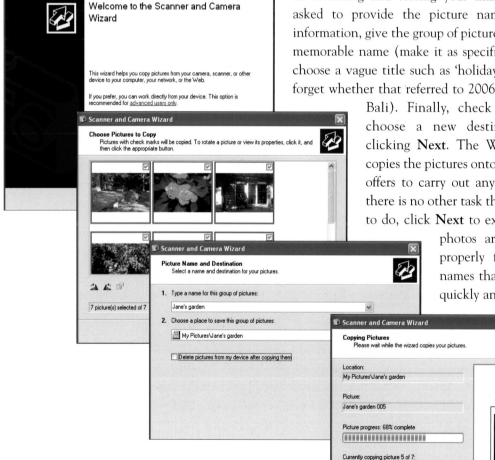

TIMELY TIP

Versatile card readers

A memory card reader – a device that reads memory cards (the small, removable, rewritable data storage devices in digital cameras and other electronic tools) – is a faster and more practical way to transfer photos to your computer because you don't have to connect the camera to a computer. Most card readers plug into a USB port. Choose one that accepts a wide range of cards so that you can download images from different brands of camera.

Rename a series of files in a single operation

It is never too late to rename photographs you have already saved.

▶ Select all the pictures belonging to the group you want to rename by clicking on the first file, holding down the shift key then clicking on the last. Now right click the mouse on the first file in the group and choose **Rename** from the shortcut menu that appears (shown below). Type the new name for the first picture (e.g. Summer 2007), and then click **Enter**. All the other pictures you selected will now all carry the same name, followed by a unique number – Summer 2007 (1), Summer 2007 (2), etc.

▶ Renaming is particularly useful for photo and image files, but it will also work for other types of computer files.

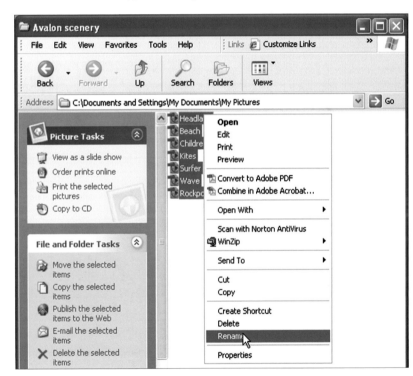

Photo-sharing solutions

▶ You can create and publish an online photo album in minutes using photo-sharing web sites such as PhotoSite, Flickr and Webshots. They are simple to use and make sharing your holiday photos with friends and family as simple as sending an email with a web link attached to it.

▶ Download free software, such as Google's Picasa, that allows you to do three things – find, organise and share your photos – and is easy to use.

▶ If all you want to do is show someone a particular image or two, don't overlook the most obvious tool for the job – your camera's LCD.

Computer care

TIMELY TIP

The stealthy invader
Dust can be the hidden enemy of computers and printers. Fans designed to draw in air to cool processors and other items also draw in dust, which can settle as an insulating blanket over components, causing them to overheat and malfunction. Use a can of compressed air to dislodge build-up, while at the same time holding a vacuum cleaner nozzle close by to suck up particles. Before opening any part of your computer, always discon-nect the mains, and don't touch any-thing with the vacuum cleaner nozzle.

Keep your keyboard and mouse in tiptop condition

A sticky key on your keyboard or a temperamental mouse are nuisances that will inevitably waste time. Your computer needs a minimum amount of regular care and maintenance to operate efficiently, and a few minutes a week spent on cleaning will pay off in the long run.

▶ Dust and dirt accumulate between the keys on the keyboard, so turn the whole keyboard upside down and shake it gently to remove larger particles. Do this once a week or so, to avoid particles becoming lodged.

▶ Use a soft brush to remove any dust sticking to the keys and the plastic case, then wipe the keys with a damp cloth or use a dust-removing spray. Wipe between the keys using wipes soaked in a cleaning solution. Never spray solution onto a keyboard or any other computer hardware, or peripherals such as a printer, as you may cause damage.

▶ To clean a mouse, turn it upside down and wipe the base with a predampened cloth. If you have a roller-ball mouse, remove the ball from its casing and clean it with water mixed with a few drops of dishwashing liquid. Rinse and dry it thoroughly. Dip a cotton bud in methylated spirits and use it to remove any grime inside the ball casing, especially around the three small contact rollers that touch the ball.

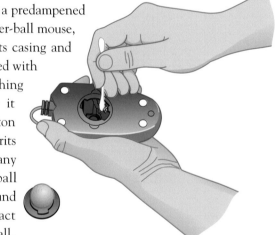

TIMELY TIP

A quick cleaning job
Keep a selection of basic cleaning materials near your computer. Having a lint-free cloth, cotton buds, a can of compressed air and a cleaning solution to hand will speed up basic cleaning and maintenance. Ready-made cleaning kits are widely available from computer outlets and large department stores, along with occasional refinements such as a mini vacuum cleaner.

It's quicker if you can see what you're doing

▶ Trying to read a dirty computer screen, particularly when light is striking it from certain angles, is difficult and can slow you down. Remove dust and finger marks using a clean, soft cotton cloth, taking particular care with LCD screens, since they are susceptible to scratching.

▶ A little clean water is all that's necessary to clean a screen, but for stubborn marks try using one of the many proprietary cleaning solutions (available from supermarkets and office equipment suppliers).

▶ The glass on a scanner should be cleaned the same way as a screen.

▶ Dust and dirt can also affect CD reader/writers, causing them to skip tracks or otherwise behave temperamentally. Avoid potential problems by cleaning the optical lens of your CD player and burner every month using a special cleaning CD. All you have to do is insert the CD into the player and follow the on-screen instructions.

Stress-free printer maintenance

Like all computer peripherals, printers can occasionally behave erratically, causing frustrating delays and wasted time. To minimise the chance of a printer slowing you down, there are a few simple things you can do.

▶ First of all, use only the best quality materials. This generally means buying the toner or ink recommended by the manufacturer, which is often more expensive. Of course it is possible to save money by buying substitutes – and many may give fault-free service – but if there's a problem, the time spent fixing it may outweigh any saving made on the initial purchase.

▶ Buy only good quality paper, since it is less likely to cause jams.

▶ Spend a bit of time maintaining a printer and you'll save time in the long run. Use cotton buds to prevent dust build-up, particularly around fan-cooling vents, rollers and beneath paper trays. Check all the parts of your printer's paper feeder to ensure they're not stained with ink.

▶ Carry out regular printing tests to check ink and toner levels, and keep spare ink or toner handy, otherwise you run the risk of running out when you're in a hurry to print an important document. If you buy in advance, you can take advantage of the best deals, too.

Papers, bills and documents

Establish an efficient filing system

The key to saving time in a home office is simple: be organised! The more organised you are, the more time you'll save looking for lost documents, dealing with expired passports and licences, and desperately trying to replace bank statements. First up, establish a system that works.

▶ Make sure you have separate files to group important papers: payslips, taxation details, mortgage or rent and insurance payments, bills, business and household expenses, subscriptions, club memberships, bank and credit card statements, documentary proof of your savings and investments, receipts and guarantees for household equipment.

▶ Depending on the amount of space you have, organise your files into a filing cabinet, filing boxes, upright files or folders (much the same as books on a bookshelf). In order to find them quickly and easily, label files according to the sort of documents filed as well as the years they cover.

▶ Remember, some financial records can now be kept for you on databases that are accessed via the Internet, using a password. This means you may be able to keep fewer paper files, only printing out a hard copy for those times when you really need it.

Find filed documents quickly

Finding records quickly can literally save you many hours of wasted time.

▶ If you work from home, you'll need to make sure that work files and household files don't get mixed up. For some, the move towards a paperless office is a reasonable goal, but for most of us filing and storing paper bills and documents is still a reality that requires a methodical approach. Two separate filing cabinets may be the answer, or a colour-coded filing system – red for work, green for home – or something along those lines.

▶ File bank and credit card statements as soon as you've checked through them, placing the most recent ones at the front of the file.

▶ If you have a cheque account, store your cheque stubs in the same file, in chronological order, so that you can find them quickly.

▶ Keep a record of the numbers of cheques in a book in case the chequebook is lost or stolen (or at least the first and last numbers).

Keep a copy on file of the telephone number you need to call to report a chequebook or a credit card that's been lost or stolen.

 Put section dividers between the main account and any other accounts you hold. This makes it so much faster to locate the document you need immediately.

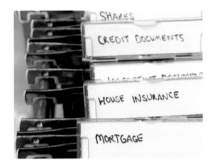

 Remember, for many accounts you can now opt to access information online, only printing off a paper statement when you really need it, which will save you time filing and retrieving paperwork.

Simplify your systems

Do you need to renew official documents such as a passport or driver's licence? Follow these tips to save time by simplifying your systems.

 Make a note in your diary or Personal Digital Assistant (PDA) when important documents are coming up for renewal, as renewal is a faster process than applying from scratch, which can result in unnecessary time-wasting delays and added work for you.

 Driver's licences are usually sent out as a matter of course, but, regardless, renew it as soon as possible, to avoid complications.

 Avoid unnecessary journeys: if you're not sure which documents you need to provide when applying for or renewing an official document, make a phone enquiry or check the appropriate web site to find out.

 Avoid waiting 'on hold' on the telephone for long periods. Check the Frequently Asked Questions (FAQs) section of a web site first, to see if you can quickly find the answer to your question.

 Prepare a passport renewal application ahead of time to avoid delays. Adult passports can usually be renewed if they haven't expired more than 12 months before the time of application. You can access and print renewal forms online (see 'Find out more', at left), but you must lodge the completed application form with the passport office, a post office or some other recognised agency, for checking of details. You will also usually need to provide three different forms of identity.

 If you lose your passport, report it immediately to your local police station or passport office. In Australia and New Zealand, you can report a lost passport on the relevant government web site and complete an application for a replacement (see 'Find out more', at left).

 Using the Internet can save a lot of time, but while most web sites – especially government ones – aim to list the most up-to-date information, also remember that regulations, such as following security reviews,

vary between countries and can change over time. You'll make life a lot easier for yourself if you take the time to read web site instructions carefully before proceeding with your task.

▶ Keep photocopies of important documents in your files, such as your birth certificate, marriage certificate, passport, driver's licence and car registration. You will save a lot of time if any of them are lost or stolen simply by being able to transcribe important information from them, such as document or passport numbers. Replacing these documents can be a lengthy process and delays can occur while checks are made by the authorities to validate your information.

▶ Prepare a 'disaster' plan. Ask a close friend or family member to keep copies of original documents in case a fire or flood destroys your records.

▶ While it's not possible to replace original birth certificates, in most cases you can obtain an official certified copy from the relevant administrative authority as proof of your birth. In Australia and New Zealand, there are registers of births, deaths and marriages for this purpose.

▶ In South Africa, download the abridged birth certificate form and fill it in before taking it to your nearest home affairs office to be processed.

Pay on time

There are several ways to help you avoid forgetting to pay a bill on time.

▶ Arrange a direct debit with your bank for all your important bills and ensure sufficient money is kept in the account to pay them; many companies will send or email you a copy of a bill automatically to remind you when payment falls due, or for your home-office files.

▶ As soon as you receive a bill in the letterbox, put it in a file marked 'bills to be paid' and note the date in your diary when the bill needs to be paid by. After you've paid a bill, file it in the appropriate place.

● Make payments over the Internet using your bank's Internet banking service, and set up automatic debits wherever possible (to make monthly payments on your home loan or a personal loan, for instance) to make the process fast and easy.

● Electronic Funds Transfer (EFT), or telephone banking services such as BPAY (in Australia), are also great timesaving methods of paying regular incoming bills. The other advantage to using these services is that they are available whenever you need them, 24 hours a day, 7 days a week.

● If you still pay bills by cheque, set aside a time each week for writing them in one go, then post them immediately.

● You can also arrange direct debit for most bill payments by supplying credit card details to the company billing you for services. Ask if this can be set up for you and simply file bills for your records.

Keeping electronic files

● Instead of photocopying important documents, scan them and store the digital files on your computer, only printing them out when it's absolutely necessary.

● Take digital photos or videos of all your most valuable possessions and keep the sales receipts for all major purchases. In the case of theft or accidental damage, this will make it easier for the insurance company to reimburse you.

● An easy way to store digital files is on a CD, DVD or a USB Flash Drive, or ThumbDrive or memory stick (they are tiny portable storage devices that plug into the USB port of your computer, and can store or back up most digital data, from photos and music to documents and presentations). File the CDs and DVDs along with corresponding receipts.

● Organise your digital files as you would your paper files, because searching your hard drive to find them can take as much time as sorting through a filing cabinet. Use separate folders for each set of documents.

▶ ▶ ACCESS GOVERNMENT RECORDS ONLINE

• **Government social security offices** display a lot of useful information on their web sites, including information regarding health and welfare payments, income support, sick leave and unemployment benefits. In most cases, if you have made social security claims you can access all your records online – stored in a database – once you have registered and obtained a password. Check the relevant government web site in your country, below, to find out if this service is available to you.

www.centrelink.gov.au

www.winz.govt.nz

www.labour.gov.za

How long should I keep documents?

Which documents you need to keep and for how long will depend on your occupation, your family circumstances and where you live. Find out from the appropriate authorities (e.g. bank or credit union, tax office, insurance company) how long you need to keep specific documents. Here is a general guide for some of the more common documents.

KEEP INDEFINITELY

Identity
● You must keep papers that establish your identity, and that of your family, in a safe place and for your whole life. If possible, keep originals in one safe place and copies in another
  ● Birth certificate
  ● Adoption papers
  ● Marriage certificate
  ● Divorce or separation papers
  ● Death certificates for family members
  ● Passports and naturalisation papers
  ● Driving licences for all family members
  ● Wills (held by a lawyer, public trustee or kept in a safe-deposit box in a bank)

Health
● Medicare card (Australia); community services card (New Zealand); health and social security card (South Africa)
● Private health care insurance policies and related cards
● Vaccination certificates
● Results of medical examinations such as pathology tests and X-rays
● Blood-group card (if you are a blood donor)

Education
● Degrees and diplomas
● Certificates of secondary, technical or other educational courses

Financial and legal
● Deeds and documents relating to property owner-ship (or unsigned copies if the originals are kept by a bank or other mortgagor)
● Copy of your will (keep original with a lawyer, a public trustee or in a safe-deposit box in a bank)

● Insurance policies for house or apartment (both building and contents cover)
● Life insurance contracts and policies
● Power of attorney
● Superannuation fund details
● Any civil or military pension entitlements. (In the case of loss, a copy of some of these documents may be obtained from the relevant authorities)

KEEP UNTIL RETIREMENT
● Pay slips, work contracts
● Letters of appointment
● Letters of dismissal
● Notification of termination of employment (and details of any Eligible Termination Payment)
● Records of unemployment or social security benefits, including those received in the case of sick leave or accident
● Lapsed insurance policies (and proof that they have been terminated)

KEEP FOR 6–7 YEARS
● Building permits
● Construction warranties on structural defects (6 years in NSW; 2 years for non-structural defects)
● Real estate agents' fees
● Bank statements
● Chequebook stubs
● Loan contracts
● Receipts of deposits and transfers relating to a bank account
● Insurance policies covering cars, income protection and professional indemnity (review annually)
● Contracts with service providers for Internet and mobile phone access
● Invoices for furniture, paintings and other valuables
● A list of assets for insurance purposes (with photographs)
● Medical file created following an accident
● Property inspection report

KEEP FOR 6 YEARS
● Debt recovery limitation on loans between individuals
● Receipts of payment of lawyers' fees

Keep for 5 years
- Taxation documents, including personal tax returns, company returns and, if registered for GST (or VAT), records of payments and refunds
- In the case of a tax audit, investigations can cover a period of up to 5 years. Keep the documents relating to your tax declarations for this period

Keep for 3 years
- Gas and electricity bills after you have left a rental property
- Documents relating to the sale and management of real estate property
- Rental agreement
- Rent receipts
- Receipt of payment of lawyers' fees

Keep for 2 years
- Invoices for improvement work carried out on your home
- Receipts for local council rates
- Insurance premium receipts
- Correspondence with your insurer regarding the payment of any claims
- Receipt of payment for medical expenses

Keep for 1–3 years
- Telephone bills
- Warranties and guarantees

Keep for 30 days
- Bills relating to moving house; claims must usually be made within 7 to 30 days. Check the policy

Personal banking

Take time to save time – and money

▶ Before choosing a bank, visit branches of several banks and ask for brochures listing their services and fees. Or take the speedy option and access all this information online, so that you can compare services.

▶ Every bank charges different fees for common services such as maintaining accounts, issuing credit cards, cash withdrawals from an Automatic Teller Machine (ATM) that is not part of the bank's own network, direct debits, bank transfers, etc. Some banks' fees are much higher than others, so don't get caught, find out beforehand!

▶ Make a list of the services that you expect to use regularly and compare the costs involved. In the end you'll save money and avoid the time-wasting inconvenience of making a wrong choice.

▶ Make sure you compare accounts or services on the same basis. Is Internet banking available? Are fee-free transactions included? If so, how many? Is there a monthly charge? Is there a fee for a service you use regularly, such as sending money interstate or overseas, and if so, what fee is charged?

▶ Be especially careful regarding fees charged if you overdraw an account without prior

CAUTION!

Is location important?
Don't choose a bank based on proximity to home or work, or misguided loyalty, either. Look for one that offers a high level of service, promptly. Banks are very competitive, so compare their services and products before you open an account anywhere.

approval, or when a direct debit is refused due to insufficient funds – the fees incurred can be ridiculously high.

▶ Do your utmost to not exceed your credit card limit. Credit cards attract high-interest fees, which can waste a lot of time to sort out, so keep this in mind when you discuss your credit limit with your bank.

▶ The more transactions you can do yourself securely via the Internet or using phone banking, the more time you'll save.

TIMELY TIP

Quick financial advice

Many of the larger banks and building societies have financial management services available to customers, to help them make decisions about accounts, loans and repayment. Having this advice (often for free) can help you to realise your financial management goals faster, though it's entirely up to you whether you act on the advice given or not. There's no obligation involved.

Banks versus other financial institutions

The big-name banks will almost certainly look after your money with a high degree of safety, but today they're not the only people who offer competitive financial services, including credit cards. Building societies, community banks, credit unions and a number of other institutions offer money-management services – many of which are available online.

Internet banking has encouraged many new services – savings accounts sometimes charge lower (or no) fees and pay better interest rates than funds deposited in conventional savings accounts. Add to that the fact that you can access them from your own home at any hour of the day or night, and you'll save on time as well as money. Paying bills online will save you hours, too.

Choose your package carefully

▶ When you open an account, your bank will offer packages grouping several services together, which will help you save time, especially if you have trouble managing your spending. (*See* 'Find out more', at left.)

▶ Organise an overdraft – some have a preferential interest rate, or a low fee or no charge at all if you have more than a specified amount in your account. In some cases there's no need to phone your bank if you're overdrawn, as an overdraft becomes automatically available.

▶ Nearly all packages include electronic banking services (Internet or telephone) that are easily the best personal-banking time savers.

▶ Be careful when choosing a package. Most offer a wide range of services, some of which you may not need, but may have to pay for. High costs can go unnoticed for some time if payment is made by direct debit.

▶ Only agree to a package if you're certain you need all or most of the services offered. If you find you're being charged for services you don't use, change the kind of account you have – or change your bank.

 FIND OUT MORE

• Check the web sites listed below and follow the links to find out how you can better manage your money and deal with bank accounts, loans and a range of other financial products.
www.understandingmoney.gov.au
www.infochoice.com.au
www.nzbdirectory.co.nz
www.finforum.co.za
www.moneyweb.co.za

Ready sources of money

▶ Need money in a hurry? If you suddenly need to make a very expensive purchase, the two most common sources of quick money are credit from your bank or money borrowed from a finance company.

▶ Online loans can be cheaper but you'll need to fill in details of your needs, assets and liabilities as well as proving your ID and financial history, all of which eat up a lot of time.

▶ Most online bank or finance company web sites have calculators that allow you to work out what loans will cost before you apply for them. The process is quick and accurate, but make sure you find out what the fees are up front so that you're looking at the total expense involved.

▶ Remember to print off copies of important documents, such as loan applications, so you have a record of what you have signed on for.

▶ Transfer money quickly from one account to another online. If you already have a mortgage or other loan account with your bank and you need money in a hurry, simply transfer funds from one account to another, just to tide you over. You can do this at any time of the day or night. (*See also* 'Manage your accounts online', on page 185.)

▶ Make a cash withdrawal from supermarkets at the same time you buy food and household items using Eftpos. There is no extra charge, and it'll save you making a separate trip to an ATM to get money out.

Solutions for fast credit

▶ If you need extra money urgently, you can choose a personal loan or a hire-purchase plan (linked to the goods or service you buy). The choice is usually between a bank or other financial institution, but be aware that many finance companies are also owned by banks.

▶ Save time by requesting credit from your existing bank, instead of shopping around other lending institutions. Be aware, though, that you may end up paying a higher interest rate for the speed and convenience.

▶ Depending on how much you need to borrow, you may be able to negotiate a good interest rate and lower fees if you have been a customer with your bank or financial institution for a long time.

▶ Get set up for Internet or telephone banking and request a credit limit increase, if only for a limited period of time. (*See also* 'Manage your accounts online', on page 185.)

TIMELY TIP

Direct transfer

If you are able to call in a favour from a family member or close friend, direct transfer of funds online from them to you is a quick-and-simple way to get money. If you're travelling overseas, this can be a very handy option.

▶ Use ATMs for a cash advance on your credit card or to transfer money from one account into another, 24 hours a day, 7 days a week. Just be aware that cash advances draw very high rates of interest.

▶ Most banks now offer services allowing you to access your accounts using a smart mobile phone or Personal Digital Assistant (PDA). You can check balances and transfer money from one account to another. But make sure you understand the costs involved.

▶ In Australia, state and territory laws govern consumer credit matters so regulations vary within each state and territory. Check with your local fair-trading or consumer authority for more information.

TIMELY TIP

Consider loan options

Before taking out a personal loan or hire-purchase finance agreement (that may charge high interest), consider organising a bank overdraft if it's a small or short-term loan you're after. It might be faster, simpler and cheaper.

Handling a bank dispute

In Australia, New Zealand and South Africa, all banks are bound by a Code of Practice under which they are required to publish and follow a complaints procedure. If you skip a step in the procedure, you risk spending more time resolving a dispute. Follow these tips to help you resolve bank disputes as quickly and painlessly as possible.

● Try to resolve any personal-banking problem by discussing it as early as possible with the appropriate representative at your bank.

● Most banks now operate an online customer feedback facility as a quick-and-easy way of clearing up minor disputes, and filling out details of your complaint online may be all you need to do.

● If your complaint can't be resolved by front-line staff at your home branch, you'll need to engage with the bank's internal disputes procedure, which is usually free of charge.

● If you don't get the result you're after, you'll be given the name and contact number of a service manager who will investigate the dispute on your behalf, and may require confirmation of your complaint in writing. The bank usually has 30 days in which to investigate the complaint.

● Keep copies of any letters you write, along with any evidence such as statements, correspondence, letters of demand and emails, etc.

● If there is no resolution, the bank has another period of time in which to investigate the dispute and offer a solution. This may take up to another 30 days.

● If a bank's dispute-resolution procedures don't solve the problem there are procedures for resolving disputes run by a banking Ombudsman, which is independent of financial institutions and guarantees that your privacy will be respected (see 'Find out more', above opposite).

● Going through the Ombudsman is free, but can take several weeks, or even months, if the complaint is a complicated one.

● The best advice is to nip any dispute in the bud as early as possible, before more time-consuming procedures become necessary.

▶ ▶ **FIND OUT MORE**

• Contact the banking Ombudsman for issues involving administration and breaches of confidentiality, negligence and general banking matters, but not matters relating to fees. The service is independent and is free of charge, but the process is time-consuming, so avoid it if you can.
www.bfso.org.au
www.abio.org.au
www.bankombudsman.org.nz
www.banking.org.za

CAUTION!

Don't get caught out

If you receive an email message from what appears to be your bank, requesting information about your password or Internet banking details, delete it. Banks and other financial institutions never request this information via email, no matter how 'real' the message might seem.

TIMELY TIP

Go broadband

For speedy Internet banking you'll need access to a fast broadband Internet connection. Dial-up speeds are much slower, causing frustration and delay. (*See also* 'Using the Internet', on page 170.)

Manage your accounts online

The Internet is economical and flexible, and is the ultimate way to remotely manage your finances quickly and efficiently.

▶ All banks offer Internet services. Get set up for online banking so you can monitor your accounts, transfer money, check foreign exchange rates, engage in online share trading, change passwords and generally stay in touch with what's on offer at any time that suits you. Go online to find out how to get started or call your bank for more information.

▶ Some banks charge a monthly fee that includes online banking transactions, though some don't charge anything for non-business accounts, so check with your bank. On the bank's web site you can securely access accounts using your ID and a password or code. Security is vital and you must comply with the bank's rules to ensure they accept responsibility if any fraud or loss occurs.

▶ Take advantage of everyday online operations: transfer money from one account to another (yours and other people's), download statements and pay bills.

▶ If you're having trouble navigating your way around while online banking, check the FAQs and troubleshooting links.

▶ Bookmark your bank's web address so you can access Internet banking fast.

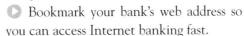
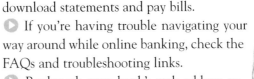

Changing banks

We're used to shopping around for clothes and cars, but not for bank accounts and other financial services. The principle is the same: choose the service, terms and conditions that best suit your needs and pocket.

▶ Before you change banks, work out what it is you're not happy about and complain, politely but firmly, and give your bank the opportunity to address your complaint. If you're still not happy, then change banks.

▶ To open an account with another bank, you'll need to provide full ID, such as passport, driver's licence, birth or marriage certificates, student card, rent notices or recent utility bills.

▶ Make a list of all your direct debits and current payments (cheques, payments using a credit card, etc.) to be deducted from the old account. Your old bank is obliged to pass on full details of your direct debits or standing orders to your new bank within a set time frame (a few days).

▶ Make sure you leave sufficient money in the old account to ensure that no payment is refused by your old bank. The time it takes for direct debits to be transferred may vary so you'll need to check this carefully.

▶ Notify all the institutions debiting money from your old account and send them full details of the new account.

▶ Have all income paid into your new account (salary, allowances, etc.) by notifying the relevant people (employers, welfare authorities, etc.). Consider topping up the old account a little to cover any outstanding direct payments, just to avoid unnecessary complications.

▶ After making sure no further transactions will be conducted on your old account, send the bank a letter via registered mail or courier (to be signed for by the bank to acknowledge receipt), confirming the account closure. Return all unused cheques, credit and debit cards cut in half.

▶ Consider the 'middle way' when it comes to bank accounts, leaving your existing accounts in place while you explore added services offered by other banks. A range of new and cost-effective services is available on the Internet, including savings accounts that can be linked to an existing account that pays higher interest and from which you can make payments electronically, or by direct debit or BPAY, etc. The new linked account may offer all the additional services you need.

TIMELY TIP

Check your accounts at any time
Use a PDA or smart mobile phone to check your account balances, or send and receive text messages or emails about your finances at any time, anywhere there's coverage. Once you're a registered user you can start saving time on your banking transactions.

Insurance and taxation

TIMELY TIP

Read your policy

The best time to read an insurance policy is when you first receive it, not when you need to make a claim. There is usually a 14-day cooling off period after signing an insurance contract, which gives you time to read the policy carefully and avoid wasting time further down the track.

Examine your options

As with most matters of commerce, the Internet has transformed the way we choose and buy insurance. Now you can shop around online.

▶ Research your insurance options online – you may save up to 10 per cent of the premium and some web sites offer direct comparisons.

▶ Find out if you're entitled to special discounts on the premiums, particularly if you have several different policies (e.g. house, car, health and life insurance) with the same provider, as many companies offer substantial loyalty discounts to multi-policy holders.

▶ Consider handing the job over to an insurance broker. They research a range of policies for you to find the most competitive premiums, which are sometimes even lower than standard rates.

▶ Once you have registered as an online client, you can manage your insurance policies yourself, researching and buying home and contents, motor, travel, health and any other insurance policies that you need. (*See also* 'Insurance brokerage', on page 189.)

The ins and outs of home insurance

Cleaning, repairing and repainting rooms damaged by accident, fire or serious storm damage won't leave you with a minute to spare. Luckily, some insurance companies offer extras that allow you to save time. Here are examples of some of those options.

● **Repairs** Instead of simply being paid money, your insurer can arrange to have the damage repaired via a network of approved companies (painting, plumbing, etc.). This saves having to find good tradesmen, which takes up added time and energy, especially when other people in your area may be looking for tradesmen, too (e.g. in the case of storm damage).

● **Security** Some insurers offer to have your house guarded until it can be made secure (after a theft, if glass has been broken or a fire, for example).

● **Temporary accommodation** If a storm or accident makes your house uninhabitable, the insurer will organise accommodation until repairs are finished.

● **A 'new-for-old' replacement** In the case of accidental damage you can be reimbursed for goods at their replacement cost, not their true value (though your premiums may be a little higher). Be aware, though, that the guarantee may only apply for a set period. Check this with your insurer.

● **Keep an eye on any claim limits** Check that your claim payout is enough to replace your goods, especially if you have recently acquired new furniture or expensive equipment.

TIMELY TIP

Older car, lower premium

If your car is old, think about reducing the level of cover, or only take out Compulsory Third Party (CTP) insurance. And be aware of the difference between 'market' and 'agreed' value. Market value is best for new cars or those with expensive accessories, whereas agreed value is better for an older car with standard equipment.

 HEALTH CARE

• **Choosing private over public.** In addition to public health care, Australians, New Zealanders and South Africans have the option of private health insurance. Visit the relevant web sites, below, for more information on health-care services in your country. www.privatehealth.gov.au www.moh.govt.nz www.southafrica.info/ess_info/ sa_glance/health/health.htm

The benefits of car insurance

▷ Subscribe to a roadside assistance scheme via your car insurer, to get you going again after a breakdown. Keep your member card on you at all times so that a quick call on your mobile phone is all that's needed.

▷ Record your insurance company's accident or customer-service helpline number in your mobile's phone book. That way you can call within minutes of an accident occurring.

▷ Make sure your membership level covers outback or country driving – if that's part of your driving pattern – to cover breakdowns in more remote locations (see 'Timely tip', on page 150).

▷ Use your insurance company to organise vehicle recovery or towing – it speeds up the process and you're less likely to be cheated by unscrupulous towing companies.

▷ Consider paying a slightly higher insurance premium for specific help, such as the loss of a windscreen, to ensure you're back on the road as quickly as possible. (*See also* 'Getting around', starting on page 150.)

Health insurance options

Many countries offer limited government-funded health services, so if you want access to full medical services and the doctor of your choice, you may choose to consider taking out private health insurance.

▷ Working out what cover is best for you and your family can be time-consuming, but there are shortcuts. Check the FAQ section of various health-fund web sites to help you work out the best option.

▷ Save time by only looking in the correct age bracket. The two most important factors in working out what level of cover you need are your age and your medical history, so don't get caught up with other details.

TIMELY TIP

Cooperative health care

Australia has reciprocal health-care agreements with a number of other countries, including New Zealand, the United Kingdom, Malta, Finland, Sweden, Norway and Italy. People visiting from these countries may be eligible for Medicare benefits while they're in Australia under these agreements. Contact any Medicare office.

Insurance brokers may find you a good value-for-money health insurance policy, but they may only represent a small range of health insurers, not all that are available.

Most private health-insurance company web sites allow you to quickly manage your own account, change your level of cover or lodge a claim online.

If you have private medical insurance and are travelling overseas, you'll need to take out a separate travel policy, although some items may already be covered. Check whether you need a new policy issued.

Insurance brokerage

Unlike an insurance agent, who works for only one company, a broker works for you in order to find the best policy in terms of cover and premiums from among all the choices on offer in the market.

Be patient when selecting a broker: finding one you can trust and who is willing to find the right policy for you at a good price is essential.

Check web sites offering comparisons between insurance companies. Many sites allow you to calculate premiums for your needs, then let an insurance broker invest the time finding you a better deal.

Take advantage of less worry and time wasted by getting your broker to manage any insurance claim in the case of an accident or a dispute.

A broker's commission is often included in the premium, so you're unlikely to pay any more than if you bought the insurance yourself.

Make the most of your insurance policies by reading them carefully. Getting a broker to buy insurance for you doesn't mean you don't have to understand the terms and conditions of the policies you've bought.

Make sure your broker understands all your cover needs. Normally, your multi-risk home insurance policy would cover you against most forms of damage, but be aware, for instance, that there is a difference between storm damage and flood damage. (Many insurance companies don't offer cover for flood damage in flood-prone areas.)

BROKERAGE

• **Discover how brokers can help** and get a quick understanding of how insurance works, by having a look at the relevant web site, below, for your country.
www.insurancecouncil.com.au
www.niba.com.au
www.ibanz.co.nz
www.insurance.za.org

Bank on insurance

Many banks have connections to one or more insurance companies, with discounts on offer to existing customers. Shop around online to check the premiums quoted by your bank are better than those you're already paying before switching insurers.

TIMELY TIP

TIMELY TIP

Note due dates

In your diary, circle the dates when your insurance policies are due for renewal, even though policies may arrive in the post. It's a good sort of insurance policy in itself!

Changing insurers

The day you make an insurance claim is the day you find out whether your insurance company is efficient at handling insurance claims or not. If you have a negative experience, think about changing insurers.

▶ Carefully weigh up the pros and cons before starting the process of ending an insurance policy, because researching a new insurer can be a time-consuming process if you're not using the services of a broker.

▶ For multi-risk home insurance or car insurance, you can terminate the policy on the renewal date, or at any other time, but it may cost you extra money. And you may need to give notice to ensure a smooth transfer to another company. Check this with your current insurer.

▶ The fastest methods are not always the best ones. Don't think that simply making a phone call or not paying a premium is sufficient to end an insurance policy before you change insurers, as it may not be the case.

▶ Send a registered letter to the head office of your insurance company. If you have an insurance broker, advise them by copying the letter.

▶ End your insurance contract in person at your insurance company's local office. They will give you written confirmation of your decision to end the policy, which you should keep on file at home.

What kind of insurance do you need?

There are two main forms of insurance: general and life. The first insures goods, property and services – houses, cars, travel and health. The second insures people – life, income, superannuation and financial security of clients.

While brokers deal with general insurance matters, for life insurance you'll need to see a qualified financial adviser, either one from a bank or some other financial institution, or one who operates independently and can advise across a range of policies offered by insurers. Using these specialist services can save you time and hassle in the long run, because of the significant investment you're making.

Take the easy way with tax returns

Whether you're preparing your own taxation return online or getting a tax agent to do it for you, get organised to avoid wasting time.

▶ Keep a separate file for all taxation documents, including receipts, any health-care claims (private and public), superannuation payments, share dividends and extra income. It'll save you hours of unnecessary hunting and gathering when the end of financial year comes around.

FIND OUT MORE

• In Australia, state-based government agencies, as well as a national Ombudsman, can help with insurance complaints.
www.insuranceOmbudsman.com.au
www.fics.asn.au
• In New Zealand, a specific office deals with insurance and savings matters. Check the web site below.
www.iombudsman.org.nz
• In South Africa, there are several industry bodies available for help, such as the Financial Services Board (FSB), which deals with complaints about financial products, including insurance. Check the web sites, below, for more information.
www.fsb.co.za
www.faisombud.co.za

TIMELY TIP

Fast tax refunds

If you can't submit your tax return online yourself, employ a tax agent to do it for you. Some tax firms specialise in obtaining fast tax refunds via an online portal to the tax office, which puts the refund money in your pocket sooner!

Insurance claim complaints

If your insurer has offered you a settlement payment for a claim that you think is insufficient, or a policy termination has not been acted upon, respond quickly to avoid unnecessary delays.

● **Re-read your policy** First make sure you really are covered for the type of insurance claim you're making. Ask your insurer to indicate the specific clause in the policy that they believe excludes them from liability, and always get it in writing.

● **Contact the customer-service department** If you are not satisfied with the insurer's response, then alert them to this fact as soon as possible so that the process can move forward to the next step.

● **Contact the industry Ombudsman** This is the next step in the process if you haven't had the desired result from contacting customer services. (*See* 'Find out more', at left.)

● **Take the matter to court** This is the absolute last resort if you have still not resolved the matter, and is to be avoided if at all possible. Proceedings are lengthy, to say the least, and can be very costly. If you do end up going down this road of action, seek legal advice as soon as possible, to expedite the process.

Use a tax agent to compile and submit your tax return. If your financial affairs are relatively simple, hiring a tax agent or accountant to do the work for you is a quick and inexpensive way to get your return in on time without the headache of compiling it yourself.

Consider submitting your return online, using e-tax. It's fast, efficient and free (the first time you lodge a return online it will take longer than subsequent times). In Australia, you can download any information you need from Centrelink, Medicare and six major financial institutions, which reduces the amount of time it takes to complete your return, not to mention a massive reduction in the volume of paperwork involved.

E-tax has the added benefit of automatically working out how tax law applies to you and what your refund or liability will be, without you having to take the time to consult a professional. You're also less likely to incur a fine or have to amend your return after submitting it.

 **CAUTION!**

Avoid late penalties
Although the Internet gives you the flexibility to prepare and file your tax return at any time, don't leave it until the last minute. You won't avoid a late fee if you submit after the due date, so make a note of it in your diary.

FILE YOUR TAX RETURN ONLINE

• Help is available if you lodge your tax details and returns online. The main advantage is that once the system is set up it can save you a great deal of preparation time. Check the web sites below to find procedures, calculators, forms and guides, and FAQs, etc., to help get you started.
www.ato.gov.au
www.ird.govt.nz/online-services
www.sars.gov.za

Buying and paying

Buying from catalogues and online

Some people love shopping, but for others it's a chore. If you're in the latter group, you'll be happy to find out how you can save time on most of your essential shopping.

▶ Shop online or using a mail-order catalogue. It's convenient and saves wasting time getting to a shop, finding a parking space and being jostled in queues. All together, that adds up to much less stress and more time to spend doing something enjoyable. And the good news is that you can buy anything from fruit and vegetables to clothes and fishing gear, almost anywhere in the world.

▶ Choose products carefully, as returning goods via the postal system isn't a timesaving exercise – you may end up getting stuck in those queues you so cleverly avoided in the first place! Study the description of the product on offer and its photo very closely, to avoid unpleasant surprises when the goods are delivered.

▶ If you're buying clothing from an overseas mail-order company, take the time to look at comparable clothing size charts on the web site (most

companies provide them), to avoid getting confused with the differences between sizing systems. The same goes for shoe sizes.

▶ Ordering from mail-order catalogues means that once you receive the package you usually have a few days in which to return the goods (often at your cost, but check the return conditions before you buy), without having to provide any reason.

▶ Return any deliveries – at the sender's expense – if they don't match your order. Most mail-order companies have a standard form that you fill in and return with the products.

Make your order clear and precise

▶ Take care when completing an order form for any goods you're intending to buy, whether online or in person, and keep a copy in your home-office files. If any disputes arise, you can quickly refer to the document to remind yourself of the terms and conditions of purchase.

▶ Ask that the full details of the company (name, address, etc.) appear on the order form, and note down the name of the salesperson you're dealing with so that you don't waste time having to explain your customer history to more than one salesperson in the event of a dispute.

▶ Ensure the description of the product is clear, along with its price.

▶ Insist on a precise delivery date (a specific day, or within certain time limits) to avoid the unnecessary frustration and time wasted involved in reorganising a new delivery time.

TIMELY TIP

Secure payment online

Secure web sites – including banks – usually display a locked padlock or unbroken key symbol indicating the site you are on is securely encrypted.

> CAUTION!

Unsolicited delivery

If you receive a package without having ordered or signed anything, there is no need to waste your time sending it back. It's considered an unsolicited delivery so you don't have to accept it.

Using secure web sites

Internet fraud and credit-card scams are definitely a risk, but you can take a number of steps to ensure your online transactions are secure.

● Make sure your web browser uses 128-bit encryption. This is specified by banks for use with credit cards and online account transactions, as it delivers a high level of security.

● Set your web browser's security preferences to alert you when it encounters a non-secure web site.

● If you're in doubt about a web site's policy on sharing data with other companies, check their privacy policy in the relevant section of the site before you buy anything.

● Credit cards are the safest way to pay for online purchases because credit-card companies usually offer customers protection against fraud.

● One way of minimising fraud is to use only one credit (or debit) card for online transactions, and to check your statements regularly – online if possible – so that you're quickly aware of all transactions. Or transfer money to a credit card for a specific purchase.

Tips for online buyers

Sorting out problems of non-delivery or unacceptable quality from Internet purchases can be very time-consuming and you may lose money into the bargain, so follow these tips to cover yourself.

▶ If you find something you like on a site such as eBay, do some research on the seller; if the feedback is positive, the seller is probably a safe bet. But if there is negative feedback, especially if it's on a small number of transactions, then be cautious about buying from them.

▶ Make sure you know exactly what you're buying: is everything you want included in the picture displayed on the web site? If not, does the seller refer to differences in their correspondence with you?

▶ Know the seller's refund policy in advance, in case the goods that arrive don't match your expectations.

▶ Find out the location of the seller. Many overseas sellers are reliable, but some are not. Sorting out problems overseas is more complicated and time-consuming than doing so within your own country.

How to handle sales

There's plenty of excitement to be had with an in-store sale, so hone your sale skills and do a bit of quick preparation to make the most of your time and effort.

▶ Make a note of the things you like the week before the sales begin. You can try clothes on calmly and ask questions about sizes and stock, etc., so that at the start of the sale you know exactly what you're going to buy without wasting time in fitting-room queues.

▶ Go to the first day or two of the sale, if you can, because the best bargains are often snapped up in the first few days.

▶ Shop with a friend. Ask your friend for advice – to avoid costly impulse buys – and take turns standing in queues, to save wasting time and to make use of the extra pair of hands. It'll speed the process up and more than likely make it more fun, too.

▶ Buy Christmas and birthday presents during sale time. Not only will you save time spent in long queues during the busy Christmas shopping period, you'll also save money into the bargain.

▶ Towards the end of a sale period, some shops further cut the price on goods that haven't already sold. That way you avoid the frantic atmosphere of sales and still bag a bargain!

TIMELY TIP

Save time at sale time

When you're shopping during sales, wear clothing that comes on and off quickly so that you can try on clothes fast, and wear slip-on shoes. A simple close-fitting top and stretch pants are even better, because you might get away with slipping clothing on top without getting changed at all!

TIMELY TIP

Go for the best option

If you have a low or fluctuating income that makes direct debit difficult, your best bet might be phone banking (in Australia, BPAY is a popular method) or Internet banking using manual transfers and payments, so that you can pay bills when it suits you or when you have the money.

Use direct debit to pay bills

Direct debits save time and hassle – utilities won't be cut off because you forgot to pay a bill. Spending a day on the phone or going to an office to have the telephone reconnected is a huge waste of time.

▶ Organise direct debits with individual companies – from your nominated bank account or credit card – so you don't have to think about factoring in the time to pay bills. Just make sure you always have enough money in the nominated account to avoid penalty payments.

▶ Set up a system of direct debit via Internet banking. All you have to do is organise a regular transfer of funds from your nominated account to that of the person or company you're paying. You'll have an automatic record of debits made that you can print out, if necessary.
(*See also* 'Pay on time', on page 178.)

Anticipate unpaid bills

Disputes with suppliers cost time and money, so if you're likely to have trouble paying a bill, take action early on.

▶ Don't leave a bill unpaid without giving your supplier an explanation. Supply reasons before the due date, and support your reasons with evidence. You'll be surprised how easily – and quickly – most matters can be resolved.

▶ Negotiate payment instalments with a calendar in front of you, to avoid any errors.

▶ Be honest and realistic when it comes to money owed. Don't agree to a system of repayment if you're not sure you can stick to it. Be upfront about what you can do, not what you'd like to be able to do. Otherwise, you'll only end up spending more time in negotiations.

▶ If things are not moving forward with the contact person you usually speak to, contact the customer-service department directly or a manager, so that the problem can be solved in the shortest time possible.

Seek help

If you feel helpless in your dealings with a supplier, ask for support from a consumer association or citizen's legal-aid bureau. For a small fee (or even no fee at all), they may be able to help you write letters and will intervene directly with a service provider, if necessary.

TIMELY TIP

Mediation helps avoid disputes
Some suppliers use mediators to resolve potential payment default problems. Contact a mediator, by letter, after you have exhausted all internal avenues and before you consider taking legal action, which is time-consuming and expensive.

Plan your work day

TIMELY TIP

Quick breakfast

Prepare your breakfast the night before work – set the table, fill the kettle or prepare the coffee. When you get up, just pressing a button will get you started.

Make use of transit time

▶ Make use of your bus or train journey to read through work files or financial or general articles in a newspaper or magazine. In short, do anything while you're in transit that is going to be useful in your working life by keeping you in touch.

▶ Think things through. If you walk or drive to work, go over your plan for the day in your head one last time, so that you're ready to get going as soon as you arrive at work.

Make your time more productive

Multi-tasking is handy for simple or uncomplicated tasks, but time management is the key concept when it comes to increasing productivity. You'll be amazed at how much time you can save.

▶ When you arrive at the office, turn on your computer before you take off your jacket or coat. And while you're entering your password or other security code, listen to the messages on your voicemail.

▶ When it comes to work, focus on doing one thing at a time and doing it well, to avoid a fractured thinking pattern, which is neither time-efficient nor productive. Multi-tasking is only for robot-type tasks.

▶ Check your email at set times. Constantly checking incoming email interrupts your work flow, resulting in a productivity slump. Close your email application and schedule times for opening it to check messages. Open, file or delete and print messages at those set times. (*See also* 'Effective management of email', on page 199.)

TIMELY TIP

Get going earlier

Most people start work on the hour, but if possible start at least half an hour earlier. The traffic will be smoother and public transport not as crowded, saving you both time and potential anxiety.

TIMELY TIP

Manage the pm slump

Not everyone can take a 'power nap' in the afternoon, but it is possible to take a quick break to walk around the block or eat a high-energy snack. Take a short break and revive rather than waste time struggling to stay awake.

▶ Use technology to help manage tasks on your to-do list, but don't get bogged down by it. Microsoft Outlook's Task Tracker desktop software allows you to keep track of tasks within a project and the people you've delegated tasks to, so that you can keep track of team projects or juggle a number of tasks within one project.

▶ Don't plan to do more than is possible in a single day. Make your timetable work efficiently by noting the time meetings start and end, then try to stick to those times as much as possible.

▶ Allow for unexpected tasks to crop up in your timetable, just as you would allow for variation in a budget.

Use biorhythms to maximise efficiency

If you want to get through as much work as possible in a day, learn to make use of your biological rhythms, which determine periods of high and low activity at different times of the day.

▶ Your most productive work output occurs in the morning, so try to tackle the most important or urgent tasks then. They'll take significantly less time to complete than at other times of the day.

▶ In the early afternoon you'll slow down while digesting lunch, and drinking coffee won't wake you up (it may even prolong sluggishness). Don't struggle to keep working, spending more time on a task than is necessary – use the time to relax, talk with colleagues or do routine work.

▶ In the middle or end of the afternoon you'll find you're able to work at medium or high efficiency, which is the time to start doing important work again.

Take a quick break

▶ Working for too long or too intensively can result in a loss of concentration, which increases the risk of making mistakes without realising it. The best and fastest solution is to take a brief break from your desk, or take a short walk to relax your muscles and get your blood circulating again.

▶ Far from being a waste of time, a break allows you to recharge your batteries. The best moment to relax is after an hour of particularly intense work. Stick to a 10-minute break, as beyond this the restorative effect will be lost.

Prioritise daily tasks

Planning your day carefully can save a lot of time. The best way to do this is to draw up a list of things you must do each day.

● Classify tasks according to two criteria: urgency and importance.

● In order to distinguish clearly what is urgent from what is important, always ask yourself, What will happen if I don't work on this file in the next few minutes or hours? What will happen if I don't take care of this myself? The first question helps you discover what is urgent, and the second what is important.

● Wherever and whenever possible, delegate tasks to other people.

Achieve more flying solo

In an office, no matter how much you want to work undisturbed, people will always interrupt you. To work effectively, analyse the main factors involved in these interruptions and solve them as quickly as you can.

▶ The problem: the telephone rings constantly and conversations go on and on without leading anywhere. The answer: let the calls go to a message bank whenever you can and send a quick email wherever possible, instead of chatting things through.

▶ The problem: your colleagues constantly come into your office to ask you questions or chat. The answer: let them know – in as diplomatic a way as possible to ensure you don't offend them – that you don't want to be interrupted… before your break!

Goodbye meetings, hello time saved

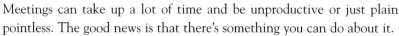

Meetings can take up a lot of time and be unproductive or just plain pointless. The good news is that there's something you can do about it.

▶ When you're called to a meeting, first make sure the meeting really is one that concerns you. If it is, then prepare thoroughly to avoid wasting time and stay focused on the reason for the meeting.

▶ If you're guilty of organising meetings for every little thing, take a different tack and try to find other ways to work that will waste less time: use memos, emails or brief small-group meetings, etc.

▶ If a meeting seems unavoidable, make sure its purpose is clear by drawing up an agenda (a task that can be delegated), without wasting time writing down a long list of points to cover. Also, give the meeting a finite length – and then stick to it.

A digital assistant

You can replace a handwritten to-do list using a Personal Digital Assistant (PDA), otherwise known as a Palm Pilot or BlackBerry (these are just two brand names among many).

These pocket computers offer an ever-expanding range of services from the basics of address book, diary, to-do lists and calendar to Internet access, emails and GPS navigation. In effect, they become a mobile office, and accessing services while on the move can save you a lot of valuable time.

Organise and file

Your work space should reflect your state of mind, with everything tidy and neatly filed away. So put an end to allowing piles of paper to accumulate in your office.

▶ Do a quick tidy-up of your office every day so you don't waste time frantically looking for the super-urgent document your head of department is asking for.

▶ Sort your paper mail into two separate piles: 'to do' and 'to read'. Deal with the things you need to do first.

Effective management of email

Email is a wonderful invention but it can also be a massive time waster. Here are a few tips and tricks to prevent you becoming overwhelmed.

▶ Set aside time to read your incoming emails at certain times of the day.

▶ To avoid being interrupted by incoming emails, deactivate the function telling you an email has arrived (usually a sound alert), or turn the volume right down so that the chime or sound can't be heard.

▶ Make the most of your anti-spam settings (or get your Information Technology [IT] team to set them up for you).

▶ Make sure your computer software is up to date, including anti-virus filters. If you're not sure how to load up or activate anti-virus filters, find out by going online, or seek professional support.

▶ Make sure your Internet Service Provider (ISP) is dealing with as much spam as possible and check the anti-spam settings on your computer.

▶ Sort incoming emails quickly, deleting as you go (always delete emails with attachments from unknown senders).

▶ Limit the use of your primary email address to avoid being flooded with spam (and jokes). Set up two addresses: one for work-related email and the other for staying in touch with friends.

▶ Unsubscribe from e-newsletters you don't have time to read.

▶ Downloading emails on a mobile phone or PDA can take a long time, but some smart phones now compress emails before they hit your inbox. This saves time, especially if pictures or documents are attached.

▶ If you need a quick reminder to do something when you get home, send yourself an email from work.

(*See also* 'Computer basics', starting on page 165.)

Anticipate tomorrow's tasks

Preparing for the next day the evening before will save you both time and worry. All it takes is a bit of forward thinking.

▶ Before leaving your office, make a list of things you couldn't finish and had to defer. Draw up a quick list of things to do tomorrow.

▶ As soon as you get home, check the battery on your mobile phone, and if it's low simply plug it into the charger.

▶ Choose clothes for the next day and iron anything that needs ironing. Use a valet chair to store these clothes, to save you hanging them up in your wardrobe or folding them into a chest of drawers.

▶ Quickly flip through and sort out which files you need to take with you to the office in the morning, and pack them into your work bag.

▶ Keep a separate bag for work so that everything you need to take with you is always ready to go. And stash your PDA and mobile phone in it so you don't waste time hunting for them in the morning.

Master time management

Enough is enough in a day

If you're having trouble getting everything done in a day, it's time to rethink your priorities.

▶ Start by getting rid of a 'good pupil' complex, always wanting to do more in the hope of being given a gold star (or a compliment). This is a real trap in the workplace, because the more you do, the more you will be asked to do. And the time you do have spare will be spent worrying about what you haven't achieved.

▶ Every day, set yourself time limits and stick to them. Put an alarm clock on your desk or set an alarm on your computer or mobile phone so that it rings when you absolutely have to leave work. If you really can't discipline yourself, ask your spouse or a friend to come and pick you up.

⟩ CAUTION!

Stick to your own job

Make a point of concentrating on your own work. The more you take on other people's work tasks, the more thinly you will spread yourself and the more time you'll lose (or spend working longer hours than you need to).

Strike a balance

Getting the balance between work and home right is key to saving time.
▶ The office is a space totally dedicated to work so the reverse should also be true; dedicate home life to your family and leisure activities.
▶ Avoid dealing with private matters in the office, or regularly taking work home: you'll only lose out in both areas, and it will cost you valuable time. The solution is to draw up limits and stick to them.

Learn to say 'no'

It's better to limit the amount of work you do rather than doing too much and doing it badly. But if you don't want to have to say 'no' too often, then give yourself time to negotiate.

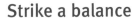

▶ When you're asked to do something, take a few seconds to think so that you can decide if you are in a position to handle the work yourself, accept the work and delegate it to one of your colleagues, or simply say 'no'.
▶ As soon as you have agreed to do a task, advise your boss and clients of the project schedule. And give them regular progress reports. If something unexpected happens, you'll be in a better position to re-negotiate your deadline.

Learn to delegate effectively

There's no doubt that delegating can be a great time saver. The trick is to know who to delegate specific tasks to and how to follow up to make sure you're kept in the work loop to check that tasks are done properly.
▶ Before you start delegating, draw up a to-do list, numbering the day's work tasks according to their importance and urgency. Then decide which person is most capable of doing each individual task.
▶ Leave only the essential tasks for yourself, and keep in touch with colleagues throughout the day to make sure tasks assigned to them are completed properly and within the correct time frame.
▶ If you're going to be held up in meetings all day, choose the person who is best qualified to take over work tasks in your absence.
▶ Make sure each person taking on a task understands the importance of what they're doing, and, if appropriate, offer advice on how they might go about doing it, to avoid time-consuming misunderstandings.
▶ Always make yourself available for help in the event of a problem arising – you'll save time by averting a disaster.

Find a job quickly

Get to know yourself

If you've recently resigned or lost your job, you'll need to be organised and methodical in order to give yourself the best chance of finding a new job as quickly as possible.

▶ Do you know which of your skills and qualifications are the most useful? Do you know the sort of work you're best suited to? Complete a few quick self-assessment tests on the Internet if that's more likely to help you answer these questions. Self-assessment is a good place to start if you're trying to decide what job might be right for you.

▶ Get assessed by a professional careers adviser: it will be more detailed than a brief self-assessment and will help you work out your aspirations, select the kind of employment that you're best suited to and, if necessary, they can make suggestions for a suitable training program.

TIMELY TIP

Stay focused

Make a quick list to help you keep abreast of your job-search efforts. It'll save time by helping you to organise your priorities, follow up on job leads and interviews and, most importantly, helps to keep you focused on your ultimate goal – finding the right job.

Are you right for the job?

Before starting your search for a job, you first need to decide if your skill levels match your aspirations. Making sure they do will prevent you wasting time chasing jobs you're not qualified to do.

Your profile
- What skills can you offer a company?
- What do you expect from an employer?
- What motivates you?
- What are your weaknesses?

The job profile
- What kind of work do you want?
- Is it in a growth sector?
- What is most important to you: the salary, job satisfaction or the working conditions?
- Think about your ideal job. What sort of company would you like to work for, a multi-national company, or a small- or medium-sized business?
- Would you be prepared to move overseas?

CV tricks that work

▶ Present your Curriculum Vitae (CV, or résumé) in a clear, concise way so that anyone reading it can see career information at a glance, while also learning something more about you.

▶ Prepare two or three customised CVs, each with slightly different information, depending on the type of position you're applying for and the company's profile, so that each one is appropriate for the job.

▶ Go online to browse web sites devoted to helping you prepare your CV or simply to update it at a job site (*see* 'Find out more', at left).

▶ Ask close friends to proofread your CV. A fresh eye and varied work experience often provides constructive criticism.

▶ Make sure everything in your CV is relevant to the job you're applying for; if not, cut it out. It'll save time for those reading it and is much more likely to land you a job faster.

Keep up to speed

Make sure your knowledge is up to date in a highly challenging workforce by finding out what's going on in your industry.

▶ Keep on top of trends and salaries in your industry, especially areas of new jobs' growth. Do this by searching the Internet and reading industry newsletters.

▶ Most recruitment agencies and companies have web sites with news and information, so do a bit of research and bookmark relevant sites.

▶ Subscribe to industry newsletters, along with individual companies and professional associations. Many offer free online subscriptions, but set up a separate email address so they don't flood your normal inbox. That way you can set aside time to read them when it suits you.

▶ Search through various relevant magazines and newspapers. You can quickly find information about changes in the labour market, the latest innovations and new opportunities.

CAUTION!

Don't wait
If you want to find a job quickly, take the initiative. Waiting for an employer to phone or simply hoping you'll stumble across a great job advertisement won't get you far. Make sure everyone knows you're looking for work.

 FIND OUT MORE

• Brush up your CV before looking for a job, and choose a layout that best suits your qualifications and experience. Follow the links on the web sites, below, to help you either compile a CV or update your CV on a job-offer web site.
www.mycareer.com.au
www.careers.govt.nz
www.resume.co.nz
www.bestjobs.co.za

TIMELY TIP

Training is the key
Find out if there are any courses that will help you find a job faster. Many short courses are available covering job application, re-training and skill development. Updating your skills can save valuable time in finding a job.

▶▶ **TRAINING TOOLS**

• **Look for work-related courses,** either government or private, that are available to you, and check if you're eligible for financial support while taking the course. Check the web sites below as a starting point.
www.centrelink.gov.au
www.seek.com.au
www.careers.govt.nz
www.worksite.govt.nz
www.info.gov.za/aboutsa/
  education

Try everything

Use every means available to move the job-research process along.

▶ Make everyone you know aware that you're looking for a job, as this can sometimes turn up unexpected opportunities.

▶ Register with a nationwide recruitment agency, but find out about their areas of expertise before calling them. Do they recruit in your field?

▶ If you register for unemployment benefits (assuming you can), don't wait 6 months before contacting an employment agency, because you'll lose more time in the job-finding process.

▶ Company CV files and databases will inevitably contain hundreds of names. So in order to get people's attention, put some personal details into your covering letter and regularly send in an updated CV. Email makes this a quick-and-easy process.

▶ Establish an agency contact and make sure they're aware of your talents and the sort of job you want. It might speed the process up a bit.

The interview – eight top tips

Being fully prepared means you'll avoid the interviewee's worst enemy – anxiety. Instead of launching into an improvised performance, it's always better to be prepared. You'll appear to be confident, calm and organised, and above all, you won't waste time and energy ruining good opportunities that may not come around a second time.

● **Personal grooming** Making a good impression is important, and looking your best will give you self-assurance.

● **Dress appropriately** Take care with your appearance to give the right impression and to give yourself a psychological boost.

● **Find out about the company** Find out as much as possible about the company before an interview – its organisation, products and financial position. A lot of this information may be found online.

● **Prepare a 5-minute summary of your work history** This trick ensures you won't have to search for words in front of the interviewers. To keep their interest, include some anecdotes, memories and good examples of your achievements.

● **Prepare brief answers to typical questions** Why have you chosen our company? What can you offer us? What salary are you hoping for? Don't be caught unprepared.

● **Train yourself** Simply by role-playing with your spouse or a close friend you can train yourself to perform well in an interview situation.

● **Remember the essentials** Take an up-to-date copy of your CV, your application letter and copies of your qualifications (and the advertisement, if there was one).

● **Arrive on time** Punctuality is essential!

Speed up your application online

By using the Internet you can contact almost anyone in a matter of minutes, without leaving your home. Recruitment companies and individual firms list job vacancies on their web sites and there are several ways to apply for a job.

● **Online** Complete an online questionnaire (recent jobs, skills, academic degrees). Expect to spend about 20 to 30 minutes per application. Keep your details on file in such a way that you can cut and paste documents to fill in the forms quickly.

● **By email** To email a job application, send a 'letter' of application with a copy of your CV as an attachment (tailored to the job). You may need to save it in two or more different formats (e.g. Word or Rich Text Format) so anyone can easily open it. Include your application letter in the body of the email so the employer doesn't have to open an attachment to 'meet' you.

● **Job-offer sites** By subscribing to an email job vacancy service you can be alerted whenever a suitable job vacancy arises that fits your profile. Often you can apply online just by forwarding your CV (remember to keep it up to date).

Learning to network

Personal contacts are an important source of information as well as a possible source of jobs. There are many ways to keep in contact with a wide range of people from various work industries, through social clubs, relatives, former colleagues or local church and community groups.

▶ It can be useful to keep in touch with old school friends by updating your details on appropriate web sites or recruitment sites. It's a fast way of being noticed by recruitment agencies and former classmates who may have a job for you.

▶ Talk to former work colleagues to find out what opportunities they are aware of.

▶ Keep in touch with anyone who may have useful information. It's easier than ever to keep in touch via telephone, email or SMS. Make sure people think of you when a suitable job arises.

▶ Attending work-related events as often as you can is more likely to keep your contacts up to date and puts your face in front of people who might have the right job for you.

TIMELY TIP

Visit trade shows

Visit recruitment or trade shows and take copies of your CV. Have business cards printed, as it's a quick way of leaving your details at stands. Personal contact is a major factor in landing a job, so collect the cards of anyone who could be helpful, then follow up with a quick phone call or email.

▶ Sporting events can be a great place to meet people who know people… who may know of a job.

▶ Company sports days are often easygoing events and offer a chance to extend your range of contacts.

▶ Say yes. If people suggest you call them about work, then make a point of doing it (unless you think it could lead to problems), as people often respond positively to someone who follows up a contact. There's always a chance it could work to your advantage.

 SPEEDY JOB PLACEMENT

• **Recruitment web sites** can quickly point you in the right direction for finding out what jobs are on offer online – wherever you live. Check the appropriate web sites, below, to find out more.

www.seek.com.au
www.mycareer.com.au
www.search4jobs.co.nz
www.bestjobs.co.za
www.careerjunction.co.za

Preparing for retirement

Superannuation – the retirees' Holy Grail

Preparing for retirement is neither quick nor easy, but there are some basic timesaving shortcuts that can help make the process simpler.

▶ Take full advantage of the magic of compound interest over many years with regular savings, in the form of superannuation contributions. This will significantly reduce the number of years you need to build up an adequate retirement fund.

▶ There have been big changes to superannuation legislation in many countries over recent years as populations age, so it's vital to know how those changes may affect you. Go online and check government web sites to find out your position in relation to superannuation, or contact your accountant and ask them to summarise that information for you.

▶ Keep all employer-funded superannuation contributions in the same fund rather than a number of separate accounts to save both time (the funds will accumulate more quickly) and money (reduced fees).

▶ Register to check what's happening to your superannuation whenever it suits you. Superannuation funds manage large amounts of your money, and online services give you the flexibility of keeping an eye on things without spending time getting in touch with your fund manager.

▶ Go online to change the mix of your superannuation fund investments, keep track of fees and update your personal details. This way you'll be able to track the progress of your nest egg without investing a lot of time in the process.

Be realistic about government benefits

▶ Don't assume you'll automatically receive a state or government pension on retirement. You need to apply for one, and there are strict rules on who qualifies for either a full or a part-pension. Check with the appropriate state or government authority for more information.

▶ Save time by asking for help. The rules on pension eligibility are complex and you may need help from the appropriate government department, to check that your eligibility has been accurately assessed.

▶ Take care when dealing with government departments; it can be a very difficult and time-consuming process to rectify errors. To avoid errors arising, ensure the information and paperwork you supply is organised and complete before you hand it over for assessment.

Getting retirement 'red tape' in order

Ironically, retiring doesn't necessarily mean you can automatically take it easy. A lot of pre-planning is required to avoid wasting time on unnecessary details that demand your personal attention.

▶ Don't put off your preparation for retirement. You'll save time by putting together your plans as soon as possible, and by doing things in advance gradually, so that everything proceeds quickly and smoothly when the time comes.

▶ To avoid paperwork dragging on, or a delay in working out your retirement date, or errors in the amount of money owed to you, be well prepared.

▶ Put together your retirement documents by collating all the papers relating to your working life. The easiest way to do this is to keep a separate home-office file and make sure the file is organised logically, with as many sub-dividers as are necessary.

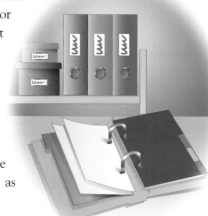

TIMELY TIP

Lost documents

If you have lost some tax statements or group certificates (issued by a company that is still in operation), ask the personnel department of your former employer to provide you with copies of the certificates, listing the amount of tax-paid contributions.

● Make sure your home-office retirement file also includes a complete record of payslips and tax details, along with documents concerning non-working periods, such as sickness, maternity leave, worker's compensation, unemployment or military service.

● If you find that important documents go missing, organise for duplicates to be made as soon as possible. Save time by applying online for government records to be sent to you, if that's possible.

File retirement documents efficiently

Use several folders to put your retirement papers in order and you'll be able to retrieve files in a flash.

● Use a different file for each type of document: one for pay and taxation, another for social security payments, etc. In each file, organise your documents in chronological order: you'll reap the rewards in time saved, especially if your paperwork is more complicated than the average (if you've changed jobs, companies or countries, and if you have had periods of illness or unemployment, or compensation payouts).

● Use coloured dividers (available from newsagents and office suppliers) as organisers within the retirement file itself, to make the divisions even clearer. For example, in your salaries' folder, separate payslips and taxation details from different employers, so that you can find any document quickly, without having to search through irrelevant files.

● If you received social security payments at some stage, separate the periods of unemployment within the file in the same way.

(*See also* 'Papers, bills and documents', starting on page 176.)

Access career records quickly

Keeping a complete record of your employment history and tax payments may save time when it comes to proving your eligibility for an age-related pension or superannuation benefit.

● To save time and storage space, keep this information in the form of electronic files that are stored and accessed on your computer, then simply email necessary forms to the relevant person. Most records are now kept this way and are faster to check than paper files. Remember to keep a backup file of these records in a secure place (on a CD or DVD).

● Most former employers, along with the tax authorities, will keep electronic versions of the files relating to your employment, and once you have established your identity they'll usually allow you to access copies of relevant files, should you need them.

Coping with bereavement

Help each other to cope better

No one is ever fully prepared for the death of a spouse or another close family member or friend. Apart from the grief and confusion of mourning, you also have to deal with making arrangements that are time-consuming and can't be put off until later. Here are some tips that may help.

▶ Don't hesitate to ask for help from those around you, as most of the arrangements can be handled just as effectively by other people. One of the most obvious ways that others can help is to contact a list of people to inform them of the death.

▶ If the deceased did not make prior contact with a funeral home, ask a close friend or distant family member to shop around and find one for you, so that you don't have to deal with unnecessary details when you're at your most vulnerable and needing time to grieve.

▶ If you feel you must make the arrangements yourself, be sure to have someone with you: the process will be faster and less painful.

▶ After the funeral, family and friends often meet together for tea and light snacks, or a wake. Ask someone close to you to organise the venue and refreshments so that you don't spend time planning it when you need the time to reflect on your loss.

TIMELY TIP

Send no flowers

Many families who have recently suffered the loss of a loved one request that friends and relatives donate money to a specific charity rather than buy flowers. Most major charities accept donations online, or you can simply phone through your credit card details.

▶▶ ▶ **HELP WITH BEREAVEMENT**

• **Help is available if you've recently been bereaved,** or if you're having difficulty living independently. In Australia, Centrelink provides access to social workers who are able to assist in this way, and similar services are available in New Zealand and South Africa. Help can also be obtained from most local councils, churches and private voluntary welfare groups. Check the appropriate web site for your country, below, for more information.

www.centrelink.gov.au

www.newzealand.govt.nz/services

www.famsa.org.za

Delegate to the funeral director

Wherever possible, and depending on how much it will cost, allow the funeral director to take over organising the necessary details. It saves time and added anxiety during an already difficult period.

▶ Take full advantage of the services offered by funeral directors. They are well equipped to provide you with help and advice at various stages after a death and with the funeral proceedings, such as applying for death certificates, booking a cremation or burials, etc.

▶ Most funeral directors offer to complete some arrangements on your behalf, but before you sign anything try to compare different services and ask for quotations (ask a friend or another family member to do this).

▶ Ask friends who have prior experience with funeral homes for advice before deciding which company to use. Some funeral homes are better than others when it comes to dealing with bereaved families and understanding their individual needs and budgets.

Plan your own funeral

▶ Consider organising your own funeral. By arranging and paying for your own funeral in advance (or simply by planning it), you can save those around you added emotional strain and time spent on formalities.

▶ Reputable funeral homes have all the information and advice you could possibly need to plan your own funeral, so shop around and find one that suits your needs, then take advantage of their specialist knowledge.

▶ Find out if you can pay off your own funeral expenses on a plan system. Check with the funeral home you're dealing with.

▶ Make the most basic decisions first: do you have strong ideas about cremation or burial? If you do, prearrange one or the other with the funeral home you've chosen.

▶ There are specific details, apart from those that concern the funeral home, that you may want to consider and organise in advance. Think about whether you'd like to have a religious service, or if you have specific music you'd like to have played at your funeral, then note it down.

▶ Lastly, make sure your next of kin know that your funeral has been prearranged, and which funeral home they should contact when the time comes. Also keep a record of these details attached to your last will and testament, either with your family lawyer or filed in an obvious place.

▶▶ FIND OUT MORE

• In Australia, the Centrelink web site has a helpful section on what to do when someone you know dies. If you are in New Zealand or South Africa, check the appropriate web site, below, for more information.
www.centrelink.gov.au
www.govt.nz/services
www.gov.za

FIND OUT MORE

• Whether you're in Australia, New Zealand or South Africa, if you're over 18 years of age you can register online to become an organ donor. It's a quick-and-simple process and will be followed up by the relevant authority. (Medicare runs Australia's only organ donor register.) Visit the relevant web site, below, to find out more.

www.medicareaustralia.gov.au
www.donor.co.nz
www.odf.org.za

Donating body organs

Time is of the essence when it comes to organ donation: when you no longer need your organs, they could signal life or death for someone who does need them.

▶ Consider becoming an organ donor (either all or some of your body organs) by registering with the appropriate authority (*see* 'Find out more', at left). They will then give you a donor's card to carry in your wallet at all times. And make sure you advise close family and friends of your decision to donate.

▶ Be aware that the removal of organs after death is authorised for therapeutic or scientific reasons, even though the law may forbid doctors from asking family members about organ donation.

◖**CAUTION!**

Donor organs

If one of your family members has made it known that they wish to donate specific body organs, the hospital authorities must be notified very quickly so they can contact the appropriate people, as the body must be transported within 24 hours.

What to do after someone dies

If someone in your family dies at home, it may be possible to get help from a public hospital, other medical authorities or welfare workers to carry out the necessary procedures at the time of death. Here is a general guide for the procedures to carry out in the hours and months after someone dies. (*See also* 'Find out more', on the opposite page.)

Within 24 hours
● Have the deceased officially declared dead (a death certificate must be signed by a doctor) and lodge the certificate with the appropriate state, territory or government authority in your area
● Keep the body at home or have it transferred to a funeral home

Within 48 hours
● Notify the deceased's employer, if applicable
● Notify relatives and close friends of the death
● Contact health insurers and any other insurance companies

Within a week
● Contact relevant local health authorities
● Notify the banks that hold the deceased's accounts

Within 3 months
● Notify the owner of the deceased's accommodation, or their landlord, body corporate and/or other tenants
● Notify gas, electricity, water and telephone companies

Within 6 months
● Notify the taxation department, giving the deceased's tax file number or similar identification whenever possible
● Transfer any joint bank accounts into a personal account
● Change all car registration and insurance documents

Aged-care options

TIMELY TIP

Help is out there

Finding out about aged-care services has never been quicker or easier if you have access to the Internet, but you can also find out about many services simply by looking in the Yellow Pages phone directory, or going to your nearest public library. All these sources provide information on special services available to seniors.

 FIND OUT MORE

• A growing number of web sites provide links to a range of worthwhile educational and other activities for older people. Have a look at the appropriate web sites, below, for more information.
www.dva.gov.au
www.health.gov.au
www.sydneyu3a.org
www.familyservices.govt.nz
www.osc.govt.nz
www.age-in-action.co.za

Living independently at home

Losing your autonomy with age does happen, but it doesn't always mean having to go into a retirement home. If you want to stay in your own home, there are some easy solutions to be found. Save time and examine your options by following these guidelines.

▶ Make changes to your house or apartment – add hand rails and make bathroom modifications – or arrange for services such as Meals on Wheels, help with housework and home nursing, to ensure the tasks of daily living are easy and not time-consuming. (*See also* 'Home care and home help', on page 215.)

▶ Allow for the fact that many of the costs for these services must be borne by you, even if you qualify for some government benefits or allowances. However, if your level of dependence is relatively low, staying in your home and receiving some form of home help will always be less expensive than moving into an aged-care facility.

▶ Stay as well as you can. Have your eyes and feet checked regularly, to avoid unnecessary falls that may result in a lengthy recovery period or the need to go into low-level care. Also, stay active by walking every day, even if it's for a short time. And establish a routine for taking your regular medication, so that you don't forget and suffer complications.

▶ Don't engage in risky behaviour, such as climbing up on chairs to access something in a high cupboard or attempting to clean out the gutters on your house – you won't save time, rather you'll increase the risk of falling. Ask someone to organise your cupboards so that everything is within easy reach and pay someone to clean out the guttering.

In good company

Loneliness doesn't have to be an inevitable part of growing older.

▶ Join a club or association in your local area. A wide range of groups concerned with the wellbeing of older people provide support in many communities. Contact your local council or community centre for more information. Local libraries and librarians can be a great source of information, too. (*See* 'Find out more', at left.)

Meet up with like-minded people and share your experiences. Many groups, including pensioners' clubs, organise activities, often with an emphasis on fitness – exercise classes, dancing or sports such as lawn bowling.

Meet new friends online. Many retirement-age people are using the Internet with enthusiasm to link up with other people all around the world, either to pursue their common interests or simply to stay in touch.

Education is also a positive post-retirement focus, with specific groups arranging excursions, speakers and access to a wide range of programs through bodies such as the University of the Third Age (in Australia) and Probus. Save time by searching online.

Many government, church and voluntary bodies are keen to promote self-reliance, part-time work and community engagement for seniors. Check with these sorts of organisations in your area to see if they have something to offer you.

Consider buying a low-maintenance pet. It's been established that people living alone are more likely to be healthy, happy and remain independent if they have a pet to care for. If a dog is too much for you to look after, think about getting a cat, a bird or a fish.

TIMELY TIP

Buy the right breed

Buying a pet won't save you time, but if you buy the right breed you can save time on their general care and minimise the time spent cleaning up after them. Look for short-haired dogs or cats that don't constantly moult, and don't buy a large dog that needs walking twice a day.

Planning for aged-care placement

Before arranging for any of your family members, friends or community members to be placed in a retirement home or an aged-care facility, carefully consider these questions first:
- Do they have special needs – medical, physical or social? Make a comprehensive list
- Can family and friends visit the aged-care facility easily?
- Does the person need access to a particular religious group?
- Does the person prefer a private or a sociable existence?
- Is security a major factor in the proposed area?
- Will the person want to take part in running the facility?
- Can visitors stay overnight at the facility if they need to?

Remote assistance

Help can quickly be at hand with emergency alarms that save precious minutes for an ill or injured person. Clients wear a small device (sometimes disguised as a bracelet or pendant), which they activate to contact a central monitoring office operating 24 hours a day.

Finding the right retirement home

Some people choose a retirement home before they need to because it provides them with autonomy and more choice. It also means having control of your own future, as opposed to being placed in a home when the decision may no longer be yours to make.

▶ Weigh up the pros and cons of moving to a retirement home. Becoming dependent is not the only reason: feelings of isolation and the question of security while you're living in your own home can also provide the motivation for making this move.

▶ Remember that there is an important distinction between low-level (hostel) care and high-level (nursing home) care, and some providers offer both levels. If you move into a low-level care facility, but at a later stage may need high-level care, find out beforehand if you'll need to move. If the home provides both levels of care you may be able to stay on, which will save the time, inconvenience and stress of moving.

▶ Make your decision in a calm and considered way so that you won't have any regrets. Take the time to compare different homes in the area of your choice, along with the services offered and the costs involved.

▶ Weigh up your financial position. Do you need to sell the family home to enter a retirement home? What sort of long-term financial investment is involved? Is there a creative financial solution available for funding your retirement without having to sell your house?

▶ Try to anticipate your changing needs as you age, as this will save you time in planning and you may be able to avoid unwelcome surprises and high prices.

▶ Try doing some Internet research, to compare services and costs across a wide range of retirement homes.

▶ ▶ CARE FOR THE CARERS

• **Governments provide a range of support services for carers** of older people, but the rules on eligibility can be complicated. The web sites below are a good starting point, but also discuss options with your GP.
www.agedcareaustralia.gov.au
www.carers.net.nz
www.services.gov.za

TIMELY TIP

Find vacancies fast

Some aged-care facility operators now offer a text message (SMS) or email service alerting customers or relatives when vacancies come up that may suit their needs. This could put you first in the queue for a suitable place.

 FIND OUT MORE

• A number of government and private agencies offer home-based care services. Check the web sites listed below to find out what is available to you or a family member who needs home care.
www.mealsonwheels.org.au
www.agedcareguide.com.au
www.ageconcern.org.nz
www.mow.org.za

Home care and home help

A range of services is usually provided by governments, local councils, churches and volunteer groups to help older people to live independently in their own homes. Some are charged for while others are provided free, but all help older people to live independently. In Australia, Aged Care  Assessment Teams (ACATs) assess the needs of those who wish to continue living at home to see what help may be required. People are often referred by their GP for assessment. The services available vary depending on where you live.

● **Home help** Get assistance with housework such as cleaning and ironing and also help to prepare meals. Home helpers are generally available for an agreed number of hours per week.

● **Nursing care** There are community-based nurses that deliver medical care as prescribed by a doctor, and help with wound dressings, diabetic medication or injections, etc.

● **Home care** This service provides help with all household tasks, often daily, but check with your local home-care provider.

● **Meals on Wheels** A meal (delivered hot or to be heated up) is delivered to the home once a day or on a fixed schedule each week. Meals on Wheels is a voluntary group. In some cases, the organisation receives government funding or commercial sponsorship. In Australia, there is a national body but there are also organisations in each state (*see* 'Find out more', at left).

Timesaving aids for carers

Caring for an aged relative or spouse can easily turn into a full-time job, so streamline your input and encourage a safe level of independence.

▶ Invest in a few 'extras'. Special aids such as a bedside commode chair, a walking frame, a device for opening tightly sealed jars, hand rails in the bathroom, a fixed chair or bench in the shower recess and an overhead bed trapeze all save time and the amount of effort required to help.

▶ If a higher level of assistance is required, ask your GP to help arrange for the relevant professional to visit your home, to suggest the most useful aids. Part of this aim is to ensure you don't save time by cutting corners, ending up with a serious injury from lifting an aged relative.

3 Cooking and entertaining

Organising cupboards

Use it or lose it

Most of the time we only use 20 per cent of the appliances in our kitchen. And 70 per cent of us keep appliances that we never use. If you're a confirmed appliance junkie, get rid of whatever you don't use. Unused appliances are a waste of space, and probably make it more difficult to store and access the ones that you do use.

Get organised by de-cluttering

Whether you're cooking for yourself or the whole family, you're going to spend a considerable amount of time in the kitchen. Make that time as productive and pleasant as possible – and save precious time for doing other things – by following these basic ideas for efficiency.

▶ If all the cake pans rush to greet you every time you open a cupboard, if you can never find the potato peeler, if you haven't made bread in your bread machine since the Christmas you got it, or if you own enough takeaway containers to open a shop, identify your specific clutter issues because you're wasting an enormous amount of time on them.

▶ De-clutter the second drawer down. Empty out each utensil and inspect it, setting aside anything that's broken or useless. Throw out broken utensils and take ones you no longer use to an op-shop or charity shop. Clean out the drawer before replacing all the remaining utensils.

▶ Sort out all the pots and pans stored in kitchen cupboards and get rid of anything superfluous. This will make room and you won't waste any more time looking for what you need at the back of a cupboard.

▶ For each kitchen gadget, ask yourself, 'When was the last time I used this?' If you can't think of the answer, don't waste any more time: give it away, throw it out or at least don't keep it in the kitchen. Only keep the things you have used in the last month. Don't be sentimental!

▶ Put the things you do use every day in places where they are obvious and most easily accessible. This way you'll always have them to hand, which saves time instantly.

Go straight for the essentials

Extra 'stuff' that clutters up your kitchen stops you from finding everyday essentials. The solution? Get rid of everything that's superfluous.

▶ Inspect everything with a critical eye and throw out the things that are no longer in good condition: glasses, plates and dishes that are chipped or have become dull over time, frying pans that are no longer flat and lids that no longer fit a matching container.

▶ Don't keep things that are no longer useful – plastic dishes that your children used years ago and trinkets that have no place in a kitchen.

The spice of life

If you don't have a specific place to store all your spices and condiments, put them in a shallow box or a plastic container without a lid and organise them alphabetically. This keeps them contained, and you'll be able to put your hands on the right one quickly every time.

▶ In the pantry, throw away the things that are no longer fit to be consumed: condiments that have lost their colour and taste, and that have been sitting in the cupboard for 10 years, and products that have passed their use-by date or that are infested with weevils.

Easily stored and easily found

▶ Choose a permanent place for everything – don't just store things where you happen to put them. If each item has a set place, you'll save considerable time: you won't have to search for items at the last minute, and the whole family will know where things are without asking... and where they should be put away after being used.

▶ Group the things that go together in the same place so you won't have to make so many small trips. For instance, store the coffee paraphernalia and the cups in a cupboard near the coffee machine, the frying pans and saucepans near the stove, and the kitchen tidy not too far from your work surface – this means you're less likely to spill scraps on the ground.

▶ Place all the containers and packages that you don't use every day at the back of cupboards, or in high cupboards, and place the foodstuffs with a later use-by date behind those that should be consumed sooner.

Seeing everything at a glance

Improving the visibility in your kitchen is such a simple thing to do and will save you an incredible amount of time.

▶ Fill up transparent, hermetically sealed glass jars or clear plastic canisters with flour, sugar, rice, pasta, biscuits, snacks and so on. This gives you a clear view of what you're looking for and what needs to be replenished when you're making a shopping list. It also has the added advantage of keeping food fresher and pest-free for longer.

▶ Opt for cupboards with glass doors. That way, you won't have to open three doors to find a saucer!

▶ Attach a horizontal bar above the work surface to hang utensils such as scissors, a grater, spatulas, skimmers and ladles, etc. Their size and shape can make it difficult to store them in the same drawer and people have a tendency to put them anywhere, which means you never know where to find them next.

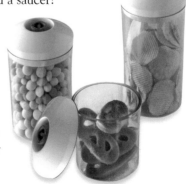

Kitchen utensils

Make the most of modern materials

To save time in the kitchen, you don't necessarily need a collection of items that resemble a kitchen catalogue, just the essentials.

▶ The utensils you do have need to be clean, efficient and in good working order. You're not going to get anything done in record time if your knives can't cut butter, your favourite saucepan has no lid and the handle keeps dropping off the potato masher.

▶ Equip your kitchen with dishes, frying pans, saucepans, glasses and household appliances that are dishwasher-safe (apart from the motors, of course!). Not only will you save time by not having to wash the dishes, but you can put them straight into the dishwasher after you use them, which keeps the benchtops clear, making the clean-up quick and easy.

▶ Choose kitchen items with a non-stick coating: oven trays, frying pans and skillets, etc. They're fast and easy to clean by hand-washing and your food will keep its shape better.

▶ Silicone containers are the best choice for trouble-free baking. These are malleable pans for tarts, cakes, sweet loaves and muffins, etc. The cake can be easily removed by gently twisting the pan, it doesn't stick and there's no need to grease the pan before baking.

▶ Choose flexible ice-cube trays that allow you to remove the cubes in an instant, and consider a non-stick cooking mat, spatulas and whisks that don't scratch, and non-slip gloves to insulate against heat.

Keep multiples of essential items

▶ Buy several chopping boards. This means you won't have to stop in the middle of preparing a recipe just to wash your one and only board and you'll also avoid the risk of contamination. Choose models that are

TIMELY TIP

Slow and steady

Slow cookers are an absolute lifesaver if you need to get a family meal on the table after having been at work all day. You simply put all the ingredients in the pot in the morning, turn it on and by the time you get home at night, dinner is ready to serve!

TIMELY TIP

Hot metal

Metal gratin dishes conduct heat better than porcelain or glass dishes, meaning the cooking time is reduced. Choose stainless steel or a non-stick surface.

easy to care for in wood or plastic. The most practical version is the cutting board that bends into a funnel shape, allowing you to pour food into a container, or to throw away peelings.

▶ Buy two or three whisks of different sizes. There's nothing better for making successful sauces, vinaigrettes, soups, mayonnaise and cake mixes in a flash.

▶ Keep two colanders in your kitchen: a small one and a large one. You can drain pasta or rice and rinse vegetables at the same time, or save a sauce that's full of lumps. Choose colanders made from steel (or stainless steel), which are not deformed by heat.

Tip-top kitchen tools

▶ Don't hesitate to change kitchen utensils regularly if they're old or worn out. You'll see the difference in work performance immediately, as you'll work more efficiently and quickly. You're also less likely to hurt yourself with properly functioning tools.

▶ Make sure all your kitchen knives are razor sharp. If they no longer hold an edge, have them professionally sharpened or invest in a new set – there's no bigger waste of time than a blunt knife.

▶ Swap your potato peeler for a blade peeler (with a U shape), which is easier to handle. It allows you to remove exactly the right amount of peel and the blade is never blocked by the peelings.

▶ Choose a new generation model garlic press that is simple to use, easy to clear out and can be washed in the dishwasher.

The right measurements

▶ Keep a set of kitchen scales handy. They're invaluable for fast and accurate weighing, and they'll help ensure your recipes always work.

▶ To measure liquids and dry foodstuffs, such as water, milk, flour or sugar, there's nothing better than a nest of measuring cups. Buy two sets: one for liquids and one for everything else. Having two sets will also save you from washing frequently as you follow your recipe. Make sure you choose cup measures that are heat- and shock-resistant.

▶ Buy a timer and forget the stress of 'overcooked or undercooked' – and no more waiting in front of the stove or oven for your dish to finish cooking. If you're worried you won't hear it, take it with you. This means you can do something else without running the risk of forgetting you have something on the stove.

Small but perfectly formed

◗ Think carefully before you invest in a multi-functional food processor with centrifugal action. When the first flush of enthusiasm has died down, it could well end up at the back of the cupboard. Instead, choose a mini processor that allows you to thinly slice your onions, chop your meat or mix soups and sauces quickly and easily.

◗ Think about investing in a hand-held electric whisk/blender. These wonderful kitchen tools are indispensable for making perfect mayonnaise, beating eggwhites or whipping cream in an instant, without dirtying another set of containers.

◗ If you're likely to use them often, an electrical can-opener and citrus juicer can also make your life easier, provided you leave them permanently plugged in so they can be used straight away. If they're readily available, they become real timesaving tools.

Get the gadgets going

◗ Keep kitchen scissors handy. They're indispensable – from opening packaging, removing the fat from meat and cutting pizza slices to snipping off herb leaves and trimming and cutting up fish. Keep them close to hand – you won't be able to do without them.

◗ Choose an apple cutter rather than an apple corer. It cuts the apple into eight segments and removes the core all in one go. It's ideal for the speedy preparation of tarts and compotes.

◗ Don't struggle trying to remove lids from jars that seem to resist all attempts at opening – buy a jar opener, and you'll avoid wasting time and losing your patience. Choose one that helps you to lift the edge of the lid slightly to let air inside, then you'll find it comes off easily.

TIMELY TIP

Great graters

The new generation of Microplane graters are more expensive, but they're also more comfortable to use, easy to clean, are extremely sharp and fast, and come in sizes to suit every grating job there is!

Sweet and fresh

When you wipe out your fridge, keep it smelling sweeter for longer by adding a few drops of vanilla to a damp cloth for the final wipe over.

The perfect saucepan set

There's no need to over-equip yourself in the saucepan department. All you really need to be able to work quickly and efficiently is decent-quality utensils with a thick base and a non-stick surface.

● **Two shallow frying pans** Choose one that is 26–28 cm in diameter and one that is a bit smaller.

● **A deep frying pan with a thick base and a lid** This sort of frying pan is very practical for all uses, including browning.

● **An enamelled cast-iron casserole dish** These pots are great for slow-cooking dishes on the stovetop and in the oven.

● **A stock pot with a lid** Perfect for pasta and soup.

● **Two saucepans** Choose one with a diameter of 22 cm and one with a diameter of 12 cm, both with their own lid.

● **An adjustable stainless-steel steamer basket** Make sure it fits inside your saucepans.

● **A pressure cooker** For fast and efficient cooking, these are impossible to beat.

The fridge

Basic care of your fridge

There's nothing more annoying than planning a meal, only to discover that half the ingredients have become inedible. So it pays – in terms of both time and money – to look after your fridge properly.

▶ Keep the fridge itself in good condition with regular cleaning and defrosting, if necessary. Keeping your fridge in tip-top condition means it'll work more efficiently, so the food inside stays fresher for longer.

▶ Fridges (and freezers) are energy-hungry appliances, so when it's time to buy, choose high-efficiency models. Compare the energy rating of different brands of refrigerators before making your final decision.

▶ Position your fridge in a spot that's away from direct sunlight and appliances that generate heat (such as ovens and dishwashers), and ensure that there's adequate ventilation all round it.

▶ Don't use sharp objects or heating appliances (such as a hair dryer) or boiling water to speed up de-frosting – these methods could damage the coils irreparably, and you would have to replace the fridge.

▶ Don't overload your fridge as the cold air needs to circulate freely.

TIMELY TIP

No more odours
Keep half a lemon or an open box
of bicarbonate of soda in your fridge
to absorb any bad odours. Change
regularly to keep it smelling fresh.

CAUTION!

In the case of a power blackout
To preserve the contents of your fridge as long as you can during a power
blackout, avoid opening the fridge door unless absolutely necessary.
The food should keep between 4 and 6 hours in the fridge and between
1 and 2 days in the freezer. After the blackout, if frozen goods have
a consistency that is a little soft to the touch, throw them out. Never
re-freeze a product that has thawed out, as it may have gone off.

▶ In normal conditions, the fridge should be set with the temperature
control on *Medium*. This should keep the temperature at 5°C or below,
with the coolest section of the fridge at 1°C. To check the temperature,
place a thermometer (for people, not for cooking) in a glass of water
inside the fridge overnight: this will give you a precise indication.

▶ In very hot weather or during periods of frequent use, you might need
to change the setting to a colder temperature.

▶ Leave the door open for the shortest possible time when you're
taking something out of the fridge.

▶ Regularly clean inside the fridge and dust the condenser coils, which
are either at the back or under, in the case of frost-free fridges, to ensure
that the motor isn't labouring under a blanket of dust.

▶ If the fridge has a freezer compartment, defrost it regularly to avoid
an excess of ice build-up in the compartment and on food inside it.

▶ Always wipe up spills in the fridge as soon as they occur to avoid
contamination or odours that can
spoil other foods stored in there.

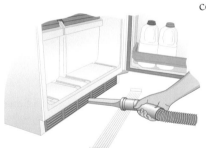

▶ Establish a leftover 'zone'
inside your refrigerator – one of
the shelves higher up – for leftovers. They're more likely to be
eaten, and you'll avoid discovering
containers of spoiled food.

A quick test for airtightness
Check the airtightness of your fridge or freezer by
closing the door on a piece of paper, then trying to
pull it out. If there's no resistance, change the seals.
An inefficient seal means an inefficient appliance,
which results in food going off inside the fridge.

TIMELY TIP

In the box

Don't waste time putting eggs in the egg compartment inside the fridge door. They'll stay fresher longer in their box on one of the shelves. You can remove the lid to make it easier to get to them – but bear in mind that the lid also helps to preserve freshness and prevent the transfer of odours through the eggs' porous shells.

The right temperature – from top to bottom

The temperature inside your fridge is not uniform, because different foods have different optimum storage temperatures. Depending on the model, it may be colder at the top or the bottom. To find out, test the temperature at different heights, then store your food accordingly.

From 0–2°C
- Meat
- Fish
- Poultry
- Deli items, such as pate
- Yogurt and milk desserts
- Egg-based foods
- Cooked food
- Food in cans and jars that have been opened

From 3–5°C
- Cooked and cured meats
- Cheese and eggs
- Cooked vegetables and fruit
- Milk and dairy products that have been opened
- Products that are thawing
- Fresh cakes
- Fruit juice that has been opened

From 5–8°C (crisper drawer)
- Fresh fruit and vegetables

From 7–10°C (fridge door)
- Jam
- Mustard and condiments that have been opened
- Butter
- Water, carbonated drinks and wine

Keeping food fresher for longer

Storing individual foodstuffs in the appropriate packaging will not only limit the risk of contamination, but also improve preservation: the food is less likely to become dehydrated, frost formation is minimised and well-sealed packaging also avoids the spread of odours.

▷ Stock up on plastic or glass containers with lids of all sizes; these are indispensable for preserving and storing small quantities of food and leftovers efficiently. And being recyclable, they're also the environmentally friendly choice.

▷ Plastic bags are simple to use and allow air to be removed easily, but to cut down your consumption of an item that is not environmentally friendly, try to use reusable packaging where appropriate.

▷ Keep plastic food wrap and aluminium foil on hand for quick storage solutions. Store them in a wall-mounted dispenser for quick access.

➤ CAUTION!

Cold-resistant bacteria

Almost 90 per cent of cases of food poisoning – such as salmonella, staphylococcus and listeria – are the result of bad food preservation. Cold does not kill bacteria, it only stops them from multiplying. And the proliferation of germs is not only a question of temperature, but also of cleanliness. So follow strict hygiene guidelines when you're handling food of any kind.

TIMELY TIP

Hot and cold

Store ground ginger, chilli powder and paprika in the fridge. Once opened, these spices lose their flavour – and heat – very quickly.

In the fridge? Yes, but...

● **Bananas** All fruit can be kept in the fridge without any problem, but bananas are affected more than others. Although their taste remains the same, their skin goes black.

● **Fruit that isn't ripe** Any fruit that isn't ripe (including peaches, tomatoes and avocados) can be kept in the fridge. This will increase the lifespan of the fruit. However, its texture will be altered and it won't ripen, so it's much better to let it ripen fully before chilling.

● **Oils** Oils become cloudy and thick in the fridge (except walnut or hazelnut oil). However, they return to their original consistency at room temperature.

● **Sliced bread** Keeping bread in the fridge delays the appearance of mould but it becomes dry and will go stale more quickly.

In the fridge? Never!

● **Potatoes** When potatoes are subjected to cold, the starch is transformed into sugar. They will therefore taste sweet when they are cooked. This is why they should be stored outside the fridge, in a dark place and never next to onions. The latter will rot more quickly if they are in contact with potatoes, while the potatoes will germinate more quickly.

● **Honey** One of the least perishable foodstuffs that exists, honey will simply thicken and crystallise in the fridge. It will return to its normal consistency after the jar has been heated for a few minutes in warm water, but there is really no reason to keep it in the fridge.

● **Onions** It's preferable to store onions in a cool dry place in an open container – away, of course, from the potatoes! In a paper bag in a cool, dark pantry is your best bet.

● **Spreads and peanut butter** After they have been stored in the fridge, they lose their taste and creaminess. However, if you don't eat much peanut butter, you can avoid rancidity by keeping it in the fridge.

Get the packaging right every time

Keep food in optimum condition while it's stored in the fridge by packing it correctly – which isn't necessarily the package it came in. Adapt the package to the product, depending on its fragility and consistency.

Type of food	Type of packaging
Smallgoods and cakes	• Airtight plastic containers
Meat and fish	• Remove from plastic bags, place on a clean plate and cover with plastic wrap or aluminium foil
Cooked food	• Plastic or glass containers with lids
Cheese and food with a high water content	• Plastic wrap. Cheese can also be wrapped in greaseproof paper or waxed paper

The freezer

TIMELY TIP

Slippery ice

After defrosting your freezer, give the interior a wipe over with glycerine. Next time you defrost, the ice will be much easier to remove.

Faultless freezing

A freezer is one of the top timesaving devices – it's right up there with washing machines. It allows you to shop less often, prepare ahead, take advantage of special prices and seasonal gluts, and to feed the family fast.

▶ Freezing must be fast. If the temperature is not cold enough, large crystals will form and the quality of the products will be affected, meaning that when they're thawed they'll be soggy.

▶ Cool warm dishes in the fridge for an hour or so before freezing.

▶ Divide large quantities into several small portions to speed up freezing.

▶ Don't try to freeze too much at one time. While items are freezing, the air must circulate freely so that the food can freeze rapidly and evenly.

▶ If you do need to freeze a number of items at one time, turn the freezer to its lowest temperature, or use the 'snap freeze' function if your freezer has one.

▶ Store each product in a suitable, hermetically sealed container. Attach an adhesive label and write the contents and the use-by date on the container. Alternately, you can write directly on the packaging with an indelible pen.

▶ To keep the motor running efficiently for longer, remember to defrost regularly (even auto-defrost models need defrosting occasionally).

TIMELY TIP

Smart stacking

Avoid stacking packages in the freezer until after they've frozen solid, so that air can circulate freely between the packages, ensuring even freezing.

Fuss-free freezing tips

▶ Get organised: aim to have enough food in your freezer to allow you to prepare meals for a minimum of one week ahead.

▶ Store fresh produce, pre-frozen products (such as spinach), small amounts of leftovers (so you don't throw them away) and food you have prepared in advance, in the freezer. This means that on the days you don't have time to go shopping, or you return home too late to cook, you have something to feed your family without getting stressed.

▶ Regularly check the contents and use-by dates of frozen foods.

▶ Store the food according to type so you can find it quickly – prepared dishes that are ready to be heated, raw meat, raw fish, vegetables and fruit, etc. – and also according to the use-by date.

▶ Keep a written inventory of what's in the freezer (stick it on the freezer door to save time checking inside) and update it when you add or remove any item so you don't waste time rummaging around.

The perfect package

Resist the urge to throw things into your freezer straight from the supermarket. A little care with the packaging of your frozen goods will not only extend their life, it will also save space in the freezer – resulting in savings in both time and money.

▶ Remove as much air as possible from freezer bags before sealing.

▶ Use plastic wrap and freezer bags for raw meat, poultry and fish. They take up less room, but more importantly, they allow you to freeze products singly, each wrapped protectively in plastic wrap. This means you can defrost a single steak instead of a whole tray.

▶ Cut the label from prepackaged meat and slip it into your bag of individually wrapped portions for easy identification.

▶ Slip a freezer bag into an empty 500-ml or 1-litre milk carton and fill it up with leftover soup or stock. When

⟩CAUTION!

Freezing and thawing – getting it right

Don't allow your dishes to cool down to room temperature before freezing them; put them into the fridge immediately (uncovered or lightly covered) for an hour or so before placing them in the freezer. If condensation has occurred during chilling in the fridge, absorb it with paper towels before sealing the food completely, then freezing. Thaw food in the fridge, or more quickly in the microwave, but never at room temperature or in hot water.

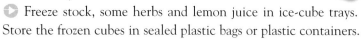

frozen, these stock 'bricks' can be removed from the carton, sealed, labelled and stacked in the freezer.

▶ Freeze raw or cooked meatballs on a baking paper-lined scone tray, then transfer them to a container, seal and pop back into the freezer. They'll stay separate and you can use as many as you want when you need them.

▶ Freeze stock, some herbs and lemon juice in ice-cube trays. Store the frozen cubes in sealed plastic bags or plastic containers.

▶ Pack kaffir lime leaves, fresh bay leaves or sticks of lemon grass into small zip-lock bags and keep them in the freezer.

Two-in-one packaging

Anything that you can cook, freeze and reheat in the same container is a definite time saver.

▶ Use containers that are suitable for both freezing and reheating, such as glass and stoneware. There's nothing to stop you from freezing lasagne in a porcelain ovenproof dish, provided you cover it well.

▶ If you're cooking a large lasagne and want to reuse your favourite dish, line the dish with baking paper and lift the lasagne from the dish when frozen. Wrap securely in plastic wrap and freeze until needed when it can be slipped back into the dish (minus the paper) for thawing and cooking without fuss.

▶ Try tipping a cooled casserole into a similar-sized dish that has been lined with a heavy-duty plastic freezer bag. Lift the bag from the dish when frozen, seal and freeze, ready to slip it back into the dish when needed.

▶ Choose microwave-safe plastic containers with hermetic seals for products that will be thawed or reheated in the microwave. Never fill the containers completely to the top, otherwise they may explode because the water in foodstuffs expands when it freezes.

TIMELY TIP

Plastic wrap on ice

If plastic food wrap drives you crazy when it sticks to itself, try keeping the roll in the freezer. This makes it easier to unroll and cut. If it doesn't adhere correctly, simply moisten the edges of the dish for a better grip.

Don't bother thawing

Frozen herbs, iced stock cubes, grated lemon zest, vegetables and small pieces of meat or fish and prawns don't need to be thawed; they can be added directly to a dish as it cooks.

CAUTION!

Freezer burn

After thawing, food can appear to have lost its colour or have a whitish tinge in places. This is freezer burn and is due to dehydration caused by contact with air. If the food has been continuously frozen, it is still completely safe to eat, but the taste may have changed so you should remove the affected part.

Timetable for optimum freezing

As long as food remains frozen at –18°C, it will last for months, but if you store it for longer than the recommended time, it may become less palatable, and its nutritional value is likely to be compromised.

Meat

Beef, veal and lamb (raw)	12–18 months
Beef, veal and lamb mince (raw)	4 months
Beef and lamb sausages (raw)	4 months
Pork (raw)	10 months
Bacon (raw)	1 month
Offal (raw)	1–2 months
Cooked meat dishes	2–3 months

Note: The fattier the meat, the less it will keep because the fat becomes rancid. Remember to remove as much fat as you can from meat before freezing it.

Poultry and game

Chicken (raw)	12–18 months
Duck, goose, turkey, guinea-fowl and rabbit (raw)	6–12 months
Game and hare (raw)	3–4 months
Cooked casseroles	6 months

Fish and seafood

White fish – snapper, flathead and cod, etc. (raw)	9 months
Fatty fish – tuna and salmon, etc. (raw)	3–6 months
Prawns (raw, shelled)	6–8 months
Prawns (cooked, shelled)	5–6 months
Shellfish (raw, shelled)	3 months
Cooked fish dishes	3 months

Note: Only freeze very fresh fish. If the fish smells suspicious when it's thawed, throw it away.

Dairy products

Butter (unsalted)	6–9 months
Margarine	3 months
Cheese with a hard skin or grated cheese	6 months
Cheese with a soft skin	3 months
Blue cheese	3 months
Milk	3 months
Homemade ice-cream	3 months
Commercial ice-cream	1–2 months
Yogurt	1–2 months

Fruit
- Fruit in sugar or syrup .... 12 months
- Berries (raw) .... 18–24 months
- Unprocessed fruit .... 6 months
- Purees and compotes .... 6 months

Note: Avoid freezing citrus fruit, avocados, tomatoes, watermelon, apples (except pureed) and kiwifruit. Freeze pears, peaches, nectarines, quinces and plums only if they are in sugar or syrup.

Vegetables
- Most vegetables (blanched, cooked) .... 10–12 months
- Cauliflower, broccoli and fennel (blanched, cooked) ...... 8 months
- Beetroot, leek and eggplant (blanched, cooked) .... 6 months
- Mushrooms (raw, braised) .... 3 months
- Onions (raw) .... 3 months
- Garlic (raw) .... 2 months
- Herbs (not blanched) .... 3 months
- Potatoes (cooked, mashed) .... 6 months

Note: To blanch vegetables, plunge them into boiling water for 2 to 5 minutes, or cook them in a steamer for 4 to 5 minutes.

Cakes, bread and dough
- Bread, croissants and other pastries .... 1 month
- Bread dough (raw) .... 2 months
- Tart pastry (raw) .... 8 months
- Tart pastry (cooked) .... 6 months
- Biscuits and shortbread .... 6 months

Note: Don't freeze cream-filled cakes. Place raw pastry rolled up in a ball in a hermetically sealed bag.

Make sure it's suitable to freeze

▷ Although both eggwhites and yolks can be frozen separately, whole eggs are unsuitable to freeze and cooked eggwhite becomes tough and rubbery.

▷ Some vegetables, such as radishes, cucumbers and avocados, don't freeze well. Potatoes (except mashed) also don't freeze very well because they tend to become watery and tasteless.

▷ Don't freeze lettuce, witlof or other salad greens. Only freeze fresh tomatoes for use in sauces or soups, because their texture changes.

▷ In general, any fruit with a high water content that you want to thaw and eat raw in a salad or dessert is not suitable for freezing because it becomes mushy. However, frozen grapes, oranges, pineapple and banana

TIMELY TIP

Keeping ice-cream creamy

Don't be tempted to lower the temperature in your freezer to make ice-cream scoopable, which is about -14°C, because you'll compromise the quality of long-term frozen food, which needs to be kept at -18°C. Instead, store ice-cream in the warmest part of the freezer – at the bottom of an upright or at the top of a chest freezer.

pieces are delicious when eaten still frozen, and frozen watermelon cubes can be blended into a delicious slushy just before serving.

▶ Don't freeze mayonnaise; it separates when it's frozen.

▶ Most thickened sauces also tend to separate when they're frozen, so try thickening them after they have thawed.

▶ Sauces made with dairy products such as yogurt and cream have a tendency to separate, so do not freeze well.

▶ Avoid freezing jelly and gelatine desserts, because they tend to become rubbery and fairly unpalatable after freezing.

▶ Avoid freezing meat or poultry that contains stuffing, as the stuffing freezes very slowly, creating an increased risk of bacterial contamination and food poisoning. If you can, remove the stuffing before freezing.

Timesaving freezer tips

▶ Measure the capacity of the ice-cube tray you're using for stock, etc., so that you know how many cubes to use when a recipe calls for a certain amount of stock, wine or lemon juice.

▶ Always leave 3–4 ice cubes in the tray and fill up the rest with cold water to quickly make new ice cubes. The freezing time will be reduced by half. Use mineral water to accelerate the freezing process even more.

▶ Buy ginger fresh, peel it and freeze it whole. It will keep indefinitely and is much easier to grate when frozen.

▶ Fill up an ice-cube tray with leftover wine and put it in the freezer. When you're making a sauce, drop a few ice cubes of wine directly into it.

▶ Cut one or more bananas into slices and freeze them. To make fast milkshakes, all you need to do is place pieces of frozen fruit directly into the blender or mixer with the milk.

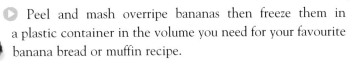

▷ Peel and mash overripe bananas then freeze them in a plastic container in the volume you need for your favourite banana bread or muffin recipe.

▷ Bread, butter, milk and pure cream can all be frozen to have on hand when supplies suddenly run out.

▷ Get into the habit of grating the zest from a lemon before squeezing its juice. Wrap the zest in a small piece of plastic wrap or a tiny zip-lock bag and freeze it in a small container. Leftover juice can be frozen in ice-cube trays, then transferred to a sealed container.

▷ Freeze leftover eggwhites in measured amounts – one, two or the number you need for your favourite pavlova recipe. Keep them tightly sealed so that they don't get tainted with odours from other foods.

▷ Mix egg yolks with a pinch of salt or a teaspoon of sugar to prevent coagulation and freeze for later use in either savoury or sweet dishes.

▷ Leftover coconut milk or coconut cream will freeze successfully in ice-cube trays. Pop the frozen cubes into a freezer bag and seal to store.

▷ Fresh herbs or fresh chillies are suitable for freezing. Simply put them into small zip-lock bags, seal and freeze until needed.

▷ Freeze single portions of cooked rice and cooked pasta in small microwavable containers. Thaw on the *Defrost* setting.

▷ Freeze chopped onion in convenient portions in zip-lock bags for when you're in a hurry.

▷ Nuts stay fresh for months in the freezer when they're sealed in zip-lock bags. And there's no need to defrost them before using.

Basic food hygiene

Being clean is part of being efficient

Saving time doesn't mean cutting corners with hygiene – being laid up with food poisoning isn't going to save anyone's time and could, in fact, leave you seriously ill and hospitalised, so don't compromise on this point.

▷ Keep your kitchen clean and tidy. You'll work better and more quickly, and at the same time you will ensure a suitable standard of food hygiene when it comes to food preparation.

▷ Don't think it can't happen to you. Studies show that, in most households, kitchens have more bacteria than bathrooms. So it's essential to do everything you can to avoid food poisoning.

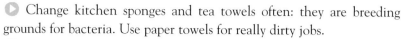

CAUTION!

Dangerous mix

When cleaning your kitchen, never mix an ammonia-based product with bleach. This creates toxic vapours, which can seriously damage your lungs and eyes.

▷ Change kitchen sponges and tea towels often: they are breeding grounds for bacteria. Use paper towels for really dirty jobs.

▷ Take care that your work surfaces, cutting surfaces and knives are absolutely clean and stored in such a way to keep them clean.

▷ Don't forget to wipe down electrical appliances after every use.

The 12 commandments of food hygiene

● Wash your hands before and after you handle food.

● Clean utensils and working surfaces with hot soapy water before, after and also during food preparation.

● Never use the same cutting board or the same utensils for raw meat, chicken or fish, and vegetables. As a general rule, keep meat, chicken and fish away from other foodstuffs.

● Never place cooked meat or fish on the same surface where you placed it raw, without cleaning the surface thoroughly beforehand.

● Thaw your food in the fridge, never at room temperature. If you defrost it in the microwave, cook it immediately afterwards.

● Never refreeze a product you have previously defrosted.

● Throw away tins of food that are dented or swollen.

● Throw away cracked eggs.

● Never eat chicken if the flesh is still red after it has been cooked.

● Close container lids and insert corks firmly before you store products in the fridge. Throw away any that show signs of mould.

● Never eat raw pastry, even to taste it.

● Put leftovers in the fridge or freezer within 2 hours of the end of a meal and if they're uneaten after two days, throw them out.

Maintain hygiene while food shopping

▷ Always start by filling your trolley with the products that are not kept in the fridge (household products, cereals, pasta and drinks, etc.) and finish with dairy products and all other refrigerated items, raw meat and fish (with perfect packaging, not ripped or dented), then deep-frozen food last of all. Think about taking along an insulated bag for the latter.

▷ Never place packages containing raw meat or fish on top of vegetables, to ensure that juices don't run out on them. Bag meat separately.

▷ Avoid non-pasteurised dairy products and stuffed chicken.

▷ Always check product labels on perishables and refrigerated foods and choose products with the longest use-by date.

Getting organised

Planned meals prepared in a flash

Saving time in the kitchen is ultimately a combination of two processes: taking advantage of various timesaving products and clever shortcuts and, when you do have some time available, making the best use of these products by being organised and preparing ahead.

▶ Prepare a list of meals for the whole week and do your shopping accordingly. It makes you a winner on every front: you won't waste time looking in the fridge every evening, asking yourself what you can make for dinner, you'll be less stressed and you won't have to do any last-minute shopping in order to get dinner on the table.

▶ Adapt the type of meal you make to your timetable. If you have more time on Sunday, cook something where the leftovers can be the basis for dinner on Monday. For evenings when you'll be home late, plan simple menus, such as steak and salad or spaghetti, or a frozen meal that has already been prepared and only requires thawing and reheating.

▶ Simplify as much as you can by using a weekly model: Monday, pasta; Tuesday, casserole; Wednesday, grilled meat; Thursday, soup; Friday, pizza, etc. This solution may sound routine, but it's tried and true! And remember, it doesn't have to be the same pasta dish every Monday.

Quick recipes for all tastes

It's faster to cook without following a recipe, but sometimes you might feel like trying something new, or you're lacking inspiration.

▶ Buy a reliable, basic family recipe book where you can quickly find the great classics: casseroles, stir-fries, pasta sauces and quiches.

▶ Choose recipes that can be easily made in less than half an hour and that have ingredients you know the whole family will like.

▶ Start your own recipe collection. Cut out and file magazine recipes that interest you, and ask friends to share their favourite recipes.

▶ There are also any number of Internet

sites with recipes on offer, along with some web sites where you simply type in the ingredients you have on hand and a recipe to match comes up, which you print out. Great for times you haven't had time to shop!

Great ideas for organising recipes

▶ Choose a simple filing method. The most efficient way is to sort recipes into starters, mains and desserts. You can create sub-categories according to product, season and type of cooking, etc.

▶ Avoid unpleasant surprises by compiling a 'tried-and-true' recipe folder where you collect all the dishes you know you cook well and that everyone likes. Use this folder on days where you don't have a minute to spare or when you have guests coming over.

▶ Store your recipe collection in a practical way – it's not time saving to wade through a shoebox full of clippings looking for the one you know is in there somewhere. The best method is a document protector, or a file with transparent sleeves, where you can easily slip in your recipes. Plastic is practical because you don't have to worry about the recipe getting spattered.

▶ Another clever idea is a stand or hanging rack for holding a recipe book open while you cook, which makes it very easy to consult and keeps the book out of the mess. And then there's always the trusty recipe file kept in a small box.

Try something new

▶ Put aside a selection of new recipes that are not too complicated and that you would like to try. Each week or so, on a day when you have a little more time, try one of them out. This will help you to broaden your repertoire, so that neither you nor the family get sick of the same old things and, who knows, you might hit on another family favourite!

Pantry basics

Indispensable ingredients for fast meals

▶ After getting all your equipment in order, this is one of the most basic steps to being super organised in the kitchen. By ensuring that you always have certain products in your pantry, fridge and freezer, you'll be able to produce easy and nutritious meals for your family or friends in next to no time. Adapt the following lists, opposite, to suit your likes and dislikes – if you don't like couscous, for instance, there's not much point in having it in the pantry, no matter how fast it might be to prepare.

Stock up on the basics

IN THE PANTRY

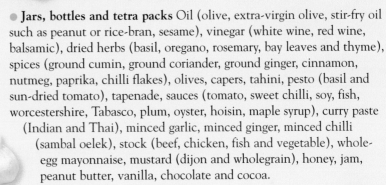

● **Dry goods** Pasta (long, short and pre-cooked lasagne sheets), rice (long grain, basmati and arborio/risotto), dried Chinese noodles, cous-cous, polenta, dried breadcrumbs, flour (plain and self-raising), cornflour, sugar (white, brown, caster and palm sugar), coffee, tea, plain crackers, flour tortillas, salt (cooking and flakes) and peppercorns.

● **Canned foods** Fruit in natural juice or light syrup, artichoke hearts, beans and pulses (cannellini, red kidney, four bean mix, chick peas and lentils), coconut milk, coconut cream, evaporated milk, fish (tuna, salmon, sardines and anchovies), tomatoes (whole, diced, passata and tomato paste), corn (kernels and baby corn), and cooking oil spray.

● **Jars, bottles and tetra packs** Oil (olive, extra-virgin olive, stir-fry oil such as peanut or rice-bran, sesame), vinegar (white wine, red wine, balsamic), dried herbs (basil, oregano, rosemary, bay leaves and thyme), spices (ground cumin, ground coriander, ground ginger, cinnamon, nutmeg, paprika, chilli flakes), olives, capers, tahini, pesto (basil and sun-dried tomato), tapenade, sauces (tomato, sweet chilli, soy, fish, worcestershire, Tabasco, plum, oyster, hoisin, maple syrup), curry paste (Indian and Thai), minced garlic, minced ginger, minced chilli (sambal oelek), stock (beef, chicken, fish and vegetable), whole-egg mayonnaise, mustard (dijon and wholegrain), honey, jam, peanut butter, vanilla, chocolate and cocoa.

● **Vegetables** Onions, potatoes, garlic and tomatoes.

IN THE FRIDGE

● **Dairy** Eggs, cheese (cheddar, mozzarella and parmesan), milk, butter, cream, sour cream and plain yogurt.

● **Fruit and vegetables** Carrots, spring onions, apples, oranges, lemons and salad greens.

● **Noodles** Vacuum-packed noodles (Singapore or hokkien).

IN THE FREEZER

● **Various** Ice-cream, a selection of fruit and vegetables, pieces of meat that can be quickly defrosted in the microwave, fish fillets or fish steaks, herbs, bread, pastry (shortcrust and puff), pizza bases, bacon, and smoked salmon.

Pantry lifesavers

Prepared vegetables and salads

Being pressed for time doesn't mean you have to live on takeaways or commercial frozen dinners. But there are a lot of clever shortcuts and prepared products that can make your life significantly easier without breaking the bank or compromising your nutrition.

▶ Don't overlook prepared and semi-prepared vegetables – although they can be slightly more expensive, they're designed to simplify your life. They allow you to skip several fiddly steps in food preparation: no more peeling, sorting, rinsing or cutting up. And their taste and nutritional quality is generally of a high standard. Weigh up the few extra cents against the cost of your time.

▶ The fresh food section of your supermarket offers a large choice of prepared salads and different salad mixes. The vegetable selection is also impressive: sliced mushrooms, sliced green beans, chopped stir-fry vegetables and coleslaw, etc. Choose the ones that suit you.

▶ Don't forget frozen vegetables – sliced onions, carrots, spinach, peas, cauliflower, green beans, zucchini, broccoli – the range is almost as comprehensive as your greengrocer's. And snap-frozen vegetables have the same nutritional value as fresh.

Taking stock – cubes and ready-made

▶ Use all kinds of stock cubes or stock powder any time you need a flavour boost. They are practical, they improve the flavour of all your dishes in a few seconds and they don't have to be full of MSG and chemicals – buy them from your health food shop.

▶ Crumble them into the boiling water you're using to cook your vegetables and pasta, or use them as a base for soups and sauces. Chicken stock cubes (the low-salt version is even better) are the most 'all-purpose' and will suit most of your dishes. But beef and vegetable are also useful.

▶ Ready-made stock in different-sized tetra packs is also a fantastic stand-by for soups, risottos, casseroles and fish poaching.

▶ For the best flavour of all, explore the frozen section of good delis or butchers for homemade frozen stock. You might not have time to make a delicious veal stock but someone has done it for you. Perfect for de-glazing and quick sauces.

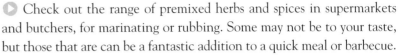

Well seasoned

....

▶ Check out the range of premixed herbs and spices in supermarkets and butchers, for marinating or rubbing. Some may not be to your taste, but those that are can be a fantastic addition to a quick meal or barbecue.

▶ There's also a huge range of ready-mixed bottled marinades, prepared curry pastes and stir-fry pastes available that can make a huge difference to the time-poor chef's culinary creations.

▶ Buy different basic flavouring ingredients, such as minced garlic, chilli, fresh ginger and chopped coriander, etc., in ready-to-go small jars. While nothing is ever quite as good as fresh, the time saved might mean that pre-prepared spices are a perfectly acceptable compromise for you.

▶ You can also buy various herbs in tube form for a quick flavour hit, but they can vary in taste and often contain quite a few additives.

▶ If you're even slightly organised, herbs of all kinds are so easy to chop and store in the freezer, either with a little water in ice-cube trays or simply packed into small zip-lock bags.

A little sauce goes a long way

....

Another fantastic idea for the cook in a hurry is to use the plethora of prepared sauces available in supermarkets today.

▶ Pasta sauces come in every flavour and amount, from large jars of classic tomato sugo and single-serve stir-through sauces to small containers of gourmet sauce from the chilled section in delis.

▶ Prepared cook-in sauces can be delicious and save you time, but always read the labels – you may not want to eat quite as much saturated fat or as many food additives as these can sometimes contain, and they can be quite expensive to buy, too.

▶ Delis often sell containers of both sweet and savoury sauces that can taste almost as good as your own – an expensive option, but sometimes a lifesaver, especially when you're entertaining.

▶ Don't forget that many leftover sauces and stocks can easily be frozen in zip-lock bags for later on.

TIMELY TIP

Nice and sweet

Try using carrots to sweeten your sauces instead of sugar, which is high in kilojoules and unsuitable for some people with special medical conditions, such as diabetes.

Shopping made easy

Note it down

Put a note pad in an obvious place in the kitchen, along with a pen. Each person can note down, day by day, the products that have run out or that are about to run out. This means that a large part of the list will already be made for you when you go shopping.

Be prepared before you go shopping

▶ Plan to do your supermarket shopping once a week, and don't forget to take a detailed list that includes all the meals you have planned for the week, as well as all the other household needs.

▶ Make a point of checking what you need. Before you leave, look in your cupboards to see how much you have of each product. Your goal is to come back with everything you need for the week. You shouldn't have to go back for something you've forgotten or for silly extras.

▶ Learn to master the 'once-a-week' method before you move on to the next step: shopping once a fortnight. This means you plan your meals for 2 weeks and you will need to put some of your fresh products in the freezer as soon as you come home from the supermarket.

Make a list

▶ Always make a list before you go shopping and you'll make fast work of the job. You won't risk forgetting a product and having to go back to buy it. And with your list in hand, you won't be distracted.

▶ Note what you need to buy while you're planning your meals. This way, you'll make sure not to forget any of the ingredients you need to prepare them. Divide your list into two columns: the first one for the name of the dish and the second one for the ingredients that are required.

▶ Before you go supermarket shopping, make a list of the products you need according to the section and you'll save time while you're shopping: fruit and vegetables, frozen food, dairy products, and so on. This means you'll move along the aisles quickly and you won't have to keep backtracking.

Keeping cool

Store a couple of insulated chiller bags or a small esky (food cooler) in the boot of your car to ensure perishable foods such as meat, fish and dairy products don't deteriorate on the way home from the supermarket (add ice bricks in really hot weather). Pack the perishables into the bags or esky, then take them straight home to unpack.

Computerise your list

Making a master shopping list on the computer is easy. Take stock of all the products you have bought at some time or other and type up the list, then cut and paste the products into categories according to set headings, such as 'fresh produce' or 'meat'. Then all you have to do is print the list and highlight all the things you need. Getting the list set up can be time consuming, but you'll save time in the long run.

Top tips for supermarket shopping

▶ If your supermarket uses pay trolleys, make sure you have the right coin for the trolley before you leave home. An even better idea is to keep a special token or coin in your purse.

▶ Don't forget to take an insulated bag with you for frozen products.

▶ Follow your shopping list strictly, and don't walk into sections where you don't need anything, or you'll get waylaid.

▶ Fill your shopping trolley methodically and you won't waste time rearranging your goods as you go (and risk squashing fresh produce). First put in everything that doesn't need to be kept cold, starting with the least fragile and heaviest things, such as bottled water or canned food.

▶ When you get to the checkout, try to group your purchases according to where they go: fridge, freezer, pantry, etc. This makes them much faster to unpack when you get them home.

Choose the best time to shop

▶ Try to avoid the busiest times at the supermarket, such as the weekends, lunchtimes and late afternoons, if at all possible.

▶ Shop outside of normal business hours if you can. Many supermarkets have extended opening hours – from very early until very late, and sometimes all night. There are fewer queues at the checkout at these times, more room in the aisles and in the car park, and often better service, too.

▶ Unless farmer's markets are simply a pleasurable way for you to shop, limit them to fresh or organic produce that you can't find in a supermarket. Markets are a more leisurely, and often more pleasant, shopping experience, but they're also a less time-efficient way to shop.

Shop online

▶ Learn to make the most of the advantages offered by the Internet. There are numerous sites where you can do all your food shopping without leaving home. Quickly compare the prices of a few products, find out about the delivery service and get started! Keep in mind that your first orders may take between 30 minutes and

1 hour to complete, although subsequent orders will be much faster.

▶ Firstly make a list of your 'favourites' (or personal base). For subsequent orders, all you'll have to do is consult this list and tick the products you need, which is very quick (and even quicker if you have a fast broadband connection). Once you've got used to the process, the savings in time and the convenience are undeniable. You can do your shopping at a time that suits you, and choose the delivery times as well.

Making the right choices

Ripe on time

▶ Place the fruit you want to ripen more quickly in a paper bag, or a plastic bag with small holes pierced in it. The plastic bag will hold in the ethylene that the fruit gives off and promote ripening. Avocados and melons ripen more quickly if you put an apple or a banana in the bag with them, because they give off more ethylene, speeding up ripening.

▶ If necessary, you can store ripe fruit in the vegetable compartment in your fridge for 3 to 5 days. However, the cold not only stops them from ripening, it can also change the texture of some fruit, especially bananas.

CAUTION!

Keep tomatoes in the shade

The rays of the sun don't make tomatoes ripen, they simply make them go soft. To keep tomatoes, you should therefore avoid exposing them to direct sunlight and store them with the stem facing upwards. Try to keep them at room temperature – putting them in the fridge changes their texture and they don't taste as good.

A guide to choosing vegetables

Take the time to choose fresh produce carefully, and you'll reap the rewards. Fresh, unblemished vegetables keep longer, which means you won't have to go shopping again quite so soon, there's less wastage and your finished dishes look and taste better.

The basic rules are simple: examine the vegetables closely, touch them and give them a sniff. Don't buy vegetables that are soft, have withered or yellow leaves, and dull or spotted skin. Similarly, avoid products that are damaged or where the smell seems strange. And don't buy pre-packaged vegetables if the package contains liquid (unless it's simply a little condensation).

● **Artichokes** The heads must be dense, and the leaflike petals tightly packed. Check that the stem is still slightly moist.

● **Asparagus** Fresh asparagus should be straight and have tight, undamaged tips and a crisp stem, with not too much woody material at the bottom of the stem. Green asparagus is coloured along three-quarters of its length.

● **Beetroot** Raw beetroot must not have skin that is too dried out. If it is cooked, the skin should be smooth and not dried out.

● **Broccoli** The broccoli buds must be as compact and fine as possible, in other words, tightly closed. The colour should tend more towards violet and never yellow: this means the vegetable is about to flower.

● **Button mushrooms** The colour of the cap depends on the variety. However, the colour of the gills, which become browner over time, should be as light as possible. The ideal is to have a cap that is so closed that you can't see the gills of the mushroom.

● **Cabbage** Comes with frizzy leaves or smooth tight leaves and can be white, green and red. The white cabbage must always be heavy and dense and its leaves must be crisp and shiny.

● **Capsicums** Can be green, yellow, orange or red, but whatever the colour, capsicums should be nice and firm to the touch with a smooth shiny taut skin – no wrinkles or blemishes.

● **Carrots** A fresh carrot must be firm and can be recognised by its intense colour and unblemished skin. If there are leaves, these should be firm and green, not wilted or pale.

● **Cauliflower** The florets of the cauliflower must be white, regular and have fine tight buds. Check the appearance of the leaves.

● **Celeriac** This root vegetable should be firm and heavy and should not sound hollow when it's tapped.

● **Celery** The leaves of celery are a good indication of its freshness. The ribs should be firm, fleshy and shiny.

(Continued overleaf)

TIMELY TIP

Try new things

Try a new fruit or vegetable next time you visit a farmer's market, and don't be put off by not knowing how to prepare or eat it – ask the market stall seller, or simply type the name of the fruit or vegetable into your Internet search engine and you'll find out what to do with it in the blink of an eye.

A guide to choosing vegetables (continued)

● **Cucumbers** Should be a nice shade of green and be firm and smooth.

● **Eggplants** Choose an eggplant that's unblemished and firm, with a smooth shiny skin and good colour – not too light and not too purple, preferably violet.

● **Fennel** Choose fennel that has lovely green, fresh feathery leaves.

● **Garlic** The heads should be full and bulbous. Check the firmness of the cloves by pressing them gently. They should not be squashy.

● **Golden shallots** Must be firm to the touch. The outer layer must be dry and shiny without any trace of mould.

● **Green beans** The pods must be fine and firm and should break cleanly when they are bent.

● **Leeks** Choose one that has a good colour. The diameter is not important: the thicker leeks are as tender as the slimmer ones.

● **Lettuce** Must be fresh and have a good colour, with no marks or bruising on the leaves. A white base is ideal.

● **Onions** Opt for white onions with fresh green leaves. A dry onion should be firm, have a shiny skin and not have any traces of mould.

● **Peas** Choose peas and snow peas with bright green, crisp pods.

● **Potatoes** Choose a regular-shaped potato without any green patches or blemishes, and that is not sprouting.

● **Radishes** Look for a bunch that's nice and green with firm roots. The colour and shape give no indication as to the hotness of the taste.

● **Spinach** The freshest spinach has deep green leaves that are fleshy without being too thick or too damp.

● **Spring onions** (Sometimes called green onions.) The white part should look shiny and the leaves should be crisp and bright green.

● **Witlof** Choose one that has firm, white leaves, lightly tinged with pale yellow. The whiter the base, the better.

● **Zucchini** Choose a zucchini that is firm, with a blemish-free skin.

A fish out of water

Use your senses when buying fresh fish – your eyes, nose and fingers will tell you immediately whether it's as fresh as it should be.

▶ Look at the skin of the fish; it should have a strong colour, and it should be moist and covered with transparent mucus. The scales should be shiny and sticky, the eye clear and shiny, the gills dark red, and the abdomen should not be taut or bloated.

TIMELY TIP

Get the pros to do it

To save time (and lots of smelly garbage), ask the fishmonger to scale, gut and fillet your fish. And ask the butcher to trim meat and chop it up, if it's for a casserole.

▶ The smell must seem fresh, not unpleasantly fishy. The smell of marine fish is much the same as seaweed or the sea, whereas the smell of freshwater fish is faintly earthy, and certainly not strong.

▶ Touch it – the flesh should be firm and elastic. If your finger leaves an indent in the fish after you've touched it, then it is no longer fresh.

▶ It's best to eat fresh fish on the day you buy it, but you can keep it for 2 days in the coldest part of the fridge, or in the freezer for longer.

Meat – a matter of appearance

▶ Start by examining the colour. A grey or brown colour indicates meat that is not fresh. Beef should be bright ruby red and veal should be pinkish white. Lamb can range from pink to dark red, depending on the food the animal ate and its age. Pork should be pink, and can be a darker or lighter shade.

▶ Look also at the fat distribution. As far as possible, choose lean meat or marbled meat: this means that the fat is between the muscles, which gives a better flavour throughout.

To everything there is a season...

Almost everything is available all year round today, so you can virtually ignore the idea of seasonal produce. If you want to avoid foreign imports or food that has spent too long in storage, use the following tables as a guide to what should be best, and freshest, in which season.

SPRING
● **Vegetables** Artichokes, asparagus, basil, beetroot, capsicums, carrots, corn, garlic, green beans, lettuce, new potatoes, peas, rocket, snow peas, spinach and watercress.
● **Fruit** Bananas, kiwifruit, oranges, pineapples and strawberries.

SUMMER
● **Vegetables** Basil, beetroot, cabbage, capsicums, celery, corn, cucumbers, eggplants, green beans, lettuce, onions, potatoes, rocket and tomatoes.
● **Fruit** Apricots, bananas, blackberries, cherries, figs, grapes, mangoes, nectarines, papaya, passionfruit, peaches, pineapples, plums, raspberries, red currants, rockmelon and strawberries.

(Continued overleaf)

To everything there is a season... (continued)

AUTUMN
- **Vegetables** Avocado, broccoli, cabbage, carrot, cauliflower, celery, corn, eggplant, fennel, green beans, leek, mushrooms, onion, pumpkin and tomato.
- **Fruit** Apple, banana, blueberries, chestnuts, fig, grapes, kiwifruit, pear, plum, quince and raspberries.

WINTER
- **Vegetables** Avocado, broccoli, brussels sprouts, cabbage, carrot, cauliflower, celeriac, green beans, Jerusalem artichoke, lamb's lettuce and mushrooms.
- **Fruit** Apple, banana, chestnuts, grapefruit, kiwifruit, lemon, lime, mandarin, pear and rhubarb.

Timesaving methods

Into the oven and you're done!

There's no doubt that some methods of cooking are quicker than others. However, your oven – along with the microwave, wok, barbecue and the stovetop – certainly has a valuable part to play in the production of fast food. Perfect your repertoire of fast cooking methods and save the long, slow cooking for the times when the clock isn't mercilessly ticking away!

▶ Use your oven as often as possible because it's one of the simplest ways to cook and there's no need to waste time wracking your brains. Preheat the oven while you're cutting a chicken into pieces – so it cooks quickly – add a few potatoes, sliced carrots and onions and it's all done! There is an endless array of combinations when it comes to roasting.

▶ Fish will cook within 15 to 20 minutes in a hot oven – just enough time to prepare a salad or some steamed vegetables.

▶ If you're pressed for time and would still like a roast, choose boned mini roasts, or individual cuts, rather than a large single joint.

▶ Create some delicious variations by covering cooked food – meat, vegetables, fish, pasta or a combination – with a bechamel sauce, grated cheese and breadcrumbs, etc., then pop it into the oven for a bubbling, golden gratin. It sounds quick, and it is!

▶ And don't forget, if you're cooking a casserole in your oven, you might as well cook two – one for now and one to freeze for later. That way you'll save energy as well as time.

(*See* 'Timesaving recipes', starting on page 265.)

Oven settings at a glance

An oven with a fan-forced setting cooks more quickly and evenly than an ordinary oven, so you need to adapt the temperatures a little. This table will help you choose the right setting for your oven.

- **Standard oven** 100°C 150°C 175°C 200°C 225°C 250°C
- **Fan-forced** 70°C 120°C 150°C 175°C 200°C 220°C

Note: Fan-forced ovens don't require any pre-heating.

Microwave miracles

You'll find that a microwave oven is not only useful for defrosting and reheating; it can also cut down on both preparation and cooking time.

▶ Don't hesitate to try recipes in the microwave. You can do (almost) anything: cakes, dishes with sauce, fish, poultry, vegetables and desserts. If you use the right containers, you'll no sooner have put the dish in the oven than the famous 'Ding' is telling you that it's time to sit down for dinner. And spatters are quicker and easier to clean up. (*See also* 'Timesaving recipes', starting on page 265.)

Getting the most from your microwave

▶ Let meat, poultry, fish and seafood sit for a few minutes out of the freezer before you defrost them in a microwave oven.

▶ Cover foods with a low water content with plastic wrap before you reheat, so they don't dry out. However, don't cover dishes with a high water content, such as soups and sauces, unless they are likely to spatter.

▶ When you reheat soup, fill the container to no more than two-thirds of its capacity, to avoid overspill on heating.

▶ Let your dish rest after you have removed it from the microwave. The internal temperature of food will continue to rise, allowing the cooking to be completed. For vegetables, wait 1 to 3 minutes; for meat, 15 minutes; and for cakes, 5 to 10 minutes.

▶ Put thicker pieces of food on the outside and the thinner ones towards the centre because cooking occurs from the outside inwards.

▶ Cut food into equal-sized pieces so it all cooks at the same rate.

(*See also* 'The microwave oven – a champion time saver' on page 18.)

Seasoning a wok

Season a new wok to prevent food from sticking. First wash it in soapy water, rinse thoroughly, then heat it. Rub all over the inside with a cooking oil and put it over high heat for a few minutes (the oil should smoke), tipping it this way and that to stop the oil from pooling. Remove it from the heat, cool a little and wipe out any excess oil with paper towels. Repeat the whole process twice more. When cleaning a wok, use hot water only – no detergent.

Full steam ahead!

▶ Enjoy carefree – and healthy – cooking using a metal steamer or bamboo steaming baskets. All you need to do is place the food into suitable containers on different levels above water that is constantly being heated.

▶ Not only will you save time – because the preparation and cooking are very fast – but you'll also have a tasty meal with very little fat.

Wok magic

If you don't yet own a wok, it's time to get one. It's the single most useful utensil for fast cooking. Even though it has been known for more than 2000 years in China, its uses are not limited to Asian cooking. A wok allows you to sauté, fry, stew and steam all sorts of dishes in just a few minutes.

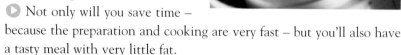

▶ You can cook all types of food – meat, vegetables, rice and noodles – quickly and at a high temperature, by moving them constantly from the centre to the edges. Then simply choose your own seasoning or add a sauce. (*See also* 'Timesaving recipes', starting on page 265.)

Become a barbecue king

Even on the smallest balcony there's room for a gas-fired barbecue. (Solid fuel ones are fine but there's a fair bit of waiting around for the coals to heat, so they're not really in the timesaving league.) A barbecue is fantastic for the quick cooking of all kinds of delicious and healthy food, and the bonus is that there are no pots and pans to wash.

▶ Pop a marinade – homemade or purchased – on meat or chicken in the morning and leave it in the fridge. By the time you get home, you'll have a fantastic meal ready to throw on the barbecue grill.

▶ Keep a selection of dry rubs and pastes for adding instant flavour to barbecued meat, chicken and fish.

▶ Add marinade to meat or chicken before you freeze it – by the time it has defrosted, it will be nicely marinated, too.

Slow and steady wins the race

If you never have time to cook casseroles or hearty soups, buy a slow cooker. You can organise it so that dinner's ready when you want it.

▶ Assemble all the ingredients in the slow cooker in the morning, turn it on and set the timer and when you get home from work you'll be greeted by the aroma of a perfectly cooked meal.

▶ This is a great option for families who arrive home at different times – a warm meal is always waiting – so you don't need to reheat food.

▶ Slow cookers are also fantastic tools for cooking delicious, creamy porridge overnight if anyone in the family prefers a hot breakfast.

One-pot wonders

▶ Simplify your life by using one pot to cook meals. You can brown meat and vegetables in the same heavy-based pan that you then use to finish cooking a casserole.

▶ Pasta can form the basis of delicious meals that are finished in the oven.

▶ Vegetables or meat can be added to rice dishes for a hearty meal cooked in a covered frying pan or a cast-iron casserole dish.

▶ Add lots of vegetables to casseroles. That way, all you need to complete the meal is crusty bread or perhaps a dollop of mashed potato.

TIMELY TIP

Use your loaf

Place a slice of bread in the drip pan when you're grilling sausages or fatty meat. The bread absorbs the fat, stops spatters and prevents the fat from catching fire.

Kitchen strategy

Develop good habits

Kitchen strategy involves some serious time saving. If you read this section and don't get at least some extra minutes out of it, you're not trying!

▶ Tidy and clean as you work – you'll maintain order in the kitchen and be organised in advance. Observe a few basic rules of hygiene: wash the sink, the work surface and utensils as soon as you have used them.

▶ Instead of piling the dishes up in the sink, put them into the dishwasher immediately after you have used them. And don't forget to turn it on as soon as it's full.

TIMELY TIP

Hold the cream and herbs
Avoid adding cream to dishes that
you're preparing to freeze: you get
a much nicer result if you add it
when reheating the dish. And for that
'just-cooked' taste, add fresh herbs
sparingly to a dish before freezing,
then scatter over a few teaspoons of
freshly chopped herbs when serving.

▶ If you don't have a dishwasher,
run a sink of hot, sudsy water
before you start cooking and wash
up as you go – when you have
finished cooking, the washing up
will be pretty well done, too.

▶ Peel vegetables over a paper
towel so you can quickly throw
the whole lot in the compost bin.

▶ Keep pets, purses, money and unpaid bills off the kitchen benchtop,
along with anything else that shouldn't be there. Not only does it add
clutter to your preparation area and make cleaning up a time-consuming
job, these things also leave germs behind, which is unhygienic.

▶ Put away all your parcels as soon as you come home from shopping
and throw away or recycle the empty containers immediately.

Variations on a theme

Prepare several variations on a theme using a single dish, all at the same
time. You can then serve one version that evening, and the other
versions on the following days, or later if you freeze them. It's a guaranteed time saver: less shopping, less tidying and more free time because
you'll only have to reheat dinner on consecutive nights.

▶ When you're preparing lasagne, which is made up of mince and
chopped onions, garlic and tomato – also part of the basic ingredients for
bolognaise sauce, cottage pie and chilli con carne – make four times the
quantity. Slice and fry the onions and garlic, brown the meat and add the
tomatoes. You can now finish each dish, or store the basic ingredients in
containers, ready to turn into whatever meal you want later on.

▶ Keep a recipe book with recipes filed by the main ingredient, say,
chicken thigh fillets, minced beef or diced lamb. You know you've got a
kilo of thigh fillets in the freezer, so what can you do with them? With
this system, the answer is at your fingertips…

(*See also* 'Timesaving recipes', starting on page 265.)

TIMELY TIP

Be prepared
Before you start following a recipe, read through it to
find out what is involved and whether you have the
skills to make it. If you do, get out all the necessary
ingredients and utensils and put them on the bench.
You'll now be able to cook without interruption.

TIMELY TIP

Daily bread

Recipes often call for fresh bread-crumbs rather than packaged ones. Simply cut the crusts from a couple of loaves of day-old crusty bread and process into crumbs in a food processor. Store the breadcrumbs in plastic containers in the freezer.

Think big when it comes to volume

If you think sufficiently big when you're cooking, you can freeze at least half of what you prepare and you'll save a lot of time.

▶ Aim to double, or better still triple or quadruple, ingredient quantities. It won't take you much more time, but you'll have one, two or three dishes that are ready in the freezer, which means that on at least this number of evenings you won't have to cook! This trick works with just about all types of dishes, from starters to desserts.

▶ If you make shortcrust pastry, biscuit dough or pizza dough, make two or three times the quantity and freeze the excess.

▶ Make double quantities of cakes and muffins – they freeze incredibly well and are perfect for including in children's lunch boxes.

▶ When making crepes, prepare a large batch and freeze what you don't eat in a stack, separated by baking paper circles.

▶ Instead of frying onions for particular meals, consider doing a large batch at a time and freezing it in recipe-sized portions.

▶ Just think, even by quadrupling only one dish once a week, you'll have up to 27 dishes in the freezer after 2 months!

Sauce without tears

▶ Whether you want to make sauces or thicken soups, choose cornflour as the thickening agent. It's the most reliable ingredient for trouble-free thickening and allows you to successfully make any sort of sauce in a few minutes – and with no lumps! Mix 1–5 teaspoons of cornflour (depending on the amount of sauce and the texture you're looking for) into a paste with a little water. Bring the sauce to the boil and stir in the cornflour mixture. Mix well and boil for 1 to 2 minutes… that's it!

Waste not, want not

▶ Get into the habit of thinking up meals for the next day or the following day using leftovers or extras from the meal you're preparing. All you have to do is increase the initial proportions and think of potential combinations to reuse one or more of the components.

▶ Think of making an omelette, a frittata or soup with leftover vegetables. Leftover boiled rice becomes the basis of fried rice, a rice piecrust, a rice salad or rice pudding; leftover meat can be added to a stir-fry, made into cottage pie or a ragout for pasta; make a delicious gratin with leftover pasta; use extra mashed potato in fish cakes or add chopped onion and parsley and fry into potato cakes.

(*See also* 'Timesaving recipes', starting on page 265.)

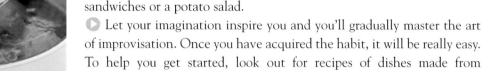When grilling or roasting chicken breasts or lamb fillets, cook a few more and use them in sandwiches the next day.

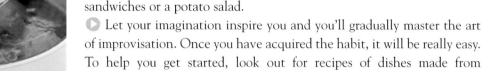Boil extra potatoes or pasta to use in potato or pasta salad.

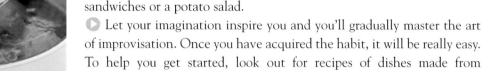When boiling eggs, cook a couple of extras to use in a tuna salad, sandwiches or a potato salad.

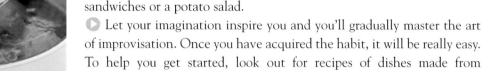Let your imagination inspire you and you'll gradually master the art of improvisation. Once you have acquired the habit, it will be really easy. To help you get started, look out for recipes of dishes made from leftovers, or just trust your instincts and invent something original. (*See also* 'Timesaving recipes', starting on page 265.)

Open a can of soup

With a can or two of soup in the pantry, you can never say that the cupboard is bare. Indeed, you can heat it up and eat it immediately, but with a little imagination, you can also use canned soup as the magic ingredient in a meal that will feed the whole family in no time.

Add some chopped cooked chicken, a fillet of frozen fish, a handful of frozen prawns or some frozen vegetables to a can of soup and you'll have a tasty dish with sauce, or a substantial main-meal soup in a flash.

Read the labels on your favourite brand of canned soup – they often have practical and easy recipe ideas for quick meals. (*See also* 'Timesaving recipes', starting on page 265.)

Cook once a month

Adopt the 'once-a-month' method, which has become increasingly popular in the US. (Type 'Once A Month Cooking' or 'OAMC' into your computer's search engine and prepare to be amazed!) This means you do all your cooking for a whole month in one single day. You need to be extremely organised and able to devote a whole day to shopping, then a whole day to cooking – but if that sounds like you, give it a go!

TIMELY TIP

Ready to eat

Use cooked dishes or ready-made foods as the basis of a super-quick meal. There are more and more ready-to-eat products available that can be eaten just as they are, or used to make other dishes and save a considerable amount of preparation time. This can be a real godsend on days when you just don't have time to make anything.

TIMELY TIP

Quick calculation

When you freeze food, write the use-by date, not the date you freeze it, on the packaging. This way you'll avoid wasting time standing over the freezer trying to calculate when each food needs to be consumed.

To start out with this method, you firstly need to draw up menus and do all the shopping in sufficient quantities. You also need to make room in your freezer to store everything.

If this all sounds a little daunting, then proceed in stages: firstly plan and cook your menus for 2 weeks, for example. Once you have mastered this without too many problems, you can move on to the next level. The results speak for themselves – you'll have a whole month up your sleeve where you won't have to think about what to make for dinner.

Indispensable cooking tips

To reduce the risk of fat splashing when you cook, put a little salt in your frying pan first. Similarly, always use a mixture of butter and oil instead of simply one or the other. It's also useful to know that margarine burns more slowly than butter, but if you prefer the taste of butter in your cooking, then try using ghee or clarified butter, because neither of them burns as readily as butter does.

Get into the habit of covering your saucepans and frying pans. Trapping the steam inside the saucepan means you keep in the taste as well as the nutrients, and it also speeds up the cooking process. Similarly, choose saucepans and frying pans that are large enough. The steam will be able to circulate more rapidly and the food will cook more quickly.

Don't burn yourself trying to remove whole herbs and spices from cooked dishes before serving. All you need to do is put cloves or peppercorns in a wire mesh tea infuser and drop it into the cooking liquid and remove it with a slotted spoon before serving the dish, or tie all the elements of a bouquet garni (the green part of the leek, parsley stalks, thyme, bay leaf and celery leaves) with string, leaving a tail for fishing it out.

Where possible, cook on a medium heat rather than on a strong heat. There'll be fewer splashes and less risk of the food burning or sticking, which means less cleaning time for you.

TIMELY TIP

Put a hole in mince

To make a mince patty cook faster, make a small hole in the middle before putting it in the frying pan. The hole disappears during cooking.

Fruit and vegetables – the secrets of fast cooking

● **Potatoes** They won't burst if you salt the water they are cooked in. The skin is easy to remove if you peel them after they're cooked. Choose new potatoes when they are in season and you won't have to peel them at all. To give mashed potato a quick lift, add a pinch of grated nutmeg and a pinch of baking powder.

● **Garlic** Cloves of garlic can be easily peeled if you place them in the microwave oven for 15 seconds. Avoid frying garlic at a temperature that's too high, otherwise it will become scorched and bitter.

● **Onions** To avoid tears, peel them under cold water and cut them next to cold running water. You can also put them in the freezer for a few moments before cutting them. To make onions brown faster, without burning, sprinkle them with sugar.

● **Green beans** Boil them for 2 minutes before peeling them and the strings will come off instantly.

● **Capsicums** To remove the skin, cook them under a hot grill until they go brown, then put them in a closed plastic or paper bag and allow to cool – the skin will simply pull away.

● **Tomatoes** To remove the skin quickly and easily, stand them in boiling water for a few seconds.

● **Lemon or orange juice** Heat lemons and oranges in a microwave oven for 15 seconds before squeezing and you'll extract more juice.

● **Oranges and grapefruits** If you soak these citrus fruits for at least 5 minutes in boiling water, the skin and the white pith can be removed much more easily.

TIMELY TIP

Remove scales in seconds
To stop fish scales flying everywhere while you're removing them, hold the fish under water. Use a knife, or even an empty scallop shell, to remove the scales by brushing over them, working against the grain.

Fish on the fly

Everyone should try to add more fish to their diet – cooking fish is quicker than meat or chicken and it's also full of omega-3 fatty acids, which are essential for a healthy heart and blood vessels.

▷ Use fillets or cutlets as often as possible for fast preparation: you don't need to remove scales or many bones.

▷ Pan-fried, stir-fried, grilled, baked or barbecued – fish lends itself to all manner of quick-and-easy cooking methods. Just choose your favourite recipe and dinner can be on the table in 15 minutes.

▶ Try cooking fish in a parcel – what the French call en papillote. It's one of the fastest, healthiest cooking methods and the result is always moist and delicious. Put your fish fillets on a square of baking paper or aluminium foil, add a few herbs and some lemon juice, and perhaps some thinly sliced vegetables. Fold the packet closed and place it in an oven-proof dish. In the time it takes to cook the rice to serve with it, your fish will be ready. Another advantage is that you can make individual papillotes, so each person can choose their own ingredients and seasoning, and the clean up is ridiculously fast and easy.

(*See also* 'Timesaving recipes', starting on page 265.)

Quick cuts for meat

▶ Choose cuts of meat that cook quickly – usually those that you cook in the frying pan, under the griller, in the wok or on the barbecue – so as not to waste time.

▶ Beef offers a huge range of choices, from skirt, rump and roast beef to fillet, sirloin, topside and mince.

▶ When you're cooking with veal, the best choices are escalopes or chops, depending on the recipe.

▶ With lamb, choose leg slices for fast grilling, or fillet, backstrap or chops, which are also good cuts.

▶ When it comes to cuts of pork, choose chops (fillet, loin), or cut a fillet into strips for a super-quick stir-fry.

TIMELY TIP

On the bone

When choosing a family-sized roast, remember that it will cook faster if the bone hasn't been removed, because the bone carries heat to the centre of the joint.

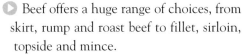

TIMELY TIP

Love me tender

The tender, choice cuts of meat are the quick-cooking ones. They are generally more expensive, but there is very little waste and if your priority is to save time, then these are the ones to choose.

Soup of the day

Turn soup into a main course simply by adding 'extras' to make it more substantial.

▶ Make your basic soup using the classic method, or start with a can or packet of soup or perhaps frozen soup, before adding to it.

▶ One of the quickest soups you can make is with a packet of frozen vegetables (peas, cauliflower, broccoli, etc.) in a cup or two of stock with a peeled, chopped potato. Puree with a hand-held blender, add milk or cream, salt and pepper, and perhaps a tablespoon or two of chopped fresh herbs. Serve with crusty bread – easy and delicious.

▶ Add your personal touch, that little 'extra' that will transform your soup and make it heartier: meatballs, chopped ham, frozen prawns or fish, vegetables, chopped cooked chicken, pasta and won tons, etc.

▶ Serve soup with toast or garlic bread, or reheat frozen rolls, savoury muffins and Turkish bread, etc.

▶ Add dumplings to a soup, or a handful of fried bread croutons.
(*See also* 'Timesaving recipes', starting on page 265.)

TIMELY TIP

Gourmet soup

Toast some slices of bread, place them in the bottom of a soup tureen and pour French onion soup (made according to packet directions) on top. Sprinkle with grated cheese and brown it under the griller or in the oven for 15 to 20 minutes. (French onion soup tastes even better if you stir in 2 egg yolks mixed with a small glass of port.)

A sparkling clean blender

To quickly clean the bowl of your blender, half fill it with hot water. Add a few drops of dishwashing liquid, close it and turn it on until it is clean.

TIMELY TIP

Gourmet express

Main meal salads

Take a quick look in your pantry, fridge and vegetable basket. You're more than likely to find enough ingredients to make a good salad.

▶ To make a full meal, all you need to do is use a carbohydrate (pasta, rice, potatoes, couscous and canned beans, etc.) and/or a basic protein (meat, fish, cheese or tofu, for example), then complement these with anything that can add flavour and colour. An appropriate dressing, some nice bread and dinner is ready!

1001 quick salads

● **Pasta salads** Tortellini, shells, farfalle, penne, fusilli… Any short pasta where the shape catches the sauce or the dressing is particularly suitable for making salads. You can add anything you like – especially what you have on hand: corn, peas, chopped tomato, ham, cheese, chicken, capsicum, tuna, anchovies, olives, capers, smoked salmon, cucumber, prawns, nuts, spring onions, artichoke hearts, marinated vegetables and hard boiled eggs, etc.

● **Rice salads** We often cook too much rice, but that can be good because it allows you to make a salad the next day. As with pasta, just about everything goes with rice. Of course, there are the classics: hard-boiled eggs, green beans, tuna, ham, tomatoes and capsicum, etc., but don't forget the little extras that can be a welcome surprise, such as sultanas, pine nuts, walnuts, sun-dried tomatoes, celery, pineapple and mango, etc. The choice is endless.

● **Warm salads** Start by lining the plate with green leaves (spinach, lettuce and rocket, for example), then scatter some fresh ingredients (tomatoes, capsicums, avocado, orange or grapefruit segments, mushroom and radish, etc.), before finishing with the hot ingredient: goat's cheese on mini toasts, strips of chicken, meat or turkey fillets sautéed in a pan, poached egg, bacon pieces, fried fish, chicken livers, grilled haloumi, and barbecued prawns or squid, etc. Delicious!

● **Salads on a theme** From the sea (prawns, sashimi, crab, smoked salmon or trout, lumpfish roe); Mexican (red beans, capsicums, guacamole, grated cheese, tomatoes, corn and grilled chicken); Greek (feta, black olives, cucumber, tomatoes, stuffed vine leaves and hummus); Asian (bean shoots, Chinese noodles, chicken, spring rolls, sesame seeds, ginger and coriander); Niçoise (tuna, cherry tomatoes, green beans, hard-boiled eggs, anchovies, potatoes and basil). Use your imagination – the sky's the limit.

No-fuss, tasty salad dressings

▶ To make honey dressing, simply mix together dijon mustard, white wine vinegar, olive oil, honey, salt and pepper.

▶ To make thousand island dressing, mix together mayonnaise, tomato sauce, sugar and garlic in a medium bowl.

▶ A simple Indian dressing is made up of curry paste or powder, plain yogurt, lemon juice and fresh coriander all combined together.

▶ Blue cheese dressing is a mixture of soft blue cheese (such as Castello, available from most supermarkets), sour cream and a dash of cognac.

▶ Make a tangy soy dressing by combining soy sauce, lemon juice, sesame oil and brown sugar together. It makes a great marinade, too.

TIMELY TIP

Pasta – fast!

If you salt the water just when it starts to boil, the pasta will cook more quickly. To avoid the water overflowing and dirtying your stove, rub vegetable oil on the rim of the saucepan before putting it onto the heat. You'll save time on the clean-up.

▶ Creamy herb dressing combines crème fraîche (or light sour cream) with lemon juice, chopped herbs (frozen) and salt and pepper.

▶ Make Russian dressing with light sour cream mixed with mayonnaise, diced beetroot, diced dill pickles, garlic and salt and pepper.

▶ A simple cream dressing is made up of pouring cream, lemon juice, mustard, salt and a pinch of sugar.

▶ Make a spicy dressing using mayonnaise, lemon juice, tomato sauce, Tabasco sauce, worcestershire sauce and salt and pepper.

A reliable staple

Pasta is one of the great fast foods. Most people like it, there are endless variations and it takes very little time to prepare, especially fresh pasta.

▶ Prepare a pasta dish using one of the many ready-made sauces available, such as classic bolognaise sauce or pesto.

▶ Use what's in your pantry, along with your imagination, for creating something more original – a tin of tuna, smoked salmon, chorizo, prawns, ham, eggs, cheese, capers, chopped vegetables, breadcrumbs, artichokes and anchovies… the list goes on.

▶ When the pantry is almost bare, you can add garlic, chilli flakes, flaked parmesan, parsley and olive oil to cooked pasta for a satisfying – and very traditionally Italian – quick dinner.

▶ Don't use two saucepans. Tip ingredients that don't need separate cooking onto the drained pasta, mix together and dinner's ready!

(*See also* 'Timesaving recipes', starting on page 265.)

Express desserts

A good dessert will satisfy everyone, young and old. But there's no need to spend hours in the kitchen to achieve impressive results.

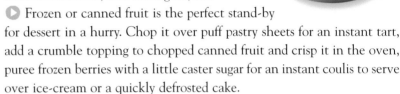

▶ Keep several different flavours of ice-cream and sorbet in the freezer. You can serve them in individual dishes and decorate them with whatever you have in store: cream, biscotti or wafers, nuts, fruit coulis, fresh fruit or fruit in syrup, caramel, grated or melted chocolate, and meringues, etc.

▶ Frozen or canned fruit is the perfect stand-by for dessert in a hurry. Chop it over puff pastry sheets for an instant tart, add a crumble topping to chopped canned fruit and crisp it in the oven, puree frozen berries with a little caster sugar for an instant coulis to serve over ice-cream or a quickly defrosted cake.

▶ Keep a packet of bought meringue nests handy – top with whipped cream and fruit for instant mini pavlovas.

▶ Impress your guests by placing scoops of assorted flavours of good-quality ice-cream in a large clear glass dish or a pretty salad bowl. Decorate the ice-cream with slivered almonds or hazelnuts, choc chips, crushed pistachio nuts or liqueur, etc.

(*See also* 'Timesaving recipes', starting on page 265.)

TIMELY TIP

Super fast, super easy
For a super-fast and delicious children's dessert, simply scrape either frozen yogurt or ice-cream between two peanut-butter flavoured or oatmeal biscuits. Hey presto! You've got an ice-cream sandwich.

Dessert tricks

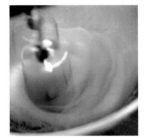

▶ Fruit tarts are fast and easy to make. Put ready-rolled shortcrust pastry into a buttered tart dish, prick the bottom with a fork and put it in the oven at 180°C. When the base of the tart is cooked, take it out of the oven and allow it to cool. Spread a layer of crème patissière, thick shop-bought custard or sweetened mascarpone on the bottom, then add the fruit of your choice, either fresh or drained from syrup.

▶ Eggwhites at room temperature (or that have been in the microwave oven for a few seconds) and that are sprinkled with a pinch of salt are easier to beat until soft peaks form.

▶ Use thickened cream, or very cold pouring cream, for whipping.

▶ Removing cakes and desserts from the tin without sticking is easily done if you sprinkle the baking tin with breadcrumbs or flour (or cocoa for chocolate cakes) after greasing it. Tip 2–3 tablespoons of bread-crumbs into the tin and turn until all the surfaces are covered. Gently tap out the excess breadcrumbs.

Useful facts and FAQs

Keeping it simple

Knowing that 1 metric cup is equal to 250 ml is not time saving in itself, but to know that fact when you're in the middle of a recipe can save a great deal of time wasting. In this section, you'll find all sorts of useful facts and figures in the one spot, so you'll always know where to look when you've got a query.

▶ Don't waste time calculating proportions that are absolutely exact. Trust yourself a little. You can rest assured that 10 grams or a few millilitres more or less won't make any difference to the way your recipe turns out.

Help! What do I do now?

Sometimes unexpected things happen in the kitchen and you panic. But before you throw everything out and start again, find out if there is something you can do to save the situation.

▶ If you've added too much salt – to the sauce, soup or water for cooking – simply double the quantity and don't add any more salt. Or while it's cooking, add a raw potato, that has been cut into large pieces, for 5 to 10 minutes to absorb the excess salt. As a last resort, try adding a little sugar to cancel out the salty taste.

▶ If your soup or sauce has become too fatty, add a few ice cubes and stir them so that the fat adheres to the ice. Pick them out again before they melt. During cooking, you can also place a lettuce leaf on the top of the soup and remove it when it's covered in fat.

▶ Tear a paper towel into strips and drag the strips across the top of a soup or sauce, one at a time, to absorb fat floating on the surface.

▶ It often happens that an egg cracks during cooking, but it can be avoided by placing a steel spoon in the water or by adding a pinch of cooking salt. If it has already happened, quickly pour a little vinegar into the water: this will make the white coagulate.

▶ To save a stew or a ratatouille, or any other dish of the same type that has burned, the best thing to do is to quickly transfer the mixture into another saucepan, without scraping or even touching the bottom. If necessary, add a little water and continue cooking, and keep an eye on it so that it doesn't burn the second time around.

▶ Got a bechamel sauce that's being difficult? To make it smooth, stir it with a fork that has a piece of raw potato on the end of it. If you aren't

TIMELY TIP

A flakey fix-it job

If you've added too much milk to your mashed potatoes and they've become runny or soggy, just add a few potato flakes or a little powdered milk. They'll come good again in no time.

entirely happy with the result, put the mixture into an empty bottle and shake well. (The easiest way to obtain a creamy sauce on the first attempt is to blend all the cold ingredients together in a blender before heating them gently. For a roux, always mix the flour with cold water.)

▶ If your mayonnaise has curdled or won't thicken, put another egg yolk in a different bowl, then gradually start adding the curdled mixture, a little at a time, beating vigorously after every addition.

▶ When pasta is sticking together, plunge it into hot water to unstick it instead of drowning it in oil. Or take 3 tablespoons of the cooking water and tip this into the dish.

▶ If you have tossed a salad and the dressing has too much vinegar in it, remove the crusts from some bread and allow the bread to absorb all the dressing. Then discard the bread and make a new dressing.

On-the-spot recipe replacements

When you're in the middle of a recipe and you realise you don't have an essential ingredient, don't waste time running to the supermarket or the corner shop. Try these little tricks.

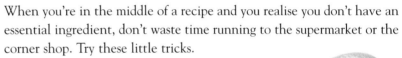

▶ Replace vinegar with lemon juice, and vice versa.

▶ If you've run out of ground coffee, try adding a small stick of cinnamon to instant coffee. You won't even notice the difference. The same trick can be used with ground coffee to enhance its flavour.

▶ When you're out of cooking wine, use 100 ml of white wine vinegar mixed with the same quantity of water, and add 2 teaspoons of sugar. Or try to replace part of the white wine with another alcohol – tequila, white vermouth, dry sherry, etc. – and the rest with stock.

▶ If you're out of red wine, replace part of the red wine volume with another alcohol – rosé, port, red vermouth – and the rest with stock.

What to do when ingredients look worn out

Do the products that you need right away have a sad and sorry look? This is how you can give them another chance in just a few seconds.

▶ If biscuits or crackers are soft, cover them with a sheet of paper towel and put them in the microwave for 1 minute.

▶ When sliced ham dries out, soak the slices in milk to soften them.

▶ If your butter seems a bit rancid or you're not sure if it's rancid, simply insert a piece of carrot in it for 1 or 2 hours: it should lose its unpleasant taste. If that doesn't work and you're short of butter, beat some thick cream in the blender with a few ice cubes. Pour off the liquid, leaving butter that you can use for most of your cooking needs.

There's nothing worse than floppy salad, but vegetables and lettuce will revive if you soak them in water mixed with vinegar (1 tablespoon of vinegar to 2 cups of water).

If the edges of some lettuce leaves you were planning to use are starting to go brown, the lettuce is no longer good enough to be served fresh. Instead, cook it as you would a vegetable, by stir-frying it quickly in a pan with a little garlic, olive oil and salt.

When bread is stale, moisten it lightly with water or milk and put it in a hot oven (not a microwave oven) for around 10 minutes.

Handy stand-by solutions

A lid that's stuck, a utensil that has disappeared… You can waste plenty of time sorting out those sorts of issues in the kitchen almost every day of the week. Instead, stay cool and try these easy hints.

If tapping firmly on the bottom of the jar with the palm of your hand hasn't worked to open the lid, put on your rubber gloves. This will definitely give you a better grip.

To release two glasses or bowls that have become stuck together, put ice cubes in the inside glass and put the outside glass into hot water. You should be able to separate them without any problem.

Who needs a nutcracker? Believe it or not, the hinges on your door can be used to crack open nuts. But be careful with your fingers and don't encourage children to do this job for you!

Simple measures

If a recipe calls for 210 g of sugar and you have nothing to measure it, don't panic. It's very simple – 210 g of sugar equals 1 metric cup. One metric cup is approximately equal to 2 small coffee cups or 1 normal teacup or medium-sized coffee mug, but check first. Always use one set of measures in a recipe.

1 cup granulated sugar	210 g	1 cup mixed dried fruit (or sultanas)	175 g
1 cup caster sugar	200 g	1 cup chopped nuts	130 g
1 cup firmly packed soft brown sugar	230 g	1 cup desiccated coconut	75 g
1 cup icing sugar, sifted	140 g	1 cup finely grated parmesan	80 g
1 cup flour	140 g	1 cup cocoa powder	140 g
1 cup rice, uncooked	200 g	1 cup basil leaves	40 g
1 cup rice, cooked	185 g	1 cup flat-leaf parsley leaves	40 g
1 cup dried breadcrumbs	125 g	1 cup cooked, shredded chicken	135 g
1 cup fresh breadcrumbs	60 g	And also:	
1 cup crushed biscuit crumbs	125 g	1 medium wine glass	200 ml
1 cup honey, golden syrup or treacle	350 g	1 cereal bowl	300 ml (1¼ cups)

Oven temperatures

Occasionally, you might find yourself consulting recipes that use a different temperature system to  the one you're used to. Keep this table close to hand – photocopy it and stick it inside a kitchen cupboard door or on a pin board – for all the conversions you might need to make.

	°C (Celsius)	°F (Fahrenheit)	Gas mark
Very slow	120	250	½
Slow	150	275–300	1–2
Moderately slow	170	325	3
Moderate	180	350–375	4–5
Moderately hot	200	400	6
Hot	220	425–450	7–8
Very hot	240	475	9

Dry weights

These imperial measurements are approximate and have been rounded for quick-and-easy reference. For example, 250 g actually equals 8¾ oz. In cases where this is likely to be critical, you need to convert more accurately.

Metric	Imperial	Metric	Imperial
15 g	½ oz	220 g	7 oz
30 g	1 oz	250 g	8 oz (½ lb)
60 g	2 oz	280 g	9 oz
90 g	3 oz	315 g	10 oz
125 g	4 oz (¼ lb)	345 g	11 oz
155 g	5 oz	375 g	12 oz (¾ lb)
185 g	6 oz	410 g	13 oz
		440 g	14 oz
		470 g	15 oz
		500 g	16 oz (1 lb)
		750 g	24 oz (1½ lb)
		1 kg	32 oz (2 lb)

Liquid measures

Don't be put off by recipes from the Internet if they use imperial or US measures. This guide helps you to quickly convert them into metric units.

Metric	Imperial	US measures
15 ml	½ fluid oz	1 tablespoon
30 ml	1 fluid oz	2 tablespoons
60 ml	2 fluid oz	¼ cup
100 ml	3 fluid oz	–
125 ml	4 fluid oz	½ cup (¼ pint)
150 ml	5 fluid oz (¼ pint)	⅔ cup
175 ml	6 fluid oz	¾ cup
250 ml	8 fluid oz	1 cup (½ pint)
300 ml	10 fluid oz (½ pint)	1¼ cups
375 ml	12 fluid oz	1½ cups
500 ml	16 fluid oz	2 cups (1 pint)
600 ml	20 fluid oz (1 pint)	2½ cups
1 litre	32 fluid oz	2 pints (1 quart)
1.25 litres	2 pints	2½ pints

Cake tin and spoon sizes

The size of cake tins varies enormously, along with the choice of non-stick, springform, loaf tins and those with holes in the middle, etc. The list goes on…

Metric	Imperial
12.5 cm	5 inches
20 cm	8 inches
22.5 cm	9 inches
24 cm	9½ inches
25 cm	10 inches
26 cm	10½ inches
28 cm	11 inches
30 cm	12 inches

1 teaspoon	5 ml
1 dessertspoon	10 ml (2 teaspoons)
1 tablespoon	20 ml (Aust) or 15 ml (NZ, SA, US, UK)

A stick of butter (US) = 4 oz (¼ lb) = 125 g

Glossary of cooking terms

Here is a brief definition of the terms you might meet as you use your recipe books or the recipes starting on page 266.

Bain-marie An indirect cooking method where one dish is placed into another larger cooking vessel containing boiling water, then cooked gently.

Bake blind To bake an empty flan or pie shell, completely or partially, before filling is added. To prevent the pastry from puffing up, the base is lined with baking paper and weighted with uncooked rice or dried beans. Remove the paper and beans halfway through the cooking process.

Blanch To plunge vegetables briefly into a large amount of simmering salted water, before removing them, and cooling quickly under running cold water. They should remain crisp.

Brine Salted water with aromatic herbs used to marinate meat, fish or vegetables.

Brown To colour food on the outside by frying to seal in the flavour and make it slightly crunchy.

Bruise To crush food (such as spices, citrus skin, garlic) lightly with a knife, rolling pin or mortar and pestle, to release the flavour.

Clarified butter Also known as ghee, this is butter with the whey and milk solids removed, allowing it to reach higher temperatures without burning.

Cook until transparent To cook something, especially onions, in butter or oil, until it becomes translucent and a light golden colour.

Coulis A thick sauce created by pureeing food, such as fresh fruit.

Cream To beat sugar and butter together until the mixture becomes pale and fluffy.

Crumb To coat food with plain flour, beaten egg and breadcrumbs before cooking it.

Decant To gently transfer a liquid from one container to another so that the sediment remains in the bottom of the container.

Deglaze To dissolve the juices that have caramelised in the bottom of a pan using liquid (wine, water or stock).

Degrease To remove the fat on the surface of a liquid, such as a sauce or stock. This can be done by using a small ladle or a skimmer or cooling the liquid and allowing the fat to solidify.

De-vein To remove the central digestive tract of prawns and other crustaceans either before or after they are cooked.

Dust To cover a cake or dessert with a finely sieved coating of icing sugar or cocoa.

Flame To pour alcohol over a dish just as you serve it, and lighting it so the alcohol burns off.

Fold To combine ingredients together very lightly and gently so that the air is not beaten out of the mixture.

Glaze To cook food with water, sugar and butter to make it shiny.

Infuse To steep ingredients in a liquid to flavour them.

Julienne Vegetables cut into very thin strips.

Macerate To soak fruits in a liquid (alcohol or wine) so that they become plumped and permeated with the liquid.

Marinate To soak food in an aromatic mixture of spices and/or liquid (a marinade) to flavour, and sometimes to soften, it.

Poach To cook food in simmering liquid (at a temperature slightly lower than boiling point).

Reduce To reduce a quantity of liquid by evaporation to make the flavours more concentrated or the sauce thicker.

Scald To heat a liquid just to boiling point.

Seal To cook meat in very hot fat, so that it browns on the outside and seals in the juices.

Season To add salt and pepper to a dish. To prepare the surface of a new wok for cooking.

Shell To remove the husk of walnuts, hazelnuts, almonds and so on, or to remove the shell from hard-boiled eggs. To remove the pod from peas, broad beans or green beans.

Simmer To cook gently at a barely moving boil.

Skim To remove the foam on the surface of a liquid using a skimmer.

Slash To make shallow incisions in the surface of fish or meat to facilitate even cooking.

Steam Cooking method consisting of suspending food in a basket or steamer over, but not touching, boiling water.

Sweat To cook food very slowly in butter or oil in a covered pan, to soften it without colouring it.

Truss To tie a chicken or other bird into a neat shape for cooking.

Zest To remove the zest (the coloured skin section only) of a lemon or orange using a potato peeler or a zester.

Recipe index

Timesaving recipes

Baked risotto

SERVES 4–6 • PT 5 MINS • CT 40 MINS

3 tablespoons butter

1 medium onion, finely chopped

3 cups (about 250 g) sliced mixed mushrooms

2 cups (400 g) risotto rice (arborio or carnaroli)

5 cups (1.25 litres) vegetable stock

¼ cup (60 ml) white wine

½ cup (40 g) finely grated parmesan

150 g baby spinach leaves

2 tablespoons chopped fresh thyme leaves or parsley

salt and freshly ground black pepper

extra parmesan, to serve

● Preheat oven to 180°C.

● Melt butter in a heavy-based casserole dish and cook onion until soft. Add mushrooms and fry for a few seconds, then add rice and stir for 1 minute. Add wine and stock and bring to the boil.

● Cover tightly with a lid and place in the oven for 15 minutes. Remove from the oven and stir, then return to the oven for a further 15 minutes. By this time the rice should be cooked and all the liquid absorbed – if not, return the dish to the oven without the lid for a further 5 minutes.

● Remove and stir in spinach, parmesan, thyme and salt and pepper to taste. Serve with extra parmesan, if desired.

Beef with noodles

SERVES 4 • PT 15 MINS • CT 15 MINS

5 tablespoons dark soy sauce

2 cloves garlic, crushed

1 tablespoon cornflour

1 teaspoon prepared wasabi paste

500 g lean sirloin steak, cut into strips

300 g soba (Japanese buckwheat) noodles

2 tablespoons sunflower oil

1 large red capsicum, seeded and thinly sliced

1 bunch spring onions, sliced diagonally into medium lengths

125 g shiitake mushrooms, sliced

3 cups (750 ml) dashi stock, made with dashi powder

1 sheet nori (Japanese seaweed), cut into thin strips

3 tablespoons chopped fresh coriander

● Mix together 3 tablespoons of the soy sauce, garlic, cornflour and wasabi in a medium-sized bowl. Add the beef and stir until well combined. Set aside.

● Bring a saucepan of water to the boil, add the noodles and cook for 5 minutes or according to packet instructions.

● Meanwhile, heat a wok until very hot, add half the oil and swirl to coat the wok. Toss in capsicum, spring onions and mushrooms and stir-fry for 4 minutes or until softened. Remove from wok with a slotted spoon. Drain noodles and set aside.

● Heat remaining oil in the wok, add beef and stir-fry for about 4 minutes or until just tender. Remove with a slotted spoon.

● Pour remaining soy sauce and stock into the wok, add noodles and vegetables with the nori and coriander. Toss well, then add the beef and toss again. Pile the noodles, vegetables and beef into bowls and spoon over the broth. Serve immediately.

Bolognaise sauce

SERVES 4 • PT 10 MINS • CT 35 MINS

1 tablespoon olive oil

1 large onion, finely chopped

2 cloves garlic, crushed

500 g beef mince

3 tablespoons tomato paste

2 cans (400 g each) diced tomatoes

½ cup (125 ml) dry red wine

½ cup (125 ml) beef stock

1 teaspoon dried oregano

1 teaspoon dried basil

1 teaspoon sugar

salt and freshly ground black pepper

● Heat oil in a large, heavy-based saucepan and cook onion and garlic until onion softens. Add the mince and cook until brown, breaking up any lumps with a spoon.

● Add tomato paste, diced tomatoes, wine, stock, oregano, basil and sugar, then stir well. Bring to the boil, lower heat and simmer, covered, for 30 minutes. Season to taste with salt and pepper. Serve with spaghetti.

TIP This sauce tastes even better if you cook it gently, covered, for 2 hours.

Bucatini all'amatriciana

SERVES 4 • PT 5 MINS • CT 20 MINS

400–500 g bucatini or spaghetti

1 tablespoon olive oil

1 medium onion, chopped

2 cloves garlic, crushed

½ teaspoon dried chilli flakes

200 g pancetta, or streaky bacon, coarsely chopped

1 can (400 g) diced tomatoes

1 cup (250 ml) red wine

freshly ground black pepper

grated parmesan, to serve

- Bring a large pan of salted water to the boil and add pasta. Cook for 12 minutes or until al dente. Drain.
- Meanwhile, heat oil in a heavy-based pan and fry onion until softened. Add garlic, chilli and pancetta and cook for a further 5 minutes.
- Add tomatoes and wine and cook uncovered for 10 minutes until sauce is thickened and reduced. Toss sauce through pasta, season with pepper and serve with grated parmesan.

Caramelised fruit

SERVES 4 • PT 5 MINS • CT 5 TO 10 MINS

2 tablespoons unsalted butter
2 tablespoons caster sugar
500 g sliced fresh fruit (strawberries, banana, blueberries, peaches, etc.)
1 tablespoon fruit liqueur

- Melt butter in a heavy-based frying pan, add sugar and stir until melted. Add fruit and liqueur and cook over moderate heat, basting with the sauce, until the fruit is warmed through and the sugar syrup is slightly caramelised.

Chakchouka

SERVES 4 • PT 5 MINS • CT 20 MINS

2 tablespoons olive oil
1 medium onion, chopped
2 cloves garlic, crushed
1 large red capsicum, seeded and thinly sliced
1 large green capsicum, seeded and thinly sliced
1 small red chilli, finely chopped
3 medium (about 450 g) large ripe tomatoes, coarsely chopped (or 1 x 400-g can diced tomatoes)
2 tablespoons tomato paste
1 teaspoon ground cumin
1 teaspoon sweet or smoked paprika
1 teaspoon salt
pinch of sugar
4 medium eggs
chopped fresh parsley, to serve

- Heat the oil in a deep, heavy-based frying pan and fry onion, garlic, capsicum and chilli gently for about 5 minutes or until softened.
- Add tomatoes, tomato paste, cumin, paprika, salt and sugar, mix well and simmer gently, uncovered, for about 10 minutes, or until thickened.
- Make four indentations in the mixture with the back of a spoon and break one egg into each hollow. Cover the pan again and simmer for 5 minutes, or until the eggs are just set.
- Sprinkle with parsley and serve immediately, straight from the pan.
TIP Add chopped ham or leftover vegetables to the basic sauce.

Cheat's roast chicken

SERVES 4 • PT 5 MINS • CT 30 MINS

4 (about 1.75 kg) chicken maryland pieces
2 cloves garlic, crushed
1 medium onion, finely chopped
1¼ cups (300 ml) chicken stock
½ cup (125 ml) dry white wine
olive oil spray
2 tablespoons butter
1 tablespoon plain flour
chopped fresh thyme or tarragon, optional

- Preheat oven to 240°C.
- Arrange the chicken pieces, skin-side down, in a large microwave-safe dish. Add garlic and onion, and pour over stock and wine. Cover dish and microwave on *High* for 10 minutes.
- Remove chicken from pan and reserve juices. Arrange chicken skin-side up in a non-stick baking dish, spray lightly with oil and roast in oven for about 15 to 20 minutes, or until browned and cooked.
- Meanwhile, melt butter in a small saucepan, add flour and cook for a minute, stirring constantly. Gradually add reserved pan juices, stirring until mixture boils and thickens. Stir in herbs, if using, and pour over roast chicken. Serve with roast potatoes and steamed green vegetables.

Cheesy potato gratin

SERVES 4 • PT 10 MINS • CT 55 MINS

4–5 medium potatoes (about 750 g), peeled and cut into medium slices
1 cup (120 g) grated tasty cheese
1 can (420 g) cream of mushroom soup
½ teaspoon paprika
½ teaspoon freshly ground black pepper

- Preheat oven to 200°C.
- Grease a shallow ovenproof dish and arrange the potatoes in overlapping rows. Sprinkle with the tasty cheese.
- Combine soup, paprika and pepper and pour over potatoes. Cover dish with aluminium foil and bake for 45 minutes. Remove foil and bake for a further 10 minutes or until top is bubbling and golden.

Cherry clafoutis

SERVES 4 • PT 10 MINS • CT 25 MINS

1 can (425 g) pitted cherries in syrup, drained thoroughly
2 tablespoons brandy
½ cup (70 g) plain flour
⅓ cup (55 g) light muscovado sugar, or soft brown sugar
1 cup (250 ml) milk
3 medium eggs
1 teaspoon vanilla extract
icing sugar, to dust

- Preheat oven to 200°C.
- Spread cherries in a 25-cm round china flan dish. Sprinkle over brandy and set aside.
- Sift the flour into a bowl and add the sugar. In a jug, beat the milk and eggs with vanilla, then whisk into the flour mixture to make a smooth batter. (Alternatively, combine everything in a food processor and process until smooth.)
- Pour the batter slowly over the fruit. Bake for 20 to 25 minutes or until lightly set and pale golden. Dust with icing sugar and serve warm with cream.

Chicken and corn soup
Serves 4 • PT **5** mins • CT **15** mins

2 teaspoons vegetable oil
1 teaspoon sesame oil
1 medium onion, chopped
1 clove garlic, crushed
2 teaspoons grated fresh ginger
1 skinless chicken breast fillet (about
   340 g), finely diced
1 can (310 g) creamed corn
1 can (420 g) cream of chicken soup
1 tablespoon soy sauce
1 cup (250 ml) chicken stock
1 medium egg, beaten lightly
3 tablespoons chopped fresh coriander
   leaves
3 spring onions, chopped

• Heat oils in a heavy-based saucepan and fry onion, garlic and ginger for about 5 minutes or until onion is softened. Add chopped chicken, creamed corn, soup, soy sauce and stock. Bring to the boil, then simmer, uncovered, about 5 minutes or until chicken is cooked.
• Quickly stir the beaten egg through the simmering soup, then serve immediately, sprinkled with chopped coriander and spring onions.

Chicken balti
Serves 4 • PT **5** mins • CT **15** mins

1 tablespoon vegetable oil
600 g skinless chicken thigh fillets,
   chopped into bite-sized pieces
1 medium onion, chopped coarsely
3 tablespoons balti curry paste, or curry
   paste of your choice
200 g vegetables (snake beans, snow
   peas, broccolini or a mixture),
   chopped coarsely
½ cup (125 ml) chicken stock
1 tablespoon tomato paste or
   tomato sauce

• Heat oil in a wok and stir-fry chicken and onion in batches until chicken is browned. Set aside. Add balti paste to the wok and fry for a minute or two.

Return chicken and onion to wok with vegetables, stock and tomato paste and stir-fry until the sauce has reduced a little and the chicken is cooked. Serve with rice.

Chilli con carne
Serves 4 • PT **5** mins • CT **10** to **20** mins

1 quantity bolognaise sauce (*see* recipe
   on page 266)
2 teaspoons ground cumin
¼ teaspoon chilli powder (or to taste)
1 can (420 g) red kidney beans, drained
   and rinsed

• Put the bolognaise sauce in a heavy-based saucepan and stir in the cumin, chilli and beans. Bring to the boil, reduce heat and simmer, uncovered, until the sauce reaches the desired consistency. Serve with rice.

Choc-caramel sauce
Serves 4 • PT **2** mins • CT **5** mins

1 large Mars bar
⅔ cup (170 ml) pouring cream

• Cut the Mars bar into slices and place in heatproof bowl with the cream. Place the bowl over a saucepan of simmering water and stir until melted. Serve immediately over vanilla ice-cream.

Chocolate cake
Serves 8 • PT **10** mins • CT **15** mins

185 g butter, softened
¾ cup (160 g) caster sugar
¼ teaspoon vanilla extract
3 tablespoons milk
3 medium eggs
1¼ cups (175 g) self-raising flour
1 teaspoon baking powder
4 tablespoons cocoa
ICING
2 tablespoons butter
2 tablespoons water
1 cup (140 g) icing sugar mixture
2 tablespoons cocoa

• Line the base of a 21-cm microwave-safe cake pan with baking paper.
• Place butter, sugar, vanilla, milk and eggs in a bowl and beat until smooth, but do not overbeat. Sift in flour, baking powder and cocoa and mix well.
• Pour mixture into prepared pan. Cook on *Medium-High* (70 per cent) for about 10 minutes or until just cooked. Stand for 5 minutes before turning out. Allow to cool.
• To prepare the icing, melt butter and water in a microwave-safe bowl. Whisk in icing sugar and cocoa. Allow to thicken to a spreadable consistency, then spread over cake.

Coq au vin
Serves 4 • PT **15** mins • CT **30** mins

1 tablespoon butter
250 g shallots or pickling onions, peeled
2 cloves garlic, crushed
125 g bacon, chopped
400 g button mushrooms, halved
1 bouquet garni
salt and freshly ground black pepper
8 chicken thigh fillets (about 800 g), halved
1 tablespoon flour
½ cup (125 ml) red wine
½ cup (125 ml) chicken stock
2 tablespoons tomato paste
1 tablespoon brandy
chopped fresh parsley, to serve

• Put butter, shallots, garlic, bacon, mushrooms, bouquet garni and salt and pepper to taste in a shallow microwave-safe dish. Cover and cook on *High* for 6 minutes, stirring once during cooking.
• Meanwhile, coat chicken fillets with seasoned flour. Place in the dish with the vegetables. Combine wine, stock, tomato paste and brandy and pour over chicken. Cover and cook on *High* for 10 minutes. Stir and rearrange the chicken pieces. Cook for another 10 minutes on *High*. Leave to rest for 2 to 3 minutes, then check that chicken is cooked. Sprinkle with parsley to serve.

Cottage pie

SERVES 4 • PT 10 MINS • CT 35 MINS

1 quantity bolognaise sauce (*see* recipe
  on page 266)
1 tablespoon worcestershire sauce
2 cups frozen mixed vegetables
4 large (about 800 g) potatoes
½ cup (125 ml) pouring cream, or milk
1 tablespoon butter

● Preheat oven to 190ºC.
● Combine bolognaise sauce with
worcestershire sauce and vegetables
in a saucepan and cook until vegetables are cooked through and sauce
is reduced a little. Transfer mixture
to a greased shallow ovenproof dish.
● Meanwhile, boil potatoes until
tender and drain. Mash with cream
and butter until smooth. Spread
mashed potato over the top of the
meat mixture and bake, uncovered,
for about 20 minutes or until top is
lightly browned.

Creamy fish korma

SERVES 4 • PT 5 MINS • CT 15 MINS

2 tablespoons vegetable oil
1 large onion, chopped
3 cardamom pods, bruised
½ cup (145 g) prepared korma curry paste
¾ cup (190 ml) chicken stock
500 g fish fillets, cut into chunks
¾ cup (190 ml) coconut cream
2 tablespoons toasted almonds, to serve
chopped fresh coriander, to serve

● Heat oil in a wok and stir-fry onion
until golden. Add cardamom pods and
curry paste and stir until fragrant.
● Add chicken stock, bring to the boil,
then reduce heat. Add fish and
simmer gently for about 5 minutes
or until fish is just cooked. Stir in
coconut cream, heat through gently.
Sprinkle over almonds and coriander
and serve with rice.
TIP Use chicken instead of fish, stir-
frying before you add the stock, and
increase cooking time to 20 minutes.

Creamy garlic chicken

SERVES 4 • PT 10 MINS • CT 20 MINS

2 tablespoons olive oil
500 g skinless chicken thigh fillets,
  chopped
1 medium onion, finely chopped
4–6 cloves garlic, crushed
2 tablespoons dijon mustard
1 tablespoon tomato paste
2 tablespoons white wine vinegar
4 tablespoons chicken stock
2 teaspoons cornflour
1 cup (250 ml) pouring cream
salt and freshly ground black pepper
400 g cooked pasta

● Heat oil in a heavy-based frying pan
and cook chicken in batches until it is
browned and almost cooked. Remove
from pan. Add onion to pan and cook
until soft. Add garlic, mustard, tomato
paste, vinegar and stock and cook for
about 5 minutes, or until fragrant and
bubbling. Return chicken to pan.
● Blend cornflour with a little cream
and stir into chicken. Gradually add
the rest of the cream and stir until
sauce thickens. Simmer until chicken
is completely cooked, then season to
taste. Serve over cooked pasta.

Creamy lemon mousse

SERVES 4 • PT 15 MINS (PLUS CHILLING TIME)

200 g good quality lemon butter (*see*
  recipe on page 272)
1 cup (250 ml) thickened cream
2 large eggwhites
salt
lemon zest, to serve
almond bread, to serve

● Spoon the lemon butter into a bowl.
Whip the cream until it holds soft
peaks, then fold into the lemon butter.
● Add a pinch of salt to eggwhites and
whisk until they form soft peaks, then
carefully fold into the lemon mixture.
● Spoon into four serving dishes and
chill overnight. Top with lemon zest
and serve with almond bread.

Creamy onion chicken

SERVES 4 • PT 5 MINS • CT 20 MINS

4 skinless chicken breast fillets, about
  200 g each
1 packet (50 g) French onion soup
¾ cup (190 ml) pouring cream
freshly ground black pepper

● Preheat oven to 175ºC.
● Place the chicken fillets in an ovenproof dish. Mix the French onion soup
with the cream. Pour this sauce over
the chicken and season with pepper.
Cook in the oven for 15 to 20 minutes.

Custard

MAKES 2 CUPS (500 ML)
PT 5 MINS • CT 8 MINS

1¼ cups (300 ml) milk
3 tablespoons sugar
2 tablespoons custard powder
2 egg yolks
1 teaspoon vanilla extract

● Combine milk, sugar and custard
powder in a microwave-safe bowl.
Cook on *Medium* for 6 minutes or
until sauce is slightly thickened,
stirring twice during cooking. Whisk
in the egg yolks and cook on *Medium-
Low* for 2 minutes until sauce is
thickened, stirring once during
cooking. Stir in vanilla extract.

Easy laksa

SERVES 4 • PT 10 MINS • CT 20 MINS

125 g dried rice vermicelli noodles
2 teaspoons vegetable oil
2 tablespoons laksa paste
3 cups (750 ml) chicken stock
1 can (400 ml) coconut milk
250 g button mushrooms, sliced
1 baby buk choy, coarsely chopped
1½ cups (200 g) chopped cooked chicken
150 g firm tofu, cut into medium cubes
250 g medium green prawns, shelled and
  deveined
1 cup (75 g) fresh bean sprouts, trimmed
2 tablespoons fresh coriander leaves

- Place rice noodles in a bowl and cover with boiling water for 2 minutes.
- Heat wok over medium heat. Add oil and fry laksa paste until fragrant.
- Add stock and coconut milk. Bring to the boil. Reduce heat to low. Add mushrooms, buk choy, chicken, tofu and prawns and cook until prawns change colour and chicken is heated through.
- Drain noodles and divide between serving bowls. Ladle laksa over noodles and sprinkle with bean sprouts and coriander. Serve with lime wedges.

Eton mess
SERVES 4 • PT 5 MINS

250 g strawberries or raspberries, or frozen mixed berries
4 tablespoons caster sugar
1¼ cups (300 ml) thickened cream
2–4 ready-made meringue nests, lightly crushed

- Hull the strawberries, if using, then sprinkle with sugar and mash a little.
- Whip the cream softly, then stir through the crushed meringue. Gently stir in the crushed fruit.
TIP Use whatever berries you have on hand for this incredibly easy dessert – frozen are fine. Fresh passionfruit also makes a tasty addition.

French onion soup
SERVES 4 • PT 10 MINS • CT 25 MINS

1 tablespoon vegetable oil
2 tablespoons butter
1 kg medium onions, thinly sliced
2 tablespoons plain flour
500 ml beef consommé
1 cup (250 ml) white wine
1 cup (250 ml) water
2 tablespoons brandy
1 teaspoon chopped fresh thyme
1 small baguette (bread stick)
1 cup (120 g) finely grated Swiss-style cheese

- Heat oil and butter in a large, heavy-based pan. Add onion and cook over a low heat for about 20 minutes, stirring occasionally, until onion is golden and slightly caramelised, but not browned.
- Stir in flour and cook for 2 minutes. Remove from heat and gradually stir in consommé, wine and water.
- Return to heat and stir until soup boils and thickens. Stir in brandy and thyme.
- Meanwhile, cut bread into medium-thick slices. Toast slices on one side only under a grill. Turn slices and top with grated cheese. Grill until cheese melts. Serve soup in bowls and top with cheese croutons.

Fried rice
SERVES 4 • PT 15 MINS • CT 15 MINS

1 tablespoon vegetable oil
3 medium eggs, lightly beaten
6 spring onions, thinly sliced
2 teaspoons grated fresh ginger
1 medium red capsicum, seeded and finely chopped
4 cups (about 750 g) cold, cooked rice
250 g cooked chicken, chopped
200 g Chinese barbecued pork or ham, chopped
200 g cooked shelled prawns
1 cup (125 g) frozen peas, thawed
3 tablespoons soy sauce
chopped fresh coriander, to serve

- Heat a wok or frying pan over medium heat. Add 1 teaspoon of the oil and swirl the eggs around the pan to form a thin omelette. Remove from pan when cooked. Roll up tightly and slice thinly. Set aside.
- Heat remaining oil in pan, add spring onions, ginger and capsicum and stir-fry for 2 minutes. Add rice, chicken, ham, prawns, peas and soy sauce and stir-fry until heated through and well combined. Scatter omelette strips over the top and serve with chopped coriander.

Fusilli with two cheeses
SERVES 4 • PT 5 MINS • CT 15 MINS

400–500 g fusilli or other short pasta
2 cups (25 g) frozen peas
½ cup (40 g) grated parmesan
2 tablespoons olive oil
1¼ cups (325 g) ricotta cheese
salt and freshly ground black pepper
chopped fresh basil or oregano, to serve

- Bring a large pan of salted water to the boil and add pasta. Cook for 7 minutes and add peas. Return water to the boil and cook for a further 3 to 5 minutes, until the pasta is al dente and the peas are cooked. Drain, reserving about 6 tablespoons of cooking water.
- Meanwhile, put the parmesan in a serving bowl, add the oil and whisk until a thick paste forms. Add the ricotta cheese and beat until well blended. Season with salt and pepper to taste.
- Add the hot pasta and peas to the cheese mixture and stir until the pasta is well coated. Add the reserved cooking water to thin the sauce. Adjust the seasoning if necessary and sprinkle generously with fresh basil or oregano.
TIP Vary it by adding finely chopped prosciutto or ham to the sauce.

Green chicken curry
SERVES 4 • PT 10 MINS • CT 20 MINS

1 tablespoon vegetable oil
500 g skinless chicken thigh fillets, cut into bite-sized pieces
1 medium onion, chopped
2 cloves garlic, crushed
1 tablespoon grated fresh ginger
1 tablespoon finely sliced lemon grass
2 tablespoons Thai green curry paste
1 can (400 ml) coconut milk
1 cup frozen chopped stir-fry vegetables, thawed
1 tablespoon lime juice
chopped fresh coriander, to serve

• Heat oil in a wok or large frying pan and brown chicken in batches. Remove from pan. Add onion, garlic, ginger, lemon grass and curry paste and stir-fry until onion is soft and mixture is fragrant.

• Return chicken to pan with coconut milk and vegetables and cook for about 5 minutes or until chicken and vegetables are cooked. Stir in the lime juice. Sprinkle with chopped coriander and serve with rice.

Harissa lamb in pita bread

SERVES 4 • PT 10 MINS • CT 10 MINS

4 tablespoons natural yogurt

4 tablespoons hummus

2 tablespoons vegetable oil

400 g boneless leg of lamb, or lamb fillets, thinly sliced

1 clove garlic, crushed

1 tablespoon grated fresh ginger

2 teaspoons harissa paste

4 tablespoons coarsely chopped fresh mint or coriander, or a combination

4 medium wholemeal pita pockets

salad leaves and chopped cucumber, to serve

lemon juice, to serve

sumac, to serve (optional)

• Combine yogurt and hummus in a small bowl and set aside.

• Heat wok until very hot, then add oil and swirl to coat. Add lamb, garlic and ginger and stir-fry for 5 to 8 minutes or until lightly browned. Add the harissa and stir-fry for a further 2 minutes. Add coriander or mint and toss together.

• Meanwhile, grill the pita breads for a minute on each side. Split the pita breads open on one side, add salad leaves and cucumber to each one, and divide the lamb between them. Top each with a dollop of yogurt mixture, add a squeeze of lemon and sprinkle with sumac to serve.

TIP Use paprika and an extra squeeze of lemon as a substitute for sumac.

Herbed fish parcels

SERVES 4 • PT 10 MINS • CT 10 MINS

½ cup chopped fresh herbs (parsley, thyme, basil, chives or a combination)

1 clove garlic, crushed

2 tablespoons olive oil

1 tablespoon freshly squeezed lemon juice

1 teaspoon grated lemon zest

4 skinless white fish fillets (about 800 g), such as snapper, bream or whiting

salt and freshly ground black pepper

4 spring onions, finely sliced

• Preheat oven to 200°C.

• In a small bowl, combine herbs, garlic, oil, lemon juice and zest. Place each fish fillet in the middle of a sheet of aluminium foil. Divide the herb mixture over the top of the fillets, season with salt and pepper and scatter with spring onions. Wrap each fillet into a secure parcel.

• Place parcels on a baking tray and bake for about 7 to 10 minutes, or until fish is cooked through.

TIP Add Asian flavours with finely chopped ginger, lemon grass and soy sauce; Spanish flavours with paprika, saffron and finely sliced capsicum; or Italian flavours with oregano, sliced mushrooms, tomatoes and capers.

Jambalaya

SERVES 4 • PT 15 MINS • CT 30 MINS

2 tablespoons olive oil

200 g chorizo sausage, cut into medium slices

1 medium onion, chopped

1 clove garlic, crushed

1 large green capsicum, seeded and chopped

1 teaspoon smoked paprika (or sweet paprika)

1 cup (185 g) long-grain white rice

1½ cups (375 ml) chicken stock

2 cups (500 ml) tomato passata, or 1 can (400 g) diced tomatoes

½ teaspoon Tabasco sauce (optional)

1 bay leaf

500 g medium green prawns, shelled and deveined, with tails intact (or frozen green prawns, thawed)

chopped fresh parsley, to serve

3 spring onions, finely sliced, to serve

• Heat oil in a deep frying pan and fry chorizo until cooked on both sides. Remove from pan. Add onion, garlic and capsicum and fry until onion is softened. Stir in paprika. Add rice and stir to coat. Return chorizo to pan.

• Add stock, passata, Tabasco sauce and bay leaf, and combine well. Bring to the boil, reduce heat, cover and simmer for about 20 minutes. Rice should be almost tender and liquid should be absorbed. If it seems too dry, stir in a little boiling water.

• Add the prawns, cover and cook for a further 5 minutes, or until the prawns have changed colour. Sprinkle with chopped parsley and spring onions, and serve from the pan.

Lamb and spinach curry

SERVES 4 • PT 15 MINS • CT 30 MINS

2 tablespoons sunflower oil

750 g lamb fillets, cut into bite-sized pieces

1 medium onion, chopped

2 cloves garlic, crushed

2 teaspoons grated fresh ginger

½ teaspoon ground turmeric

1 teaspoon ground cumin

2 teaspoons ground coriander

½ teaspoon ground chilli

1 tablespoon garam masala

1 cinnamon stick

5 whole cloves

2 medium ripe tomatoes (about 300 g), coarsely chopped

salt and freshly ground black pepper

1 cup (250 ml) thickened cream, or natural yogurt

250 g baby spinach

4 large naan breads

• Heat oil in a large saucepan over moderate heat. Fry meat in batches, until browned. Remove from pan. Fry onion and garlic until softened.

- Add grated ginger, turmeric, cumin, coriander, chilli, garam masala, cinnamon stick and cloves. Cook for a further 1 minute.
- Add the tomatoes to the pan and cook over gentle heat for about 7 minutes, or until cooked down to a pulp. Return lamb to pan.
- Season with salt and pepper, pour in the cream and simmer, uncovered, for a further 15 minutes.
- Meanwhile, put the naan bread under the griller to heat through.
- Add the spinach to the curry and stir continuously until it wilts. Bring to the boil, then remove the pan from the heat at once. Serve with the naan.

TIP Buy naan from the bread section of most supermarkets.

Lamb kebabs

SERVES 4 • PT 15 MINS • CT 15 MINS

½ cup (125 ml) olive oil
juice of 1 lemon
2 cloves garlic, crushed
1 tablespoon dried thyme
1 tablespoon dried rosemary
salt and freshly ground black pepper
600 g boned leg or shoulder of lamb, cut into bite-sized pieces
3 medium onions, cut into medium chunks
250 g large cherry tomatoes, halved
1 medium capsicum (red or green), seeded and cut into medium chunks

- Soak eight bamboo skewers in water while you prepare the meat.
- Put the oil, lemon juice, garlic and herbs into a bowl and season with salt and pepper. Add the meat and the vegetables. Cover and leave to marinate for 1 hour in the fridge.
- Prepare the skewers by alternating pieces of meat, chunks of onion, tomato halves and capsicum.
- Cook on a heated oiled grill plate on the barbecue or under the griller for 10 to 15 minutes, or until done as desired, turning them from time to time.

Lamb stew

SERVES 4 • PT 10 MINS • CT 60 MINS

2 tablespoons olive oil
1 onion, chopped
2 cloves garlic, crushed
800 g boned leg or shoulder of lamb, diced
3 tablespoons tomato paste
1 cup (250 ml) red wine
2 sprigs fresh rosemary
1 teaspoon dried marjoram
salt and freshly ground black pepper
2 medium red capsicums, seeded and chopped

- Heat oil in a heavy-based casserole and fry onion and garlic until soft. Add the meat and brown. Stir in tomato paste, wine, herbs and season with salt and pepper to taste. Cover and simmer on a low heat for 30 minutes. Add the capsicums and cook for a further 25 minutes or until lamb is tender. If sauce seems too thick, add a little water; if too thin, simmer with the lid off. Serve with steamed potatoes, rice or pasta.

Lasagne

SERVES 4 • PT 10 MINS • CT 50 MINS

1 quantity bolognaise sauce (see recipe on page 266)
2 tablespoons butter
2 tablespoons plain flour
2 cups (500 ml) milk
salt and freshly ground black pepper
125 g mozzarella or cheddar cheese, grated
¼ teaspoon ground nutmeg
250 g packet instant lasagne
½ cup (40 g) grated parmesan

- Preheat oven to 190°C.
- To make the cheese sauce, melt butter in a heavy-based saucepan, stir in flour and cook, stirring, for 2 minutes over gentle heat until mixture is dryish. Remove from the heat and gradually stir in milk to make a smooth sauce. Return to heat and cook gently until sauce boils and

thickens. Season with salt and pepper. Remove from heat and stir in cheese and nutmeg.
- To assemble the dish, spread one-third of the bolognaise sauce over the base of a lightly greased baking dish. Cover with a layer of lasagne sheets, then top with one-third of the cheese sauce. Continue layering, ending with cheese sauce. Sprinkle with grated parmesan and bake, uncovered, for about 45 minutes, or until golden and bubbling.

TIP This dish can be covered and frozen before cooking.

Lemon butter

MAKES ABOUT 2 CUPS (500 ML)
PT 4 MINS • CT 8 MINS

125 g unsalted butter
1 cup (210 g) sugar
¾ cup (190 ml) lemon juice
grated zest of 2–3 large lemons
4 medium eggs

- Place butter, sugar, lemon zest and juice in a large microwave-safe bowl. Cook, uncovered, on *Medium* for 3 minutes, stirring once during cooking. Allow mixture to cool a little.
- Whisk eggs into lukewarm mixture. Cook on *Medium* for 5 minutes, or until the mixture thickens, checking and stirring every 30 seconds. Cool and store in clean jars.

Linguine with smoked salmon

SERVES 4 • PT 5 MINS • CT 15 MINS

400–500 g linguine
1 tablespoon olive oil
1 medium onion, chopped finely
200 g smoked salmon, coarsely chopped
3 tablespoons sun-dried tomato pesto
1 cup (250 ml) light sour cream
chopped fresh parsley, to serve

- Bring a large saucepan of salted water to the boil and cook pasta for 12 minutes or until al dente. Drain, reserving a little of the cooking water.

• Heat oil in a heavy-based saucepan and fry onion until soft. Add smoked salmon, pesto, sour cream and drained linguine to the pan and stir gently until combined and heated through. If the sauce seems too thick, add a little cooking water. Sprinkle with chopped parsley to serve.

TIP Keep 200-g packets of smoked salmon in the freezer; it thaws quickly.

Macaroni cheese

SERVES 4 • PT 10 MINS • CT 30 MINS

2 tablespoons olive oil
3–4 rashers bacon, chopped
1 medium onion, finely chopped
3 tablespoons butter
⅓ cup (50 g) plain flour
3 cups (750 ml) milk, or a mixture
    of milk and cream
2 teaspoons dijon mustard
salt and freshly ground black pepper
2 cups (240 g) grated cheddar cheese
4 cups cooked macaroni, or other
    short pasta

• Preheat oven to 200°C.
• Heat olive oil in a heavy-based saucepan and fry bacon and onion until onion is soft. Remove from pan and set aside.
• Melt butter in the same saucepan. Stir in the flour and cook for a minute until mixture bubbles. Remove from heat and gradually stir in milk. Return to heat and stir until sauce boils and thickens. Stir in mustard, salt and pepper to taste and half the cheese. Stir until cheese melts, then add cooked pasta and stir to combine.
• Spoon the macaroni into a shallow ovenproof dish, scatter remaining cheese on top and bake for 20 minutes or until golden and bubbling.

TIP Buy ready-grated cheese. For a crunchy top, mix 1 cup (60 g) fresh breadcrumbs with the topping cheese. To cook it even faster, brown the top under a pre-heated griller instead of in the oven.

Marinated kebabs

SERVES 4 • PT 10 MINS • CT 15 MINS

2 tablespoons olive oil
2 tablespoons lemon juice
1 clove garlic, crushed
1 tablespoon chopped fresh rosemary
2 tablespoons chopped fresh parsley
salt and freshly ground black pepper
1 kg firm fish, such as swordfish, tuna
    or blue-eye, cut into medium cubes

• Soak eight wooden satay sticks in water while you prepare the marinade for the fish.
• Combine oil, lemon juice, garlic, herbs and salt and pepper to taste in a large glass bowl. Add fish, cover and refrigerate for 10 minutes.
• Thread fish onto satay sticks and reserve marinade. Cook on a barbecue plate or chargrill pan, turning frequently and brushing with reserved marinade.

TIP Try adding peeled raw prawns to the kebabs, as well as chunks of vegetables, such as onion, capsicum, mushroom and zucchini. If you enjoy spicy flavours, add a chopped fresh chilli or dried chilli flakes to the marinade.

Mediterranean tuna

SERVES 4 • PT 10 MINS • CT 20 MINS

250 g cherry or grape tomatoes, halved
1 tablespoon capers, drained
⅓ cup (50 g) pitted black olives, halved
1 tablespoon fresh thyme leaves
2 tablespoons olive oil
freshly ground black pepper
4 medium tuna steaks (about 650 g),
    skin removed
lemon wedges, to serve

• Preheat oven to 210°C.
• Combine tomatoes, capers, olives, thyme, olive oil and a good grind of black pepper in a bowl.
• Place the fish steaks in a single layer in an oiled ovenproof dish. Cover with the tomato mixture. Bake

for 20 minutes, or until fish is just cooked – do not overcook. Serve with lemon wedges.

TIP Try this recipe with salmon fillets or a firm, white fish. Or add different herbs and seasonings.

Nachos

SERVES 4 • PT 5 MINS • CT 10 MINS

1 quantity chilli con carne (*see* recipe
    on page 268)
1 avocado
1 teaspoon Tabasco sauce
lime juice, to taste
250 g packet corn chips
1 cup (120 g) grated cheddar cheese
½ cup (125 ml) sour cream
½ cup (125 ml) salsa in a jar
chopped fresh coriander, to serve
lime wedges, to serve

• Mash avocado with Tabasco sauce and lime juice to taste.
• Arrange corn chips around the rim of a flat, flameproof dish. Spread the beef mixture in the centre and sprinkle with cheese. Place the dish under a hot griller until cheese melts. Top with sour cream, mashed avocado and salsa. Sprinkle with coriander and serve with lime wedges.

Pan-fried fish

SERVES 4 • PT 5 MINS • CT 10 MINS

4 skinless white fish fillets (about 800 g),
    such as snapper, bream or barramundi
plain flour, for dusting
125 g butter
juice of 1 lemon
1 tablespoon chopped fresh parsley

• Dust fillets with flour. Heat half the butter in a heavy-based frying pan and fry fish until cooked on both sides, turning once.
• Add the rest of the butter to the pan with the lemon juice and parsley and cook until it foams, taking care not to burn it. Pour over fish and serve immediately.

Pantry pasta

SERVES 4 • PT 5 MINS • CT 12 MINS

400–500 g pasta (penne and spirali)
2 tablespoons olive oil
1 medium onion, finely chopped
2 cloves garlic, crushed
1 small red chilli, chopped, or a pinch
    of dried chilli flakes
1–2 large ripe tomatoes, chopped, or
    1 can (400 g) diced tomatoes, or
    prepared tomato-based pasta sauce
3 anchovy fillets, chopped finely
1 tablespoon capers in brine, drained
½ cup (75 g) pitted black olives
1 can (185 g) tuna in oil
chopped fresh basil (optional)

● Bring a large pan of salted water
to the boil and add pasta. Cook for
12 minutes or until al dente, then drain.
● Meanwhile, heat the oil in a heavy-
based saucepan and fry onion, garlic
and chilli until onion is softened. Add
tomatoes and cook for a few minutes
to soften and reduce.
● Add remaining ingredients, except
basil, and heat through. Toss sauce
through cooked pasta and sprinkle
with basil.

Pear and chocolate tart

SERVES 6 • PT 10 MINS • CT 30 MINUTES

1 sheet ready-rolled sweet shortcrust
    pastry, thawed
80 g dark chocolate
3 medium eggs
6 tablespoons crème fraîche
2 tablespoons milk
1 large can pear halves (825 g), well drained
butter, for greasing

● Preheat oven to 180°C.
● Place the sweet shortcrust pastry
in a buttered tart dish. Break the
chocolate into pieces into a small
heatproof bowl. Melt it gently over
a saucepan of simmering water or in
the microwave. Allow to cool a little
and add half the crème fraîche and
the milk. Stir until well combined.

● Spread this mixture over the pastry
then place the drained pear halves
evenly on the chocolate. Mix the eggs
with the rest of the crème fraîche and
pour over the tart. Bake for 30 minutes.
TIP Crème fraîche is a slightly sour
cultured cream, now available in
delicatessens and many supermarkets. Make your own by warming
1 cup of heavy cream, then adding
1 tablespoon cultured buttermilk and
allowing the mixture to thicken at
room temperature for 24 hours.

Penne with broccoli

SERVES 4 • PT 5 MINS • CT 15 MINS

450 g broccoli, cut into small florets,
    stems discarded
400–500 g short pasta, such as penne,
    fusilli or orecchiette
60 g drained anchovies in oil, plus
    2 teaspoons oil from jar
1 clove garlic, crushed
1 small red chilli, chopped, or a pinch
    of dried chilli flakes
2 tablespoons chopped fresh parsley
¾ cup (65 g) grated parmesan
1 teaspoon lemon zest
1 tablespoon lemon juice
freshly ground black pepper, to serve
olive oil, to serve
extra parmesan, to serve

● Bring a large saucepan of salted
water to the boil and drop in the
broccoli for 1 to 2 minutes until bright
green but still crisp. Remove broccoli
with a slotted spoon and reserve.
● Return the water to the boil and
add pasta. Cook for 12 minutes or
until al dente, then drain.
● Heat anchovy oil in a large frying
pan and cook anchovies, garlic and
chilli for 1 minute until fragrant. Add
this mixture to drained pasta with
parsley, parmesan, lemon zest and
juice and toss to combine. Serve
with freshly ground black pepper,
a drizzle of olive oil and extra
parmesan, if desired.

Pizza

SERVES 4 • PT 10 MINS • CT 30 MINS

30-cm pizza base
½ cup (140 g) tomato-based pizza sauce
chopped fresh herbs (basil or oregano)
toppings, such as sliced mushrooms,
    capsicum and salami; chopped ham and
    artichoke hearts; and black olives, etc.
1 cup (120 g) ready-grated pizza cheese

● Preheat oven to 220°C.
● Spread pizza base evenly with
sauce and chopped fresh herbs.
Sprinkle with half the cheese.
Arrange desired topping choices
over the top, then sprinkle with the
rest of the cheese.
● Bake for 30 minutes until base is
crisp and cheese has melted. Cut into
wedges to serve.

Pork with lemon and garlic

SERVES 4 • PT 5 MINS • CT 10 MINS

2 tablespoons olive oil
400 g pork fillets, cut into strips
2–3 cloves garlic, crushed
salt and freshly ground black pepper
½ cup (125 ml) dry white wine
juice of 1 lemon
chopped fresh parsley, to serve

● Heat olive oil in a wok or frying pan
and seal pork. Add crushed garlic and
season with salt and pepper. Sauté
for 5 minutes, then add the wine.
Bring to the boil and add the lemon
juice. Sprinkle with chopped parsley
to serve.

Quick fruit crumble

SERVES 4 • PT 15 MINS • CT 40 MINS

700 g fruit, such as apples, apricots,
    strawberries, raspberries or a mixture
⅓–½ cup (70–100 g) caster sugar
CRUMBLE TOPPING
1½ cups (210 g) plain flour
90 g unsalted butter
¼ cup (50 g) caster sugar
1 teaspoon cinnamon (optional)

- Preheat oven to 200ºC.
- Peel the fruit and cut into medium-sized pieces. Mix with the caster sugar and place in an ovenproof dish. Sprinkle over the crumble topping and press down lightly.
- Bake for 35 to 40 minutes or until topping is golden brown. Serve hot with custard, cream or ice-cream.

Quick gazpacho
SERVES 4 • PT 15 MINS

1 thick slice dry-textured bread
4 tablespoons olive oil
3 tablespoons red wine vinegar
salt and freshly ground black pepper
1 tablespoon paprika
2 cans (400 g each) diced tomatoes
1 medium red onion, coarsely chopped
4 cloves garlic
1 fresh or dried red chilli
1 large cucumber, chopped
1 each of medium red, yellow and green capsicum, seeded and chopped
1¼ cups (300 ml) iced water
12 ice cubes, if required
6 large basil and/or mint leaves

- Remove crusts from bread. Place bread, olive oil, vinegar, salt, pepper, paprika, undrained tomatoes, onion, garlic and chilli into a food processor and process until combined.
- Add chopped cucumber and capsicum. Stir in enough iced water to make mixture soup-like, but not too thin: it should be quite dense. Leave to chill, or stir in the ice cubes and serve immediately, topped with shredded basil or mint, and croutons.

Quick roast potatoes
SERVES 4–6 • PT 10 MINS • CT 30 MINS

1 kg desiree potatoes, peeled and chopped into quarters, or smaller chunks
2 tablespoons olive oil
1 tablespoon chopped fresh herbs, such as rosemary or thyme

- Preheat oven to 240ºC.
- Cook potatoes in a large pan of salted boiling water until just tender and a bit crumbly on the outside (this will make them crisp in the oven), then drain.
- Arrange potatoes on an oven tray or in a shallow baking dish and toss with oil and fresh herbs. Roast for 20 minutes or until golden and crisp, turning them occasionally.

Ratatouille
SERVES 4 • PT 15 MINS • CT 20 MINS

3 medium zucchini, thickly sliced
2 medium eggplants, cut into small chunks
5 medium tomatoes, or 2 x 400-g cans diced tomatoes
1 medium red capsicum, seeded and coarsely chopped
1 medium onion, coarsely chopped
2 cloves garlic, crushed
2 tablespoons chopped fresh basil
2 tablespoons chopped fresh parsley
salt and freshly ground black pepper
3 tablespoons olive oil
1 tablespoon balsamic vinegar

- Combine all ingredients, except oil and vinegar, in a large microwave-safe bowl, and season with salt and pepper. Cook in the microwave oven for 10 minutes on *High*, mix again, then cook on *High* for a further 10 minutes. Pour off excess liquid. Add the olive oil and vinegar.

Ratatouille frittata
SERVES 4 • PT 15 MINS • CT 20 MINS

6 medium eggs
2 tablespoons sour cream
salt and freshly ground black pepper
200 g leftover ratatouille (*see* recipe above)
butter, for greasing

- Preheat oven to 190ºC.
- Whisk the eggs and cream in a bowl until just combined. Season with salt and pepper, to taste. Add the cold ratatouille and mix well. Grease a 20-cm cake tin with butter and pour in the mixture. Cook in the oven for 20 minutes or until mixture is set. Allow to stand for a few minutes, then slice and serve with a green salad.

Risotto balls
SERVES 2 • PT 5 MINS • CT 10 MINS

1½ cups leftover risotto
1 medium egg, lightly beaten
grated parmesan, to taste
salt and freshly ground black pepper
dried breadcrumbs
oil, for shallow frying

- Mix the risotto with beaten egg, a little grated parmesan and salt and pepper to taste. Roll the mixture into small balls with your hands, roll them in breadcrumbs and shallow fry until browned all over. Serve hot or cold.

Salmon patties
SERVES 4 • PT 10 MINS • CT 10 MINS

2 portions (about ⅔ cup) mashed potato
1 can (210 g) pink salmon, drained and flaked, bones removed
½ medium onion, finely chopped
1 tablespoon whole-egg mayonnaise
1 medium egg, lightly beaten
1 tablespoon finely chopped parsley
salt and freshly ground black pepper
1 medium egg, extra
2 tablespoons milk
2 tablespoons plain flour
½ cup (60 g) dried breadcrumbs
oil for shallow frying

- Combine the potato, salmon, onion, mayonnaise, egg, parsley and salt and pepper to taste. Shape mixture into six patties.
- Beat extra egg and milk in a flat bowl. Dip the patties into flour, then egg and milk mixture, then breadcrumbs.
- Heat oil in a frying pan and fry patties on each side until golden brown. Serve with a green salad.

Self-saucing pudding

SERVES 4–6 • PT 10 MINS • CT 40 MINS

1 cup (140 g) plain flour
2 tablespoons cocoa
½ cup (100 g) caster sugar
3 tablespoons butter
½ cup (125 ml) milk
1 medium egg, lightly beaten
½ teaspoon vanilla extract
SAUCE
¾ cup (175 g) firmly packed soft brown
   sugar
4 tablespoons cocoa
2 cups (500 ml) boiling water

● Preheat oven to 190°C.
● Sift flour and cocoa into a bowl and add sugar.
● Melt butter in a saucepan over low heat. Remove from heat and add milk, egg and vanilla. Gradually add butter and milk mixture to dry ingredients and mix to a smooth batter. Pour batter into a lightly greased ovenproof pudding dish.
● For the sauce, combine sugar and cocoa in a bowl and sprinkle over the surface of pudding batter. Carefully pour boiling water over the pudding.
● Bake for 35 to 40 minutes. Serve with cream or ice-cream.

Smoked trout kedgeree

SERVES 4 • PT 10 MINS • CT 20 MINS

3 tablespoons butter
1 medium onion, finely chopped
1 clove garlic, crushed
2 teaspoons curry powder or mild
   curry paste
1⅓ cups (250 g) long-grain rice
2⅓ cups (600 ml) fish or vegetable stock
salt and freshly ground black pepper
½ cup (60 g) frozen peas, thawed
300 g ready-to-eat smoked trout, flaked
2 tablespoons chopped fresh parsley
1 tablespoon lemon juice
4 medium hard-boiled eggs, quartered

● Melt butter in a heavy-based sauce-pan and cook onion until softened.

● Stir in garlic and curry powder and cook another minute, until fragrant. Add the rice and stir to coat. Pour in stock and salt and pepper to taste. Bring to the boil, reduce heat, cover and cook over very low heat for about 15 minutes.
● Fluff up rice with a fork, add peas, trout, parsley and lemon juice and stir through. Top with hard-boiled eggs to serve.

Spanish-style chicken

SERVES 4 • PT 10 MINS • CT 45 MINS

2 tablespoons olive oil
1 kg skinless chicken thigh fillets,
   halved
100 g chorizo sausage, thickly sliced
1 medium red onion, chopped
1 clove garlic, crushed
1 large red capsicum, seeded and sliced
1 large yellow capsicum, seeded and
   sliced
1 tablespoon sweet paprika
1 can (400 g) diced tomatoes
⅔ cup (170 ml) white wine
2 tablespoons pitted black olives
salt and freshly ground black pepper
chopped fresh parsley, to serve

● Heat oil in a large flameproof casserole and fry the chicken thigh fillets over high heat until golden. Remove from pan.
● Add the chorizo slices to the pan and fry until starting to colour. Remove from pan.
● Add onions, garlic and capsicum to pan and fry until onion is lightly browned and softened. Stir in paprika and cook a few moments until fragrant.
● Return chicken and chorizo to the pan. Stir in the tomatoes and wine and bring to the boil. Simmer gently covered for about 15 minutes, then remove the lid and simmer for a further 15 minutes, or until chicken is cooked through. Stir in olives, season to taste and scatter with chopped parsley.

Speedy stroganoff

SERVES 4 • PT 10 MINS • CT 50 MINS

1 tablespoon vegetable oil
500 g beef strips
1 medium onion, finely chopped
1 clove garlic, crushed
2 teaspoons paprika
2 tablespoons tomato paste
1 can (420 g) cream of mushroom soup
1 tablespoon worcestershire sauce
250 g button mushrooms
2 tablespoons sour cream
salt and freshly ground black pepper

● Heat oil in a heavy-based casserole and fry beef in batches until browned. Set aside. Add onion to pan and fry until soft. Add garlic and paprika and cook for 1 minute. Stir in tomato paste, soup, worcestershire sauce, mushrooms and browned beef. Bring to the boil, reduce heat and simmer for 40 minutes or until meat is tender.
● Stir in sour cream. Serve with pasta.

Spicy prawns

SERVES 2 • CT 5 MINS

2 tablespoons vegetable oil
1 teaspoon curry paste of your choice
400 g medium green prawns, shelled
   and deveined
2 tablespoons pouring cream

● Heat oil in a wok. Fry the curry paste for a minute or until fragrant. Add the prawns and cook quickly until just changed colour. Stir in the cream, let it bubble for a few seconds to heat through, then serve immediately.

Tagliatelle with breadcrumbs

SERVES 4 • PT 5 MINS • CT 12 MINS

400–500 g tagliatelle
½ cup (125 ml) olive oil
3 cloves garlic, crushed
⅓ cup (60 g) pine nuts
3 cups (180 g) fresh breadcrumbs
4 tablespoons chopped fresh parsley
2 tablespoons chopped fresh oregano

2 tablespoons chopped fresh chives
salt and freshly ground black pepper
grated parmesan, to serve

● Bring a large pan of salted water to the boil and add pasta. Cook for 12 minutes or until al dente, then drain.
● Meanwhile, heat 3 tablespoons oil in a heavy-based frying pan. Add garlic, pine nuts, breadcrumbs, herbs and salt and pepper to taste, and fry mixture for 5 minutes, or until breadcrumbs are lightly browned but still quite soft.
● Toss drained pasta with remaining oil, scatter with breadcrumb mixture and toss again. Serve with parmesan.

Thai-style soup
SERVES 4 • PT 5 MINS • CT 15 MINS

1 tablespoon vegetable oil
1 medium onion, finely chopped
1 clove garlic, crushed
3 tablespoons red curry paste
2 teaspoons grated fresh ginger
1 small red chilli, finely chopped
1 tablespoon finely chopped lemon grass
2 cans (420 g each) cream of pumpkin soup
1 can (400 ml) coconut milk
1 cup (250 ml) chicken stock
500 g medium green prawns, shelled and deveined
2 tablespoons chopped fresh coriander

● Heat oil in a heavy-based pan and cook onion until softened. Add garlic, curry paste, ginger, chilli and lemon grass and fry a minute or two longer.
● Add soup, coconut milk and chicken stock and stir until combined. Bring to the boil, reduce heat and add prawns. Simmer gently until prawns have just changed colour. Serve with coriander.

Tortellini soup
SERVES 4 • PT 1 MIN • CT 15 MINS

2 cans (420 g each) tomato soup
1 teaspoon dried basil
½ teaspoon dried oregano
375 g cheese tortellini
freshly ground black pepper

● Heat soup. Add the herbs and pepper. Add the tortellini and simmer for 5 to 10 minutes, until pasta is al dente.

Tuna casserole
SERVES 4 • PT 15 MINS • CT 40 MINS

250 g shell pasta, or other short pasta
1 can (425 g) tuna in brine, drained and flaked
1 cup (125 g) frozen peas, thawed
2 tablespoons butter, softened
salt and freshly ground black pepper
1 can (420 g) cream of mushroom soup
1 cup (250 ml) milk
1 cup (125 g) dried breadcrumbs
1 cup (120 g) grated tasty cheese
2 tablespoons chopped fresh parsley

● Preheat oven to 190°C.
● Bring a medium saucepan of salted water to the boil and add pasta. Cook until al dente, then drain.
● In an ovenproof dish, mix cooked pasta, tuna, peas, butter and salt and pepper to taste.
● Combine soup and milk and stir into tuna mixture. Combine breadcrumbs, grated cheese and parsley and sprinkle over the top. Bake for 25 to 30 minutes or until lightly browned and bubbling.

Veal parmigiana
SERVES 4 • PT 15 MINS • CT 20 MINS

2 tablespoons milk
1 medium egg
2 tablespoons plain flour
½ cup (60 g) dried breadcrumbs
4 veal schnitzels (about 400 g)
2 tablespoons olive oil
1 cup (280 g) tomato-based pasta sauce
1½ cups (180 g) grated pizza cheese

● Preheat oven to 200°C.
● Beat egg and milk together in a shallow bowl. Dust each veal schnitzel with flour, dip in the egg mixture, then coat in breadcrumbs.
● Heat oil in a heavy-based frying pan and cook veal until lightly browned on both sides.

● Arrange veal in a single layer in a shallow ovenproof dish. Top each slice with one quarter of the pasta sauce, then top with the cheese.
● Bake, uncovered, for about 15 minutes, or until cheese is melted and veal is heated through.

Vegetable omelette
SERVES 2 • PT 10 MINS • CT 5 MINS

leftover cooked vegetables, chopped finely
1 teaspoon butter
extras, such as bacon, chopped ham, etc.
4–5 medium eggs
salt and freshly ground black pepper

● Heat leftover vegetables in a frying pan with the butter. Add any extra ingredients and fry a minute longer.
● Beat the eggs lightly together and season with salt and pepper, to taste. Pour over the vegetables and cook on a high heat, tipping the pan to allow the uncooked egg to flow underneath.

Vegetable stir-fry
SERVES 4 • PT 5 MINS • CT 10 MINS

450 g hokkien noodles
1 tablespoon vegetable oil
2 cloves garlic, crushed
1 medium red capsicum, seeded and coarsely chopped
1 bunch baby buk choy, coarsely chopped
250 g fresh baby corn
200 g snow peas
100 g shiitake mushrooms, halved
3 tablespoons kecap manis
2 tablespoons soy sauce
1 tablespoon oyster sauce

● Cover noodles with boiling water and leave until softened, then drain.
● Meanwhile, heat oil in a wok and add garlic, capsicum, buk choy, corn, snow peas and mushrooms and stir-fry for 3 to 5 minutes.
● Combine kecap manis, soy sauce and oyster sauce in a small bowl. Add to vegetables, along with noodles, and stir-fry for a further 5 minutes.

Preparing to entertain

Be realistic when it comes to dinner parties

▶ Don't invite more people than you can cope with in conditions that will be uncomfortable for everyone.

▶ If you haven't had much experience with entertaining, don't think about organising a large formal dinner party, which is more likely to be long and difficult to manage. And if you're not used to cooking for large numbers, start by inviting four to six people.

▶ Choose a simple menu composed of dishes that you always make successfully. And there's no need to spend hours making a dessert if desserts aren't your specialty.

▶ Buy as many ready-made meal components as you can: dips and starters, sauces and desserts, etc. You'll save time and be a lot more relaxed with your guests.

Easy menu planner

Entertaining can become a nightmare very quickly, so make keeping things on track easy for yourself by compiling three lists.

● **List the complete menu** Write a list from start to finish, including drinks, side dishes, bread and coffee, so that you're prepared.

● **Make an action plan** Work out how long each dish will take to cook, what you need to do when and how far ahead you can do it.

● **Write down every single ingredient** Before you go shopping make a comprehensive list of everything you need to buy, divided into fresh and non-perishable, and in the correct amounts of each ingredient.

Plan ahead

The most important decision is to plan what you're going to serve several days ahead of time. Everything else follows on from this choice: the shopping, the wine, the table decorations, etc.

▶ Plan the menu according to both the season and the occasion – a hearty casserole on a hot summer's night isn't a good idea, neither is a four-course formal dinner when it's a casual meal with a couple of friends.

▶ Try to balance the courses and don't get too complicated, to ensure that your menu isn't too rich; isn't too reliant on a single ingredient, such as eggs; and isn't reliant on a single mode of cooking, so that everything doesn't need to be in the oven at the same time.

▶ Maintain a balance of hot and cold dishes on the menu, to make things quicker and easier when it comes to serving the food on time.

▶ Choose a theme to help with planning decisions. You might choose a seafood theme, or a barbecue or vegetarian food.

▶ Plan your menu around a particular cuisine: Spanish, Italian, Greek, Chinese, Japanese, Mexican, Moroccan or Indian. This will help you decide which dishes to prepare for each course, what drinks to serve and even give you ideas for table decorations.

TIMELY TIP

Check first

Some of your guests may have special food restrictions, or perhaps they simply don't like certain foods. Find out when you invite them, so you're not suddenly faced with trying to produce a quick replacement dish in the middle of your dinner party.

Ideas for themed menus

● **Italian** Antipasto or carpaccio as an entree, lasagne or other pasta as the main course, tiramisu for dessert.

● **Spanish** Gazpacho, tortilla or a selection of tapas as an entree; paella, calamari or chorizo quiche as a main course; Catalan cream for dessert.

● **Greek** An assortment of hors d'oeuvres as an entree (taramasalata, tzatziki, hummus, eggplant dip and vine leaves, etc.), moussaka or lamb kebabs as a main course, Greek pastries for dessert.

● **Moroccan** Harira soup or briouats (fritters with minced meat or cheese) as an entree, tagine or couscous as a main course, fruit salad or Middle Eastern pastries (baklava) for dessert.

Watching the clock

Just because you're pressed for time doesn't mean you have to panic over last-minute details or open packets at the table! There are easier solutions.

▶ Make dishes that allow you to spend the minimum amount of time in the kitchen and the maximum amount of time with your guests – many cookbooks have this aim in mind, so do a bit of research.

▶ Choose recipes you can prepare and cook in advance, which means you'll only have to heat them up.

TIMELY TIP

Get the timing right

Timing can be one of the hardest things to get right. So avoid choosing two dishes that both need to be cooked in the oven at different temperatures – especially if it takes you longer to cook the second one than to eat the first!

Keep a diary

For each of your dinner parties, note what you served, who was there, how everything went and whether you'd do anything differently next time. You won't run the risk of serving the same thing to the same guests twice, and if the meal was a success, you won't have to look for other recipe ideas for different guests.

▶ If you're planning a traditional dinner with an entree, main course and dessert, do the timer test: 5 minutes to do the finishing touches and serve the entree, 8 to 10 minutes to clear away the entree and serve the main course, and 5 minutes to present and serve the dessert. Simply by choosing dishes that correspond to this timetable, you'll save time as well as make the most of your guests and the meal.

▶ If you have very limited time, plan to prepare only one course yourself, say, the main course. Buy the first course and the dessert and add your own touches: pack bought chicken liver pate into individual ramekins and serve with homemade herbed or garlic crostini; or top bought meringue nests (available from most supermarkets) with fresh berries, a quick berry coulis and whipped cream.

Only do what's necessary

If you prepare everything in advance, the only thing you will have to do is take the dishes out of the fridge and reheat them.

▶ In summer, choose cold soups, terrines, antipasti, cold seafood or salads as an entree.

▶ Allow for the possibility of guests being late. For example, for the main course choose a dish that can be left to simmer. And remember that you can make this type of dish a few weeks in advance, when you have time to spare, then keep it in your freezer until the day of the dinner party arrives.

▶ For dessert, choose things that can be kept in the fridge or in airtight containers: ice-cream, cakes, tarts, fruit salads, panna cotta and pavlova, etc.

▶ Prepare the cheese platter in advance and leave it, covered, at room temperature.

Every detail counts

Save time by thinking ahead – and making a list – of everything that is needed at the last minute. Many of these jobs can be done before the guests arrive: the vinaigrette for the salad, chopped herbs for garnish, a saucepan of boiling water (left on a low heat) to cook the rice or pasta, slices of bread placed in the grill pan, precooked vegetables ready to go into the microwave, and so on.

TIMELY TIP

Well-mannered guests

If guests offer to help, by all means let them – it will save time and make the whole experience more fun. Allow them to bring the dessert, the wine or a pre-dinner nibble. Or let them help you serve the drinks, or clear away dishes while you're preparing the dessert. People are usually more than happy to help, and it keeps things running smoothly when your hands are full.

Cooking ahead

Keep a file of tried-and-true dishes that can be cooked in advance and reheated, or prepared ahead and cooked to perfection in good time and without too much more attention. The following list is a good example of what you can prepare ahead when you're in a hurry.

Entrees
- Hot or cold soup
- Pate, terrine, savoury mousse
- Quiche, flan, frittata
- Salad
- Antipasti and deli items
- Raw or smoked fish
- Carpaccio
- Shellfish and seafood

Main courses
- Stew, casserole, hotpot
- Goulash, stroganoff
- Curry
- Stuffed vegetables
- Osso buco
- Moussaka, lasagne
- Beef bourguignon
- Shepherd's pie
- Chilli con carne
- Veal parmigiana
- Coq au vin, chicken cacciatore
- Cassoulet
- Easy-carve roast

Accompaniments
- Gratin (potato or vegetable)
- Puree or mash
- Ratatouille
- Tabouli
- Precooked vegetables
- Salad

Desserts
- Ice-cream, sorbet, parfait
- Tart
- Sweet mousse
- Fruit crumble
- Tiramisu, trifle
- Panna cotta, crème caramel
- Dessert cake
- Pavlova
- Fruit salad, poached fruit
- Cheesecake

Self-serve for simplicity

▶ If you have a lot of guests or you want to make things informal and easy, a buffet is the perfect solution. There's no end to the possibilities, and they're very simple to do.

▶ Give free reign to your imagination: serve only cold dishes, or a mixture of hot and cold, or follow a theme, such as a curry party. You could choose a buffet composed of 100 per cent salads, or serve a whole ham with crusty bread and different condiments on the side. Each guest is then free to make up his or her own plate to suit their personal taste.

▶ The ultimate timesaving option is to call on a caterer to provide the buffet dishes for you. Or choose dishes that can be cooked in bulk and then frozen. Just make sure you present them well and serve lots of fresh bread and a few salads, too.

In the right order

On the buffet table, place the plates at one end of the queue, and the cutlery, glasses and serviettes at the other end. Guests will have a free hand to serve themselves without having to juggle a glass, plate and cutlery.

Get your priorities right

Your guests would rather spend time with a relaxed host who serves them something simple than with someone completely frazzled. Making a few advance preparations will save time and avoid you getting flustered.

▶ Set the table the night before, if you can, and fold the serviettes.

▶ Before your guests arrive, set out the glasses for pre-dinner drinks and make sure the wine is in the fridge, the bottle opener is on hand and that you have lemon slices and enough ice.

▶ Finish the last-minute presentation of the first course so that it can be served as soon as everyone is seated.

▶ Organise a place to put jackets and coats, so you won't have to look for coathangers or make room in a wardrobe at the last minute. If you have children, get them to take care of guests' jackets and coats.

▶ If everything is laid out, ask your guests to help themselves to drinks.

▶ Set out dips and nibbles so that no one goes hungry while you're greeting the arriving guests. (Don't forget a small bowl for olive pips.)

▶ Light the table candles just before guests are due to arrive.

▶ Tidy up, and get out everything you need so that all you have to do is prepare the plates or reheat the dishes.

What's that smell?

Make sure your guests smell the lovely cooking aromas coming from the kitchen, not the bad ones, by trying these quick tricks.

▶ Avoid spreading the hideous smell of cauliflower throughout the house by placing a piece of bread in the cooking water, or 1 tablespoon of flour, a cork or a bay leaf.

▶ Is fish on the menu? Soak it in lemon juice for 20 minutes prior to cooking. This is a clever trick that also reduces the cooking time.

▶ Place a bowl of white vinegar in the room to absorb bad smells.

▶ Burn a few drops of your favourite essential oil in an oil diffuser.

Moving right along

If you have friends living nearby, you might like to try a progressive dinner as a way of saving on preparation time.

▶ Pre-dinner drinks and nibbles are at one person's house, the first course is served at the next person's, the main course at the one after that, dessert the one after that, and coffee and petit fours are then served at the last person's house. Each person is only responsible for preparing one thing, which must be organised in advance so that everyone can sit down at the table as soon as they arrive. Easy.

▶ If moving from house to house is impractical, you can still organise a dinner where everyone is responsible for only one course – the dishes simply need to be transportable to wherever the dinner is being held. This is the perfect solution for when everyone is pressed for time but would still like to get together.

▶ Save time and energy by using a trolley on wheels to transport what you need to and from the table and the kitchen.

TIMELY TIP

Perfect hands

You can easily get rid of the cooking smells on your hands. If you have handled onion or garlic, rub them with stainless steel 'soap' or the back of a stainless steel spoon under running water before washing them with soap. To eliminate fish smells, rub your hands with salt and vinegar.

TIMELY TIP

Hot plates

You can warm plates for serving by placing a wrung-out damp paper towel between each one (do it ahead of time), then microwaving them for about 30 to 60 seconds. Do not microwave plates with metal rims, and if you don't want to use paper towels, place a container of water in with the plates.

TIMELY TIP

Cool the bubbly

To chill champagne or sparkling wine more quickly, add a handful of cooking salt to the ice in the ice bucket.

Five good reasons to start a wine cellar

Even if you know very little about wine, you should start a wine cellar – your local wine outlet will be more than happy to give you advice, and you'll save a great deal of time and money in the long run.

▶ Anyone can start a cellar. It doesn't have to be a stone-lined cavern in the basement – a cool cupboard will do the trick – and you don't need dozens and dozens of bottles to have a good supply at home.

▶ You can buy wine at the discounted dozen price, and home delivery is often included in the cost. Some outlets will also deliver a regular tasting dozen to your door.

▶ Many wines that have aged well are nicer to drink and are usually worth considerably more than you paid for them originally.

▶ With a cellar, you'll always have wine on hand to serve to guests.

▶ Matching wine with the right food becomes a breeze.

TIMELY TIP

A good drop

Keep an eye out for special discounts on your favourite wines, then order a couple of cases over the phone and have them delivered. Some wine merchants and bottle shops will waive their usual delivery fee if you order more than one case.

Setting the scene

Minimum effort, maximum effect

Creating a welcoming and relaxed place for receiving guests is a simple matter if you follow a few easy guidelines.

▶ Don't spend hours cleaning your house or dreaming up elaborate presentations to impress your guests. A couple of details are enough to create a pleasant atmosphere or a specific theme.

▶ Clear newspapers and pet hair off the sofa, and clean the bathroom and toilet, but forget the rest if you don't have time. The important thing is that your guests feel comfortable right from the first drink and they won't if they can see you've worn yourself to a frazzle getting everything ready and cleaning the family silver.

▶ If you feel compelled to clean anywhere else, give the hall a quick once-over and put a bunch of fresh flowers near the front door for a good first impression (and stow away any clutter blocking the hallway).

▶ Create a cosy atmosphere by dimming the dining room lights and placing candles or tea lights everywhere – including a few in the garden if it's visible from the house. And remember to protect wooden surfaces.

▶ Lavender essential oil (or any other favourite essential oil) in a couple of strategically placed oil burners will give a subtle, fresh fragrance to the air.

▶ Put a new cake of guest soap and a clean handtowel next to the bathroom sink.

▶ Another bunch of fresh flowers in the living room will also do wonders for ambience.

▶ Use table lamps, rather than overhead lights, for subtle lighting.

▶ Put on your favourite music – but not too loudly.

▶ Don't forget to add fresh, green touches to the meal – garnish your dishes with sprigs of fresh herbs, lemon slices and so on. It takes very little effort and a minimum of time, but it's these finishing touches that ultimately make all the difference.

▶ Lastly, don't overload the plates with sauces or accompaniments – good, simple food, simply presented is always a winning choice.

A simple setting

You can create a beautiful table setting in very little time using just three elements: candles, serviettes and flowers.

▶ Choose candles that aren't too tall, so they don't interrupt the line of sight of your guests. They should match the theme of the meal or be the same colour as your serviettes and/or flowers.

▶ Similarly, avoid floral arrangements that are too high and ornate and that will prevent the guests from seeing each other, as well as flowers with an overwhelming perfume. Choose a simple centrepiece or perhaps place a small flower next to each plate or over a flat-folded serviette.

▶ If you don't have time to launder table linen, use good-quality paper serviettes instead and fold them nicely.

How to fold a serviette in 5 seconds

Paper serviettes are ideal when you're trying to save time: no washing or ironing, and they come in a fantastic range of colours and designs. Present them in an original way, though, rather than simply placing them flat on a plate. And rest assured that you don't need to be an origami expert to do it: this fold can be done in 5 seconds flat.

- Open out the napkin completely
- Pinch the middle of the napkin between your thumb and forefinger
- Shake it and place it in a glass
- Fold the ends over a little if the glass is quite small

Easy ideas for instant atmosphere

Colour and simplicity are the key elements of successful table setting.

▶ Complement the theme of your dinner by setting the table along the same lines. Scatter a few shells on the table for a seafood dinner, add large fresh chillies or small cactus pots for a Mexican meal, and bamboo place settings with a few beautiful smooth stones for a Japanese meal.

▶ Special occasions (Christmas, Valentine's Day, Easter, Halloween) are generally a great source of inspiration and the accessories are easy to find: stars, hearts, eggs and pumpkins – the list is almost endless.

▶ Always keep in mind that your guests are coming to eat the food, not the decorations, so don't waste time being too elaborate or overloading the table with unnecessary items.

Pre-dinner drinks

The perfect choice

▶ Save time by serving everyone the same drink for an aperitif. You will only use one sort of glass and you won't have to take out – and put away – different sorts of alcohol and fruit juice.

▶ Stick to the classics. Think about offering traditional pre-dinner drinks that are always appreciated – champagne or a simple champagne cocktail, such as kir royale or bellini, or a martini.

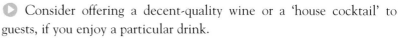

Consider offering a decent-quality wine or a 'house cocktail' to guests, if you enjoy a particular drink.

If you know that your guests have such a wide range of tastes that one single sort of drink is unlikely to be acceptable, then offer a choice – but remember, you could waste a lot of time mixing different drinks, so aim to keep the choice of drinks on offer as simple as you can.

Use a little imagination: prepare sangria or punch, or even a jug of Pimms on a sunny day when you're eating outdoors.

Whatever your choice, don't offer too many alternatives – except, of course, to those guests that don't drink alcohol.

Serve appetisers instead of a first course

A clever timesaving trick is to offer a good selection of appetisers and finger food. This means guests will serve themselves, you won't have to prepare an entree, you can wait for late-comers without dying of hunger and there will be less washing up to do.

Choose hors d'oeuvres that don't require any preparation. This is one area where there is no need to have a theme or a pattern – simply serve a selection of nibbles that are quick and easy to prepare and serve, although it's not difficult to stick with a theme if you'd prefer.

Serve crackers, olives, dips, guacamole, taramasalata, tapenade, sliced salami and cabanossi, antipasti and different crisps, etc.

A wheel of brie or a beautiful vacherin, served with crackers and a little fruit or fruit paste, is also a very easy and popular pre-dinner snack.

Pick up a selection of ready-made morsels from your local deli or check out the supermarket frozen goods that can be heated in the oven, such as mini quiches, spinach pastries, pastizzi and dim sum.

Think about offering mini blinis, or buy mini toasts and put various toppings on them.

Fresh oysters and small peeled prawns with a couple of dipping sauces are always popular and are easy, timesaving appetisers into the bargain.

TIMELY TIP

Manage your neighbours
Disputes with neighbours can waste a lot of time and energy, so if you think your party could end up being a bit noisy later in the evening, warn your neighbours and thank them in advance for their understanding – or think about inviting them.

Quick savoury pastries

Spread a sheet of butter puff pastry with tapenade, sun-dried tomato pesto, basil pesto or very finely chopped smoked salmon. Sprinkle with grated parmesan and roll the edges of the pastry towards each other from opposite sides, forming a scrolled tube. Cut into 1-cm slices, sprinkle with a little more cheese and bake on a baking paper-lined tray at 230°C for 15 minutes. Any unsliced rolls can be frozen.

Fast and fuss-free dips for chips

Buy ready-made dips and simply add sour cream, herbs, chopped bacon, nuts and soy sauce, etc. Garnish with chopped chives, a sprig of basil or parsley, and sprinkle with chilli, paprika, sumac or curry powder. When making dips yourself, use sour cream, light cream cheese, smooth ricotta cheese, yogurt, whole-egg mayonnaise, soft goat's cheese or crème fraîche as a base, then add flavourings such as these.

- **French onion** Add a packet of French onion soup mix and chopped parsley.
- **Chive** Add chopped chives and salt.
- **Mustard** Add dijon mustard, wholegrain mustard and mayonnaise.
- **Curry** Add Indian curry paste, salt and garlic.
- **Asian** Add green curry paste, soy sauce, garlic, chopped coriander and fish sauce.
- **Salmon** Add smoked salmon, lemon juice, salt and chopped dill.
- **Tex-mex** Add tomato paste, garlic, chilli, cumin, grated cheddar and salt.
- **Cocktail** Add mayonnaise, tomato sauce, worcestershire sauce, sugar and garlic.
- **Provençal** Add tomato paste, chopped rosemary and basil, chopped black olives, capers, salt and pepper.

Minimal-effort entertaining

Community effort

Entertaining doesn't have to be all about slaving over a hot stove for days. Entertaining friends can be informal, friendly and so easy.

▶ Often the most successful parties are those where the guests do most of the work – without even realising it, because they're relaxed and having fun. So if you're time-poor, don't think you can't possibly entertain, just gather all the ingredients and let your guests do the cooking!

▶ There are lots of ways for guests to get involved: fondue, Swiss raclette, barbecues, Japanese sukiyaki, shabu-shabu and teppanyaki, Mexican tacos or tortillas, and homemade pizzas.

▶ You probably won't need a first course with this type of meal, but pay special attention to the accompaniments – condiments, sauces, bread, vegetables and salads – because they can make all the difference.

▶ Make sure you always have enough of the main ingredients, whether they be cheese, meat, fish or vegetables. Running out of ingredients in the middle of the dinner can end in total disaster.

FIND OUT MORE

• You'll need a tabletop raclette grill, but it's a quick and fun way to entertain on a winter's night as guests melt their own cheese. All you have to do is buy the cheese and accompaniments, and the only ingredient you have to cook beforehand is the potatoes. www.raclette.com.au

TIMELY TIP

The kindest cut

The Japanese dish shabu-shabu calls for very thin slices of meat. To enable you to cut the meat more easily, place it in the freezer for 1 or 2 hours ahead of time or ask your butcher to slice it.

Fondue and raclette

Fondue is one of the most famous of the tabletop cooking methods, while raclette is a popular traditional meal from Switzerland, but isn't generally as well known. (*See* 'Find out more', at left.)

▶ With an inexpensive fondue maker – a special saucepan set over a tabletop heat source – you can vary the ingredients of the fondue to suit your taste. Meat or cheese fondues are the best-known recipes, but you can also explore less traditional ideas, such as Japanese-style or seafood fondues, and even chocolate fondues.

▶ Raclette is a delicious melted cheese served over cooked potatoes, and is usually accompanied by side dishes of gherkins, pickles, onions, deli meats and fresh tomatoes, etc.

Guest chefs

▶ A do-it-yourself pizza party is a great timesaving way to entertain. Just supply small pizza bases (make them yourself or save time and buy them) and lots of different toppings. Guests add their choice of toppings to a base before the pizzas go into a hot oven to cook. Serve antipasti to nibble on while the pizzas are cooking, add a green salad and dessert, and dinner is done in a minimum of time.

▶ On a summer's evening, why not offer a variety of gourmet sausages (or perhaps ready-made kebabs or chops), plenty of crusty bread, tomato sauce and a couple of salads? Fire up the barbecue or electric grill and allow guests to cook the sausage that takes their fancy.

▶ Go Mexican. Provide soft flour tortillas and bowls of refried beans, chilli con carne, grated cheese, grated onion, chopped tomato and avocado and shredded lettuce. Guests simply choose the ingredients they want and wrap them in a tortilla.

▶ Look for recipes for Japanese tabletop dishes, such as grilled teppanyaki, which can be cooked on a portable electric grill, or shabu-shabu – the Japanese equivalent of fondue, in which meat and vegetables are cooked at the table in a hot broth. Go online to find recipes and ideas.

Say cheese!

▶ For a simple supper, organise a large platter with several varieties of cheese, some ripe pears, grapes or dried fruit, a few nice bottles of wine and a couple of different types of fresh bread and crackers.

▶ It's better to offer larger pieces of just a few really delicious cheeses in peak condition, rather than small chunks of too many ordinary cheeses. And the same goes for the fruit – take advantage of what's in season and choose from the nicest samples.

▶ To put together a good cheese platter, choose a hard cheese such as aged cheddar, a blue cheese such as stilton, a creamy soft cheese such as brie, and perhaps also a small goat's cheese.

▶ If you think cheese will not be quite enough to eat for the gathering you've got planned, organise a pot of soup (homemade or a good-quality bought one), a nice green salad and find some special chocolates or other sweet treats to serve with coffee.

▶ Take your cheeses out of the fridge at least 1 hour before serving so they have the perfect soft and creamy consistency. Serve them on a natural surface (wood, wicker, marble, glass, etc.) so as not to interfere with the taste.

▶ Heat some crusty bread for a few minutes before the beginning of the meal and put small containers of butter on the table.

Beside the seaside

If you enjoy seafood, one of the quickest and easiest ways to present a sumptuous feast is to visit your local fish market.

▶ You can put a cold platter together – or ask the fishmonger to do it for you – with very little trouble or time spent at all. Most fishmongers will be happy to open oysters, supply cooked prawns, dress crabs and lobsters ready for serving, and will often also have a couple of ready-made sauces to go with it all.

▶ Many fishmongers also sell prepared sushi and sashimi, which make a delicious addition to a mixed seafood platter.

▶ If you prefer to have some of your seafood hot, one of the fastest and easiest methods is simply to cook it on the hotplate of an oiled barbecue.

▶ Remember to also serve lots of fresh bread, salted butter, a good vinaigrette, mayonnaise, lemons… and finger bowls!

TIMELY TIP

Self-cleaning shellfish

To remove the sand from shellfish, place them flat in a colander and stand them in a basin of salted water. They'll think they are in their natural environment and will open and close several times, flushing the sand out.

Outdoor entertaining

Getting ready for al fresco dining

Take advantage of beautiful spring or summer weather and pleasant surroundings by organising your gathering outdoors, either in the garden or at a lovely picnic spot – it's an informal and relaxed way to entertain.

▶ Make sure there is adequate shade for both guests and food – use a market umbrella or, for larger groups, consider hiring a shelter or awning. And always have a tube of sunscreen on hand.

▶ Create a mood quickly for evening outdoor parties by lining garden paths and the driveway with candlelight – place tea lights in empty jars. Or festoon fences, tree branches and awnings with outdoor fairy lights.

▶ Don't invite flies and mosquitoes. Burn mosquito repellents, such as coils or citronella, and supply personal insect repellent for your guests. Keep a supply of light throwovers to protect food from flies.

▶ When the weather is likely to be on the cool side, buy or hire a gas-fired patio heater.

Barbecuing – a timesaving tradition

A barbecue is a great way to entertain outdoors in fine weather. It's quick, easy and informal, there's usually less mess to clean up, and you can produce an almost endless variety of food.

▶ A gas-fired (or electric) barbecue is the quickest and easiest barbecue option, but as long as you allow extra time for heating, a solid-fuel barbecue will also do a good job (and you don't have to wait around for it to heat up – just light some heat beads and let the fuel fire up).

▶ If you have a barbecue with a hood, you can extend your repertoire, as the hood allows the barbecue to act as an oven.

▶ Keep your barbecue clean, covered and in good working order – clean it while it's still warm – so it's always ready to use. Keep the implements nearby as well.

▶ If your barbecue runs on bottled gas, invest in a spare full bottle so you never run out.

▶ If you use solid fuel, make sure you've always got enough heat beads and firelighters on hand.

▶ The simplest and quickest barbecue solutions are plain chops, sausages and steaks, etc., but it takes very little extra time to plan a marinade or tasty sauce to make things much more interesting.

A great way to get everyone doing their own thing is to provide all the makings of a tasty hamburger – meat or chicken patties, tomato, lettuce, cheese, onions, beetroot, pickles, tomato sauce and bacon, etc. – and let everyone cook and assemble their own burger.

Buy from butchers and supermarkets that carry an extensive range of barbecue-ready food, such as marinated meat, boned and stuffed roasts, 'butterflied' poultry and game, pre-threaded kebabs, pre-mixed hamburger meat and gourmet sausages, and you'll save a lot of time.

Use ready-made marinades, dry 'rubs' and sauces, which are readily available from supermarkets, delis and even some butcher shops. Or pre-mix your own and freeze it.

Visit your local fish market for inspiration – seafood cooks quickly and beautifully on a barbecue, whether you're cooking tuna steaks, salmon fillets, whole sardines, sizzling prawns or baby calamari.

Vegetables are also delicious barbecued – they can be char-grilled directly on the grill plate or wrapped in foil and roasted until tender. Try eggplant, zucchini, baby squash, mushrooms, tomatoes, sweet corn, capsicum, onions and, of course, potatoes.

CAUTION!

Taste test

No matter how much of a hurry you're in, don't be tempted to cook on a barbecue while the firelighters are still burning – everything will taste of kerosene.

Fabulous fast chicken

Pour a good dollop of Thai sweet chilli sauce over chicken thigh fillets. Add a slurp of soy sauce and a good sprinkle of sesame oil, then turn the chicken to coat. Allow to marinate for an hour or two, then cook on the barbecue and sprinkle with chopped coriander to serve. (If you can't wait for marinating time, simply cook it straight away.)

Perfect picnics

Don't waste time trying anything too elaborate when you're planning a picnic – remember you're going to transport everything you require to the chosen spot, before unpacking, cleaning and then repacking.

Choose food that can be cooked ahead and eaten cold, preferably with your fingers, such as chopped raw vegetable sticks and dips, cooked and sliced chicken pieces, individual quiches or pies, sandwiches, cold cooked sausages or cutlets and so on.

Pack salads loosely into rigid containers to prevent crushing. Transport the dressing separately in a screw-top jar or plastic container.

○ Instead of a whole cake or tart, pack cupcakes, a batch of biscuits or a pre-cut slice for a quick-and-easy picnic dessert.

○ Choose square food containers where possible, since they are easier to stack than round ones and take up less space.

○ Disposable plates and glasses are lighter and safer to carry than crockery and save time and effort on washing up – but if you think this is environmentally unfriendly, invest in a light plastic picnic set and simply reuse it.

○ If you like tea or coffee, take a vacuum flask of boiling water and teabags or coffee – making it at the picnic avoids an over-stewed taste. And don't forget the sugar and milk.

○ Keep a picnic basket or backpack permanently packed with essentials so that it's ready to go: salt and pepper, a corkscrew, a sharp knife, plastic or paper plates, paper serviettes, glasses and cutlery, serving spoons, a picnic rug, a packet of disposable wipes, insect repellent, plastic rubbish bags, a small first-aid kit and a torch.

TIMELY TIP

Use your loaf

Instead of packing individually filled rolls, split a long baguette lengthwise. Drizzle the surface with olive oil and add savoury fillings, such as deli meats, cheese and antipasti, then tie the baguette with string to hold it all together, and wrap tightly. Slice it into portions at the picnic site.

TIMELY TIP

Frozen assets

Keep plastic containers of frozen juice or water in your freezer so that you can pack them straight into the esky or food cooler with the picnic food – the bottles act as ice bricks and can be drunk as they thaw.

Cooking for a crowd

Make a quick list

Some special occasions dictate that you must entertain, even though you've got a dozen other commitments, tight deadlines at work and very little time to spend organising, so make the most of the time you have.

○ Prepare ahead. Whether it's a special anniversary, a milestone birthday, a child's party, your turn to host the family Christmas or even a family wedding, you'll save time and feel more in control if you take the time to plan carefully and make a few lists to work with.

○ The most useful list is the long-term to-do list: write down everything that needs to be done up until the day of the celebration, then re-organise it into a chronological action plan for the lead-up to your party.

Instant cake stand

If you don't have a cake stand for a buffet table, use a large plate or platter. Stand it on an upturned sugar bowl or soufflé dish. Make sure the plate is absolutely central and secure the two together firmly using Blu-Tack.

If you can delegate, do it. Distribute the various jobs on your list amongst helpers and put their names next to the job they're doing. Tick them off as they get each job done.

Do as many things as you can as far ahead as possible – it's no good wishing on Christmas Eve that you'd bought a patio umbrella, painted the bathroom or planted a garden bed of flowering annuals.

Be realistic – if you've got 12 months' notice and you want to paint the bathroom, then put it on your list and get it done, but if you're faced with planning an imminent event, prioritise only what needs to be done. Ask yourself, would guests prefer to eat something or admire the newly painted bathroom? Consider what you can do in practical terms.

Follow your long-term plan with a shopping list and a to-do list for the actual day itself, remembering to include every last detail. It's easy to forget things when you've got lots to remember.

Large-scale entertaining

The most important advice when it comes to entertaining large numbers is to keep it simple, or you run the risk of wasting time unnecessarily.

Don't overestimate your own capabilities, and don't plan too many different dishes – augment the main dish with simple accompaniments, such as salad, vegetables and bread.

Look for recipes that are not too complex and that can be cooked ahead and frozen. It'll save you time and help keep things organised.

Remember to keep in mind that you will need the capacity to reheat frozen food – will everything fit in the oven or on the stove? If not, consider a combination of cold and hot dishes.

Handy facts for planning

- A loaf of bread has 18–20 slices
- A long baguette will serve about 10 people
- About 2 tablespoons of butter will cover eight slices of bread
- A large iceberg lettuce will serve about 10 people, a large cos will serve about eight people and a butter lettuce about four
- A 2-kg celebration cake can be cut into approximately 50 slices
- A 750-ml bottle of wine fills at least five wine glasses
- A 750-ml bottle of champagne fills six champagne flutes
- A 1.5-litre bottle of water fills at least six water glasses
- About 200 g of ground coffee makes about 40 cups
- Some 10 kg of ice will cool two cases (24 bottles) of wine or 48 small bottles of beer

TIMELY TIP

Easy hire

If you need to hire wine glasses, you can often do so for free or a small fee from your local wine merchant, if you are also ordering wine (the wine and glasses can be delivered together). Remember to order more glasses than you need – people have a habit of putting them down and forgetting.

▶ Don't make too large a quantity of a dish at one time. If you find a recipe that serves 10, make two batches rather than double the recipe – you might find that your pots and pans simply aren't big enough or that such a large quantity is too difficult to freeze or reheat in one lot.

▶ If you've planned ahead, you can do the cooking and freezing over a period of time, which makes the whole task considerably less formidable.

▶ Ensure that at the time you want to fill your freezer with prepared food, you haven't filled it to the brim with other frozen goods. Either allow it to 'run down' ahead of time or organise with friends and neighbours to have access to their freezers.

▶ Don't put numerous hot dishes into the freezer at once – cool them in the fridge, or in a sink of water and ice cubes, then freeze them.

Estimating quantities

This is always a tricky area because, oddly, the more guests you have, the less they tend to eat per head, especially at a buffet. If you're catering for 100 people, for instance, allow full quantities for about 85. And when trying to estimate quantities of alcohol, ask your local wine merchant – not only will they give you good advice, many are often prepared to sell you alcohol on a sale-or-return basis.

BUFFET FOODS	10 PORTIONS	20 PORTIONS	40 PORTIONS
● **Soup, hot or cold**	2 litres	4 litres	8 litres
● **Cold, sliced meats** (off the bone)	900 g	2 kg	3.5 kg
● **Boneless meat** (for casseroles)	1 kg	2.5 kg	4.5 kg
● **Roast meat, hot or cold** (on the bone)	2 kg	3 kg	6.5 kg
● **Poultry on the bone** (oven-ready weight)	3.5 kg	7 kg	14 kg
● **Fish, filleted** (in cooked dishes)	1.5 kg	3 kg	5 kg
● **Rice or pasta** (uncooked weight)	500 g	1 kg	1.5 kg
● **Vegetables** (uncooked weight)	1.5 kg	3 kg	5.5 kg
● **Fresh fruit or fruit salad**	1.5 kg	3 kg	5.5 kg
● **Ice-cream**	1.5 litres	2.5 litres	5 litres
● **Cheese for a cheeseboard**	500 g	1 kg	1.5 kg
● **Biscuits for cheese**	500 g	750 g	1 kg

TIMELY TIP

Delicious duck

If you live near your city's Chinatown, pick up all the makings for very quick Peking Duck – small pancakes, chopped cooked duck and hoisin sauce. Roll up small amounts of duck with a spring onion and sauce in each pancake, then warm slightly before serving. It's fast and impressive finger food that requires very little effort.

How to throw a cocktail party

A drinks or cocktail party is a great idea for a special occasion, since it's an easy way to entertain a group of people in a set period of time.

▶ Specify arrival and departure times so that guests don't overstay their welcome, and don't seat them at tables – it's not necessary.

▶ Finger food should be just that – food that can be eaten with the fingers, and preferably in one or two bites. This means you can serve it with paper serviettes – make sure you have lots of them – but you won't have to worry about supplying individual plates or utensils.

▶ Plan to serve about 4–5 pieces of finger food per person for the first hour and about 4 pieces per person for every hour after that.

▶ When you're devising a menu, be sure to include both hot and cold finger food, so that one dish can be served while another is being heated.

▶ Choose recipes that can be prepared ahead and heated quickly.

▶ If you're serving coffee at the end of the evening, serve sweet finger food to go with it – or cut a celebratory cake into tiny portions and serve.

▶ Try to include a few things that can be set out before guests arrive, such as antipasti, a cheese platter, dips, nuts, olives and so on.

▶ Don't forget the humble sandwich – nicely presented, of course. They're easy, inexpensive, versatile, alcohol-absorbent and always popular.

▶ Make sure you have an attractive fruit-based, non-alcoholic 'mocktail' on offer as well.

▶ Don't serve too large a selection of cocktails and prepare ahead by pureeing or cutting up fruit, squeezing juice or making sugar syrup.

▶ Consider hiring a couple of bar staff to serve the drinks and food, even if you're planning to prepare it all yourself.

Children's birthday parties

Foolproof preparation

With a few tricks up your sleeve, hosting a children's birthday party can be done without too much stress or time spent. All that's required is sound organisation – and a few deep breaths!

▶ The ideal solution is to organise the party in your garden, or perhaps a local park. The children will be more relaxed and you'll save yourself many long hours of cleaning and tidying.

TIMELY TIP

Fast sandwiches
Cut loaves of unsliced white bread lengthways and spread the slices with cream cheese and/or ham. Put the slices together to form a sandwich and cut them into small fingers. To serve them quickly and avoid any spills, put them on a tray and cover the sandwiches with plastic wrap until they're served.

▶ The first thing you need to do is ask another adult or two to help you. You won't be able to keep an eye on the children, organise games, open the door, show or take children to the bathroom and serve food all at once.

▶ If you're having professional entertainment, look on the Internet or in the Yellow Pages phone directory for a magician, a clown or a fairy, for example, and make sure they're available for the chosen date before you send out invitations.

▶ Three weeks beforehand, send small invitation cards by mail: they're less likely to get lost among the debris in the bottom of a school bag and you'll receive an answer more quickly.

▶ Send a group email invitation with the click of a button. You can get creative and design an invitation that's sent as an attachment, using digital photos and word processing software.

▶ Write yourself a list of planned activities that will last the duration of the party. Alternate quiet games with active ones to reduce energy levels but, depending on the children, keep things as structured as possible.

▶ Plan the party food, and keep it simple. Excited children do need to eat, but they tend to be easily distracted. Avoid expensive junk food and don't spend hours making traffic-light sandwiches – most children will just as happily eat a plain cheese or ham sandwich.

▶ Start shopping for the party several days – or even weeks – ahead. Buy all the non-perishable items: drinks, cake candles, balloons and other decorations, a paper tablecloth and serviettes, paper cups, plates, sweets, loot bags, large rubbish bags and the things you need for the games.

▶ Prepare simple take-home 'loot bags' well ahead of time. You don't need expensive ones – brown paper bags with a sticker or two on them are fine. Fill them with a few lollies and an inexpensive party favour.

▶ Choose some appropriate music CDs. If you have a collection of music on your computer, or you have access to an online music store, you can quickly compile and burn a party CD that includes all your child's favourite songs and some suitable music for party games.

CAUTION!

Don't leave presents lying around
To avoid having some of the younger guests investigate (or break) birthday presents, store them away from the party area or put them into a large box as they arrive, remembering to quickly write who it was that gave each present on the presents themselves, in case cards get lost in the pile.

TIMELY TIP

A helping hand

Consider inviting parents as well as their children to your child's party, especially if it's an informal gathering outdoors. In return for serving a glass or two of wine and some finger food, you'll get plenty of help and sanity-saving adult company.

Clever games – outside or inside

▶ Start the party with the more boisterous games and move gradually to the quieter ones as the children tire (especially smaller children) and it's time to calm them down before they go home.

▶ Outside, try games that would be difficult to play inside, but which don't require very much equipment: a treasure hunt that you or your child has prepared earlier, a sack race (using garbage bags), relay races in teams (running, walking backwards, hopping on one foot, on all fours, wheelbarrow) and throwing objects into a basin of water, not to mention classic games such as Simon Says, hide-and-seek and blind man's bluff, which are always more fun to play outside.

▶ A magnetic fishing game can be just as much fun inside as outside: all you have to do is replace the water with polystyrene beanbag beans.

▶ Inside, you don't need to have professional equipment to organise games that will entertain young children. Try pass-the-parcel, pin the tail on the donkey, musical chairs and the mummy game (using several rolls of the most inexpensive toilet paper you can find).

▶ Slightly older children often like playing memory games, or the chocolate game, where they dress in various items of clothing and eat a piece of chocolate with a knife and fork after throwing a six with a dice – if you're short of inspiration, browse the Internet.

▶ Organise mime or face-pulling competitions.

▶ If there aren't too many children, get them to make up a story: the first one starts and the next one continues, until everyone has had a turn. Tape the story and play it back to them later on.

▶ Serve the food halfway between each long game sequence and if the children get over-excited, calm them down by sitting them in front of a video or DVD of an age-suitable movie.

A ready-made birthday party

You can organise a successful birthday party without spending hours preparing everything at home. And it doesn't have to cost the earth.

▶ If you are only inviting a few children, why not take them to see a show – theatre, cinema or circus, depending on their age – and then go for cake afterwards in a nearby cafe?

▶ Think about spending the afternoon in a theme park or at the zoo.

▶ Some fast-food outlets offer inexpensive parties, including entertainment for young children, so if this option isn't in opposition to your thoughts on junk food, it's definitely a fast-and-easy alternative.

Family Christmas

TIMELY TIP

Let there be light

If you have lights on your Christmas tree, make sure you have a few spare tiny bulbs to replace the ones that inevitably blow on Christmas Eve.

Christmas is coming…

If it's your turn to host the family Christmas, remember that not leaving everything to the last moment saves an enormous amount of time and money – not to mention sanity!

▶ Ask family members to share the tasks with you, so that everyone contributes, rather than allowing the whole burden to sit on one person's shoulders.

▶ Share the food preparation so that you, as the host, can concentrate on making the setting as festive as possible. It's not as if the date changes from year to year, so it should be easy to plan well ahead for the Christmas celebrations.

▶ Don't wait for December to buy presents. As soon as you see something that's perfect for someone in the family or a friend, buy it and put it aside.

▶ Keep a small notebook in your bag and note down your purchases so you don't forget by November that you bought something for Uncle Fred in the January sales.

TIMELY TIP

Don't forget the batteries

If you buy toys that require batteries, don't forget to put a few in the present before you place it under the tree. And keep a few extras on hand as well. It'll save any tears on Christmas morning!

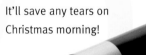

▶ Visit the Christmas fetes, stalls and markets during the lead-up to the festive season. You'll find all sorts of inexpensive and unusual articles for decorating the house or your dinner table, along with gastronomic and hand-crafted goodies that make lovely gifts.

▶ If you like a traditional Christmas fruitcake and pudding, bear in mind that they can be stored for up to a year (a cake in the freezer, the pudding in a cool place), so make them in winter, when you've got more time and it's going to be pleasant spending the day in a warm kitchen.

▶ Buy wrapping paper, ribbon, cards, bonbons or crackers and decorations when they go on sale immediately after Christmas, and save them for the next season. You'll save time on next year's preparations.

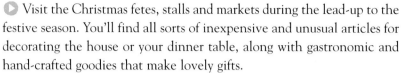

Smart gift giving

There's no doubt that shopping for Christmas presents can be one of the most time-consuming and sometimes frustrating activities at an already busy time of the year. Children love receiving and opening presents, but quite often, adults would just as happily enjoy a Christmas get-together. If your whole family feels this way, do a bit of lateral thinking…

▶ Suggest that everyone donates a certain amount of money that can then be given to a charity or charities of everyone's choice, or subscribe to one of the Third-World Christmas schemes that give goats, clean water, housing or education on your behalf.

▶ Set a price limit on the presents that can be bought – it's fun to see how inventive everyone can be with just 5 or 10 dollars.

▶ Organise a 'Kris Kringle' – each person has to buy a gift (up to a certain value) for just one other specified person. The recipients' names can be drawn randomly from a hat or suggested by the host well ahead of Christmas day so that you have time to go shopping.

▶ Make it a rule that all gifts must be edible or drinkable!

Make it a cool Yule

Christmas is often a very busy time of year, so if time is tight, let your family know that you are not going to be serving hot roast turkey and all the trimmings. Opt instead for a cooler, do-ahead alternative.

▶ You don't have to go without turkey altogether: roast it ahead of time and serve it cold, or look for recipes for smaller cuts of turkey that can be served cold. Cold turkey cuts are often considerably moister and tastier than a whole roasted bird, anyway.

▶ Rare fillets of beef, roasted poultry portions, poached salmon, marinated pork fillets and tandoori lamb cutlets, etc., are all delicious served cold and a selection of these meats is perfect for a cold buffet.

▶ Glaze and bake a whole ham, serve it at room temperature and allow guests to carve it themselves.

▶ Think outside the usual meat dishes, and instead serve a mixed seafood platter – as sumptuous as the budget will allow.

▶ Prepare a selection of simple salads to accompany your main dish, or better still, get other family members to bring them.

▶ Skip the whole hot pudding thing and opt instead for desserts that can be made ahead and refrigerated or frozen.

▶ If people are pining for a touch of tradition, offer Christmas cake or mince pies – both of which can be purchased ready made – with coffee.

A family wedding

TIMELY TIP

Wedding photos

If you've hired a professional to photograph the ceremony, but you want to carry on the celebrations in a more intimate setting, ask friends to take photos and perhaps even a video, or leave a disposable camera on every table for guests to take lots of informal snaps.

A well-planned wedding

Even if you don't plan to hold the wedding at home, you will still need to make decisions about an enormous number of details. Thorough planning is essential, whether you're inviting 20 or 200 guests.

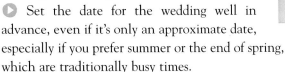

▶ Set the date for the wedding well in advance, even if it's only an approximate date, especially if you prefer summer or the end of spring, which are traditionally busy times.

▶ To give you some idea of the setting for the reception and the necessary budget, get yourself some practical guides devoted to planning a wedding (search online bookshops such as Amazon.com), along with a list of reception venues and lists of competent professionals.

▶ Buy a printed wedding planner (or use the one overleaf as a start). These are readily available from larger newsagents and bookshops and are absolutely invaluable for providing a chronological checklist for all the things you need to do in the lead-up to a wedding.

▶ Consult the many bridal magazines on offer and go to a bridal show, if there's one, before the wedding date.

▶ Don't forget that useful advice about what you should and shouldn't do often comes by word of mouth – consult friends who have recently married or been involved in organising a family wedding.

A basic wedding planner

A wedding planner is essential for the smooth running of any wedding. Tailor this one to suit your own particular needs. It will not only save you time, it will also help to maintain your sanity!

15–12 months ahead
- Plan one or several family meetings to decide on the type of wedding you want and to set a budget
- Set the final date for the wedding
- Roughly estimate the number of guests
- Research ceremony and reception venues
- Book the ceremony and reception venue/s you have chosen as quickly as possible
- Contact the priest, marriage celebrant or registry
- Set the timetable for the various events of the day (ceremony, toast and reception, etc.)

12–6 months ahead
- Choose bride and groom's attendants
- Set aside time for trying on wedding dresses
- Draw up a draft list of guests
- Start looking for a caterer and ask for quotations (unless this is handled by the reception venue). Confirm the different services offered first
- Choose a florist
- Book a photographer and videographer, if you're having a video shot
- Contact professionals who can provide entertainment for the evening
- Organise music for the ceremony

6 months ahead
- Order the wedding dress
- Organise outfits for the wedding party
- Draw up the final guest list
- Finalise the caterer and the entertainment
- Choose and book your honeymoon destination

4 months ahead
- Order the wedding rings
- Choose and order wedding invitations and stationery
- Choose and order a wedding cake
- Start drawing up your wedding gift registry
- Select hotels for interstate or overseas guests
- Organise clothing for the groom

- Have a map printed showing the location of the reception so that guests won't get lost
- Organise a 'going away' outfit and choose some accessories to go with it
- Book the wedding cars

3 months ahead
- Book the wedding rehearsal
- Submit a wedding gift registry that the seller posts on the Internet, to save time choosing and buying
- Book a hairdresser for the wedding day
- Finalise flowers with florist

2 months ahead
- Send the invitations, the maps indicating the location of the ceremony and the reception, and the list of accommodation that has been reserved
- Collect all the documents you need to submit
- Prepare the ceremony with priest or civil celebrant
- Settle the final details concerning the decorations at the different locations where the ceremony and reception will take place
- Organise any final details concerning the entertainment at the wedding and reception
- Try on the wedding dress once again

1 month ahead and up until the wedding day
- Finalise the decorations on the wedding cars
- Order or make bonbonnière, if using
- Make sure all food details are finalised and confirm numbers
- Draw up an initial seating plan
- Have the final dress fittings
- Refine the timetable for the wedding day
- Discuss timetable details with the Master of Ceremonies
- Break in the wedding shoes, to avoid blisters
- Send thank-you notes for gifts received
- Draw up the final seating plan
- Re-confirm with the different participants in the wedding to ensure the timetable works
- Pick up your wedding rings from the jeweller
- Pack your honeymoon suitcase
- Have the wedding party outfits delivered
- On the morning of the wedding, put yourself in the hands of your beautician and your hairdresser

Don't get swamped
Even if you have a lot of help to
prepare a wedding, try to do things
gradually. Draw up a personal
schedule and follow it to the letter
to avoid running out of time as the
wedding day approaches. Send a
thank-you note as soon as you receive
a gift and put a few cards aside for
any last-minute gifts.

Merge technology with tradition

Don't underestimate the power of the Internet for helping you to plan
all the details of a wedding, and saving a huge amount of time spent
running around. It offers the contact details of an enormous variety of
service providers and you'll be able to find what you need in a few clicks.

▶ Search for wedding-planner and organiser sites that offer download-
able software packages to help you plan your wedding.

▶ Find celebrants and examples of wedding services.

▶ Get some fresh or traditional ideas for ceremony and reception music.

▶ Look at photos of reception venues, restaurants or honeymoon spots.

▶ Compare catalogues of dressmakers who specialise in weddings.

▶ Have a look at examples of the work of wedding photographers.

▶ See samples of invitations and wedding stationery.

▶ Get some instant inspiration for wedding cakes (and their cost).

▶ Compare prices and designs of jewellery designers.

▶ Find instructions for DIY wedding craft.

A wedding at home

If you or one of your children is getting married in spring, summer or
autumn, you have a beautiful garden and you want to keep your wedding
day intimate, why not organise a wedding at home?

▶ After you have calculated the number of guests, rent a marquee. This
is essential in case the weather turns wet, unexpectedly cold or windy.
Enquire whether heating the marquee is an available option, too.

▶ Rent mobile toilets if your house has only one bathroom.

▶ Choose a caterer who works in your local area and ask them to
provide all the crockery and cutlery, including serving plates.

▶ Rent enough tables and chairs for a sit-down reception, and make
sure that the price you are quoted includes delivery, setting up of tables
and chairs and also dismantling and removal after the wedding.

▶ Get a local florist to supply, deliver and arrange the floral table
decorations, along with the bouquets for the whole wedding party.

When the going gets tough...

▶ Delegate the coordination of events to a professional. This person
will handle your choices, take care of all the practical questions, monitor
orders, hire musicians and photographers, and generally take the stress
out of the planning by coordinating everything. If you're at all
concerned, check that details have been taken care of before your
wedding day, to avoid panicking when you should be enjoying yourself.

4 Maintaining your home

Good planning

Start out on the right foot

Any building or renovation job requires good planning. Mistakes can be costly, not to mention a colossal waste of time.

▶ Work out your priorities, a budget and a time frame. You should also consider how much disruption construction will cause to your normal routine and in what order the work should be done.

▶ Once your priorities are established, take some measurements and make a few sketches or hire an architect or draughtsman to draw up plans for you. These can be shown to your local council to determine what is permitted before you hire a professional to do the final plans.

▶ If the changes you're making are minor, approved plans may not be required, but in Australia, New Zealand and South Africa major structural changes require council approval, which can take about six weeks. (Contact your local council before undertaking any construction work, to find out what regulations may limit your building and renovation plans.)

▶ Talk to other family members and decide whether you can stay at home during the construction period or whether you need to relocate.

Get the professionals

Most plumbing and electrical work must be done by a licensed tradesperson, but requirements for builders and contractors vary.

▶ Be aware of the contractor's legal obligations concerning personal liability, workers' compensation and property damage.

▶ A builder's licence usually means there will be insurance cover for residential work, but it always pays to ask. Don't accept verbal promises – get everything in writing and check construction progress regularly.

TIMELY TIP

Stay on task

When working on jobs yourself, limit interruptions by engaging a babysitter to look after your children – away from the house – and taking the phone off the hook. Work to a list, in the correct order, and complete one task before starting another.

Contract tips

Follow these five simple tips and you'll save time, and avoid the biggest headache of all – contract work gone wrong!

● Give yourself plenty of time to read the contract and make sure you understand it before you sign – and get legal advice if you're unsure.

● Agree on materials, a time frame and a fixed price.

● Agree on clean-up procedures so you're not left with a mess.

● Final payment should be delayed until after the building inspector has given approval to the building or renovation work.

● Make sure there are no blank spaces that can be filled in later!

▶ If you're not happy with some aspect of the construction or workmanship, speak up as soon as possible, because delays can make mistakes more difficult and time-consuming to fix.

Being an owner-builder

▶ If you decide to build or renovate yourself, you'll first need an owner-builder's licence, which your local building authority can advise you on.

▶ Once you start the building or renovation, begin with the most time-consuming tasks while you're still enthusiastic.

▶ When employing tradespeople, shop around and go by recommendation. Ask for references and inspect previous work – for a big job, get at least three or four quotes.

▶ Draw up a schedule for the job and try to book your tradespeople well in advance to avoid delays.

▶ Stay in close contact with the tradespeople working on your job, as things can change daily and good communication is key to saving time.

Surviving a renovation

Follow these simple tips to minimise the disruption from renovating.

▶ Remove as much clutter as possible from the areas you'll be living in.

▶ Clear the working area to make the job easier and safer for everyone.

▶ Vacate the area being worked on. For example, if it's the kitchen, use a microwave oven and an electric frying pan in the laundry during the renovation, to avoid accidents in or damage to the work area.

▶ Simplify your lifestyle to reduce stress – don't invite your extended family to stay during a renovation, and set out a play area for children.

▶ Keep your children's routine simple and uninterrupted.

The basic tool box

- Double-sided adhesive tape (1)
- Staple gun and staples (2)
- Shifter (3)
- Stillson wrench (4) (Also known as a jaw wrench or adjustable pipe wrench.)
- PVA glue
- Utility knife (5)
- Set of 5 or 6 open-end spanners (6)
- Spirit level or laser level (7)
- Measuring tape (8)
- Sandpaper (9)
- Hammer drill (10) For concrete.
- Cordless drill (11)
- Electric sander (12)
- Small workbench (13)
- Pliers (14) Including one set of cutting pliers.
- Caulking gun (15)
- Glue gun (16) With glue sticks.
- Insulating tape (17)
- Teflon tape (18)
- Broadknives (19) Have two sizes.

NAILING AND DE-NAILING
- Mallet (20)
- Hammer and nails (21)
- Pincers (22)

SCREWING
- Phillips screwdriver (23) Have several sizes.
- Flat screwdriver (24) Have several sizes.
- Screwdriver tester (25)
- Screws (26) Wood screws, screws and plugs of different sizes, screws and plugs for hollow partitions.

SAWING
- Mitre with matching saw (27)
- Wood file (28)
- Hacksaw (29)
- Handsaw (30)

PROTECTIVE EQUIPMENT
- Gloves (31)
- Goggles (32)
- Mask

Renovating your kitchen

TIMELY TIP

Microwave up
Free-up valuable bench space by mounting your microwave oven on the wall or using a purpose-built cupboard or shelf. Include a space for storage and quick access to microwave dishes and utensils.

The basic shapes

Your new kitchen's layout will depend on the space you have available, and will be determined by the traffic flow, the minimum space between benches and the amount of wall space you have.

▶ Plan your kitchen renovation down to the last detail. A kitchen should be practical and easy to use, so it's important to position the stovetop, refrigerator and work surfaces in a logical order.

▶ Conserve energy and save time by creating an efficient work-flow plan based on the 'work triangle' between the fridge (and pantry), the stove and the sink (*see* 'Plan the work flow of your kitchen', starting on page 12.)

▶ A U-shape is the most efficient design as it excludes through traffic. And an island bench will help to further divide it from a larger area.

▶ An L-shaped kitchen is the best option in situations where you're limited to one corner. It easily accommodates the work triangle and also allows easy access to other rooms.

▶ Galley kitchens with parallel benches suit long narrow spaces, but it's important to remember that 1 metre is the absolute minimum workable space between two benchtops.

(*See also* 'The kitchen', starting on page 12.)

Quick cupboard solutions

Renovating is expensive and time-consuming enough, without having to have custom-made cupboards fitted. Today, you have the choice of ordering stock cupboards and cabinets that can be assembled relatively quickly and with the finishes of your choice.

Adequate bench space

Here is a rough guide to assist you when planning kitchen benches:
● 300 mm on both sides of the stovetop, for safety
● 1200–1800 mm for preparation areas
● 450 mm for unloading beside fridges, wall ovens and pantries
● 300 mm for serving two plates and 600 mm for four plates

FIND OUT MORE

• Ready-made modular units are a quick built-in solution for most situations. They come in cabinet form or wire-rack form, with all the necessary components for quick construction. The web sites below supply planning tips and products for flat-packed units available in Australia and New Zealand. (Flatpax supplies kitchen units that can be adapted to suit wardrobe storage.)
www.ikea.com.au
www.flatpax.com.au

TIMELY TIP

Hard-wearing surfaces
Kitchens get a major work-out on most days of the week, so shop around for work surfaces that are resilient and durable – before you start renovating – and you'll save time on cleaning, maintaining and repairing your kitchen benchtops.

▷ Purchase units that only require finishing, or select pre-finished versions ready for installation.

▷ Standardised dimensions and modular designs simplify the job – just measure the available space, order a series of units that come close to fitting it, then make up the difference with fillers between cabinets.

▷ Take advantage of manufacturers, such as Ikea and Flatpax, who provide layout grids for planning purposes (see 'Find out more', at left).

▷ Heights are standard and designed to suit the average person, but there are plenty of choices in cupboard widths. Although the standard bench height is around 900 mm, you can always raise it by building your cupboards on higher plinths or kickboards, since many prefabricated cupboards have adjustable legs that the kickboards clip onto.
(See also 'Get the height right', on page 13.)

Planning tips for accessible storage

Renovating gives you the chance to better organise your kitchen for maximum efficiency, so carefully consider your cooking habits to determine what your storage needs are, and translate that to easy, practical solutions on your kitchen renovation plan.

▷ Try removing doors to create open shelving – it's easier to see items that are running low and need replacing.

▷ Insert drawer dividers to save time sorting through cutlery items.

▷ Install extra benchtop pull-outs that maximise wasted space.

▷ Convert an existing cupboard to a walk-in pantry. This can be a time-efficient and cost-saving solution for reuse during renovation.

▷ Build overhead cupboards right to the ceiling – you might need a step ladder to reach them, but you will maximise your storage space and eliminate the problem of grease and dust collecting on top, thus cutting down on time spent cleaning.

⊃ CAUTION!

Don't take risks – keep children safe
Paying attention to safety aspects is always of prime importance when it comes to renovating, especially if there are young children living through the renovation, too. Gas burners, electric elements, hazardous materials and sharp implements should be kept well out of their reach.

▶ Install an appliance cupboard that sits on the benchtop, so appliances that are used regularly are quickly to hand – and fit a pull-down roller shutter to quickly hide the clutter when guests arrive.

▶ Consider an island workbench if you have room – it'll double your workspace and give you additional storage on all four sides.

▶ Fix a lattice grille onto the wall above your workspace and hang everyday utensils on it for quick access.

(*See also* 'Clever kitchen storage', on page 16.)

Renovating your bathroom

Get it right the first time

A bathroom can be as small as you like, but there are recommended sizes to make it acceptable, and there are some important legal issues to consider before you start any renovation.

▶ Check with local council before undertaking any building or renovation work in your bathroom, as requirements may vary from area to area.

▶ Internal bathrooms without windows or doors opening to the outside need ventilation, either in the form of a skylight or a mechanical ventilation system (*see* 'Essentials of efficient ventilation', on page 14).

▶ Always use licensed plumbers and electricians: doing these jobs yourself may be illegal and is also time-consuming.

Minimum size recommendations

In Australia and New Zealand, the minimum size recommendations for bathrooms are as follows:

- 2.2 square metres for a shower recess or bath with basin
- 2.9 square metres for a shower or bath plus toilet and basin
- 3.5 square metres for a bath as well as a shower, toilet and basin

Renovate to minimise everyday cleaning

Bathrooms need to be hygienic and fresh, as warm, humid environments provide a perfect breeding ground for bacteria. With careful planning, your renovation will save time on day-to-day cleaning.

▶ Install a toilet that has the cistern hidden either in the wall or in the ceiling – this will save space and reduce cleaning surfaces.

TIMELY TIP

The two-in-one heater

While you're renovating the bathroom, install a heated towel ladder. They don't take up much space and are relatively simple to install (especially if someone else does it for you!).

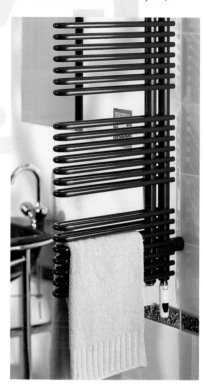

▶ Select easy-to-clean, durable materials that will survive regular family traffic and the occasional bath overflow. And floor materials need to be slip-resistant.

▶ In Australia and New Zealand, instead of installing small, circular floor drains, which can clog and make using large tiles tricky, think about installing a drainage channel that runs the width of the room – using larger tiles means less grout to keep clean, too.

▶ Replace a traditional shower cubicle and glass screen with an open shower bay and you won't have to scrub soap scum off glass surrounds.

▶ Look for porcelain-enamelled cast iron, stainless steel and vitreous china surfaces for your bathroom renovation: they're all durable finishes for bathrooms and are easy to care for.

▶ Opt for white and ivory-coloured fixtures – they're often less expensive and are easier to clean, while dark colours tend to show marks.

▶ Consider installing a bathroom vanity with a benchtop that includes an integrated and seamless ceramic wash plane – no place for soap and dirt to hide, maintaining a clean, hygienic surface.

▶ Install hand-held shower heads in the shower cubicle, set into the bath hob, so that you can quickly rinse down surrounding surface areas, which will save time on cleaning by reducing the build up of soap scum.

▶ Heated towel rails simply plug into a power point and help to make towels stay fresh longer, which cuts down on washing time.
(*See also* 'The bathroom', starting on page 19.)

Fast makeover ideas

If you're renovating other parts of your house and the budget won't stretch to a new bathroom, give it a quick 'makeover' renovation or at least try these tips to make it appear bigger, with little work involved.

▶ Eliminate shadowy corners with adequate lighting. The room will appear higher if you can focus low-wattage, indirect lighting on the ceiling (*see* 'Lighten things up', on page 22).

▶ Swap large fixtures for smaller ones – a full-size bath for a corner shower or a large vanity for a pedestal basin.

▶ Use no more than two dominant horizontal lines.

▶ Keep your choice of materials simple and consistent to give the impression of space, and put any clutter out of sight.

▶ Replace small mirrors with large ones, to reflect and create more space (*see* 'Mirror, mirror on the wall', on page 22).

Timesaving renovation solutions

▶ Ready-made vanity cupboards with integrated basins in a solid surface top can be simply plumbed into place.

▶ Install prefabricated shower compartments, which come with two or three fibreglass reinforced walls combined with the tray.

▶ Use gloss and semi-gloss paints because they repel water and clean up easily, which will cut down on maintenance and cleaning time.

▶ For timber areas, choose panels coated with melamine, which is water-resistant and easy to clean.

▶ Think about using glass bricks in your bathroom renovation, as they provide an instant window for light while maintaining privacy.

▶ Install a single mixer tap with a dual function, instead of separate controls for bath and shower (*see* 'Multi-service taps', on page 21).

TIMELY TIP

New life for an old bath

Instead of replacing an old bath (especially an attractive claw-foot one), think about having it resurfaced. It'll give your old bath new life and you might save some money.

Quick fixes for the bathroom

You'll need a plumber to install your bathroom fittings, but there are a few maintenance jobs you can do yourself while you're renovating, to save both time and water (*see also* 'Plumbing', starting on page 359). Anything that can be fixed is something that doesn't have to be replaced!

● Change a washer in a leaking tap
● Fix a leaking toilet cistern
● Unblock a drain
● Unclog a blocked shower head

Walk-in and built-in wardrobes

Key planning and organisation

Before you plan a bedroom renovation, don't forget to look through your wardrobes and everything in them. What sort of storage habits do you have? Which ones need to change, and which ones are OK? How can you best use the space you have?

▶ Based on your needs and lifestyle, decide whether to put in more drawers than shelves, or more compartments than hanging space, etc.

▶ If you prefer to hang shirts rather than fold them, simply plan to have additional hanging space, rather than accommodating extra shelving in your new wardrobe. Shirts require about half the length of trousers.

Make a detailed list of the things you need to store: how many pairs of shoes, clothes to hang, how much space they take up in height, etc. This helps you to choose the different elements and their size.

Once you know what you're looking for, shop around large storage specialist shops, such as Ikea and Howards Storage World, and consult online catalogues (*see* 'Find out more', on page 16). You'll save a lot of time if you choose units that you can install yourself. And the choice is vast, so you're sure to find what you need.

Match modular units with your personal touch. Some large do-it-yourself centres sell panels and shelves that you can cut to your own size, along with kit elements, such as baskets and brackets or pre-drilled panels for screws, braces, etc., that you can adapt according to your needs.

The right measurements

WARDROBE CONTENTS
Maximise wardrobe hanging space and organise your clothes at the same time by constructing compartments in your robe that allow for just the right amount of length for each type of clothing.

950 mm	1200 mm	1600 mm
Shirts	Trousers (cuff)	Long dresses
Blouses	Garment bags	Dressing gowns
Skirts	Long skirts	Overcoats
Shorts (cuff)	Dresses	Coats
Jackets		
Suits		

Make use of extra space

If you have extra space after renovating, think about installing a wardrobe for storage (to include linen, paperwork, winter clothing or anything else that doesn't fit somewhere else). The more stuff you have stored away, the less time you'll spend cleaning and dusting.

Go for the minimum if that's all you need. A typical shallow wardrobe is about 550–600 mm deep by 1500–2400 mm wide and usually offers a single rod, a shelf above and a pair of sliding doors.

A walk-in robe requires a 600 mm-wide access corridor so more space is needed. If you have enough room, double your hanging space by installing a double tier of rods along one wall for suits, shirts and other shorter items. Rods are usually hung 300–350 mm from the wall.

Fit shelves to the end wall for folded clothes – space them at 180 mm to minimise rummaging. Seldom-used items can be stored on shelves fixed above the rods, and a sloping shoe rack will help keep pairs tidy.

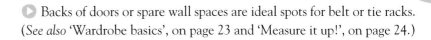

> Backs of doors or spare wall spaces are ideal spots for belt or tie racks. (*See also* 'Wardrobe basics', on page 23 and 'Measure it up!', on page 24.)

Better organisation equals faster installation

Usually, modular units are easy to install, even if the instruction sheets are not always explicit or easy to follow. But with a little forethought and organisation, you'll work more quickly to get the job done fast.

> Clear enough space in the room where you're going to construct the installation: you should be able to spread all your components out flat on the ground so that you can see each part.

> Group the screwing elements together in categories (wood plugs by size, and the same for screws, etc.), and in the order in which they will be used, so that they're ready to go. Count them to ensure none are missing.

> Keep your tools close to hand. You'll need at least a measuring tape, flat-head and Phillips-head screwdrivers, a hammer, spirit level and shifter. And if you use a cordless drill you'll make the job move along faster.

Kit doors – a speedy solution

The type of doors you choose depends on the available space in the room being renovated. You can install hinged, sliding or folding doors in any part of your home.

> Hinged doors need a rebated jamb, a pair of hinges on each door and enough room to swing to provide adequate access.

> Sliding doors are usually timbered or mirrored and take up the least amount of space, plus you can install them yourself on a track system.

> Folding doors require a track system and need hinges to allow the doors to concertina along the track. They're usually panelled or louvred.

> The fastest solution is to buy a pack that includes the doors and track system or hinged components ready to install. But before you do anything, take all the measurements and talk to your supplier.

Putting up shelves

Correct support

A shelving unit is only as good as its support system. This will depend on weight and space needed, end or rear mounting, fixed or adjustable brackets, and the method by which they will be attached to the wall.

▶ Most shelf brackets and tracks have several mounting holes to choose from, but they need an anchor that stays fast when you tighten the screw.

▶ It's always best to fix a shelf to a stud or framework to support heavy weights, but if you have to mount a shelf onto plasterboard, use a mechanical anchor to give it support.

▶ Heavy objects should be fixed using metal toggles. These screw into position, then as you tighten the mounting screw, the metal flange pops out and is drawn in tight to the back of the plasterboard. You can remove the shelf and the bracket for painting at any time, and the anchor remains in place ready to use again.

Sample support systems

Renovating provides the opportunity to rearrange shelving. Make sure you know which shelf support system to use to avoid shelves collapsing, which not only wastes time, but is also potentially dangerous.

▶ Rigid, pressed-steel angle brackets are suitable for medium weights – always mount them with the longer leg against the wall.

▶ Brackets clipped into slotted standards make shelving adjustable and able to carry heavy loads (they come in 200-, 250- and 300-mm sizes).

▶ The simplest and quickest way to hold shelves inside cupboards or bookcases is to install cleats at each end.

▶ Pin-type supports fitted into pre-drilled holes will carry quite heavy loads on 750 x 20-mm thick boards.

▶ Tension poles can wedge between a floor and ceiling and be used to support shelves when you don't want to make holes in walls.

▶ Folding brackets let you drop a shelf out of the way.

TIMELY TIP

Find studs quickly

It's best to anchor shelf supports into solid timber if you can – an electronic stud finder is a handy tool that will save time and prevent mistakes. If you can't get hold of a stud finder, run an electric razor across the wall; when it crosses the stud, the razor's buzzing sound will change.

Suitable shelving

Shelves come in many forms so you'll need to select the correct one for the job. Here is a quick reference guide on shelving spans suitable for a full load of books. You can buy ready-made shelving units complete with brackets and hardware, or have the shelf components cut to your specified dimensions by a specialised cutting service.

Material	Maximum span
17 mm plywood	800–900 mm
300 x 25-mm timber	500–600 mm
300 x 50-mm timber	1200–1350 mm
18 mm particle board	600–700 mm
10 mm glass	400–450 mm

TIMELY TIP

Limit dusting

Adjustable shelving cuts down on the need for frequent dusting, as you can tailor the space exactly to fit the objects being stored.

Hanging pictures

Secure mounting

Take into account both the nature of your walls and the size of the paintings: the full-length portrait of your great grandfather requires a different attachment system from the coaster with a holiday snap on it!

 Any picture weighing more than 10 kg should be hung from two points on the wall with hanging devices attached to corresponding points on the frame. Fix the hanging devices into a stud, if possible, even if it's just for one side of the picture. If you're unsure about the weight, use a pair of hooks spaced about 250 mm apart on the wall. This also prevents a picture from tipping if it slides on the wire.

For lighter frames, there's a whole range of triangular hooks (picture hooks) of all sizes and for all surfaces, and all you have to do is nail them in. If you make a mistake, you can easily remove them by pulling them upwards because they're fixed on an angle. And because the nails are extremely fine, they're unlikely to damage wall surfaces.

TIMELY TIP

Portrait gallery

Before hanging frames of different sizes, do a 'dummy run' on the ground so you can visualise the effect without wasting your time with failed attempts on the wall. If you're dealing with a lot of frames, sketch a plan to organise spacing between the paintings, to ensure consistency of height, while allowing for variations in size.

▶ Consider hanging pictures from a picture rail. A picture rail is a fine rod fixed near the top of the wall. Battens that carry hooks are suspended from this, allowing you to adjust the height, so you can change the position of your pictures without touching the walls.

Hang it right the first time

Experts recommend that paintings should be hung so that the centre of the painting is at eye level, but just whose eyes those are will depend on the viewer. A good general formula that is guaranteed to work every time with just one nail hole is:

● Write down 1500 mm on a piece of paper.
● Measure the height of your frame in millimetres and then divide the measurement by two. Add this to the 1500 for a new total.
● Measure the distance between the hanging wire at full tension and the top of the picture frame, then subtract from the total.
● Measure this distance up from the floor, then bang in your picture hook right there. Perfect!

Solid fasteners provide peace of mind

▶ With large paintings, it is advisable to place fasteners on both back edges. Screw in two closed hooks then join them with brass wire. Do a trial run: the top of the painting should hide the hook. If it's visible, tighten the wire a little bit. When you have reached the right height, remove the painting from the hook and firmly attach the brass wire by pinching it with special rings. You'll find complete systems with hooks, wire and rings in most hardware shops.

▶ Some frames are sold with a fastener already in place on the upper support. But this is not always the case. If necessary, you can nail small brass triangles, using tiny nails. Don't take any risks: remove the glass before you pick up your hammer.

▶ You will also find adhesive fasteners that can adhere to the frame. These are easy and quick to use but are only suitable for very light frames. Make sure you wait for 1 hour before you hang the picture otherwise the glue won't hold. Take care to find the exact centre where you're going to nail or glue the fastener: if it's off-centre, the painting will be uneven and you'll have to start all over again.

TIMELY TIP

Easy placement

Before you start banging in nails, decide what pictures you want to use in a grouping and cut out paper templates and fix them to the wall with Blu-Tack, then rearrange them until you're happy with the result. No more having to say, 'A little to the left... no, up a bit...'

How to hang a mirror

Hanging a mirror doesn't present any particular difficulties, apart from the fragility and weight of the object. Make it an easy job with these tips.

▶ Most large mirrors have fixing brackets as an integral part of the frame. Drill and screw – rather than nail – the fixings and match the size of the screws to take the weight of the mirror.

▶ You can forget about all the double-sided adhesive attachment options unless you're fixing a very small, lightweight mirror. Mirrors are generally very quick to put up, but if they don't hold firm you'll have a catastrophe on your hands!

▶ Use traditional mirror clamps. They come in different sizes to suit the thickness of the mirror. For a decorative mirror, four should be sufficient: two on the bottom and two on the sides – these should be placed closer

to the top. However, if you're installing a full-length mirror, don't skimp – double the number: two on the bottom, two on each side and two on the top. These clamps are made up of a support that has to be attached to the wall by a screw and a cover that springs back on top.

▶ Be careful not to force too much when you screw on clamp covers, because the pressure on the mirror could result in a crack. A clever trick is to insert a thin piece of card behind each screw as a tightening gauge.

Curtains and blinds

Ready-made curtains are perfect

▶ You'll find ready-to-hang curtains in a number of shops – they come in a variety of fabrics and styles, which means you don't have to get out the sewing machine. However, they're usually only available in standard sizes, so there's no point considering using them if your windows are an

TIMELY TIP

Quick calculation

Using the standard widths of windows (1200 mm) and fabric (1400 mm) in Australia and New Zealand, we know that three lengths of fabric are sufficient in most cases, in other words, one-and-a-half widths per drop. For washable material, add 5 to 10 per cent extra length to allow for shrinkage.

CAUTION!

Watch the weight

Some fabric is heavy enough to make a curtain rod bend, or even pull away the system attaching the rod to the wall. To avoid this happening, provide a third point of attachment, in the centre.

unusual size. If you do opt for ready-mades, take your window measurements with you – avoid approximations when you're shopping. A little extra in width is of no consequence, but length is another matter: if a curtain is too short, it won't look good, and if it's too long, you'll need to spend time re-doing the hem.

▶ Consider what type of hanging system is most practical. You'll be able to choose curtains and drapes to suit both rod and track installations and each of these systems has a wide selection of headers to choose from.

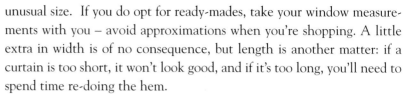

Make curtains part of the plan

Window dressings are an important part of the finishing process during a renovation, not to mention money-savers when it comes to keeping the warmth in during winter. Your options include a wide range of drapes and pelmets, curtains and valances, and various styles of blind including verticals, venetians and shutters. The most important considerations when choosing curtains are:

● **Function** What is the main function of your window coverings: privacy, insulation or light control?

● **Budget** If you set a budget for curtains and blinds it'll narrow your choices and save you time when it comes to shopping around for available options. Do some Internet research to get an idea of pricing.

● **Theme or style** Think about whether you're going to adopt a theme or particular style before you begin renovating. Whether your renovation is purely cosmetic or it involves major structural changes, you'll need to refer back to your plan to make sure that all the elements, including curtains and blinds, continue the theme using ornamental cords to hold drapes back or decorative pelmets, etc. These small touches can add a great deal to the overall effect.

Top tips for sewing your own curtains

▶ Measure windows carefully. To work out how much fabric you need, measure the height between the curtain rod and the ground, then add 300 mm for the header and hem. For the width, allow at least two-and-half times the width of the window, with three times being the ideal.

▶ Choose good-quality materials that are easy to work with and you'll save time. Slippery fabric, for example, is very difficult to sew because you need to tack it by hand before machine sewing it together, to ensure that your seams are straight and that the fabric doesn't pucker.

▶ Consider buying a close-weave fabric, to avoid the need for lining, and steer clear of fabrics where the pattern must match – it can eat up hours of your time trying to get it to look right!

▶ Choose a fabric that can be machine washed, rather than a dry-clean-only fabric, because it's faster and cheaper to launder it yourself.

▶ Wash the curtain fabric before you cut it. This is very important as it stabilises the fabric and allows you to wash the curtains after they have been hung for a while, without the risk of them shrinking.

Easy-to-use curtain rods

Not sure whether to use rods or tracks? Both are easy to install.

▶ Simple rods and curtain tracks have a sliding system. To hang curtains, sew on curtain tape (available from fabric-supply shops such as Spotlight), which allows you to pleat the material or the netting, and in which you place small hooks.

▶ Choose curtain rods that fit your decorating theme. They're available in different materials and shapes – often with highly decorative ends – and they can be used with different attachment systems for the curtains, including traditional rings, claws that clip onto the material and still others made from materials that you put together yourself.

▶ To choose the right length for the rods, measure your window and then add another one-third. Always place curtain rods at least 150 mm above the window so they won't interfere with its opening. Before attaching the brackets, check that the rod is perfectly horizontal. Adapt the attachment system to your type of wall – in principle you should always drill and plug to ensure solid fixing.

Get quick cover with a roller blind

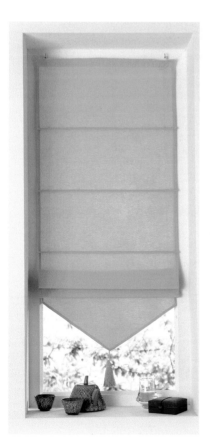

Blinds can completely transform a room, so if your renovation budget is limited, put blinds at the top of the 'must-have' list.

▶ You can fit blinds onto windows or glass doors. Trim them to suit the shape of the window or door after you have attached the supports.

▶ For roller blinds, cutting the roller bar is simple. Measure between the supports, deduct 8 mm, cut, then attach the supplied end, which is used to attach the roller bar to the supports.

▶ Blinds are very adaptable because they work with almost any type of material: vinyl blinds for the bathroom and fabric blinds for the bedrooms or the living area.

▶ Make your own blind. Just remember to choose material that doesn't rip or fray, because you'll save time on hemming the edges.

Slick slats

▶ Venetian blinds come with timber, custom wood and plastic or aluminium slats, and they're solid and easy to maintain. As with roller blinds, you can easily adapt the size of plastic or aluminium venetians to the dimensions of your windows, both in height and width.

▶ To adjust width, take the measurements after attaching the supports. Firstly, shorten the upper and lower cover strips. Remember to protect the slats when you're cutting the cover strips.

▶ Hang up the blind and trace the new width on the lower slat. Cut the slat then trim the others, starting from the bottom and working up. Use the offcut from the first slat to mark the cutting position for the following slats.

▶ Adjust the height by removing the end protectors from the lower cover strip, cut the cord, then completely release the strip. Remove the superfluous slats and put the cover strip back in position, followed by the cord and the protectors. Cut the excess cord.

TIMELY TIP

An economical temperature

The temperature you choose on a reverse-cycle airconditioner thermostat – each degree cooler in summer and warmer in winter – can increase the running costs by as much as 10–15 per cent, and it takes longer for the unit to achieve the chosen temperature. Opt for a temperature you're just comfortable with, say, 25°C in summer and 20°C in winter.

Airconditioning

Save time making your choice

The best time to install most airconditioning units is while you're building or renovating, but don't get bamboozled by the wide choice on offer out there. Check this list of what's available so you can narrow your choice and save time shopping around.

▶ The simplest option doesn't require installation – portable units that move from room to room. They plug into a regular power point.

▶ A wall or window model airconditioner is usually installed in a window or on an external wall.

▶ A split-system airconditioner consists of a compressor unit that's installed outside, and one or more air outlets installed inside.

▶ A ducted system is usually installed in the roof or outside on the ground, then ducted to air outlets throughout the house.

▶ Reverse-cycle airconditioners cost a bit more than cooling-only models, but you can also use them for heating in winter.

▶ Conventional airconditioners work by regularly switching on and off in order to maintain the chosen room temperature. 'Inverter' airconditioners, on the other hand, remain switched on and adjust their working capacity in order to maintain the room temperature.

Get the most out of your airconditioner

Follow these quick tips for getting the most out of an airconditioner.

▶ Ensure your airconditioner operates correctly by getting a specialist airconditioning dealer or contractor to carry out the installation. They will also be able to advise you on the best placement of the indoor and outdoor units to ensure the unit reaches its maximum lifespan.

▶ Ideally, an airconditioning unit should not be placed in direct sunlight, as this will reduce its efficiency. It's best to install it on the shady side of the house, or shade the unit itself.

▶ Close all doors and windows and draw the curtains or blinds to prevent unnecessary heat getting in and cool air escaping.

▶ Choose the 'air-recirculate' setting to prevent hot or cold air from being drawn in from outside.

▶ In summer, adjust air vents to point towards the ceiling, because cold air falls. In winter, point the vents towards the floor as warm air rises.

▶ Shade your windows during hot summer days (to keep the heat out) and during cold nights (to keep the heat in).

▶ When an unusually hot day is forecast, turn on the airconditioner early, rather than waiting until your home heats up. Similarly, start heating early when you're expecting a cold day.

▶ Take advantage of an airconditioner's energy efficiency. For every kilowatt of electricity consumed, two or more kilowatts of heating or cooling capacity can be produced. Window and split-system models must carry an energy-rating label, and the more efficient it is, the lower its running costs are. Ducted systems are expected to meet minimum energy performance requirements, but they don't carry the energy-rating label. (*See also* 'Compare energy-efficiency ratings', on page 66.)

⮕ CAUTION!

Frost-free
If you live in a cold area, look for a model with an automatic de-icing feature, or you may have problems with frost building up on the outdoor heat exchanger coils in winter.

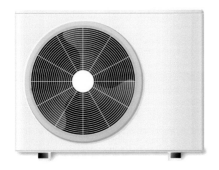

Regular maintenance checklist

Avoid malfunction and time-consuming repairs by doing a bit of regular maintenance on your airconditioner. This includes cleaning the air filter and dusting return-and-supply air grilles to maintain a clear airflow. Most components of airconditioning systems involve mechanical moving parts that also need regular maintenance and adjustment to ensure they operate properly.

● Keep condensers, evaporators, cooling coils and heater elements clean
● Regularly check controls such as timers and thermostats
● Ensure dampers and valves are opening and closing fully
● Maintain refrigeration equipment to keep it working efficiently
● Fix leaks in ducts and pipes, and keep insulation in good condition

The candle test

On a windy day, slowly move a lighted candle in front of each window and door-frame joint. As soon as the flame flickers, you know you have a draught coming in. Once it's identified, use a gap sealant to fill the joint.

Sand lightly

Don't be too heavy handed when it comes to sanding back a wall surface or you might create visible scratches in the plasterboard.

What to do about draughts

Reduce the length of time it takes to warm a room up with your air-conditioner by eliminating draughts. Give each door a quick inspection to check if light is coming in from the outside. If it is, you know you need to put something there to stop a draught coming in.

▶ Install a weather strip – a self-adhesive rubber tape that fits around doorways and windows. It's inexpensive and simple to install yourself, and comes in different thicknesses and different colours.

▶ Attach a weather seal to suit your particular door. Firstly, identify your door type so that you buy the correct type of seal. Some are only draught seals while others are also rain-proof. Check with your local hardware shop if you're not sure which one you need.

▶ The fastest way to stop a draught coming under a door is to use a 'door sausage' to seal the gap between the door and the floor. You can kick it into position in a flash and then stow it behind a couch or along a wall when it's not needed.

Preparing walls

Getting off to a good start

▶ Before decorating any surface, make sure it's clean and smooth. Painted plasterboard in good condition will probably only need dusting and a light sand. Walls and ceilings in heavy-traffic areas or near fire-places or cooking areas may have a greasy film that needs to be removed.

▶ Clean dirty walls thoroughly using sugar soap (following the manufacturer's instructions), water, a sponge, a bucket and rubber gloves.

▶ Remove all hanging objects from walls and clean off cobwebs with a feather duster or the dusting accessory on your vacuum cleaner.

▶ Cover a broom end with an old flannelette pillowcase or shirt, securing it with a large rubber band, and dust the ceiling and walls – flannelette is textured enough to grab dirt fast. Change the pillowcase or turn it inside out when it gets dirty.

▶ Remove old wallpaper (*see* opposite page) and repair any damaged walls before painting them.

▶ If you have to remove wallpaper before painting, remove a small section in an inconspicuous corner first, using a scraper –

there may be several layers! This will also give you a better idea of how much time it's going to take and if necessary, you can change your plans.

▶ Remove several layers by hiring a steamer, and make sure you remove all the glue and residue from the walls afterwards, by washing them with sugar soap (available from supermarkets and hardware shops).

▶ Fill small cracks with a good-quality filler that can be painted over when dry. Larger cracks (more than a finger thickness) will need a couple of coats of spackle or compound (available from hardware shops), which will need to be primed before painting.

▶ Don't forget to dust or vacuum and wash skirting boards and windowsills, too, because they are major dust catchers.

Removing wallpaper the easy way

▶ Many wallpapers are 'strippable', which means they can be removed easily. Pry up a seam edge using a utility knife and tug gently, pulling down at an angle, keeping both hands close to the lifting edge. If it comes off easily, peels in a long sheet and leaves no adhesive residue, then your job will be a simple one-step operation.

▶ Soak older papers and newer ones applied with standard wallpaper paste, to soften the paste. It'll make your job faster. Use warm water and liquid detergent and add a handful of cellulose paste to each bucket of water – it helps to hold the water on the wall. Leave it on for at least 5 minutes, then use a scraper to lift off the paper.

▶ Score washable and wipeable wallpapers with a serrated scraper (or an old dinner fork), so that water can penetrate.

▶ Consider hiring a steam wallpaper stripper to tackle materials that are difficult to remove, or if the wall is covered with layers of old paper. It may make your job faster and easier.

▶ Remove wallpaper that's been covered with paint using a chemical stripper designed for textured coatings – wear protective gloves and goggles.

▶ Vinyls are usually easier to strip off a wall – the vinyl skin can be pulled from its backing, then the backing soaked away. With some modern papers and vinyls, the backing can be left on the wall as the lining paper for the next wall covering. This only works if the paper is well stuck – if there are any loose areas, strip them off.

TIMELY TIP

Clean as you go
Protect the floor with a drop sheet, and put lengths of dampened wallpaper in garbage bags as you go so you're not walking on sticky paper.

TIMELY TIP

Quick wet-down
Wet the wallpaper with a hand spray: it's much quicker than applying water using a brush or sponge.

Fill and sand quickly and efficiently

▷ To fill holes and cracks, use a filler that's ready-to-use. They come in a flexible tube or a tub and are practical for small surface areas.

▷ When the filler is dry, it retracts, so when you spread it make sure you exceed the surface you need to fill. This means you won't have to add any more later on. The idea is to slightly overfill and then sand back.

▷ Save time by working with two spatulas: one on which you place the filler and a smaller one to spread the product into the hole.

▷ Sand back all the rough parts you can feel with the flat of your hand.

▷ Use a sanding block to help you sand evenly. Most hardware shops sell cork blocks, but you can make one using a flat piece of wood about the size of your hand. Fix a strip of sandpaper to it using drawing pins. For larger surfaces, save time by using an orbital sander with a vacuum bag attached to catch the dust.

Painting

The best time to paint interiors

▷ It's a good idea to paint the ceiling (which can be a messy job) before stripping any wall coverings. But this is the only exception to the rule that all preparatory work must be done before you start painting. So check all surfaces are stable, as smooth as possible, primed where necessary, and are clean and dry.

▷ Work in natural light whenever possible, so you can see the new areas and avoid going back over covered surfaces unnecessarily.

▷ Avoid painting when the temperature is dropping – choose a warm, dry day for optimal drying conditions.

▷ When painting outside choose to work after a dry spell, as paint will not take to damp surfaces. Avoid windy days and finish working 2 hours before sunset so the paint has a chance to set before evening dew forms.

▷ In winter, follow the sun around the house, working on the east and north sides in the morning and the south and west sides in the afternoon, to maximise drying time and reduce glare. On hot summer days work in the opposite order.

The right tools for the job

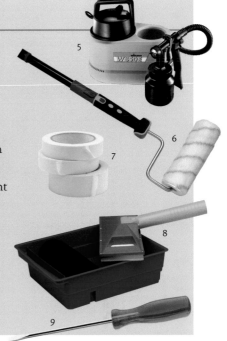

- **Flat tray or small paint bucket** (1)
- **Clean rag**
- **Thinner** Choose the thinner to suit the type of paint you're using.
- **Sponge** (2)
- **Sheets of sandpaper** (3) Have a few sheets each of fine- and medium-grain sandpaper.
- **Brushes** (4) You'll need two flat ones of different widths and a round one for the corners.
- **Spray gun** (5)
- **Roller and telescopic handle** (6)
- **Masking tape** (7)
- **Paint pad** (8)
- **Flat screwdriver** (9)

Quick paint calculation

To estimate the amount of paint you'll need, add the surface area of the floor and that of the walls (without deducting anything for the windows if they're of normal size – it's better to have too much than not enough). Then check the covering capacity of the chosen paint: this is the quantity of paint for 1 square metre, indicated on the paint can.

Handy hints to make the job an easy one

▶ Remove all fittings – power-point cover plates, handles and latch plates – before painting. If you can't do this, rub them with a thin smear of petroleum jelly to keep them free of paint spatters.

▶ Use plastic wrap to cover odd-shaped things such as telephones, doorknobs or lights. You may have to tape some things, but because you can see through the wrap you'll still be able to use them.

▶ Apply masking tape around window panes for a neat edge when painting. If you prefer not to tape them, allow the paint to flow against the glass then use a single-edge razor blade to scrape it off before it dries. Hold the blade at a 45-degree angle and wipe it clean as you go.

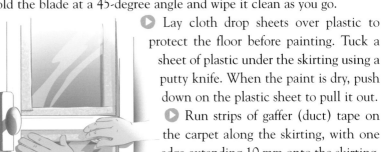

▶ Lay cloth drop sheets over plastic to protect the floor before painting. Tuck a sheet of plastic under the skirting using a putty knife. When the paint is dry, push down on the plastic sheet to pull it out.

▶ Run strips of gaffer (duct) tape on the carpet along the skirting, with one edge extending 10 mm onto the skirting. Tuck this edge down between the carpet and the skirting using a putty knife, then pull up the tape when the paint is dry.

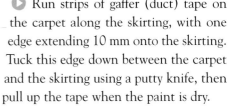

Ten top tips for a great paint job

- Always prepare surfaces thoroughly.
- Use the correct paint system – don't take risky shortcuts.
- Buy the best-quality brushes and rollers you can afford – poor-quality tools often result in an unsatisfactory result.
- Stir the paint well before use, pulling the pigment up from the bottom to the top.
- Check with your local paint shop to see if you need an additive to make the paint stick or flow better.
- Always cut-in (paint around the edges) before rolling a wall or ceiling.
- Always work from top to bottom.
- Never paint when the temperature is falling.
- Always paint over any filled holes to help seal the filler. Patched areas should be sealed before painting.
- Allow adequate drying time between coats of paint.

TIMELY TIP

No cleaning necessary

Forget about cleaning your brushes every time you take a break from painting. Wrap brushes or rollers in aluminium foil or plastic wrap and they won't dry out for several hours.

Choose the right paint

As a general rule, most professional painters prefer flat acrylic paints for ceilings, low sheen-finish acrylic paints for walls and semi-gloss or gloss acrylics for woodwork, which is a handy guideline for do-it-yourselfers.

▶ Acrylic paints have a number of advantages over their oil-based counterparts, which contain solvents causing pollution. They're water-based, meaning they rarely need to be thinned; brushes and any paint drips clean up easily with just soap and water; they emit almost no fumes or vapours when applied; and they dry fast. No contest!

▶ Flat paint has the advantage of providing a soft, glare-free finish and it tends to hide minor surface irregularities. It's easy to apply and is the best choice for ceilings and walls in low-traffic areas.

▶ Low-sheen (satin finish) paint combines the soft finish of flat paint with the washability of semi-gloss. It's easy to apply and can be used in high-traffic areas and wherever a lustrous finish is desired.

▶ Semi-gloss paint is reasonably easy to apply and provides a highly washable surface. It's usually used on windowsills, doors and trim, and in kitchens and bathrooms, where you need moisture resistance and washability.

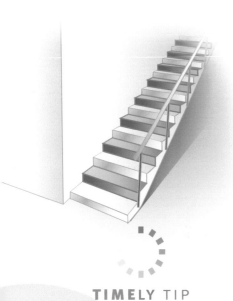

TIMELY TIP

Take the easy way

Instead of waiting for your family to leave before you repaint stairs, think about painting every second step and its corresponding riser. Wait until they're thoroughly dry and then paint the remaining steps.

High-gloss paint is highly reflective and resists grease and moisture. It has the advantage of being able to be washed repeatedly and handles knocks well. However, it tends to show flaws or streaks, so it requires meticulous application on a well-prepared surface.

A systematic approach

Aim to be systematic when you're painting and start with the ceiling.

Paint in strips, starting near the window that lets in the most light, then move to the walls, starting with the wall with the most open space and least trim. Paint the wall from top to bottom, beginning at one end.

Once the ceiling and walls are painted, move on to the woodwork, which should have been prepared beforehand. If walls are to be papered, extend the paint about 10 mm onto the wall around door and window frames, above skirting boards and below any picture rail or coving. This disguises any gaps that may occur between the wallpaper and timberwork.

If the cornices and the ceiling are to be painted in different colours, paint the ceiling first. If the cornices are to be the same colour as the ceiling, paint them first. Run the paint about 25 mm onto the ceiling so that the roller doesn't damage the new work.

Paint the ceiling using a roller that's suited to the paint. And attach the roller to a telescopic handle so you don't have to climb up and down a stepladder to recharge it.

To ensure even rolling, paint in zigzags. On the ceiling, make the first diagonals in a W pattern then fill in the spaces with uniform criss-cross horizontal and vertical strokes. For walls, use an inverted W and fill in between, reloading the roller with paint whenever it starts to paint unevenly.

Save time by using specially designed pressure rollers containing paint, or shaped pads for vertical corners of room walls, and where the ceiling and walls meet in the same colour.

Tint the primer

When painting timber, cut down on the number of finish coats by getting the primer tinted to about half the colour density of the final shade.

TIMELY TIP

Minimise the amount of paint you use

▶ Don't overload a roller or paintbrush with paint. You'll only end up with paint runs, stains and excessively thick layers of paint, meaning more work for you later on.

▶ When using a paint tray, only pour paint into the dish section. Run the roller over the ridged part of the tray to remove any excess paint before application.

▶ Dip a paintbrush into the can only up to two-thirds of its length. Instead of wiping off the excess on the side of the paint can, rub it over a metal wire that you attach to the two fastening points of the can's handle. It'll be easier to close and open the lid again on a clean tin.

Paint the door off its hinges

A door is faster and easier to paint when it's off its hinges and the handles have been removed, so try to do that if you can.

▶ Place the door flat on a table or on trestles and paint one side at a time. The fastest way to paint doors is with a 6-mm nap roller, then immediately 'lay off' (flatten) the stipple left by the roller with a paint-moistened 75-mm synthetic brush. Take long, light strokes starting from the top of the door and then from the bottom, gently lifting the bristles off the surface at about the middle.

▶ It's usual for the edges to be the same colour as the room in the direction the door opens. However, the internal edges should be the same colour as the adjoining room. Use a small flat brush (about 25 mm).

Wallpapering

Choose wisely and save time

The fastest way to change the character of a room is by hanging wallpaper. With practice, the proper tools and the right papers, even a novice can master the basics needed to do a good job in a short time.

▶ Choose high-quality, machine-printed, pre-trimmed papers, which tend to be the most problem-free, so you'll save time putting them up.

TIMELY TIP

Easy does it

One of the best timesaving wall-papering solutions is dry-peelable paper, where you can change your wallpaper as often as you like simply by peeling off the top vinyl layer to expose the backing layer, which is then ready to have the next paper hung straight on to it.

Flocked and foil papers, or wallpapers with selvage edges that must be trimmed on the job, are challenging and best left to the professionals.

▶ Patterns that are 'straight' are easier to hang than 'dropped' patterns. Straight patterns are so-called because neighbouring panels meet in a straight line, while dropped patterns have design repeats that need to be matched panel to panel, which can be time-consuming, and they often also require more wallpaper.

▶ When you buy your wallpaper, also buy a compatible paste and paste brush, or buy a water trough if your paper is pre-pasted.

Smooth hanging

Before you start any wallpapering job, get the walls prepared to save time on the clean-up, and to avoid unnecessary damage to wall fixtures.

▶ Clear the room as much as possible: take down shelves, turn off electrical power and remove cover plates from switches and power points. Protect the floor with drop sheets – plastic is slippery when wet, so place it under cloth sheets to prevent any spills damaging flooring.

▶ Make sure that the walls are in good condition before you start: they should be clean and smooth. Wash them with sugar soap, then rinse. Repair any dents or cracks in the walls and mask off the trim.

The right tools for the job

If you're going to do a good job of hanging wallpaper yourself, in the shortest time possible, you'll need to gather together the essential tools. You'll need the following:

- **Wallpaper brush** (1)
- **Glue brush** (2)
- **Tape measure** (3)
- **Scissors** (4)
- **Utility knife** (5)
- **Sponge** (6)
- **Spirit level or laser level** (7) Include a piece of wood to serve as a ruler.
- **T-shaped ruler**
- **Seam roller** (8)
- **Buckets** (9) One for the glue and one for the water.
- **Gluing table** (10)
- **Water trough** This is to use with pre-pasted papers.

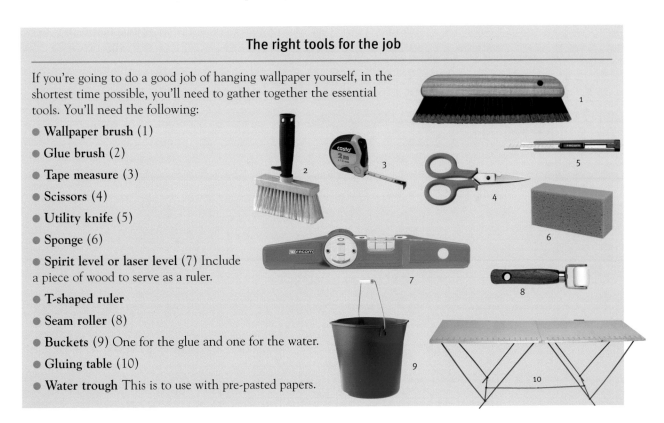

▶ Apply size (a glutinous substance that's used to penetrate and seal fibres in porous materials such as wallpapers and fabric) to the walls that are going to be papered, cutting-in the edges and corners with a brush. Allow it to dry overnight.

Cut wallpaper lengths quickly

Follow these three tips for success.

▶ Measure the height of the walls and add 100 mm at both ends to allow for trimming – this will be the size of each length. You'll be able to cut them on the gluing table (at this stage, it's still clean). Trace the cutting line on the reverse of the paper with a T-shaped ruler and at the top write the letter T. Cut the length with a cutter (utility knife), resting the blade against the ruler. Mark the top of all the following lengths with the letter T. This will allow you to hang them all in the same direction, without having to check each one.

▶ Make the job go faster and more smoothly by marking measures. By making marks directly onto the gluing table itself, you won't have to constantly use your tape measure.

▶ Consider preparing the special cut-outs in advance – for doors, windows, etc. – and number them, and the job will go faster, too.

TIMELY TIP

Find the attachment holes

To find the position of attachment holes, place wooden toothpicks in them and make sure the points stick out by a few millimetres. They will come through the paper and make it easy to reposition any hanging items.

International code of wallpapering symbols

Wallpapers are identified using this international code of symbols, so you can easily determine the one that will best suit your needs.

⌣⌣	Pre-pasted	≈≈	Washable
▸|0	Random side joins	∼	Spongeable
▸|◂	Straight side joins	▮◟	Strippable
↓↑	Reverse hang alternate lengths	▮◟	Wet removal
▸|.	Half-drop side joins	⌒⎍	Paste-the-paper
☼	Moderate light-fastness	▮▸	Paste-the-wall
☼	Good light-fastness	▮◟	Easy-peel (dry-peelable)

TIMELY TIP

Lightning fast tracing

The ultimate tool is the laser level, which is also easy to use. It projects a level line onto the wall and all you have to do is trace over the line! It's fitted with a spirit level, so you can make plumb and horizontal lines.

The right amount

Most standard wall coverings are sold fully trimmed in rolls that are 10 metres long by 530 mm wide, though the size may vary by 5 per cent, depending on the manufacturer. Buy all your paper in one go (colour batches can vary), and buy an extra roll for patching, or two if you have tricky cuts or angles. Order extra paper for repeats of more than 600 mm, to match. To order, measure the perimeter (including doors and windows) and the height of the room being wallpapered.

| Perimeter | NUMBER OF ROLLS | |
	Height (up to 2.5 m)	Height (from 2.5–3.2 m)
12 metres	7	8
15 metres	8	10
18 metres	10	11

A quick estimate can be made if you have a leftover roll of standard wallpaper. Measure the height of a wall and work out how many drops one roll will cover. Then walk around the room, holding the roll of paper against walls, windows and doors as a measuring stick, to see how many widths you need. Divide the number of widths by the drops per roll to give the number of rolls.

Perfect pasting

▷ As soon as the glue is ready, start to coat the paper. You'll work faster by gluing three lengths at the same time. Place them on the table with a little overlap so that the surface of the table is completely covered. This means there will be fewer glue spills and therefore less cleaning up afterwards.

▷ Apply the ⅔–⅓ rule: glue the length and fold over a first third, then the following two thirds. Then fold in two.

▷ When you're gluing wallpaper, remember to leave a small part with no glue in the upper corners, because you'll need to keep your hands clean a little longer in order to hang it up without a problem.

▷ As soon as the first length is glued, fold it according to the ⅔–⅓ rule (mentioned above), and leave it to stand for the time it takes to glue the second, and so on.

▷ Place a broom handle between two chairs to provide a temporary hanging rail, as it's not always easy to find a place to put the glued paper before attaching it.

Choose wallpaper that is pre-pasted. There's less mess involved and the sheets only need to soak in a water trough for the time specified on the label. Drain and allow the sheets a few minutes to relax before hanging them as per the manufacturer's instructions.

Use a plumbline for a good finish

The most important thing when hanging wallpaper is to start perfectly plumb (perfectly vertical and straight). It's rare for the ceiling and walls to be absolutely straight, and a few millimetres of difference at the beginning can turn into a major catastrophe at the end!

Firstly, draw a line on the wall. Start in a corner and measure the width of the paper minus 15 mm and mark a perfectly vertical line. Your first strip of paper will be positioned hard against the plumbline and the opposite edge will then wrap around the corner by 15 mm onto the adjoining wall.

The plumbline must be accurate. You can use a spirit level and a straight edge, or a plumb bob, to mark the line to work from, to keep the wallpaper lengths in alignment.

Tricks for hanging wallpaper

Having a few tips and tricks up your sleeve before you start out on any do-it-yourself project will make the job faster and more successful. And that is especially true of hanging wallpaper, which can become a nightmare if you don't know what you're doing.

Glue the wall before placing wallpaper on it. This will allow the paper to slide more easily into position.

TIMELY TIP

Bubbles be gone!
Pierce air bubbles with a sharp blade, then inject glue with a syringe or apply it with a small, flat brush. Smooth with the wallpaper brush then with the seam roller. Finish by wiping away the excess glue.

▶ Always brush the wallpaper using a wallpaper brush, working from from the centre to the sides and from the top to the bottom to ensure that all air bubbles are removed.

▶ Glue each consecutive length edge-to-edge, and run the roller from top to bottom over the seam to ensure that the paper adheres well. Sometimes there isn't enough glue on the edge so you should always have a pot of glue handy, and use a small, flat brush to apply it.

▶ Leave a 100-mm overhang at the top and bottom. Mark a crease at the cornice and at the skirting with the rounded tip of a pair of scissors. These overhangs can be cut with a utility knife, but cutting them with scissors reduces the chance of a tear. All you need to do is unstick the paper lightly, cut along the mark, then reglue it.

▶ Clean the ceiling and skirting board immediately after the job is done, using a damp sponge, and throw the offcuts of glued wallpaper into a garbage bag as you work, to save time on the clean-up and to avoid getting into a gluey, tangled mess.

Shortcuts to cut-outs

▶ For windows and door frames, hang a full length of wallpaper so it overlaps the frame. Flatten the paper on the wall and make diagonal cuts at the corners of the frame. Lift the flaps of paper, crease the paper at the edges of the frame, then trim.

▶ To paper around a power point or a switch, don't waste time cutting out the length beforehand. Place it directly over the object, make two diagonal cuts with a utility knife, then cut the paper with scissors. The small overhang will be hidden under the power-point cover.

▶ Using scissors, make notches in the wallpaper to neatly follow the curves of an archway. If you make a lot of notches, the paper will follow the shape of the wall perfectly.

Wall tiles

Problem-free tiles

Ceramic tiles are a functional wall covering for bathrooms and kitchens, and come in a wide range of sizes, colours and price ranges.

▶ Measure the area to be tiled and try to work it to full tiles in order to minimise cutting. Allow for a 2-mm tiling joint in your measurements.

▶ Buy your tiles all at the same time to ensure an exact colour match – even white tiles vary from one product batch to the next. Allow an extra 10 per cent in your calculations to cover any breakages and cutting requirements; it could save you a lot of time and unnecessary hassle. Store them after your renovation is complete, in case you break a tile further down the track.

▶ If you can't get exact colour matches, mix the tiles from different boxes – any variations in tone will be less noticeable.

▶ If it's necessary to add a few rows of tiles to an existing surface, choose a matching colour and mark the border with mosaics that are decorative or of just the one colour.

TIMELY TIP

Quick mix
Mix tile adhesive quickly and efficiently using a power drill with a mixing blade attachment.

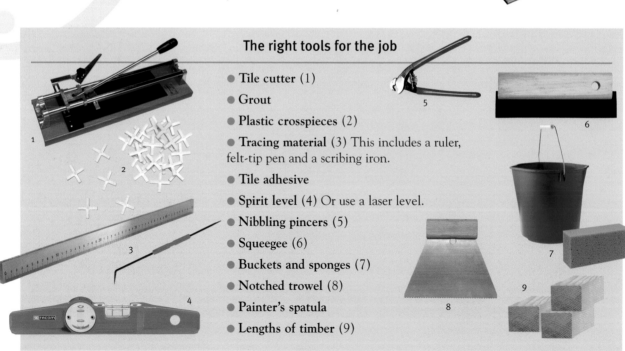

The right tools for the job

● **Tile cutter** (1)
● **Grout**
● **Plastic crosspieces** (2)
● **Tracing material** (3) This includes a ruler, felt-tip pen and a scribing iron.
● **Tile adhesive**
● **Spirit level** (4) Or use a laser level.
● **Nibbling pincers** (5)
● **Squeegee** (6)
● **Buckets and sponges** (7)
● **Notched trowel** (8)
● **Painter's spatula**
● **Lengths of timber** (9)

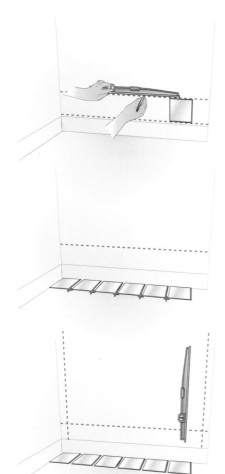

Begin with a good base

▷ Use wet-area wallboard products around showers, baths and wet areas. In these places, walls and floors should be waterproofed to meet current Australian and New Zealand standards. Check with your local authority before undergoing any renovation involving tiling.

▷ As with painting and wallpapering, always begin with a sound base before tiling walls – fill any holes and cracks, and ensure that all surfaces are smooth, clean and dry before you start working on them.

▷ Painted or papered walls aren't suitable for tiling, as the adhesive will only be anchored to the paint or the paper and not the wall. You'll only waste time having to re-prepare the walls before retiling them.

The right start

▷ Start with walls that allow uninterrupted laying. Straight lines are crucial when tiling, so measure carefully to determine the starting point.

▷ Trace a horizontal line above the floor or the skirting board, using a spirit level. The maximum distance between the line and the skirting board must be equal to the width of a tile plus 2 mm, which is the thickness of the tile spacer (plastic crosspiece).

▷ Distribute the cut tiles at each end. Lay a row of tiles on the ground along the wall, placing the spacers in between each tile. Measure the difference in length between the last tile and the wall, divide by two and transfer this measurement to the beginning and the end of each row.

▷ Trace two vertical lines to indicate the first and last rows of full tiles using a spirit or laser level to ensure they are plumb.

Square set-up

▷ To save time as you work, use a right-angled support. You can lean the first tile on it and ensure that everything is vertical.

▷ On the vertical and horizontal lines that you've drawn, attach temporary lengths of timber with a couple of nails fixed only slightly into the wall. Having this guide is a handy time saver when it comes to gluing the tiles, as you won't have to constantly check the alignment of the edges.

▷ Pick up the adhesive with a spatula, place it on the edge of the trowel and only cover the wall a square metre at a time. Spread the glue with the notched trowel to give an even layer over the area.

TIMELY TIP

Cutting correctly

Place the tile that needs to be cut with the glazed side up against a tile in the last row. Position at the wall, or on the ground, and mark a line that aligns with the full tiles. Allow 2 mm for the spacer, then cut.

Laying tiles the easy way

▶ Glue the first row and place the spacers as you go. Work from bottom to top completing each row of tiles in turn.

▶ Systematically scrape away the excess adhesive in the joints with a match – this will take longer if you allow the glue to dry.

▶ Remove timber guides and spacers before the adhesive has fully dried.

▶ To finish, tile the sides and the last (bottom) row. In principle, you should only have to glue whole tiles, but floors aren't always straight. If you do have to cut tiles for the last row, place the cut side facing the ground.

▶ Work in the same way when you come to do the side tiles, gluing the cut tiles in sequence. And remember that on the sides it's faster to put adhesive on the back of the tile and not on the wall.

Neatly cut curves

Save time on a tiling job by using four tiles instead of two to cut around pipes, floor grates and plumbing fixtures. It's easier to cut a quarter of a circle than half a circle.

Mark the rounded shape, and the part that has to be removed, with a scribing iron or permanent marker. Cut the piece little by little using the nibbling pincers after the bulk of the waste has been removed with a small grinder. For a perfect finish, file the nibbled edge.

Great grouting

▶ Don't try to grout all the joints in one go because grout sets quickly.

▶ Prepare a small quantity of grout in a bucket by pouring water onto the powder, and not the opposite. This will allow you to control the consistency more easily – crush any lumps with your hands. Fill another bucket with fresh water and keep two sponges handy.

TIMELY TIP

Seal bathroom joints

Some joints or gaps (around a sink, basin, bathtub, etc.) must be filled with flexible silicone. Tape either side of the joint and fill with silicone using a caulking gun, then smooth it using your finger. Dip your index finger in soapy water as you go, to make the job faster and easier. Remove the tape as soon as you've finished.

▶ As soon as the grout is ready, pick it up with a spatula and spread plenty of it over the tiles to cover a small area. Continue with the rubber squeegee, moving it in all directions to force the grout into the joints until they're filled.

▶ Using a clean sponge, eliminate the excess as soon as it starts to set, wiping it over flat so as not to hollow out the joints. If you wait too long, it will be much harder to remove from the tile surface.

▶ Make another batch of grout and cover another small area, then keep working this way until you've finished the job.

▶ When you've finished, wipe a damp sponge over the joints. To remove the final smears, mix a cup of white vinegar with a bucket of warm water and polish the tiles with a clean towel.

How to drill a tile

▶ To avoid breaking a tile when you're drilling a hole in it, place a piece of tape marked with a cross on the position for the hole.

▶ Get the hole for the drill bit started off by tapping a nail gently to just break the surface of the enamel, then drill with an electric drill, on a low-speed setting using a masonry bit.

Timber panelling

Use MDF panels for speedy installation

Medium-density fibreboard, or MDF, is a versatile building material.

▶ Change the look of a room quickly by installing large, lightweight panels of moisture-resistant MDF. The panels come in a range of sizes and styles to suit both contemporary and traditional decors.

▶ Buy panels that have already been primed, to save time with both preparation and painting of the panels.

▶ Consider laying sheet wall panelling in a variety of timber finishes as an alternative to MDF panels. The sheets are randomly grooved to give the look of individual board panelling, and are also pre-finished, so you don't need to apply any stain or finish once they're fixed to the wall.

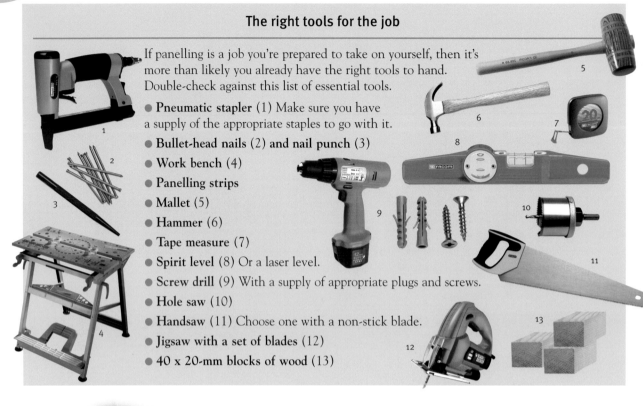

The right tools for the job

If panelling is a job you're prepared to take on yourself, then it's more than likely you already have the right tools to hand. Double-check against this list of essential tools.

- **Pneumatic stapler** (1) Make sure you have a supply of the appropriate staples to go with it.
- **Bullet-head nails** (2) **and nail punch** (3)
- **Work bench** (4)
- **Panelling strips**
- **Mallet** (5)
- **Hammer** (6)
- **Tape measure** (7)
- **Spirit level** (8) Or a laser level.
- **Screw drill** (9) With a supply of appropriate plugs and screws.
- **Hole saw** (10)
- **Handsaw** (11) Choose one with a non-stick blade.
- **Jigsaw with a set of blades** (12)
- **40 x 20-mm blocks of wood** (13)

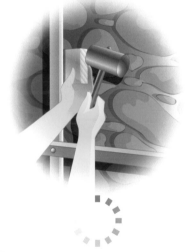

TIMELY TIP

Free material at hand

Save offcuts of timber for packing behind framework battens to bring them back into alignment.

The finish is only as good as the base

Be warned: timber panelling is not a mask to hide all evils – the walls must be sound before you even think about covering them.

▶ Masonry walls are usually easy to work with – the panelling can be fixed directly to the wall surface using panel adhesive, as long as there's no loose or damaged mortar involved.

▶ On plasterboard walls, it's advisable to provide a level and plumb surface for the panelling by fixing battens to the wall studs.

▶ Using battens fulfils two purposes – they provide a level support for the panelling, and they create space between the panelling and the wall to provide adequate ventilation.

An uncluttered work space

▶ Save time by working in a room where there's no furniture, so you can handle panels more easily and avoid damaging anything.

▶ Strips of panelling are sold by the lineal metre. To avoid running short, allow for extra in your final calculation.

▶ Remove the panels from their packaging and leave them in the room for 48 hours before attaching, so they can adapt to the humidity level.

▶ Remove any power points and switches before attaching the panelling. When you install the timber strips, all you'll have to do is to make a mark and cut the position of switches using a hole saw.

A problem-free frame

▶ For masonry walls, fix battens using masonry nails or plugs and screws.
▶ On plasterboard walls, nail or screw battens to the wall studs – use a stud finder to help find studs quickly (*see* 'Timely tip', on page 317).
▶ Horizontal battens should be spaced at 400-mm centres.
▶ Check the battens are plumb using a spirit level. If not, use packing pieces behind the battens to maintain a level laying surface.

Attaching the panels

▶ The position of the first strip determines the position of the others. Firstly, remove the tongue, which doesn't serve any purpose. Make a vertical mark 5 mm from the wall, draw a line, run a bead of panel adhesive 500–600 mm along each batten, then position the first strip and attach it.
▶ Fit the tongue of the second strip into the groove of the first one. Tap lightly with a mallet to avoid damage to the edge. To ensure a snug fit, take an offcut from a strip, put it in position and give it a few light blows with a wooden or rubber-headed mallet. Repeat this at various heights.

▶ If you're using nails, use bullet-head nails. Hammer them at an angle into the tongue on each strip and sink the nail head using a nail punch.
▶ Using a spirit level or a laser level, check that the panelling is plumb every three or four strips, because it can get out of alignment very easily and you'll then have to waste time going back over what you've already done to realign the panels.

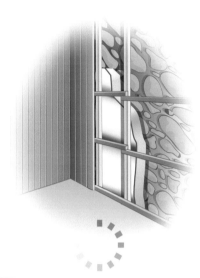

Fast finishing touches

▶ If you end up with an uneven finish at the top and the base, mask small defects at the base by fitting a skirting board. For the top, use mouldings, cornice or a simple quartered timber strip.

▶ Cut out the positions of the switches and power points with a hole saw, and put the fittings back into place. Don't be tempted to do any electrical work – it's illegal – get a qualified electrician. And remember to check the length of the attachment screws, as you have to take into account the extra thickness of the frame and the panelling.

TIMELY TIP

Like butter
Nails and screws are more easily screwed into hardwood if they have been pressed into household soap beforehand. It's amazing how effective it is!

Levelling floor surfaces

TIMELY TIP

A fast and simple solution
Choose self-levelling mortars: they're fast setting, self-levelling floor toppings specifically formulated for levelling concrete prior to laying carpet, vinyl, tiles or timber-laminate floating floors.

The basic preparation

▶ Find out what the floor you're walking on is made of and if it's level before installing a new floor covering.

▶ Make sure that the floor's base surface is not full of humps and hollows, otherwise you'll be wasting your time and run the risk of spoiling the finished appearance of your new floor.

▶ Check that a timber or particle-board floor is level, and fix any squeaks or loose boards. High spots can be sanded down.

▶ With concrete floors, even a dip or rise of 3 mm over 1 metre needs to be repaired before the floor can be covered. Any high spots should be ground off and low spots filled with a self-levelling compound.

 **CAUTION!**

Start at the correct end
Remembering to start at the correct place will always save time – there's no point finding yourself stuck in a corner in the middle of a job. Work backwards and start from the side opposite to the door.

The right tools for the job

- **Cleaning materials** A vacuum cleaner, broom, detergent, etc.
- **Self-levelling mortar**
- **Glue brush or roller** (1)
- **Drill and mechanical mixer** (2)
- **Bonding agent**
- **Bucket** (3)
- **Stainless-steel float** (4) This is used for spreading the mortar.

Getting ready

▶ Place a straight edge over the surface and identify high or low spots. Mark them, then grind off high spots and fill low spots.

▶ Clean the floor to remove traces of grease, which can prevent bonding.

▶ Spread a layer of bonding agent on the areas to be treated. This will ensure a good bond between the concrete and the mortar topping. Leave it to dry according to manufacturer's instructions.

Making the floor level

▶ In a bucket, add water to the mortar and mix well – save time and energy by using an electric drill with a mixing attachment. The mixture shouldn't be too liquid. Leave it to rest for a while.

▶ Gently pour the contents of the bucket onto the floor. Using a float, spread it out to a maximum thickness of 3 mm. Start again and work in small sections until all hollows are filled.

▶ Use a stainless-steel float for spreading mortar correctly. Don't worry about any marks it leaves; these will disappear as the mortar self-levels.

How long does it take?

Knowing how long different agents take to dry can save you quite a lot of time if you factor this into the planning.

- Drying time for the bonding agent — 30 minutes
- Setting of the self-levelling mortar — 30 minutes
- Hardening — 2–3 hours
- Before laying the floor covering — 24 hours

Wall-to-wall carpeting

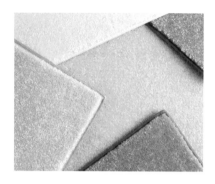

TIMELY TIP

Stop creases
Make sure carpet is unrolled and
stretched before it's laid. This will
remove any creases that may have
settled in during transport.

Make a few basic decisions

Carpets come in a variety of colours, styles, patterns and quality finishes.
You can choose from synthetic or wool, with the latter usually being
more expensive. Follow these tips to save time choosing the right carpet.

▶ Always choose carpet according to the room it's being used in.
Carpet in high-traffic areas needs to be more resilient than carpet in a
bedroom (*see* 'The star rating system', below).

▶ Once you've narrowed your choice according to wearability, consider
how much you want to spend. You'll make your decision faster by not
wasting time looking at carpeting out of your price range.

▶ For a professional finish, and when laying high-quality, expensive
carpet, hire a professional to do the job for you. It's not only faster, it'll
ensure you get the best results, too.

▶ If you have cheap carpet that's OK to use in a spare room, but you
don't want to go to the expense of getting someone to lay it for you, do
it yourself – it is not a particularly difficult or time-consuming job
(depending on how skilled you are, of course).

The star rating system

Carpets sold for residential use in Australia and New Zealand are rated
according to wearability using a system of stars. Check the list, below,
before you head out to buy carpet, to find out how many stars you
should be looking for. It'll help you narrow your choice and save time.

- **One star** Light duty
- **Two stars** Medium duty
- **Three stars** Heavy duty (lower to mid range)
- **Four stars** Heavy duty (mid to higher range)
- **Five stars** Extra heavy duty (lower to mid range)
- **Six stars** Extra heavy duty (mid to higher range)

Classes of carpets

Australians and New Zealanders can make fast work of choosing carpet
for the home or office, thanks to current classing and labelling of carpets.

▶ Don't spend time wondering whether the carpet you're choosing is
suitable for a specific area – take advantage of information supplied by

CAUTION!

In the right direction
Carpet always has a direction –
you see it when you vacuum:
when going against the fibre the
shade always seems darker. Be
careful if there are joins – you'll
need to position the second
piece of carpet so that it runs
in the same direction as the first
or the seam will be visible.

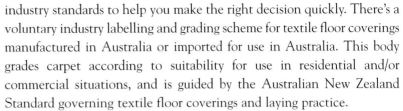

DIY carpet laying

Stretching and seaming of carpet is best done by a qualified, professional carpet layer, but carpet with attached cushion can be laid by most do-it-yourselfers. With just a few simple, inexpensive tools and double-sided adhesive tape, you can lay your own carpet in reasonable time.

industry standards to help you make the right decision quickly. There's a voluntary industry labelling and grading scheme for textile floor coverings manufactured in Australia or imported for use in Australia. This body grades carpet according to suitability for use in residential and/or commercial situations, and is guided by the Australian New Zealand Standard governing textile floor coverings and laying practice.

▶ Yellow and blue labels identify carpets that have been graded for residential use. Residential ratings can have a maximum of six stars (*see* 'The star rating system', on opposite page). The star system allows you to quickly decide which carpet is suitable for your needs.

▶ If you need carpet graded for commercial (contract) use, look for gold and black labels. Commercial ratings carry a maximum of four stars.

▶ Be aware that there is occasional crossover and some carpets will carry both residential and commercial gradings.

▶ There is also an Environmental Classification Scheme (ECS) for carpet. The ECS covers Volatile Organic Compound (VOC) emissions, noise reduction and thermal insulation properties that relate to a carpet's environmental performance.

Careful planning equals time saved

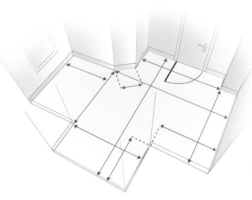

▶ Make an exact plan of the room to be carpeted, including all the recesses, the position of the doors and windows, etc. Measure to the centre of doorways and to the back of cupboards, then add 10–15 cm to the dimensions of the room. This information will help the retailer advising you, particularly with regard to the direction in which the carpet should be laid, and therefore the resulting dimensions.

▶ If you buy good-quality carpet, make sure it's properly laid, or its look and performance will be severely undermined. Problems such as poor

The right tools for the job

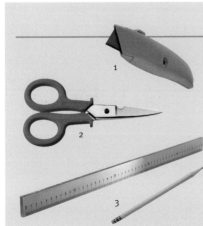

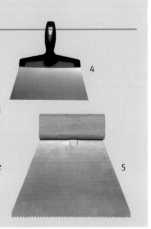

- **Utility knife or carpet cutter** (1)
- **Scissors** (2)
- **Tracing material** (3) A ruler and pencil, etc.
- **Double-sided adhesive tape** Alternately, you can use carpet adhesive.
- **Broadknife** (4)
- **Notched trowel** (5) You'll need this if you're using carpet adhesive.
- **Carpet edging strip**

TIMELY TIP

No more accidental cuts

If you're cutting carpet yourself, avoid the risk of making accidental cuts by placing a large spatula flat on the carpet and cutting gradually, moving the spatula as you work – it also acts as a straight edge.

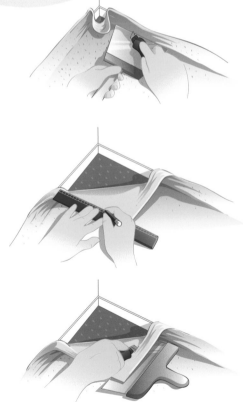

joins, badly matched patterns, rucking and lumpy underlay can arise as a result of poorly laid carpet.

▶ Buy the very best underlay you can afford. As a general rule, the better the underlay, the longer the carpet will look good. It's counter-productive to have the quality of your carpet undermined by a sub-standard underlay, which could reduce your carpet's life by years. (*See also* 'Getting a good result', below.)

Get carpet into position first

▶ Before laying carpet, remove any doors opening into the room being carpeted. The bottom of the doors may have to be trimmed to allow them to swing freely over the new carpet after it's laid.

▶ Position the carpet so that it's centred in the room and allow 4–6 cm surplus run-up on the walls on all sides. Make sure the carpet is well centred and that there are no creases in it.

▶ If one wall has no doorways or recesses, it's OK to butt the carpet up to the wall and then simply trim the other three sides.

Careful cutting

▶ Measure the room before cutting the carpet, then pre-cut the carpet 8–12 cm larger than the room size.

▶ Mark the angle formed by the floor and the wall with the rounded part of a pair of scissors. Then cut the overhang with a carpet cutter. Stop around 20 cm from the corner angles, so that you cut them last.

▶ When you have finished cutting a straight edge, fold back the corner. Using a ruler and pencil, trace a line on one side that follows the cut that has already been made. Cut along the line, protecting the carpet underneath by placing the broadknife in between. Do the same thing on the other side of the corner angle.

Getting a good result

Cushion or underlay is a critical flooring component. It's the foundation for your carpet, and is responsible for enhancing both its comfort and durability. Underlay is constructed of several different materials, including sponge rubber, foam rubber, urethane foam, bonded urethane and felted combinations of hair and jute. In order to handle the traffic on the carpet, select underlay of an appropriate thickness. In a bedroom, a thick, soft underlay works well, but in a family room with heavy foot traffic, a thin underlay works better.

TIMELY TIP

Tiles are ideal

Carpet tiles are durable and have a thick backing – so they hold using their own weight, which means you don't have to attach them. If there's a stain on one tile, all you need to do is remove it, then clean it or replace it.

Using adhesive correctly

▶ Choose any good-quality, low-VOC, multi-purpose adhesive. Carpet seam-sealer adhesive for seams can be purchased from carpet suppliers or home-improvement centres that sell carpet.

▶ Once the carpet is in position, fold one half of the carpet back over itself and apply the adhesive (following manufacturer's instructions) to the floor. After proper 'tack time' lay the carpet onto the adhesive and then do the other half of the room.

▶ Get it right the first time, because once you have glued down carpet, it's difficult to unglue it! If you have to unglue carpet, you also have to remove all traces of glue, which is a time-consuming process.

▶ For a small room, double-sided adhesive tape is faster. Put tape around the perimeter of the room and place 30 x 30-cm crosses of tape at 1-metre intervals in the middle of the room, leaving the protective cover on the tape while you position the carpet.

▶ Fold one half of the carpet back over itself, peel the protective cover off the tape and replace the carpet, smoothing it from the centre of the room towards the walls. Repeat on the other half.

Vinyl floor coverings

Make an informed choice

Vinyl flooring is also called 'resilient' flooring because it characteristically bounces back from the weight of objects that compress its surface. In general, there are two types of vinyl flooring: sheet and tile.

▶ Available in 3- and 4-metre widths, domestic sheet vinyl comes in many colours and designs and a variety of qualities. It's the most popular of domestic vinyl floors due mainly to the 'loose-lay' method of installing – generally in one piece in an average-size room.

▶ Sheet vinyl is a great option because it can also be glued down, and is ideal for laying over the top of old flat floors, ceramic tiles and concrete, giving an instant effect for a minimum of effort and cost.

▶ If you're laying sheet vinyl over timber floors, a 6-mm hardboard underlay needs to be installed first, to ensure the floor surface is flat and to eliminate 'mirroring' of the floorboards.

▶ Consider buying latex-backed vinyl tiles (either semi-rigid or laminated) because they're supple, easy to handle and lay, and are comfortable to walk on. They come in a range of colours and designs, some imitating other materials such as stone and timber. You can use them in any room, but they're best for kitchens and bathrooms.

▶ If you're looking for durability, choose semi-rigid vinyl tiles. They're highly resistant to indentation, gouging and other physical damage and wear, which ultimately is a great timesaving feature. These tiles are often found in laundries, toilets and entryways because they're hard-wearing.

▶ If you want to go more for look or even custom design your own floor, opt for laminated vinyl tiles. They're available in wood, marble, slate and stone finishes, which is a quick-and-easy way to continue an interior design theme. They come in squares and plank form.

Opt for versatility

As a general rule, a versatile product is a timesaving product because it provides a single solution to a number of different issues. For this reason, vinyl floor coverings are a winning choice for use in the home.

▶ Use vinyl on kitchen and bathroom floors – it's durable, easy to maintain and more moisture-resistant than many other materials.

▶ Match vinyl flooring to your decor. Virtually any look can be obtained, including classic looks that simulate wood and ceramic. And custom-made designs are easily created using sheet vinyl flooring.

▶ Save time finding costly noise-reduction solutions by laying vinyl, which is great for cutting down on the noise made by most hard floors, especially if you live in an apartment block.

▶ Take advantage of vinyl's low-maintenance qualities. It's tough, resistant to scratching, scuffing, staining, indentation and other daily abuse, which saves you time on cleaning and making repairs.

▶ When compared with alternative materials, vinyl offers reasonable installation costs, and it's relatively cheap to maintain throughout its life.

TIMELY TIP

Get the temperature right
Your floor will bond faster if you lay vinyl when the room temperature is between 18–29°C for at least 48 hours previous to, during and 48 hours after installation of the floor.

The right tools for the job

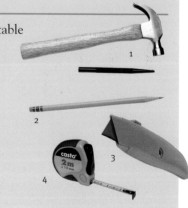

- **Self-levelling mortar** You'll need this if you're working with concrete sub-floors.
- **Timber filler**
- **Double-sided adhesive tape**
- **Vinyl seam sealer**
- **Hammer and nail punch** (1)
- **Straight edge**
- **Floor sander** If you're working with timber sub-floors.

- **Adhesive** Buy one that's suitable for vinyl floor coverings.
- **Pencil** (2)
- **Utility knife** (3) Make sure you have a spare set of blades.
- **Long metal ruler**
- **Tape measure** (4)
- **Hard rubber roller**

Best layout

Sketch your room to scale, measuring the length and width of the floor and checking each measurement twice. Decide if the vinyl sheets will run the length of the room or across the room, then lay them out so the pattern looks right when you walk into the room. Always add a safety margin of at least 10 cm to allow for matching patterns and making joins in the vinyl.

Start from a good base

Vinyl sheeting can be laid over most types of sub-floor, but first check that the sub-floor surface is dry and hard, and free of any loose dirt or other material – sweep or vacuum it thoroughly.

▷ If you're working with a concrete sub-floor, check the surface for imperfections and make sure it's level. Spread a self-levelling mortar over the floor, if necessary, to start with a smooth surface (*see* 'Making the floor level', on page 343). Follow the manufacturer's instructions on the packet and allow sufficient time for the mortar to cure properly.

▷ If you're working with a timber sub-floor, check that the boards are securely fastened by punching all the nails below the surface using a hammer and nail punch. Fill any holes, knots or imperfections with a good-quality wood filler, then sand it smooth.

▷ If timber boards are cupped or very uneven, get a professional to level them out for you, or hire a floor sander and do it yourself.

▷ A quick fix for timber sub-floors is to simply cover the existing floor with special hardboard underlay, staggering the sheets and nailing at 10-cm intervals. Once laid, sand the underlay until it's smooth.

For a perfect finish

▷ When the job's done, replace any architraves or skirting that was removed from the floor prior to laying the vinyl sheeting.

▷ Use plenty of double-sided tape under heavy movable objects, such as washing machines or freezers, when 'loose laying' (not using glue).

▷ Do not wash the floor for at least 24 hours after laying vinyl, to allow the seam sealer to dry completely.

Fixing vinyl to the sub-floor

● Sweep and vacuum the sub-floor surface. Unroll the new vinyl flooring and allow it to sit flat in the room for at least 24 hours prior to laying.

● Trim the sheets to size by starting at the corners of the room and around fixtures – aim to have a gap of 1–2 mm to all vertical surfaces. Try practising with offcuts to get the knack of cutting to size around corners or fixtures.

● If you have an awkward shape, make a template of the whole room from cardboard and use it to cut your vinyl to fit.

● Sweep the vinyl flat with a soft broom and if necessary, make additional release cuts to ensure the vinyl sheets lie perfectly flat.

● To cut the sheets around pipes or a toilet, first make a template with cardboard or paper. Stick the template to the vinyl sheet and cut out the shape, then secure the sheet using double-sided tape.

● If using adhesive, plan to glue the vinyl down in two equal sections.

● Apply adhesive around the perimeter, using a trowel, then fill the middle with an even coat, finishing in a straight line along the rolled-back vinyl.

● Allow the glue to set for the recommended time, before rolling the vinyl back over it and smoothing out any bubbles with a hard rubber roller.

● Repeat for the second half.

Self-adhesive tiles – the easy option

▶ Self-adhesive tiles are fast and easy to install – simply pull off the backing paper and press them into place.

▶ Make sure you place each tile directly into position without sliding or you'll find yourself wasting time pulling them up to reposition them properly.

▶ Always butt up the edges of tiles closely, or dirt and grime will get stuck between them, which will increase the time you spend cleaning and vacuuming!

▶ Firmly press down all over the surface of each tile with the palm of your hand to ensure good even adhesion and they'll be more likely to stay in position.

▶ Cut vinyl tiles the quick-and-easy way: first, use a sharp utility knife to score through the surface, then carefully bend back the tile – it should snap cleanly along the score line.

TIMELY TIP

Make a double cut

If you have to make joins, save time by letting the two pieces overlap by a few centimetres, then cut the two thicknesses at the same time. Rest the utility knife against a metal ruler and keep the blade firmly in the cutting groove. Remove both offcuts and butt the two pieces together then glue either side of the join.

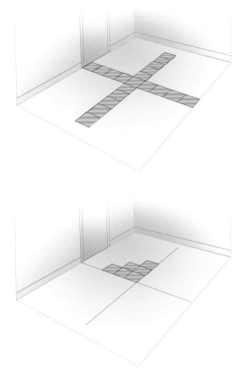

Follow a sequence

▶ Tiles look best centred in the middle of the room with any narrow tiles at the edges. So your first task is to find the centre of the floor. If you simply begin from a corner you may end up with whole tiles along one side and narrow tiles along the other.

▶ Carry out a trial installation. Place two rows of tiles in a cross, laying them from the central point out towards the walls. The tiles on the edge should be the same width against the two opposing walls, so move the rows of tiles until you find the exact position for the first tile, which should be approximately in the middle of the room. Trace around the tile.

▶ Remove the backing paper on the first tile, press it into position and smooth it down. This is your guide for laying subsequent tiles.

▶ Retrace the two perpendicular axes in relation to this new position. Position a second tile next to the first, along the line. Then a third above the first. Continue working like this in a stair formation, making sure the tiles are a snug fit and checking constantly to ensure they are aligned. Complete a quarter of the room at a time.

TIMELY TIP

How many tiles?

Vinyl tiles are usually 300 x 300 mm square and sold in packs of multiples. If the room is an irregular shape, divide it into rectangles and measure each one separately, then make a scale drawing on graph paper. This will allow you to work out the number of tiles you need and help you set out an attractive design.

Change a damaged tile quickly

Don't rush to rip up a damaged tile. Follow these three easy steps and do it properly the first time around. It will save you wasting time in the long run.

● Heat the centre of the tile using a heat gun or an iron over aluminium foil, to soften the plastic and glue. Remove the tile and scrape the space clean.

● Once the sub-floor is clean and dry, check that the new tile

fits perfectly, then remove the protective paper and fix it into position.

● Smooth and cover the tile with a board, then place a heavy object on top. Wait for a few hours before removing the heavy object.

TIMELY TIP

Spare tiles

Plan to buy at least 15 per cent extra when shopping for tiles. If you need to change one later on you may not be able to match your pattern or colour exactly.

Fast edge cutting

▶ Place a tile exactly on top of a glued tile. Place another one on top of that one, but move it back so that it touches the wall: this will serve as a guide for cutting the middle tile (against the edge of the top tile). The offcut that is obtained will exactly fit the space you need to fill. Break the cut, remove the protective paper and fix it in place.

▶ If you manage to have exactly the same space all around the room, you can skip the previous step and add a frieze. It's better to lay the frieze tiles after you have finished laying the rest of the tiles.

Floor tiles

Do it like an expert

A tiled floor is attractive, hard-wearing and easy to clean. And today's choice means you'll quickly find the type of tile you want, in the colour or pattern to suit almost any decor.

▶ Provided the surface is suitable and you prepare it correctly, laying tiles requires no special skill, especially with modern adhesives.

▶ Choose the adhesive you use to match the tiles you've chosen, and make sure it's appropriate to where they're being laid. For example, choose water-proof adhesive in damp situations, such as shower units, where ceramic tiles will get a thorough soaking. With underfloor heating, choose adhesive that is heat-resistant. Check manufacturer's specifications and follow the instructions carefully.

Carefully does it with round cuts

TIMELY TIP

If you have to make round cuts in tiles prior to laying, particularly for tiling around the toilet bowl, draw a template on a piece of cardboard and use an angle grinder fitted with a continuous diamond blade. Trim up the cut neatly using tile pincers.

The right tools for the job

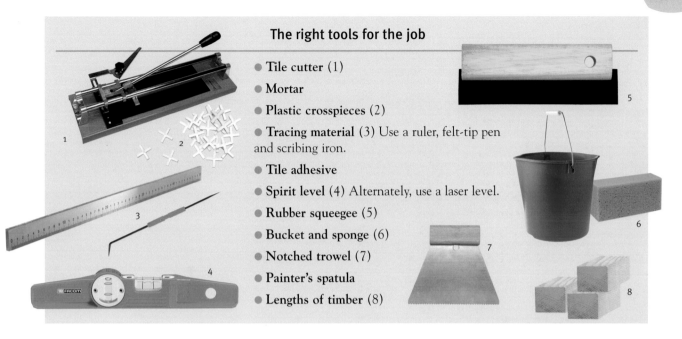

- **Tile cutter** (1)
- **Mortar**
- **Plastic crosspieces** (2)
- **Tracing material** (3) Use a ruler, felt-tip pen and scribing iron.
- **Tile adhesive**
- **Spirit level** (4) Alternately, use a laser level.
- **Rubber squeegee** (5)
- **Bucket and sponge** (6)
- **Notched trowel** (7)
- **Painter's spatula**
- **Lengths of timber** (8)

TIMELY TIP

Try coloured grout

Using coloured grout is a great way to quickly change the look of a room and do it at a fraction of the cost of retiling. All you need to do is remove the old grout with a grout rake (available from hardware shops) and replace it with grout of another shade.

Know your options

There are two distinctive types of tile: ceramic and porcelain. The most commonly used tile is ceramic, made of clay baked in a conventional kiln. Porcelain tile, made from fine white clay fired at an extremely high temperature, is much harder and often has the lustre of stone, and is usually quite resistant to staining.

▶ Choose from either glazed or unglazed ceramic tiles, depending on where they're being used. Unglazed tile, such as quarry or terracotta tiling, has an earthy, natural look.

▶ Glazing gives a tile better resistance to water and stains and makes the surface look brighter and more vibrant. But glazing can also make tiles slippery. When tiles are intended for an area where this might be a problem, it pays to choose a texture that is slip-resistant.

▶ Don't skimp on laying tiles – the job needs to be done properly. If you have any doubts about your ability to do it yourself, save time, hassle and complications by hiring a professional to do it for you.

Classification of tiles

Resistance to scratches, scoring, wear from people's feet and general deterioration from the hard objects that move over the ceramic tile surface is tested according to the PEI method. For glazed tiles, the Porcelain Enamel Institute (PEI) method used to measure abrasion resistance is rated by the following scale:

● **PEI 1** Tiles for areas with light traffic and without abrasive dirt, such as bathrooms and barefoot traffic areas.

● **PEI 2** Tiles for areas with light traffic, little abrasive dirt, soft-sole shoe area, such as bathrooms and bedrooms.

● **PEI 3** Tiles for areas with medium traffic, such as residential (domestic only).

● **PEI 4** Tiles for areas with medium to heavy traffic, such as residential and light commercial.

● **PEI 5** Tiles for areas with intense traffic, such as residential and commercial.

A successful set-out

▶ The best way to set-out is to lay a row of tiles dry (without adhesive) to see how the pattern will work across the room. Ensure the gaps are accurate and even, and position the tiles against a straight edge to keep them aligned. If the desired set-out with full and half tiles against the border doesn't work, you can either open or close the joints, or try adjusting the border-tile width.

▶ To determine the position of the first tile, use a chalk-line to mark two perpendicular lines that cross in the middle of the room.

▶ Place the first tile at the intersection of the lines, and the following tiles along the lines until you reach the walls, adding the crosspieces to take into account the spaces for the joins. The space between the walls and the last tiles must be the same everywhere. If this is not the case, slide the tiles until this is achieved.

▶ Draw the outline of the first tile and retrace the perpendicular lines, which will serve as a guide for the other tiles.

Tips for success

▶ Draw a scaled plan on graph paper. This will allow you to choose the best design for your situation and work out how many tiles you need.

▶ Accurate set-out before laying is essential and helps to avoid wastage and excessive cutting (*see* 'A successful set-out', above).

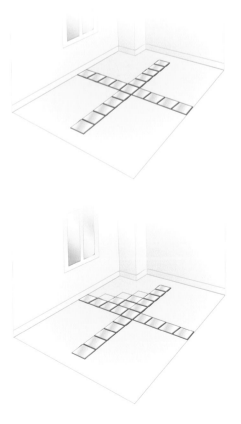

▶ Minimise the number of cut tiles, keep the diagonal cuts to halves and make the pattern symmetrical to the room's prominent wall.

▶ The set-out must be exactly square, otherwise the gap between the tiles will gradually open or close as the job proceeds.

▶ You'll save time by laying large tiles, but your surface must be completely level before they're laid or they will crack.

▶ If laying mosaic tiles, buy them in sheets to save time.

▶ Add an extra margin of 10 per cent for potential mistakes and breakages. Buy all the tiles at the same time and mix up the different packets to allow for any variations in shade.

Smooth laying

Begin by laying whole tiles, working from the centre outwards.

▶ Spread a bed of adhesive with a notched trowel according to the manufacturer's instructions. Spread only enough adhesive to cover an area of about one square metre so the adhesive doesn't dry out before you reach the end.

▶ Press the first tile into position, twisting it slightly to firmly 'bed' it into the adhesive. Place the second tile alongside with the same gentle twisting motion, using a crosspiece between them to obtain evenly spaced gaps. Continue until you've reached the edge of the adhesive, then spread another layer of adhesive over a further square metre.

▶ When all the tiles are in position, start cutting tiles to size. Place the tile to be cut exactly on top of the last whole tile in a particular row.

CAUTION!

Correct joints

Don't get caught out: wall tiles need a 2–3-mm joint, while floor tiles usually need 5–8-mm joints, so make sure you use the correct spacers for each job.

Top tips for grouting quickly

● Start from a corner of the room and work backwards.

● Using a bucket, mix ingredients to a runny consistency and then use a squeegee to spread the grout over the surface to fill the joints.

● Allow it to set for 10 to 15 minutes, then clean the tiles twice with a sponge and water: the first sponging will level the grout in the joints and clean the corners and skirtings; the second cleans the tiles. Allow to dry. Sponge again to remove smears left after drying. For large areas change the cleaning water often.

● To remove the final smears, clean with a cup of white vinegar in a bucket of warm water, then polish the tiles using a clean towel.

▶ Place a second tile over it, this time butted up against the wall or skirting board (place your tile spacer against the wall to allow for grouting). Use the edge of the top tile to make a line on the tile to be cut. Score across the line with a scribing iron, then snap the tile with a heavy-duty tile cutter for a clean break.

▶ Combine adhesive on the back of the cut tile and press it into position hard against the wall or skirting. To cut an L shape, score the surface carefully and nibble away the waste with tile pincers.

Floating floors

TIMELY TIP

A job for a pro

Unlike carpet, laying a traditional parquet or timber floor can be a long and difficult process, so leave it to the professionals. It'll save you both time and trouble.

Fast installation of floating floors

Floating floors are finely engineered flooring systems manufactured to exact specifications, and consist of pre-cut panels that fit together.

▶ Choose panels made of solid timber, veneer, plywood or with a laminate surface. They usually interlock with tight joints via a click or tap-together tongue-and-groove system.

▶ Take advantage of a fast floor makeover. This type of flooring can be successfully laid over concrete, tiles, vinyl, timber or particle-board floors, so you can change the look of your floors quickly.

▶ Floating floors are suitable for use in any internal areas, except wet areas such as bathrooms and laundries.

▶ Save time on regular maintenance. Timber and laminate floating floors are pre-finished, so they don't need sanding, oiling or sealing.

▶ Be guided by the manufacturer's instructions when it comes to installation – these floors actually do float, expanding and contracting in response to the moisture content of the surrounding air. Because of this, the floors are not glued or fixed at any point, and need expansion gaps around the perimeter, and every 8 metres in longer rooms.

CAUTION!

Quality will last longer
Be aware that cheaper laminate flooring cannot be sanded and resurfaced in order to extend its lifespan, so consider this before making a decision.

The right tools for the job

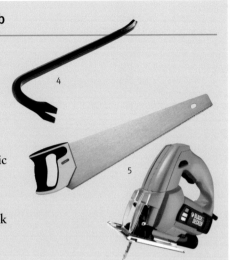

- 10-mm thick spacers
- Hammer (1)
- Combination square (2)
- Sliding bevel (3)
- Pry bar (4)
- Rolls of waterproofing plastic and insulating underlay
- Jigsaw or handsaw (5)
- Pulling bar and tapping block
- Stringline

Preparation and decision-making

▶ Clear the room and vacuum the existing floor surface thoroughly to make sure there's no dirt or particles on it.

▶ Calculate the area of the room to be covered, then work out the number of floor packs required to do the job. (Each pack will indicate floor coverage per square metre.)

▶ Transition pieces will need to be placed wherever the new floor meets different existing floor surfaces such as tiles or carpet. These usually occur in doorways or adjoining rooms.

▶ Remove skirtings and trim door jambs to allow the new floor to float under them, or cover the expansion gap with quad beading.

Start with a good surface

▶ A timber or particle-board floor will need to be checked to make sure it's level before laying a floating floor, and any squeaks or loose boards should be fixed. Any high spots can be sanded level.

▶ Concrete floors need to be checked to ensure they're flat. Any unevenness of more than 3 mm over 1 metre needs to be repaired. High

TIMELY TIP

Buy extra boards
Buy an extra pack of floorboards, to ensure you don't run short during installation, and to replace any that get damaged further down the track.

spots should be ground off and low spots filled with a self-levelling compound to correct any unevenness.

▶ If you're planning to lay a floating floor over a new concrete slab, make sure it has time to dry out first – a good rule of thumb is one month for each 25 mm of slab thickness.

▶ Measure the moisture content of a concrete slab – poor drainage or damaged pipes can cause problems later on.

Use underlay for a better result

▶ If the floor is being laid over a concrete base, it needs to be separated from the concrete surface by a waterproof plastic membrane. A layer of 200-micron thick black plastic will do, but check the manufacturer's recommendations. Overlap the joins, turn the membrane up at the walls and carefully fold it in at the corners. Keep the upturn slightly less than the height of the skirtings so it will be hidden when they're replaced.

▶ Provide an impact cushion and sound insulation for late-night dancing, by layering at least 2-mm thick polyethylene underlay over the plastic membrane. Buy the best quality available, or as recommended by your manufacturer. Butt the underlay joins rather than overlapping or taping, to give a smooth finish. Leave a gap of at least 10–20 mm around walls.

▶ Save time by buying a combination waterproof-insulating underlay – and tape all the joins to ensure adequate waterproofing.

Quick-click installation

▶ Before laying of the floor can begin, you'll need to calculate the width of the last row of boards. If it's less than 50 mm, reduce the width of the first row to increase the width of the last row. When making your calculations, always remember to allow for the 12–15-mm expansion gap on either side of the room.

▶ The first row of boards must be laid against a straight wall. If the wall is curved, you will need to scribe and trim the first row of boards to match the wall before continuing to lay the other boards.

▶ Check your starting corner is square to keep the halves in perfect alignment otherwise you may have to go back and redo the job.

TIMELY TIP

Quick moisture check

Tape a 600 x 600-mm square of black plastic to the concrete base and leave it for 24 hours. After removal, droplets or a darkening of the slab's surface would indicate the presence of moisture that needs to be checked out.

TIMELY TIP

Timesaving tools

The best tools to buy from your hardware shop are a pulling bar and a tapping block. These are especially made for fixing the last row of boards in place.

⊙ Lay the first and second rows, keeping the tongue of the boards facing the wall, using spacers to maintain the required expansion gap.

⊙ Follow the manufacturer's directions, laying the boards in sequence. Finish each row completely before beginning the next.

⊙ Click or tap the long sides together before closing the end gap.

⊙ Use a pulling bar to close up the last end joint.

Plumbing

Stick to the limits

⊙ There are some plumbing jobs home owners can do, but in Australia, New Zealand and South Africa, regulations are very strict when it comes to plumbing. A licensed plumber and gas-fitter must carry out all installations and major repairs. Check with the water-supply authority in your area to find out what do-it-yourself plumbing jobs you can safely undertake at home.

Spot the leak

All pipe connections – between pipes, to a tap, to drainage, etc. – are potential sources of leakage. Any soggy areas of ground or unexplained rises in your water bill may indicate broken or cracked pipes.

⊙ Be attentive and trace leaks. A little seepage of water can cause major problems further down the track, especially when it comes to fine cracks, as they're difficult to see at first.

⊙ Locate the origin of the leak, turn off the water at the mains and call a licensed plumber to fix the problem.

⊙ Dripping taps and a running cistern may simply need a new washer.

TIMELY TIP

Grease the thread

When you reassemble a U-bend under a sink, put vaseline on the thread. It'll be much easier to undo the next time.

CAUTION!

Risky business

Australian and New Zealand residents can change their own tap washers lawfully, but make sure you know what you're doing. If water leakage results in an insurance claim, the claim may be rejected if a licensed person didn't carry out the work. And if flood or resultant water damage occurs, you're not covered.

TIMELY TIP

Plumber's helper

Provide your plumber with a detailed floor plan before he starts on any work. If you know the layout of existing pipes and outlets, mark these on the plan.

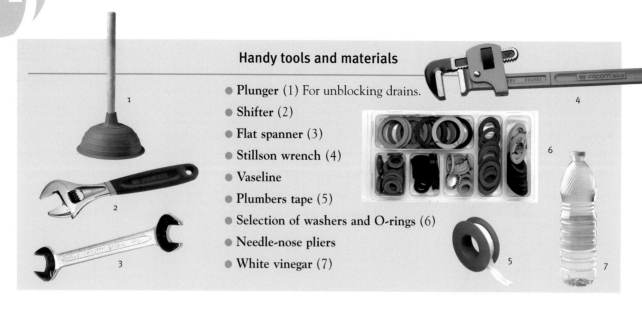

Handy tools and materials

- **Plunger** (1) For unblocking drains.
- **Shifter** (2)
- **Flat spanner** (3)
- **Stillson wrench** (4)
- **Vaseline**
- **Plumbers tape** (5)
- **Selection of washers and O-rings** (6)
- **Needle-nose pliers**
- **White vinegar** (7)

Stop the drips

When a tap drips, turning it off even tighter only makes the problem worse – it probably needs a new washer put in.

▶ Shut the water off at the mains. If you live in a house, the water meter will probably be near your front boundary. If you live in a unit, apartment or townhouse complex, the mains tap may be inside. Turn on a tap to check that the water has stopped running. If the water hasn't stopped running, call a plumber.

▶ Once the mains water has been shut off, undo the main nut on the leaking tap using a shifter.

▶ There are three washers to replace. These are: the large-body washer (usually red or orange), the O-ring on the spindle (use a pair of needle-nose pliers to remove it), and the tap washer, which should simply drop out of the spindle.

▶ Lubricate the spindle with vaseline, then reassemble the unit.

▶ Once the tap is reassembled, partially open it and turn the mains back on. If your tap is still leaking it means the seat is probably pitted and it will have to be reground. (Seat-grinding kits are available from most hardware shops, or pay a plumber to do it for you.)

▶ CAUTION!

Put a stop to scale

If you live in a hard-water area, you need to regularly descale the shower rose and tap nozzle, along with the aerator screwed onto the taps, by soaking them overnight in white vinegar (*see* 'Timely tip', on page 54).

TIMELY TIP

No more clogging

Install a removable screening basket system to filter out and retain any solids being discharged from the sink. The system ensures that only screened waste water can be discharged to the drain.

Fix faulty flush systems

Toilet cisterns overflow because the inlet valve doesn't shut off when the water reaches its correct level. In this case, check the first four points listed below, but if water runs continuously from the cistern into the pan, the outlet valve is the problem, so check the last three points.

▶ If the water level is too high, bend the brass float arm down a little to lower the water level in the cistern.

▶ The inlet valve washer may be faulty, so replace it.

▶ The inlet valve may be clogged, so dismantle and clean it.

▶ The float may be fouling the inside of the cistern, so bend the float arm so the ball is clear of all obstacles.

▶ Dirt or water-borne minerals may clog the valve, which you can fix quickly by simply cleaning it out.

▶ In old cisterns there is a tiny groove in the brass plate under the suction washer, which may need cleaning out. Check if this is the case.

▶ A reduced flush can result from either the water level setting being too low, so adjust the brass float arm upwards, or the outlet valve suction washer may be faulty, so replace it. If the latter is the case, you'll hear the valve fall back into place just after flushing starts.

How to handle sink and basin leaks

If water is leaking from a sink or basin into the cupboard below, check the waste pipes first, because it's probably due to a leaky joint or fitting. If not, check the water-supply pipes, as a connector may have loosened. Lastly, check the vanity benchtop to see if water is leaking under the seal.

To reseal a waste fitting:

● Unscrew the S trap underneath, then undo the lock nut holding the waste fitting in place.

● Smear plenty of mastic filler round the sink outlet hole.

● Bind the threaded tail of the waste outlet fitting several times anti-clockwise with plumbers tape for at least 25 mm up the tail.

● Put the waste fitting through the hole with the body slots facing back and front.

● Bed the rim in the mastic filler.

● Under the sink, slip a flat plastic washer over the protruding tail of the outlet, then fit another washer.

● Screw on the back nut, holding the grid from above with long-nose pliers while you tighten the back nut with a spanner.

● Remove surplus mastic filler with a damp cloth.

Clearing blockages

There are various ways to unblock sinks or basins.

▶ U-bends are generally made out of plastic and have an access cap that you can unscrew to remove whatever is causing the blockage, but remember to put a bucket underneath as there'll be water in the bend that you'll have to clean up if it doesn't land in the bucket.

▶ If the blockage is further along, run a length of wire (coathangers are perfect for this) to clean out the pipe.

▶ If that doesn't work, use a plunger. Place a plunger over the clogged drain. Add enough water to cover the plunger lip and form a seal. Plunge straight up and down several times and 'pop' the plunger away. Repeat this method a few times to free the blockage. Remove it by hand and discard.

▶ You can also use one of the many chemical products available on the market. These cleaners are made primarily from caustic soda. Read the label on the drain cleaner and follow the manufacturer's instructions carefully. After using a chemical cleaner, flush the cleaner from the pipes using hot water.

TIMELY TIP

Effective plunging

In the bathroom, even if you are unblocking the basin, don't forget to close off all the openings connected to the pipes: the plughole in the shower or the bath, the drainage for the washing machine, etc. This will make your plunger more effective.

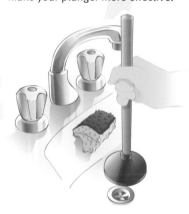

Electrical work

Stick to the letter of the law

Australian, New Zealand and South African regulations are very strict when it comes to electrical work undertaken in residential settings.

▶ Check with the electricity-supply authority in your local area to find out what do-it-yourself work you can safely undertake in the home, but don't overestimate your skills when it comes to electricity.

> **CAUTION!**
>
> **Always play it safe**
> Electricity is dangerous and the electrical installations in a house or an apartment are governed by very strict regulations. A licensed electrician must carry out all installations and the power supply must be disconnected before any work commences.

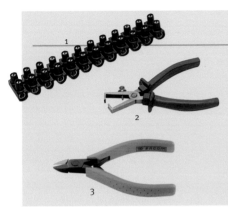

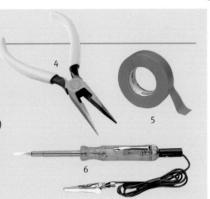

Handy tools for minor repairs

- Connectors (1)
- Stripping pliers (2)
- Cutting pliers (3)
- Long-nose electrician's pliers (4)
- Insulating tape (5)
- Screwdriver tester (6) To check where the current is flowing.

TIMELY TIP

Dial before you dig!

'Dial 1100 Before You Dig' is a free service providing information on most underground networks across Australia. In New Zealand, you can ring the Cable Location Service on 124 for information, or get a Telecom contractor to come on site and mark out where the underground cables lie.

Don't hesitate to get the advice of a qualified electrician if you're unsure about any electrical problems in your home.

Before beginning any excavation work, it's essential to identify all underground services to and within the property, and locate the position of gas, electricity, water and other underground services.

Underground cables installed on your property (see 'Timely tip', at left) should be accurately recorded and information placed in the meter box. If no record is evident, a registered electrical contractor may be able to assist in locating the cables for you.

Power boxes and fuses

Know where your power box is located on your property in case of an emergency. And keep a torch handy in case the power blows at night.

If a fuse blows repeatedly in your house, have a registered electrical contractor or licensed electrician carry out a safety check.

Be careful when replacing rewirable fuses, and make sure the main switch is turned off first.

Label all switches, circuit-breakers or fuses in the switchboard to identify the area of the property they control and protect.

Switch the power off at the mains when you're renovating or carrying out any maintenance jobs.

Have a licensed electrician inspect your switchboard if it has a strange smell or if there are any signs of heat scorching, burn marks or worn wires.

Economical bulbs

When you have to replace a bulb, think about switching to energy-saving bulbs that last as much as 10 times longer.

CAUTION!

A storage issue

Always store your extension cords indoors, even if that means a garden shed. Exposure to the elements can result in deterioration of the protective covering, and even minimal exposure to wiring can result in an electrical burn or shock.

Circuit-breakers and fuses

Circuit-breakers can replace ceramic fuses and are reset at the flick of a switch. A circuit-breaker provides short-circuit and over-current protection such as when a power point is overloaded. However, they are designed to protect the wires not people. If the power has been tripped by the circuit-breaker, it indicates faulty wiring or a faulty appliance. Unplug the appliance or call an electrician.
To change a fuse, follow this procedure.

● Turn off the power.

● Pull out the ceramic fuse block and check for wire damage.

● Using a screwdriver, unloop the bit of broken wire and remove it.

● The maximum number of amps you can use will be written on the board. Choose the correct wire and replace the damaged one by looping it back over the screw. On the other side of the fuse block, pull the wire reasonably tight and nip off the excess wire, then return it to the box.

● Turn the power back on.

Note: If there are no maximum amps written on the board or fuse block, use the following as a general guide: light circuits use 8-amp fuses and general power either 10 or 15 amps, although stoves and airconditioners may require higher amperage. Always check first.

Before a blackout happens

Don't wait for the day when you have a blackout to realise that a bit of simple advance planning can get you out of a pickle quickly – minus the drama associated with stumbling about in the dark!

▶ Keep a supply of fuses of different amperages in the meter box.

▶ Keep an emergency number for the electrician next to the phone.

▶ Have an assortment of replacement bulbs for the whole house on hand, and get into the habit of replacing used ones.

▶ Always keep a torch in the same place – and easily accessible when the lights are out – so that you can grab it and find your way to the fuse box without accident.

Take care when extending

▶ Take care to always fully unwind extension cords, to avoid overheating. Use cords long enough for the job so you don't have to join several cords together, but make sure you don't exceed the maximum safety length. If the cord needs to be longer than 25 metres, check with a licensed electrical contractor.

▶ Extension cords, adaptors and power boards should be used only for temporary purposes, and not for high-powered appliances such as dishwashers, fridges and microwaves.

▶ Never use extension cords where they could be splashed by water, fall into water or be exposed to wet weather – if your extension cord does get wet, switch it off at the power point, unplug it, dry it out and have it checked for any permanent damage.

▶ Never lay extension cords on the ground where they can be walked on or driven over by a vehicle. There is the hazard of tripping over them and also the possibility of crushing or damaging the insulation material. Preferably, cords should be suspended 2.5 metres (about 8 feet) above the ground, attached to other fixtures by taping or using cable ties or similar.

▶ Keep on the lookout for situations where physical damage to the cord could occur, such as sliding doors, and avoid them. You want to avoid damaging the insulation and exposing live conductors.

▶ Never use twin flex (two wires) as an extension cord – always use a cord that has earth, active and neutral wires in it, with a regular three-pin plug and socket attached.

Safety switches for security

▶ Safety switches look similar to circuit-breakers, but they provide extra protection from electric shock by monitoring the flow of electricity and if any irregularity is detected, the electricity supply is immediately cut off.

▶ If you have children in the home, or a backyard workshop with power connected, consider installing safety switches to reduce the risk of electrical accidents. In Australia, new homes are required to have safety switches installed.

▶ Licensed electrical contractors can install switchboard-mounted safety switches in older homes at a reasonable cost.

▶ Think about buying portable safety switches for appliances and extension cords, to protect against unnecessary accidents.

▶ A licensed electrical contractor is the only person who should install switchboard and power-point safety switches.

TIMELY TIP

See-through plugs
Clear plastic three-pin plugs allow the wiring to be checked without first having to undo the plug, which instantly saves time (and money, if an electrician is doing the work for you).

5 Caring for your garden

Garden planning and design

First decide what you want to achieve

The first step to creating a garden that's both easy to maintain and rewarding is to put some simple design ideas in place. Whether you're starting with bare earth or an established garden, formulate a garden plan.

▶ Identify your garden needs, then design and plan accordingly. Think carefully about what you want to do in your garden: is it a space for inviting friends and relaxing, a play space for children or pets, a small piece of wilderness in the middle of the city, an area reserved for cultivating flowers, or somewhere to grow your own organic produce?

▶ Discuss your plans with all the family. Take notes and pay attention to everyone's expectations. Planning, construction and planting happens more quickly and calmly if everyone is in agreement.

▶ Draw up a list of the things you like and don't like in your current garden, and accept a few compromises or short cuts to avoid endless work and major expense when trying to modify the aspects you don't like.

▶ Plan for the future by making your design flexible. Think about how your garden may need to change over the years if you have a growing family, and take that into consideration during planning.

▶ Consider pets and hobbies. If you have pets or special interests, take them into account during the planning stage, too, if necessary.

Recycle your favourite plants

Before undertaking major landscape work, identify the plants already in your garden that you like and that can be reused in the new garden. It'll save you having to go out and buy more plants than you need.

▶ Dig up and store those plants that are in the way of new work.

▶ If possible, move established plants in winter when most plants are dormant or have slowed their growth.

▶ Plants higher than 2 metres may need special equipment to be moved safely. Save time by checking this beforehand.

▶ Hold transplanted trees in large pots in potting mix, or keep their roots wrapped in hessian. Water the root ball regularly, particularly in hot or windy weather, as the roots will dry out faster.

▶ Reduce the stress on plants caused by moving by spraying them with an anti-transpirant product (available from most garden centres). This reduces water loss through the leaves.

▶ Replant as soon as possible when your new garden is ready.

TIMELY TIP

Use what's there

Trees can take many years to grow large enough to provide shade and colour in a garden, so taking care not to damage existing trees during rework saves you time and money. Make existing trees the focal points of your new design.

Protect existing trees

By taking steps to ensure existing trees are protected, you'll save time spent tending to a damaged tree or, worse still, having to remove and then replace a tree that is damaged during the reworking process.

▶ Keep heavy equipment away from tree trunks and root systems by erecting a barrier around special trees. Protect the area within a 1–2-metre radius around the base of each tree trunk.

▶ Take care not to raise the soil level over the tree roots or to bury the trunk by piling up soil around it.

▶ Avoid digging drains or excavating near tree roots.

▶ Don't alter drainage patterns in your new garden to the extent that existing trees suddenly receive a lot less or a lot more water.

Define your style

Garden style can be dictated by your personal preference, the existing style of your home or plants you already have in place.

▶ Decide if you want to have a formal (laid out in a balanced, geometric style) or informal (less structured and more rambling) garden, or a combination of both – with more formal spaces closer to the house and more informal areas further away from it.

▶ Keep in mind that formal spaces defined by neat, clipped hedges can be time-consuming to maintain, so take that into account if you're going to be the one responsible for the garden's upkeep.

▶ Once you've defined a preferred style, it's quicker and easier to make specific plans. Then, before making each new decision, simply ask yourself whether it's going to fit in with your overall garden plan.

CAUTION!

Tree roots grow

Include trees in your garden design plan, but do some research before planting certain species, to avoid long-term damage to foundations and overhanging roof spaces, or disruption to paving or paths. Allow room for roots and branches to spread unhindered, by checking the height and width of trees you plant. The spread of tree roots usually reflects the spread of the branches.

TIMELY TIP

Colour tip

If you're unsure of colour choices, take a photo of your house, garden wall or courtyard with you when you're buying paint. Some paint specialist shops use computer enhancement of photos to show you how a colour scheme will look. This can save you both time and money.

Find north

Find and locate north (your sunny aspect) and mark this on your garden plan. Patterns of sun and shade dictate how you use your garden and the type of plants you can grow.

A seasonal advantage

Rework your garden at any time of the year, but plan to do major planting during the cooler months (autumn to early spring), when plants (and gardeners) are under less stress from the heat. It'll make the best use of your time and resources. Schedule major construction work for the dry times of the year to avoid wet-weather delays. And avoid the busiest times, such as the lead-up to Christmas.

Factor in environmental impact

Gardens today should be designed with environmental impact in mind. Consider how your design and planting choices affect your surroundings and you'll avoid time-consuming complications.

▶ Avoid planting or construction that causes extreme shade. You'll end up wasting time finding solutions for dealing with the shade problem.

▶ Make sure what you plant is sustainable and suits your climate – it'll save you the extra time spent watering and maintaining your garden.

▶ Include room for a compost heap in your design so you can recycle grass clippings, prunings and kitchen scraps to use as mulch or organic fertiliser. (*See also* 'Don't forget the compost', on page 375.)

Planning saves time

Carefully planning a design layout saves a considerable amount of time when creating a new garden because once work has begun, it's both difficult and time-consuming to make changes.

▶ Save time creating a plan by using your house plans as a template. Mark the direction of north, along with existing features such as trees, access points and services such as water supplies.

▶ Draw the plan of your garden to scale so you can quickly figure out the best solutions before starting work.

▶ Use a scale that's easy to understand, such as 1:100 (1 cm on the plan equals 100 cm or 1 metre in the garden).

▶ Make a few copies of the garden plan, cover it with a layer of tracing paper and then sketch in your ideas. Use several layers of tracing paper to try out different ideas until you hit on the one that works best.

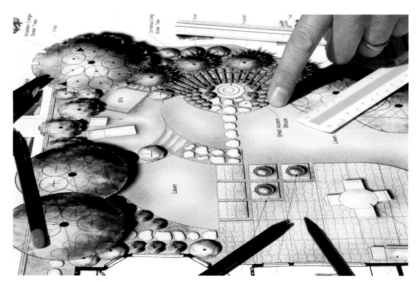

TIMELY TIP

Getting it done on time

If you're trying to have your outdoor work completed to meet a deadline, such as an outdoor wedding or the long summer holidays, plan the work in stages and figure out an achievable schedule. If time is short, prioritise the work. And always allow for the usual hold-ups such as wet weather or unavailability of materials.

▶ Using coloured paper, cut out surface areas to scale for the elements that you want to include in the garden: a terrace or deck, a barbecue, play equipment for children, a garden shed, a storage area for the garbage bin, an area for water tanks or a compost heap, a clothes line, a swimming pool, or other feature elements.

▶ While you're drawing up a plan, consider that the barbecue should be accessible from the kitchen, water tanks should be located near down-pipes from the roof but out of sight, and garbage and recycling bins should have easy access to the street front.

▶ Plan for any future changes, such as a swimming pool, when the budget allows. Consider access and location, and keep that area available for future development so that minimum reorganisation is required.

▶ In Australia, phone 'Dial Before You Dig' on 1100, to identify the location of all services on your property including gas, electricity, water and phone lines. (*See* 'Find out more', at left.) In New Zealand, you can ring the Cable Location Service on 124 for information, or get a Telecom contractor to come on site and mark out where the underground cables lie on your property.

▶ Use your garden plan to show tradesmen or contractors what you've got in mind and to help you compare quotes.

Work in stages

▶ If improvements to your garden require earth moving or major construction, spread out the work over two or three years, but ensure new work doesn't undo previous work.

▶ If your garden has drainage problems or difficult access, call in a landscape designer or landscape contractor before reworking it. A long-term plan drawn up by an expert

is a great time saver, even if you intend to do the work yourself in stages.

▶ Start by digging trenches to carry water pipes, electricity conduit and other services, then work outwards from the immediate vicinity of the house, undertaking work on the patio or deck. Also get started on the urgent tasks, such as laying turf or paving, if your garden is a sea of dirt.

TIMELY TIP

Computer design

There are computer programs available that allow you to plan and model garden design ideas. It's a great timesaving option if have reasonable computer skills.

TIMELY TIP

Stop the dirt

If you've just moved into a newly built home and you're surrounded by dirt, laying turf will keep the dirt under control and can give you the time to plan your garden or save up for more expensive paving, decking and structural work. Turf can be easily removed or reused later on.

Make outdoor living spaces work

Make the most of outdoor living spaces by locating them as best you can.

▶ Position a terrace, patio or deck on the same level as your access from the house and near the kitchen or living room. Positioning an outdoor eating area close to the kitchen saves time when you're entertaining.

▶ Take regular weather conditions into account, particularly the need for shade and rain protection. Consider covering part of your terrace with a vine-clad pergola or a fixed roof, which avoids the need to use large umbrellas to control sun and shade. (*See also* Vergolas in 'Home automation services', on page 37.)

▶ Include attractive vistas beyond your garden – a tree, church spire or city lights – by framing them and making them a focal point.

TIMELY TIP

Keep a record

Make a garden book or keep a folder with space to save plant labels, planting ideas, maps and garden plans. If you're computer savvy, scan this information into a computer file and save it. Having this ready reference saves time and hassles.

Garden essentials

Put up a shed

Keep tools safe and secure, and always to hand, in a garden shed.

▶ If you don't have an existing backyard shed, include space on your garden plan for a prefabricated shed from a hardware shop or shed specialist, which you can either install yourself or have built. The simplest ones are made out of sheet metal or polypropylene, but you can buy sheds made out of wood, too.

▶ Make provision to install electricity in your garden shed. This means you can equip it with lighting and plug in an electrical appliance, providing a safe and convenient power source in your garden.

Everything in its place

To make the most of your shed or storage area, have a place for everything. This means less time wasted searching for tools when they're needed, and it's quick and easy to put them away.

▶ Reserve the shed for storing gardening materials, not household stuff. You need a place to put the lawnmower, tools, pots, seeds, products, etc.

▶ Be safe: install a closed cupboard or shelving out of reach of children for pesticides and other chemicals.

▶ Make a set place for the lawnmower and other bulky tools, attach hooks to the wall for long-handled tools and fix reels on the wall for hoses.

▶ Use trays or plastic boxes stacked one on top of the other to store small things that are easily lost, such as opened seed packets, string, labels, rope, a dibbler and various small tools.

Catching water

With the cost and availability of water being an issue for gardeners in many regions, the installation of tanks to capture rainwater, or equipment to recycle grey water, is also part of setting up an efficient backyard.

▶ Utilise out-of-the-way spaces for rainwater tanks – between the house and a fence or under a deck.

▶ Position water tanks close to downpipes to reduce the need for additional and expensive plumbing.

▶ Make sure power is available adjacent to the tank, to run a pump that provides enough pressure for water to be used in all parts of the garden and for drip-irrigation systems, which cut down on maintenance.

▶ Install filters to keep debris from getting into your tank as fresh water flows in. It's vital to regularly check and clean filters to avoid wasting time and water (water overflows when inlets become blocked).

TIMELY TIP

Maintenance-free shed

Although a wooden shed may blend into the natural decor of most gardens better than metal does, raw wood needs to be maintained – with a protective coat of paint or oil each year. Save time by choosing a treated wood or maintenance-free metal shed.

TIMELY TIP

Keep it clean

Install and regularly clean filters on tank pumps at the outlet, to ensure your water supply stays clean and to prevent blockages when the system is up and running.

Practical and discreet storage for bins

Minimise any unpleasant impact from handling bins, both for garbage and recycling, by preparing a special corner for bins in your garden.

▶ Choose a place that's easily accessible from the kitchen and that's near the street, but out of sight and sheltered from hot sun.

▶ Hide bins behind a hedge of fast-growing evergreen shrubs, or put up a trellis that can be disguised with evergreen climbing plants.

Fast-growing shrubs and climbers to hide bins

If you've got a designated garbage and recycling-bin area that you'd like to shield from view, try planting one of the following shrubs or climbers:

	COOL CLIMATE	WARM CLIMATE
EVERGREENS		
Acalypha (*Acalypha wilkesiana*)	✗	✓
Bottlebrush (*Callistemon* Hybrids) (1)	✓	✓
Cherry laurel (*Prunus laurocerasus*)	✓	✗
Croton (*Codiaeum variegatum*)	✗	✓
Juniper (*Juniperus* 'Skyrocket')	✓	✓
Lillypilly (*Acmena smithii, Syzygium* spp.)	✗	✓
Murraya (*Murraya paniculata*)	✗	✓
Odontonema (*Odontonema tubiforme*)	✗	✓
Pittosporum (*Pittosporum* 'James Stirling')	✓	✗
Plumbago (*Plumbago* 'Royal Cape')	✗	✓
Sasanqua camellia (*Camellia sasanqua*)	✓	✓
EVERGREEN CLIMBERS		
Actinidia (*Actinidia kolomikta*)	✓	✗
Allamanda (*Allamanda cathartica*)	✗	✓
Bleeding heart (*Clerodendrum splendens*)	✗	✓
Bougainvillea (*Bougainvillea* spp.) (2)	✗	✓
Carolina jasmine (*Gelsemium sempervirens*)	✓	✓
False sarsparilla (*Hardenbergia violacea*)	✓	✓
Ivy geranium (*Pelargonium peltatum*)	✓	✓
Pandorea (*Pandorea jasminoides*)	✓	✓
Passionfruit vine (*Passiflora edulis*) (3)	✓	✓
Potato vine (*Solanum jasminoides*)	✓	✓
Pyrostegia (*Pyrostegia venusta*)	✗	✓
Star jasmine (*Trachelospermum jasminoides*) (4)	✓	✓
Wonga wonga (*Pandorea pandorana*)	✓	✓

Invisible bins

Hide a bin quickly by assembling wooden panels or lattice using posts and braces. Use treated timbers to reduce the need for ongoing maintenance, or try a bamboo screen.

Don't forget the compost

Compost made from kitchen scraps, weeds, grass clippings and prunings is a good way to feed and mulch your garden and also reduces your waste.

▶ Set aside an area for the compost bin that's out of sight but easy to access from the kitchen. Make sure there's room to wheel in a wheelbarrow to speed up delivery of garden refuse and the distribution of finished compost (*see* 'Quick homemade compost', on page 415).

▶ Compost bins should be built or positioned directly on soil (not on a concrete or paved surface).

▶ Save time and space by buying a bin made from recycled plastic.

▶ The fastest way to make reusable compost is to have the heap well ventilated, so select or build a bin that's aerated or easy to access for quick turning using a garden fork or spade.

▶ If space permits, make room for two compost bins: one that's composting and one that's being filled up with recyclable materials.

Paths and driveways

Clever lines

Providing good, clear access to your house through the garden is essential to ensure convenience and to avoid navigating dangerous routes.

▶ Design and build pathways so that you can move around the garden easily and without encountering any physical obstacles.

▶ Don't rush to lay a pathway – be guided by general traffic habits around your home. After a few months, traces of foot traffic and wear on the grass will show the obvious place to trace a pathway. These worn areas are almost always the most natural and direct paths to use.

▶ Use lengths of garden hose to 'draw' your paths. Unroll two lengths of hose between the points that you want to join up, leaving them slack so as to round out the shapes. As soon as you're happy with the shape, keep the hose in place with U-shaped wires, then mark the line (using

TIMELY TIP

Quick surfaces

Think about using gravel or thick mulch if you have to make (or remake) pathways. For areas of occasional access, use stepping stones set in the grass or across soil. These are great for coping with traffic without creating wear and tear.

light-coloured sand, lime or spray-on marker paint). This is much faster and just as efficient as using small garden stakes and cord.

▶ Think about constructing a couple of small steps where there are changes in the ground level, for safety and to avoid wear and tear.

▶ Allow for narrow pathways between hedges and fences, behind banks or around a vegetable garden, so that you have access to planted areas you need to trim or structures you need to repaint. These paths should be 60–80 cm wide to be able to use an edge trimmer or a hedge cutter. Using these paths will help save time on fence maintenance, too.

Weigh up the cost

Sometimes it pays – in more ways than one – to choose carefully.

▶ To make paths and driveways low maintenance, make sure they're built on a level surface with a firm foundation.

▶ Weigh up the installation costs against timesaving benefits associated with the longevity of the finish. For example, compacted sand is cheap and easy to install, but leads to higher ongoing maintenance than a solid surface, such as concrete or compacted granite, which costs more initially.

Edging plants for paths

PLANT NAME	EXPOSURE	SEASONAL INTEREST	CLIMATE
Bergenia	Semi-shade	Late winter to spring	Cool
Candytuft (1)	Sun	Year-round	All
Common thrift (2)	Sun	Summer	Cool
Cranesbill (*Geranium* spp. and Hybrids)	Sun or semi-shade	Spring to summer	Cool
Dianthus	Sun	Spring to autumn	Cool
Golden alyssum	Sun	Spring	Cool
Helianthemum (3)	Sun	Summer	Cool
Liriope	Sun to shade	Year-round	All
Lomandra	Sun	Year-round	All
Mondo grass	Sun to shade	Year-round	All
Nasturtium, dwarf	Sun	Spring to autumn	All
Snow-in-summer	Sun	Summer	All
Thyme	Sun	Summer	Cool
Winter savoury	Sun	Summer	Cool

▶ Include expansion joints in paths and along driveways – wherever possible – to avoid the surface cracking in the future.

▶ Before starting construction on a driveway, take weight bearing into account, especially in a driveway that doubles as a car-parking area.

Pathway basics

▶ Don't change pre-existing paving, cement, asphalt or gravel pathways if the shape is suitable and the surface is in good condition, especially if you're redesigning your garden. It'll be one less change you need to make.

▶ Define the width of your pathways by keeping in mind that you will use them with a wheelbarrow or lawnmower.

▶ Keep in mind that the ideal pathway measures 1–1.2 metres wide.

▶ To make your path easy to navigate, make sure it has broad curves and clean angles and perhaps even a gentle slope.

▶ As a quick-fix after a period of heavy rain, lay down boards or spread gravel over very muddy areas. If drainage and access is a problem in certain parts of a pathway, address these issues in the longer term.

Low-maintenance care of paths

▶ Build path edges made from bricks, logs or treated timber (old railway sleepers work well), to prevent garden soil falling onto a path or to stop gravel from a pathway making its way into garden beds.

▶ Before building a pathway, lay a weed mat between the borders of the path to prevent weeds from emerging, then cover it with about 2 cm of gravel. This will save you several weeding sessions a year.

▶ Keep shady paths safe by treating them with an anti-moss solution once a year. If possible, remove overhanging branches and install drains to remove or redirect water so that paths stay as dry as possible.

▶ Dress up the edges of your pathways using clumps of sprawling ground-cover perennials, which are great for breaking up angular lines and providing a flash of colour throughout the year.

▶ Choose small perennial or herbaceous plants that flower or look good for a long time without needing any special care, such as liriope, lomandra or mondo grass (*see* 'Edging plants for paths', on the page opposite). All you have to do is trim them back if they become too invasive.

TIMELY TIP

Once-a-year treatment
Problem weeds can be kept out of paths using a pre-emergent herbicide. One application at the time of path construction stops or delays seeds from germinating, which beats the weed cycle.

Soft surfaces

▶ Think about your surface options. Grass paths are attractive and inexpensive, but they require mowing (unless you get someone to do it for you). Other options include mulch, gravel or compacted granite.

▶ Reserve grass for pathways with the least traffic and that are easy to mow. Heavy wear on grass inevitably leads to patches of earth to replant, which is a time-consuming job.

▶ Avoid using lawn for pathways that tend to be damp or sloping, as they can become too slippery to walk on.

Safe, easy driveways

Make your driveway easy to negotiate with the family car by taking safety into consideration, along with location, layout and plantings.

▶ To grow plants alongside a driveway, select species without thorns or sharp leaves that may scratch you, your family or the car.

▶ Keep clear vision in mind at all times when you're planning where to locate the driveway, particularly if you need to cross a path or walkway.

▶ If you've got the space, consider installing a circular drive, to save you the time and trouble of backing or turning your car.

▶ Never locate a child's garden play area near a driveway.

Lighting and power

Let there be light

Adequate lighting and power make your garden easier to manage and maintain, and more enjoyable to spend time in.

▶ Make your garden safer and more versatile by installing lighting. It means you can make the most of hot evenings by being able to sit and eat outdoors, which often saves time on cleaning up.

> ➤ **CAUTION!**
>
> **Don't skimp on safety**
> Don't take risks with electrical equipment. Use only materials suited to outdoor use, make sure you have a circuit-breaker attached to the mains and hire a licensed electrician to carry out installations – it's illegal not to.

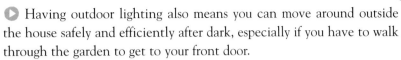

Having outdoor lighting also means you can move around outside the house safely and efficiently after dark, especially if you have to walk through the garden to get to your front door.

Don't stop at outdoor lights, install power points as well. With outdoor power it's possible to use timesaving outdoor appliances, extra lighting and pumps associated with rainwater tanks.

TIMELY TIP

DIY alternatives

Where it isn't practical to install a mains system, safe low-voltage and solar-powered alternatives are available, which can be easily connected and installed, even by inexperienced do-it-yourselfers.

Earth works first

The best solution to delivering light and power to all parts of the garden is the underground network. Have it installed when your house is built or when you're developing the garden. In an existing garden you can reduce disturbance by installing light and power when you redo pathways or alter the garden layout. In fact, the easiest and most recommended place to run the cables is under paths. In any case, don't play around with electricity: have the network installed by a licensed electrician. (*See also* 'Find out more', on page 371.)

The right light in the right place

Install lights in high-traffic areas outdoors, particularly in risky spots such as stairs or where there's a change in ground level.

Consider the safety and sturdiness of outdoor lights, because this is of prime importance. They'll be expected to withstand weather conditions over a long period of time, and if you have children, them too.

Consider installing garden lights with sensors, which switch on as soon as someone approaches. These aren't a good idea if you have pets, but are practical near the house, where traffic tends to be heavier.

Think about using solar lighting, particularly for pathways. They work using small solar panels that store energy during the day, then release it at dusk. The stored energy provides light for several hours. And they're fast to install, as there's no connection and no excavation, so no need for an electrician to organise underground cables.

CAUTION!

Too much night light

There is nothing more unpleasant than being blinded by a bright light, so before installing garden lighting, check that you're not going to disturb your neighbours with lights that are too powerful or set at an intrusive angle. Do a quick trial run with a portable floodlight to check where the light falls.

Fences and hedges

Dress up fences in a flash

Fences and hedges fulfil numerous roles around the house and garden: they provide privacy and security, mark property boundaries, and often conceal areas you don't want to have on show. They also keep children and pets in the backyard and deter unwanted visitors.

▶ For unattractive wire fences that you'd like to camouflage, choose climbing plants that will trail up and cover the wire.

▶ In front of solid walls, sow flowers with tall stems or arrange plants in pots in a very tight arrangement so that there aren't any gaps. This is a great way to spruce up your garden in a very short time.

Plants to hide a fence

SPECIES	TYPE	COLOUR	HEIGHT
● Dahlia	Bulb	Many colours	70–90 cm
● Hollyhock (1)	Biennial, seed	Many colours	1.5–2 metres
● Lavatera	Annual, seed	Pink, white	1 metre
● Nasturtium	Annual climber, seed	Orange, yellow	2.5 metres
● Ornamental tobacco	Annual, seed	White, red	70–80 cm
● Sunflower	Annual, seed	Orange, yellow	2 metres
● Sweet pea (2)	Annual climber, seed	Pink, blue, white	2 metres

▶ Weed and hoe the ground along a fence (about 20 cm from the fence) to give your garden a fresh new look in a minimum of time.

▶ A lick of paint quickly transforms a tired fence and can provide an attractive backdrop for garden plants.

▶ Disguise an ugly paling fence in a flash by using solid boards or woven screening material. Outdoor-rated or maritime boards are quick and easy to attach to existing fence posts and can be painted or rendered. Woven reed or bamboo (available by the metre from garden centres) can also be attached to existing fence posts for instant effect.

Sharing a fence

Most dividing fences are made of timber or metal and the shared cost is usually based on the average fencing type in your neighbourhood. If you want to build a more expensive style of fence and your neighbour objects to the cost, you may have to pay the difference. Remember, too, that fences are subject to regulations that control acceptable heights. Before replacing a fence, call your local council for more information. If you do find yourself in dispute over a fence, there are usually resolution services available.

Masonry walls – cool and decorative

Walls made of stone or brick need little maintenance and bring coolness and privacy to a garden. They also act as a barrier to noise.

▶ Don't allow climbers to scale masonry walls, as they can damage the wall fabric and result in ongoing maintenance problems. Instead, mask or soften the wall using lattice to train climbing plants, such as potato vine or mandevilla, or train an espaliered camellia or fruit tree up the wall.

▶ Go for effect with an annual climber such as sweet pea or nasturtium.

▶ Brighten up bare walls by planting flowering shrubs at their base or arranging a few clipped potted plants, such as lillypillies or box.

Long-lasting fences

▶ For small fences made from palings or lattice (especially suitable for a smaller garden), choose a hardwood that's suited to outdoor use. And to avoid unpleasant surprises, find out how the colour changes over time as it weathers. To keep a timber fence looking new, apply a protective seal and repaint regularly.

▶ Treat fencing timber against insects and fungus to ensure its longevity. Untreated timber can be eaten by termites or attacked by rot.

Hedge your bets

▶ Consider planting a hedge as a long-lived fence or privacy screen for very little effort or cost. Hedges can be either formal, which means they are regularly shaped by clipping and pruning, or informal, which means they take on the natural shape of the shrub.

▶ Clipped hedges are neat and take up less space than informal hedges, but tend to take up more time in regular maintenance. If you prefer a formal hedge, invest in future maintenance with timesaving pruning equipment, such as electric or powered hedge trimmers, or pay a professional hedge trimmer twice a year – in spring and late summer or autumn – to trim hedges for you.

▶ Plants suited to formal clipped hedges include many conifers, laurel, photinia, sasanqua camellia, box, bougainvillea (tropical and subtropical climates only), lillypilly, murraya, New Zealand Christmas bush and pittosporum. Informal alternatives include oleander, grevillea, melaleuca, abelia and rugosa or hedge roses.

Trouble-free hedges

▶ As a guide to ongoing maintenance, pay attention to the ultimate size and shape of plants used as hedges by doing a bit of research first.

▶ Choose small-growing or dwarf cultivars, because they require less training and pruning than an unnamed species.

▶ For uniformity, plant all the same variety from the same supplier.

▶ Buy a few extra plants and grow them elsewhere in the garden, or in pots, in case part of the hedge needs to be replanted at a future date.

▶ To provide the best start in life for your new hedge, prepare a trench rather than dig individual holes. By doing this, the soil right along the row can be improved with manure and organic matter before planting.

TIMELY TIP

A twittering hedge

An easy way to attract a range of native birds to your garden is to plant informal hedges. Select dense or prickly plants that provide both food and shelter for birds. Good choices include hakea, grevillea, melaleuca and bottlebrush in Australia and New Zealand, or num-num and kei-apple in South Africa.

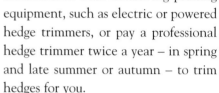

Instant screening

While you're waiting for hedges to grow and mature, make a temporary screen using garden lattice or tall annuals such as sunflowers or hollyhocks.

TIMELY TIP

TIMELY TIP

Just add water
When planting a hedge, install a drip watering system with several drippers to each plant. You'll save time watering and the plants will be more likely to survive. Adapt the system as plants grow and observe local water restrictions.

▶ Space plants according to their ultimate size and also how quickly you want the hedge to form. Hedge plants that grow to around 3 metres high are best planted 1 metre apart. With taller-growing hedge plants, space them 2 metres apart. Lower-growing or smaller plants can be grown more closely together – around 50–80 cm apart.

▶ To reduce weed competition after planting, surround new hedge plants with weed matting or a 5–7-cm layer of organic mulch (take care not to build it up around the trunks or stems of the plants).

Fast-flowering hedge plants

PLANT NAME	SEASON	BEST CLIMATE
● Bougainvillea (1)	Any time	Subtropical to tropical
● Camellia (2)	Autumn to winter	Cool to subtropical
● Hibiscus	Summer to autumn	Temperate to tropical
● New Zealand Christmas bush	Summer	Cool to subtropical
● Oleander	Spring to autumn	Temperate to tropical
● Plumbago	Spring to autumn	Temperate to subtropical
● Rose	Spring	Cool to temperate

TIMELY TIP

Low hedges
A row of low-growing shrubs can make an attractive edge to a garden bed or along a path. Good choices include dwarf box, dwarf lillypilly, dwarf camellias and honeysuckle (*Lonicera nitida*).

Paving and decks

Seasonal care

Paving and decking are great time savers because they are practically maintenance-free – no mowing, watering or feeding involved!

▶ Look for paving material that's non-slip, weather- and stain-resistant and that doesn't scratch. By choosing a durable surface that is easy to maintain, you'll save both time and money.

▶ If your outdoor living area is only used during the warmer months, give the area a quick spring clean at the end of winter.

▶ Spruce up paving or decking with a high-pressure cleaner (water restrictions permitting), or give it a quick wash using a bucket and a stiff outdoor broom. During the rest of the warmer months, a daily sweep

with a broom is all that's needed.

▶ Re-oil, re-stain or repaint the external woodwork once a year, to extend its life.

▶ Treat surfaces that are damp and shaded in winter to avoid the build-up of moss, which can make paving or decking dangerously slippery after rain. To make the most of your time, choose an anti-moss treatment that needs to be applied only once a year.

Don't get flooded

To avoid flooding after heavy rainfall – along with time-consuming damage-control measures – ensure paving is set out correctly.

▶ Paving should be cambered (slightly arched) to allow water to flow away from the house and other structures. A gentle slope of 1:100 is sufficient to encourage good drainage.

> If it's possible, redirect the natural flow of water to lawn or garden areas and you'll save time on watering.

> Lay paving stones on sand rather than concrete, to allow some water to soak directly into the soil below the paving. Unless there's a problem with drainage, water shouldn't collect on top of pavers.

TIMELY TIP

Paver revival
Give old paved areas a facelift by turning the pavers over. As long as your pavers are laid on compacted sand, this is a quick and easy way to make paved areas look clean and new.

Ponds and ornamental pools

TIMELY TIP

Use a filter
Installing a good filtration system and pump reduces the need for completely cleaning out a pond on a regular basis. Just clean the filter at set times and enjoy crystal-clear water without all the hard work and time invested.

Clean your pond once a year

When the weather begins to cool from late autumn through to early spring, it's time to clean your pond.

> Cut the grass and pull out ground-cover plants and weeds that have invaded from all sides. Remove branches and dead leaves from the bottom of the pond and skim out floating weeds. All this material can be added to your compost heap.

> Water plants in pots should be taken out, cleaned up and repotted into fresh soil. Cut back those that have died down for the winter.

Make your water feature water-wise

Follow these simple tips for making your water feature water-wise.

> Instantly reduce the amount of water lost through splashing by simply adjusting the flow of fountains, if possible.

> Make sure the water in your water feature is captured in a pond or basin so that it can be recycled. Do this by surrounding the fountain's splash zone with a waterproof membrane, then disguise the material with

pebbles. This area captures water and then allows it to drain back into the pond or the water reservoir under the fountain.

● Don't run a fountain on windy days.

● Where possible, use rainwater to replenish ponds and water features.

Give your pond a thorough cleaning

If your pond is looking murky or is leaking and needs to be completely emptied out for cleaning, here's how to go about it.

● Drain the pond by siphoning the water out with a hose (reuse the water on lawns, shrubberies or trees).

● Save some of the water by siphoning it into buckets, to retain some of the natural pond life for replacing after cleaning.

● Using a small garden spade, shovel out mud and debris from the base of the pond and scrub the sides with a scrubbing brush.

● Repair leaks or damaged areas as necessary.

● Refill with fresh water and add the original water that was saved.

● Test and adjust the pH of the water before adding fish to the pond (seek advice from aquarium specialists or online).

● Replace all the pond plants.

Note: water is lost from ponds and other water features through evaporation, so top up the water level regularly, especially in summer.

Quick-and-easy kits

● To install an ornamental pool, buy the whole thing as a kit (from a garden centre or aquatic specialist) and you'll make fast work of putting it together. You'll find everything from thermally moulded pools to the connectable parts for cascades and streams. This method costs more than simply installing matting or a waterproof pond liner on a bed of sand, but you save valuable time.

▶ Kits are quick and easy to install: dig a hole corresponding to the volume and shape of the ornamental pool and then choose the elements of your decor, without forgetting the main item, the pump. To make it work, don't forget that you need an electrical power supply and access to water for regular top ups (never let the pump run dry).

Create a cool oasis

Fountains and water features can provide a wonderfully calming focus in your garden, without you needing to invest hours of your time maintaining them.

▶ Choose the simplest time-saving solution: the kit. Garden centres offer a wide range of water features fitted with pumps that operate on a closed circuit.

▶ An advantage of a fountain over a garden pond is that it contributes to oxygenating the water – fish will love it and the water is less likely to become choked with algae, which means less time spent cleaning.

▶ Plants, and particularly water lilies, aren't suitable to use in fountains as they generally prefer still water. However, there is a way to have plants and moving water coexist: locate a fountain in the deepest part of a pond, where there are the fewest plants.

▶ To make a water feature child-safe, simply fill it with large river pebbles to reduce the water depth to less than 30 cm. It will still look attractive and be capable of supporting plant growth.

Plant in baskets to guarantee success

In water, it's preferable to plant in baskets rather than in traditional pots.

▶ Choose baskets with handles. In spring, when it's time to lift out the plants to divide clumps or refresh planting mixes, simply lifting the basket out by its handles makes the job fast and easy.

▶ Opt for 'special' pond baskets (available from garden centres) to hold plants, or use laundry or storage baskets, which are cheaper.

TIMELY TIP

Keep out weeds

Take care not to introduce weeds with water plants and you'll cut down on extra work. Also, rinse all material going into the pond and only buy from reputable nurseries. Don't be tempted to add floating plants, such as azolla, which become a weed menace on the water's surface. And never put aquarium weeds into ponds.

Keep children safe

Each year, children are victims of backyard accidental drowning. It is imperative that you install a safety fence around any water installation in your garden, in line with local council regulations. Fences must be childproof and include a self-closing gate.

Plant in the right part of the pond

A pond contains four main planting areas: at the edge (in the ground), on the surface (floating plants), in shallow water (10–20 cm), and in deep water (30–50 cm). Here is a list of what to plant in each area.

EDGE
- **Astilbe** (*Astilbe* Hybrids)
- **Canna** (*Canna* Hybrids)
- **Day lily** (*Hemerocallis* Hybrids) (1)
- **Gunnera** (*Gunnera manicata*)
- **Hosta** (*Hosta* Hybrids)
- **Knobby clubrush** (*Isolepis nodosa*)
- **Marsh marigold** (*Caltha palustris*)
- **Papyrus** (*Cyperus papyrus*)
- **Primula** (*Primula* spp.)

SURFACE
- **Marsh flower** (*Villarsia* spp.)
- **Nardoo** (*Marsilea drummondii*)
- **Water lily** (*Nymphaea* Hybrids) (2)

SHALLOW WATER
- **Japanese water iris** (*Iris ensata*)
- **Water buttons** (*Cotula coronopifolia*)

DEEP WATER
- **Flowering rush** (*Butomus umbellatus*) (3)
- **Pickerel weed** (*Pontederia cordata*)

▶ Line water baskets with hessian, coir or perforated plastic to prevent the soil from spreading into the water. Fill the baskets with a mixture of garden soil and compost (or select a potting mix for aquatic plants).

▶ Place plants on the bottom of an ornamental pool, pack down the surface and then cover it with small stones or pebbles. This prevents the plants from coming up and fish from searching around the roots.

▶ Elevate shorter-growing plants on bricks or large river stones to enable them to reach the surface of the water.

Careful positioning

Don't position a pond at the bottom of a slope because water run-off from your garden could contaminate the pond water and poison the aquatic life.

TIMELY TIP

Swimming pools

Find the best position

▶ Site a swimming pool away from large trees so that it's less likely to be deluged by leaves and dirt, which can eat up hours in pool-cleaning time. Overhanging trees provide summer shade, but also drop material that has to be regularly removed, such as leaves, twigs and flowers.

▶ Get shade, without the leaves, by investing in a shade sail that can unfurled fully or partially, or erect a permanent structure such as a pergola over part of the pool.

Consider your options

Deciding to have a swimming pool is just the first of many related decisions. Save time and complications up front by carefully considering your options.

▶ Above or below ground? Pools can be sunk into the ground or built above ground. Your choices involve not just cost (in-ground pools are more expensive) but also space, access for excavation and the length of time you want a pool in your backyard.

▶ Investigate the advantages and disadvantages of concrete or fibre-glass, which are the two main options for in-ground pools, before beginning construction. It could save you time and money.

▶ How will the pool be filtered and cleaned? Filtration and cleaning systems vary not just in their mode of action but in the amount of input you have to devote to maintenance. Way up the short-term costs over long-term convenience for minimum maintenance.

▶ Think about what sort of pool fencing you need and want – timber, metal or glass – taking the cost and look into consideration, along with maintenance. In a small area, or where there are external views, glass fencing can turn your swimming pool into a garden feature, and it's easy to clean and maintain, without ongoing costs.

TIMELY TIP

Cover up

Pool covers provide protection from fallen leaves and other debris, particularly when the pool is not in constant use, as well as reducing evaporation of the pool water.

TIMELY TIP

Light up

Lights in and around swimming pools not only make swimming after dark safer, they can also transform your pool into a striking garden feature after dark.

Great plants to grow near pools

Soften the look of a swimming pool – and provide extra garden space – by planting around it. The trick is to select plants that aren't going to pollute the pool with leaves or flowers, that have few thorns and that look good in summer when the pool is in constant use.

PLANT	DESCRIPTION	CLIMATE
Agapanthus (1)	● Heads of blue or white summer flowers, strappy green leaves year-round ● Great as a border	Frost-free
Camellia (2)	● Tall evergreen shrubs with white, pink or red flowers from late summer to spring ● Good screening choice	Cool to subtropical
Hibiscus	● Shrub with flamboyant flowers from spring to autumn	Frost-free

TIMELY TIP

Renovation or removal
Before removing a swimming pool, decide if it can be given a facelift with new tiles or a new surround. If you do decide to remove your pool, think about making the space a water-storage area for your garden.

▶ In Australia and New Zealand, it is compulsory to fence in swimming pools and ornamental pools that are more than 30 cm deep (40 cm in New Zealand) – check regulations with your local council. (In South Africa, check current pool fencing regulations with your local authority.) These areas must be fitted with childproof gates that are kept shut at all times. Never prop open a safety gate in case children gain access.

Don't forget the environment

Make your swimming pool as environmentally friendly as it can be by including power- and energy-saving features. You'll save both time and money in the long run.

▶ Install a rainwater tank to catch water for topping up the pool. You won't be relying on expensive mains water and you won't be bound by water restrictions during dry periods. Tanks can collect water from nearby roofs. Position the tank away from the pool to reduce its visual impact.

● Opt for solar heating. Heat from the sun is available for many months of the year, it's free and can be efficiently harvested to heat a swimming pool. Plus, having warm pool water throughout the cooler months of the year extends the use and value you get from your swimming pool. Go online to research your best options.

● If you live in a bushfire-prone area, you can access the water in your swimming pool for fire-fighting using a petrol-powered pump (electrical power often fails during bushfires) and suitable hosing. Practise using the pump so you save time by acting quickly in an emergency.

Trees and shrubs

Right tree, right place

● Select trees carefully and don't plant too many. The first thing to do is establish the height and spread of each species, its mature size and upkeep needs so that you can picture your garden in 5 to 10 years time.

● Before planting a tree, assess whether the shade it casts will be welcome (screening your entertaining area from hot summer sun), or if it will cause a problem (blocking winter sun).

● Check for overhead wires before planting any tree, and consult your house plans for the location of services such as electricity and sewer lines, to avoid wasting time if any services are damaged or interrupted. (*See also* 'Find out more', on page 371.)

● Allow each tree enough space to spread its limbs and root system. Trees that don't have enough room often grow tall and spindly, which means they're unstable and a strong gust of wind could blow them over, resulting in damage to your house or garden.

TIMELY TIP

Shady solution

Shade is important for garden play areas for children, so find a spot that receives summer shade, or plant trees, shrubs or vines on the northern or western side of your garden.

TIMELY TIP

Name your choice

Save time by making the right choice first time around, and buy named varieties of trees. They grow to a known height and spread, unlike seed-grown trees, which can vary enormously.

Care-free garden trees

PLANT	DESCRIPTION	CLIMATE
Agonis flexuosa	● Silvery drooping leaves; flowers in spring	Cool to temperate
Crabapple	● Spring flowers; autumn fruit	Cool to temperate
Crepe myrtle ('Indian Summer' series)	● Summer flowers; autumn colour; attractive winter bark; deciduous	Cool to subtropical
Eucalyptus ('Summer Beauty')	● Large pink-red flowers in summer; evergreen	Cool to subtropical
European mountain ash (1)	● Very decorative in winter; attracts birds	Cool
Evergreen ash	● Spring flowers, drought-tolerant; evergreen	Cool to subtropical
Forest pansy	● Heart-shaped leaves; autumn colour; low-growing	Cool to temperate
Frangipani (2)	● White flowers; evergreen	Subtropical to tropical
Fruitless mulberry tree	● Umbrella-shaped with large leaves	Cool to subtropical
Ginkgo (3)	● Slow-growing tree; magnificent autumn colours	Cool to temperate
Japanese maple	● Cut-out leaves; flamboyant colours	Cool to temperate
Judas tree (4)	● Mauve flowers on the wood; rounded leaves	Cool to temperate
Liriodendron (Tulip tree)	● Remarkable summer flowers; superb autumn colours	Cool to temperate
Magnolia (5)	● Fragrant flowers; deciduous	Cool to temperate
Silver birch (6)	● Delicate leaves; a choice of elegant varieties	Cool
Sophora	● Umbrella-shaped or weeping; deciduous	Cool to temperate

TIMELY TIP

Bumpy roots

Don't lay hard paving on the ground under trees: the roots can dislodge paving, making it uneven and dangerous to walk on. Instead, use mulch around the roots and save time on both watering and repair and maintenance.

Gentle care of trees

▶ Don't lop a tree to reduce its height; employ a qualified tree surgeon to remove some of the branches. This will lighten the tree's canopy without destroying its overall shape and impact.

▶ Trim climbers and ground-cover plants regularly so they stay where you want them to, and discourage them from climbing into trees, or they could cause serious complications. Be particularly vigilant with ivy, wisteria and bougainvillea.

Basic maintenance for shrubs

▶ With the huge choice of great shrubs on offer, save time by choosing only those species that are suitable for the year-round climate in your area, the condition of your soil and the aspect of your garden.

▶ Find out about a plant before you buy. If you fall in love with a particular species, check its characteristics and, if necessary, choose a similar one that may be better suited to the conditions in your garden.

▶ Pay attention to position. Don't buy a plant for a specific part of your garden if it's intolerant to the extremes of heat and cold in that area.

▶ Save time choosing the right plants by asking for help at your local plant nursery or garden centre: they often employ experienced gardeners and landscapers, so take full advantage of the free expertise on offer (and avoid making costly, time-wasting mistakes!).

Observe and choose

▶ Choose shrubs you can enjoy in different ways each season: coloured stems (such as *Rubus cockburnianus*, *Cornus alba* 'Sibirica'), winter blooms (such as *Chaenomeles japonica*), spring flowers, fragrances (such as daphne for winter and gardenia for summer), and different types of leaf colour, shape and texture, or autumn colours.

▶ Observe nearby parks and gardens: they're a good source of inspiration and the best way of checking the hardiness of certain species. As soon as you notice an interesting shrub, find out its name and make a note of it – you'll have a preselection if you need it.

Star shrubs through the seasons

	PLANT	DESCRIPTION	CLIMATE
WINTER	Camellia	● Pink, red or white flowers; evergreen shiny leaves	Cool to subtropical
	Daphne odora	● Pink flowers and spicy perfume	Cool to temperate
	Japonica (1) (*Chaenomeles japonica*)	● Magnificent red or pink flowers; spiny shrub; deciduous	Cool to subtropical
	Poinsettia	● Red, pink or white flowers	Temperate to tropical
	Witch hazel	● Yellow fringed pompom flowers; original and perfumed varieties	Cool
	White dogwood	● Bright red decorative bark	Cool
SPRING	Azalea (2)	● Pink, red, mauve or white flowers, some perfumed; evergreen leaves	Cool to subtropical
	Forsythia	● Yellow flowers; striking at the beginning of spring	Cool to temperate
	Lilac (*Syringa* spp.)	● A range of colours to choose from; shiny green, wedge-shaped leaves; perfumed	Cool
	Weigela	● Pink, red or white flowers on arching canes; some varieties have variegated foliage	Cool to temperate
SUMMER	Buddleia (*Buddleia davidii*)	● Clusters of white, blue or lilac flowers that attract butterflies	Cool to temperate
	Gardenia	● White flowers; perfumed; evergreen	Temperate to tropical
	Hydrangea	● Heads of blue, mauve, white or pink flowers (colours can vary with soil pH); deciduous	Cool to subtropical
	Kolkwitzia (3) (*K. amabilis*)	● Superb pink blooms at the beginning of summer	Cool
	Mexican orange blossom (*Choisya ternata*)	● Evergreen leaves; orange flowers; perfumed	Cool
	Mock orange (*Philadelphus* spp.)	● Highly perfumed white flowers	Cool to temperate

Star shrubs through the seasons (continued)

AUTUMN 	**Amelanchier**	● Exceptional flowers, fruit and autumn colours	Cool
	Banksia (*Banksia ericifolia*)	● Tall spires of orange, candle-like, long-lasting blooms; attracts birds	Cool to subtropical
	Fothergilla	● Changing coloured foliage	Cool
	Sasanqua camellia	● Pink, white or red flowers	Cool to subtropical
	Smokebush (4) (*Cotinus coggygria*)	● Rounded shape; attractive leaf colours; decorative flowers held on bush	Cool to temperate

TIMELY TIP

Read the label

File plant labels so you don't have to go searching elsewhere for specific plant information. Keep them in a garden resource book or diary, or file scans of them on your computer for quick reference.

Perennials

Quick-and-easy care tips

There are two basic types of perennials: herbaceous, which die down in winter but regrow in spring, and evergreen, which are leafy all year.

▶ If you live in a cold or frost-prone area, herbaceous perennials are the best choice, as they're often dormant when the weather turns cold.

▶ Find out about plants in a flash by checking the plant label: all the necessary information is provided, including height and width, colour, flowering period, best aspect, and type of soil required.

▶ Pay particular attention to the height and spread of perennials, as most grow rapidly before blooming and need to be allocated the correct space at the time of planting (when they are usually much smaller).

▶ Choose perennials not only for their flowers but also for attractive foliage and interesting plant shapes. That way you won't spend more time than is necessary on filling in gaps in your garden design.

TIMELY TIP

Instant rewards

Perennials are easy to grow from root cuttings or by dividing clumps, but for an instant effect – and to save time – buy plants in pots in spring, then watch them grow and bloom faster.

TIMELY TIP

A minimum of care
Once in the ground, perennials are great time savers: they're not particularly prone to disease and only require a good clean-up in late winter to eliminate dead branches and leaves (to make way for new spring growth). Give them a good dose of slow-release fertiliser at the same time.

Size does matter

▶ Size garden beds sensibly so you can access perennials throughout the year. Not only will your plants have room to grow and look their best, but you can tend the beds easily and efficiently, without squashing plants in the process. (*See also* 'Dividing perennial clumps', on page 419.)

▶ Edge beds using a border of bricks or paving stones. In spring, remove invasive plants such as grasses, which may have accumulated on the border, and your garden will immediately look clean and tidy again.

▶ If you don't have a permanent border in place, outline garden beds simply by cutting the edge with a hoe or sharp garden tool. You'll get a very satisfying, clean look.

Well-composed perennial plantings

▶ Create interesting planting schemes featuring perennials by first getting inspiration and ideas from plant catalogues, magazines, web sites and specialised books, carefully taking note of pictures and plant combinations that appeal to you.

▶ If the plants you find in a picture aren't suitable for your garden or climate, get advice from your local nursery, garden centre or online, and find replacement plants of a similar size, colour and flowering time.

▶ Don't be too scattered. Using too many different plants in the same area can look messy. Aim at planting groups of five to seven identical plants (according to the size of the adult clump) and calculate the space between them so they can all flourish – it'll give an impression of abundance and mass, and caring for the same plant group is faster.

▶ Not all perennials die down over winter – many are evergreen and look good all year round, especially in frost-free gardens. So if it's year-round colour you're looking for, include clumps of clivia, agapanthus, kangaroo paw, flax and day lily.

TIMELY TIP

Photo finish
Organise your garden beds in the same way you would a family photo: the large plants at the back and the small ones in front. You'll save time finding filler plants and dealing with a hotchpotch of plant sizes.

The benefits of mulching

● Lay mulch in your perennial garden – it's a great time saver (cover soil with a layer of organic matter 5–7 cm thick). It keeps the soil and root systems cool in summer, eliminates excessive water evaporation (meaning less watering), breaks down to feed plants and condition the soil, and prevents the growth of weeds by depriving them of light. That all translates to healthy plants and less maintenance.

● Spread mulch around young perennials or grow a filler plant – such as early spring-flowering bulbs – while you're waiting for them to grow.

● Take advantage of the fact that mulch also provides a decorative surface and opt for a material that blends in well with your garden.

● The choices of mulch include: grass clippings, homemade compost or shredded local organic waste, such as sugar cane, cocoa shells, pea straw or composted bark. Avoid large wood chips, though, as they can make the soil acidic and water-repellent.

(*See also* 'Quick homemade compost', on page 415.)

Annuals and bulbs

TIMELY TIP

Speedy results

For instant colour, fast results and fuss-free selection, buy advanced flowering punnets of annuals, and plant them in garden beds or pots.

Fast and reliable flowering

Annuals are best-known for their colourful flowers and seasonal rewards with a minimum of effort required from gardeners.

● Get good results from seeds. Opt for annuals when you need garden plants that grow quickly and readily from seed.

● Choose seedlings bought in punnets from a garden centre or nursery if it's a fast solution you're looking for, but don't forget that many vegetables and flowering plants grow quickly and easily from seed, too.

● Brighten up a shady summer garden by planting impatiens. All you need is five plants in separate pots and within a couple of weeks you'll have beautiful clumps of pink, white or orange. Their water and fertiliser requirements are minimal and they're guaranteed to flower without any trouble until autumn frosts arrive.

● Take advantage of instant colour. Use annuals in combination with permanent plants in a pot, or make up a feature pot, hanging basket or window box with a seasonal display of flowering annuals.

● Plant annuals in a picking garden so that you have blooms available for indoor arrangements throughout the growing season. Poppies, stocks, sweet peas and calendulas are all great choices.

Early flowers

In warm, frost-free climates, seeds of spring- or summer-flowering annuals in cold-climate gardens – such as sweet peas and petunias – can be planted in late autumn for flowers as early as late winter.

Colourful plantings

Sow seeds of annual flowers such as alyssum, nasturtium or cosmos directly into the ground to fill bare spots quickly and cheaply, and in the right colour scheme for your garden.

HEIGHT	WHITE TO PINK	BLUE TO MAUVE	YELLOW TO RED
High (more than 60 cm)	Cleome / Cosmos (1) / Lavatera	Cornflower / Larkspur / Salvia	African marigold / Rudbeckia / Sunflower
Average (40–60 cm)	Candytuft / Clarkia (2) / Impatiens	Canterbury bells / Dahlia (dwarf) / Statice	Calendula / Poppy (3) / Zinnia
Low (less than 40 cm)	Alyssum (4) / Bellis / Primula	Forget-me-not / Nigella / Viola	Eschscholzia / Marigold / Nemesia
Climbing	Sweet pea (5)	Cobea	Nasturtium (6)

Bulbs – winning time savers

Bulbs are synonymous with fast, easy gardening – all that's needed for flowering and growth in the first season is already contained in the bulb.

▶ Bulbs come complete with a reserve of energy from stored nutritional reserves in the bulb itself (or a corm or tuber, depending on its botanical nature). Opt for the classics and reap the rewards: tulips, daffodils, begonias, crocuses and anemones.

▶ Leave bulbs in the ground from one year to the next, as long as your soil is well drained. There's no need to lift and store bulbs that are suited to your climate after their growth has died down. Simply protect them by covering the ground with a layer of mulch.

▶ Be aware that large clumps may occasionally need to be lifted and divided to encourage better flowering the following season.

Fast, fuss-free removal

In some instances, bulbs are best removed for storage instead of being left in the ground.

▶ Dig bulbs up carefully when the plant leaves become drier, and store them in a dry place until replanting the following year.

▶ Some bulbs are very sensitive to wet or hot conditions: many tulips, daffodils, gladiolus and some dahlias, for instance, survive best if they're lifted (because they become dormant), then stored away until the next season.

▶ Save time by preparing for bulb removal at the time you plant. If you decide to plant a group of flowers in a clump or a lawn, place them on a bed of good soil in a small plastic pot. Make a hole with a flat bottom in the ground to bury the container at the right depth. To remove them, just lift up the container with a fork to pull out the whole clump together and take the bulbs away to store.

Top tips for good buying

▶ Be wary of tempting offers at the end of the season when bulbs are sold at very low prices. If a deal seems too good to be true, it probably is!

▶ Look carefully at the size of the bulbs and their freshness: if they're small, dry or withered, they probably have little chance of flowering.

▶ Check the state of health of the bulbs. Keeping them for too long or storing them in bad conditions encourages the development of fungus and bacteria, which can contaminate your healthy plants.

Indoor bulb displays

▶ Encourage early indoor flowering of bulbs such as hyacinths, crocuses or narcissus. Self-sufficient bulbs only need a support, such as a bulb jar, and moisture, to flourish indoors and provide a stunning show of blooms.

TIMELY TIP

Early treats

At the beginning of spring, place dahlia and tuberous begonia bulbs on a bed of damp peat in a well-lit place; shoots will begin to form. After planting, they'll already have young shoots coming up and will flower several weeks early!

TIMELY TIP

Mark the spot

If you're leaving bulbs in the ground, slip a plant label or marker into the spot before the bulb dies down so you don't dig it up by mistake over summer.

▶ Get the show going. Put a bulb on gravel at the bottom of a vessel or in a narrow vase or bulb jar so that the water touches the base of the bulb. Put the bulb in a cold dark place for a few weeks (flowering is triggered when the bulb has received enough cold), before moving it into a sunny position to encourage growth and flowering.

▶ Save time and buy pre-prepared bulbs that have already had their flowering triggered in a cold room.

Lawn and lawn alternatives

TIMELY TIP

Blitzing weeds

Selective herbicides are a great time saver for dealing with lawn weeds such as bindi-eye and flat weeds. One spray at the right time and there's no need for weeding.

Do you need a lawn?

▶ Get rid of it or reduce its area. Lawns are incredibly time-consuming, so the best way to save time (and money) is to do away with them! Or, make your lawn area smaller by enlarging garden beds and planting shrubs, which are the least demanding garden plants.

▶ Ask yourself these questions first. If you answer yes to all three, make space for lawn; if not, think twice. Do you have young children or pets? Do you enjoy lawn care? Do you like the look of green lawn?

A care-free lawn

▶ Choose a mixture of grasses that corresponds to your needs. This is the key to a lawn that's easy to maintain. There are different species with varying degrees of fineness, resistance to trampling and adaptability to shade. If you

have a sunny garden and children who like to play ball games, choose a sporting mix. In the shade and under trees, it's absolutely essential to sow a mixture for shady ground. Don't hesitate to buy several sorts of mixes for your lawn: you'll save time and avoid problems in the long run.

Mow less often

To cut down on mowing, choose a slow-growing grass variety that suits your climate, such as dwarf buffalo or one of the fescue-based, cool-season lawn mixes.

TIMELY TIP

TIMELY TIP

Fortify beds

Keep runners out of garden beds using barriers sunk into the ground around each garden bed, or by maintaining the edges with regular digging, cutting the grass with an edger or by using a glyphosate-based herbicide (don't apply it on windy days, and only apply it to the very edge of the lawn).

▶ If you have repeated trouble growing a good lawn under trees due to shade and root competition, give up and look at alternative ground covers. Consider replacing lawn with mulch, gravel or paving.

▶ When you plant your lawn, think about maintenance: it's better to put all the lawn areas together rather than have a small strip of lawn that is impossible to mow and constantly encroaches on flower beds.

▶ For efficient mowing, you must be able to go over the whole surface without performing acrobatics: there should be no sharp angles and no cramped passages between two patches of lawn.

▶ If you have a tiny patch of lawn – under 9 square metres – a hand mower is the quickest option. There's little maintenance, no fuel to be bought and stored, and the mower is easy to store away.

A quick reviver

With a few tricks up your sleeve, in spring your lawn will be as good as new and you'll avoid a more time-consuming revamp.

▶ If your lawn is invaded by moss and weeds, give it a quick renovation in autumn. On a day when there's no wind, apply a selective lawn weed-killer and leave it to work for around 10 days (check all lawn products to make sure the one you use suits your lawn variety).

▶ Borrow or rent a scarifier (a powered one for more than 100 square metres of lawn). Water the lawn to loosen the soil, then five days later go over it thoroughly lengthways and widthways with the scarifier fitted with a catcher to eliminate moss.

▶ Scatter coated grass seeds in the bare areas and spread slow-release fertiliser granules (that gradually release their nitrogen) over the whole surface of the lawn.

▶ The repeated addition of lawn foods can result in soil becoming acidic, which favours weeds, so add lime to your lawn occasionally to reduce acidity and cut down on time spent weeding.

TIMELY TIP

Instant lawn

To lay a lawn quickly, use turf, which comes in rolls much like carpet. Simply prepare the ground before laying it and hey presto! You've got instant lawn.

Month-by-month lawn-care guide

● **Early spring (September)** Do the first mowing as lawns begin to regrow with warmer weather. Remove weeds and moss from damp areas. Naturalised bulbs will be flowering (don't mow these areas).

● **Spring (October to November)** Mow regularly, maintain edges near paths and garden beds, and spread fertiliser if there's been rain.

● **Summer (December to February)** Water at night or in the early morning once or twice a week. Don't water an established lawn during drought – let it survive on its own (lawns from running grasses regrow once rain returns). Mow regularly and maintain the lawn edges.

● **Autumn (March to May)** This is the best time to revive your lawn, treat it for compaction and re-sow damaged areas or lay a new lawn. Plant bulbs for naturalising if desired. Fertilise in early autumn to encourage strong growth as the season cools.

● **Winter (June to August)** Mow occasionally, treat emerging weeds – especially bindi-eye – and other prickly lawn weeds, and aerate compacted lawns. Expect warm-season lawns to brown off in frost (they'll re-green in spring). Cool-season grasses are green and lush throughout winter. Water occasionally.

Make mowing count

▶ From the end of spring, mow every week or two. It's more efficient and timesaving to mow frequently, but leave the grass a little longer rather than scalping it. The grass will be lusher and more drought-hardy and have fewer weeds if you mow a little and more often rather than the other way around.

▶ Don't put off mowing for too long. Long grass clogs the mower, which makes the job harder and more time-consuming.

▶ Think about paying someone to mow the lawn for you – it's a quick and relatively cheap option!

TIMELY TIP

Easy edges

A brick or stone border that is slightly lower than the level of the grass provides an efficient mowing strip that is both aesthetic and very practical: the grass won't invade planted areas or pathways, and you get a clean cut by mowing right up to the edge, with the two outside wheels on the border.

TIMELY TIP

Leave off the catcher

When you're mowing, save time by not connecting the grass catcher so you won't have to keep stopping to empty it. The cut grass left on top of a mown lawn quickly dries and breaks down to feed the roots.

Lawn alternatives

Here are some great timesaving alternatives to a traditional green grassy lawn. Make the change and say goodbye to mowing forever!

- Massed plantings (1)
- A bush garden of native plants and mulch
- Paving or decking
- Inorganic mulch such as compacted granite or gravel
- Ground-cover plants such as Australian native violet (*Viola hederacea*)

The vegetable garden

TIMELY TIP

The mulching reflex

The secret for quickly ridding a vegetable garden of weeds is mulching. And it's also the cheapest (read: free) and easiest of materials to acquire. Homemade mulch is made up of composted grass clippings, leaves, well-chopped prunings and food scraps.

Fast-growing plants

Growing vegetables is a highly rewarding form of gardening, and with the right preparation, you won't need to spend long hours doing boring jobs.

▶ Choose seedlings rather than sowing seeds. They may be more expensive, but planting advanced seedlings saves time and avoids the uncertainties of sowing. And staggering plantings of seedlings over several weeks will provide variety and extend your harvest, so you won't be eating the same sort of lettuce two weeks in a row!

▶ For a terrace or small garden, buy single plants. This means you can buy as many different varieties of each plant as you please. Look for small, early-cropping varieties for pots.

TIMELY TIP

Two for one

There's an easy way to keep enjoying fresh salad with just the flick of a wrist: cut lettuce leaves off at ground level and they'll grow back a second time.

Simple tricks

Save time on thinning out – removing excess plants that have germinated to leave just one strong seedling to grow – by mixing the seed with sand before scattering it along a row, or using seed on seed tapes, which guarantees even spacing.

Get the temperature right

To ensure success, sow seed when the ground is at the correct temperature for each crop. Here is a list of common vegetables to plant in spring and autumn, with their corresponding ground temperature.

VEGETABLE	TEMPERATURE (°C)
Peas	8
Lettuce	10
Carrots	10
Watercress	10
Fennel	10
Parsley	10
Cabbage	10
Leek	10
Spinach	12
Radish	12
Turnip	15
Zucchini	15
Pumpkin	15
Tomatoes	15
Beans	15
Sweet corn	16
Cucumber	20
Capsicum	23

▶ Opt for fast crops or ones that can be harvested over a long period, such as spinach, silverbeet, soft-hearted lettuce or aromatic herbs, especially if you don't have very much space, instead of filling your vegetable garden with crops that take a long time to mature, such as onions, potatoes, pumpkin and cabbage.

▶ Try cultivating sun-drenched tomatoes, perfumed strawberries and crisp little radishes for their superior flavour. It'll mean easy access to fresh produce and fewer trips to the supermarket.

Green fertiliser

Never leave the ground in your vegetable garden bare. If you don't want to plant a crop, sow a green fertiliser such as beans, clover or alfalfa to add nitrogen to the soil and protect it from erosion. To get the benefit, dig the green manure into the soil before flowering.

Easy-to-cultivate seasonal vegetables

In most warm climates, year-round crops can be grown for a constant supply of vegetables. Summer-harvest vegetables can be sown from late winter to spring, but sow autumn harvest in spring to summer, and winter/spring harvest in summer to autumn.

YEAR-ROUND HARVEST

Cabbage
● Time to harvest is 8–16 weeks
● Chinese cabbage is the easiest to grow and can be harvested in 8 weeks

Carrots (1)
● Time to harvest is 12 weeks
● Avoid shallow, pebbly soil that deforms the roots. If growing in pots, choose round carrots

Lettuce
● Harvest mature leaves 5 weeks after planting
● Stagger plantings over several weeks to keep crops coming

Radish
● Time to harvest is 6 weeks
● Never let the ground dry out, otherwise radishes become hollow and too peppery

Rhubarb (2)
● Time to harvest is 8–12 weeks
● Plant crowns in winter; fertilise and water regularly to keep cropping

Silverbeet (chard)
● Time to harvest is 8–12 weeks
● Harvest older outer leaves to keep cropping

SUMMER HARVEST

Capsicum
● Time to harvest is 10–16 weeks
● Grows year-round in warm climates. Protect from fruit fly in problem areas

Cucumber
● Time to harvest is 8–12 weeks
● Grows year-round in warm climates

Green beans (3)
● Time to harvest is 10 weeks
● Sow two or three times from spring to early summer for staggered harvests from summer to autumn. For fastest crops select dwarf beans

Potatoes
● Time to harvest is 3–4 months
● When the young plants measure 15 cm, place a mound of earth around each one to bury the base of the stalks

Tomatoes (4)
● Time to harvest is 12–20 weeks, depending on variety
● In warm climates, sow a second crop in late summer for fruit throughout autumn

Zucchini
● Time to harvest is 8–14 weeks
● Pick the fruit when it's young and tender (they increase in size very quickly)

(Continued overleaf)

Easy-to-cultivate seasonal vegetables (continued)

AUTUMN HARVEST

Leek (5)
- Time to harvest is 12–20 weeks
- Make successive sowings to stagger harvest and fertilise every two to three weeks for quick growth. In warm to tropical zones grow through winter

Pumpkin
- Time to harvest is 14–16 weeks
- Vines need plenty of space to spread. Can be grown through winter in tropical areas

Sweet corn (6)
- Time to harvest is 12–16 weeks
- Plant in blocks for good cob formation

Sweet potato
- Time to harvest is 12–16 weeks
- Vine spreads over large area and is highly frost- and cold-sensitive. Grows year-round in tropical areas

WINTER/SPRING HARVEST

Broccoli
- Time to harvest is 12–16 weeks
- After cutting the tops, side growth continues for many weeks

Onions (7)
- Time to harvest is 6–8 months
- Select suitable varieties for your area for trouble-free growth. Harvest as tops yellow and bend over

Peas
- Time to harvest is 12–16 weeks
- In cold areas continue planting in late winter to early spring for spring and early summer harvests

Spinach (English)
- Time to harvest is 8–10 weeks
- In cool areas continue planting through winter for early spring harvests

Aromatic herbs – great rewards for little effort

▶ Divide the ground reserved for aromatic plants into three parts. Reserve the first part for annuals (such as chervil, dill and coriander) and the second for biennials (such as curly and flat-leaf parsley, and root herbs), which, by definition, have a life cycle of two years. Lastly, in the third part, plant the perennial species (such as rosemary, tarragon, thyme, winter savoury, chives and oregano), which will last several years.

▶ Save time on sowing herbs and buy small plants instead. That way you'll be able to harvest them from the first summer.

▶ Set up a small pot of herbs on a terrace or patio, close to your kitchen, especially if your vegetable garden is way down at the bottom of the garden. This means you won't have to make endless trips back and forth to pick commonly used herbs.

Fruit trees

The basics of growing fruit

Fruit trees can be both productive and ornamental.

▶ If you want to grow productive trees in a small space (unless you have a big garden), select dwarf varieties or plants that are grafted onto dwarf rootstock. You'll save time climbing up a ladder to pick fruit or prune the tree, too. Good choices include citrus, apple trees, mangoes, avocados, pears, peaches and apricots.

▶ Fruit trees can be complex to manage in an orchard or where production is the number-one aim, but in an average-sized backyard, general care and management is much easier. As a rule, prune fruit trees after they have produced a crop. And always remove suckers or any dead, diseased or broken branches as soon as you notice them.

▶ Whenever you buy a fruiting plant, check whether a pollinator is required. Many fruit trees only bear fruit if another variety is nearby to provide cross-pollination.

▶ The simple way to cross-pollinate is to have two varieties grafted on one plant.

Net your crop

▶ Physical barriers, such as nets or wire cages, are a fast and easy way to protect your crop from predators such as birds, bats and even possums. Check nets regularly to release animals that may have become trapped, and use the appropriate netting for your crop. Once you've harvested your crop, remove the net and store it for the next year.

TIMELY TIP

Lovely lemons

A lemon is probably the most useful of all fruit trees to grow. There are small-growing varieties to suit pots or court-yards and larger varieties to suit bigger gardens.

A fruity harvest

Plant fruit trees in autumn rather than spring – it'll save you 12 months in terms of fruit bearing because the tree will have more time to mature.

TIMELY TIP

TIMELY TIP

Water without staining

An easy way to water your indoor plants is with ice cubes, without the risk of water leakage or staining of indoor surfaces. Simply put a couple on top of the pot soil and leave them to melt.

Indoor plants

Choose the right room

▶ Look for the best place in the house for each plant, and don't be afraid to try different locations until you find the right spot.

▶ Forget about rooms that are too dark or that don't have any natural light: most indoor plants originate in tropical or subtropical regions (in particular equatorial forests), and they need filtered light. In front of a large bay window exposed to the west or east is ideal, with the light filtered by netting if necessary.

▶ Plants requiring the maximum amount of sun should be positioned on a windowsill facing north. Always check moisture levels and that the leaves are not being burned by the sun. At the slightest sign of withering, move the plants back towards the middle of the room.

▶ Ferns and moisture-loving plants are best suited to bathrooms.

▶ Don't position indoor plants in draughty areas or near ducted heat or airconditioning outlets.

The secrets for success

▶ Only water when the potting mix feels dry to the touch: over-watering is often the cause of indoor plant death. Check by pushing your finger into the soil – if it comes out without any trace of soil on it, start watering.

▶ Gently mist plant foliage using an atomiser. Indoor plants benefit greatly from ambient moisture.

▶ Pay attention to drainage. Place your indoor plant pots on a gravel surface (in a saucer or a tray), which is kept moist.

▶ Feed indoor plants with small amounts of fertiliser. The fastest and simplest solution is to use complete liquid fertiliser in special doses ('green plants', 'flowering plants', 'orchids', etc.). Apply every two to four weeks or according to the manufacturer's instructions.

▶ Remember to water your indoor plants more often during the hot summer months and less during winter.

Easy indoor plants

PLANT	CHARACTERISTICS	MOISTURE	LIGHT
African violet (1)	● Small flowering plant with downy leaves	++	Semi-shade
Chlorophytum	● Clump of long variegated leaves	++	Strong
Cissus	● Climbing or hanging	+	Semi-shade
Croton	● Boldly coloured leaves	++	Strong
Cyclamen	● Winter flowering	+	Strong
Ferns (2)	● Large choice of leaf shapes and shades of green	+++	Semi-shade
Ficus (F. elastica, F. benjamina, F. pumila, etc.)	● A huge family ranging from shrubs with large leaves to hanging plants with very small leaves	++	Strong
Kalanchoe	● Flowers in autumn and winter	++	Strong
Peace lily	● Green leaves, white flowers	+	Strong
Pineapple	● Clump of long thorny leaves	++	Strong
Poinsettia (3)	● Naturally winter flowering	+	Strong
Radermachera	● Cut-out shiny leaves; can spend summer outdoors	++	Strong
Schefflera	● High stems with shiny-palmed leaves	+	Semi-shade

TIMELY TIP

Give plants a shower

If you do ask a neighbour to water your indoor plants over a weekend, make it a quick and painless job for them by putting all your pot plants in the shower recess or bath. One quick burst of water from the shower or a watering can and the job is done!

Water while you're away

▶ The quickest, easiest and simplest solution is to get a friend or neighbour to come in and water your indoor plants for you when you're away.

▶ Try watering using thick string. Wet the string and bury one end in a few centimetres of soil with the other end curled in a dish of water. Capillary action draws water to the plant.

▶ Put all your indoor plants together in a room that stays light even when the house is all closed up, and give them a good watering before you head off.

▶ Set up your own 'automatic' watering system. Buy porous terracotta irrigation cones – from a garden centre, hydroponic specialist or online – that screw onto plastic water bottles. Fill the bottles then leave them to do their work.

React quickly to problems

▶ Watch out for pests and diseases. When you notice a problem, take the affected plant outdoors to a sheltered spot and away from other indoor plants, to avoid cross-contamination.

▶ Apply pesticide a.s.a.p. Use a general low-toxic insecticide or spray oil for insects such as aphids, scale or two-spotted mite. Apply a fungicide for fungal problems. If in doubt, look for all-purpose products.

▶ Don't use an excessive dose of insecticide, and follow the label instructions. Most require repeat spraying in 7 to 10 days.

▶ Always be suspicious of new plants – they may harbour pest or disease problems. Put a new arrival to one side for a few days: if there's a problem, it will be easier to treat in isolation.

Simple potting tips

▶ Feed and care for a pot plant properly and it will fill the whole volume of its pot.

▶ Transplant potted plants that have outgrown their container into a larger one with new potting mix.

▶ Repot your plants in spring, and in the case of flowering plants, after they have flowered.

▶ Copiously water a pot plant a few hours before it's repotted. To remove the plant more easily, turn the pot upside down in your hand.

▶ Don't try to save time by putting a small plant in a big pot. It won't thrive and is a waste of potting mix and space, and you'll only have to repot further down the track.

▶ When repotting, always use a bagged mix that's formulated for the type of plant you're growing (such as orchids or African violets).

▶ Check that the pot has a drainage hole (if not, drill or make holes in the base of the pot). To prevent soil leaching from the pot, cover drainage holes with a square of mesh or flywire.

TIMELY TIP

Rain on down

Save time on regular maintenance by taking indoor plants outside on a rainy day, especially during the warmer months. The plants get a good watering and the leaves will be washed and dusted in a flash. Let them drain before bringing the pots inside, but don't leave them outside when the sun comes out, or you risk burning their leaves.

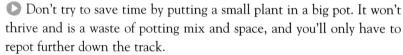

TIMELY TIP

Top it up
Make indoor plants thrive by giving them a good watering after repotting, and add more potting mix or soil if the soil level drops after watering.

Gardening tools

TIMELY TIP

Save your energy

With ratchet secateurs and pruners (large, long-handled secateurs), cutting branches is child's play. because this system literally gives you 10 times the strength. You'll work faster and won't tire so quickly.

Tips for buying tools

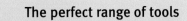

▶ Go for quality and you'll save time. It's better to have a limited number of good-quality tools than a multitude of useless gadgets.

▶ Choose tools that are properly adapted to your build. In particular, take note of tool handles (spades and forks for instance): regardless of whether they're made of wood, metal or plastic resin, handles need to be solid and light, and always suitable for your hands.

▶ Motorised tools, such as leaf blowers, are great time savers, though they're often quite noisy. Use them appropriately and in moderation.

CAUTION!

Disposable blades

Tools with stainless-steel blades are practical time savers because they're easier to maintain. Just be aware that you'll have to replace a worn blade because you won't be able to sharpen it.

The perfect range of tools

You don't need a complete range of garden tools, but what you do have should be sturdy and functional. Buy tools to suit your specific gardening needs. Well-maintained tools will last you many years.

Working the soil
- Flat spade (1)
- Fork (2)
- Rake (3)

Removing weeds and aerating
- Hoe (4)
- Weeding hoe (5)

Pruning
- Long-handled pruner
- Pruning handsaw
- Secateurs (6)

Planting
- Garden claw (7)
- Trowel (8) and fork
- Bulb planter (9)

Watering
- Watering can with a rose
- Hose and trigger nozzle (10)

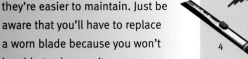

Simple tips for gardening tools

▶ Choose brightly coloured tools. Mark green or blue tools, or those with plain wooden handles, with coloured adhesive tape so you can find them quickly amongst greenery.

▶ For steel cutting tools (spades, forks, hedge trimmers or hoes), fill a box or bucket with sand soaked in oil (use the leftover oil in containers of car engine oil, for example). Stand the tools vertically in the sand next to each other. The sand will remove the soil from the tools and the oil will protect them from rust.

▶ Do a bit of general maintenance on garden tools during winter. It'll only take half a day to brush and wipe them using an oily cloth, sharpen any blades, oil wooden handles, tighten screws, etc. You'll be ready for the big jobs in spring and summer, without any time wasted.

TIMELY TIP

Getting the edge

Use an edge trimmer to finish off pathway edges and banks after mowing: they're easy to handle and can fit everywhere for a clean result in the blink of an eye. If you have a lot of edge trimming to do, opt for a lightweight trimmer.

▶ CAUTION!

Prevent the spread of disease

After pruning diseased plants, wipe the secateur blades with a rag soaked in alcohol, disinfectant or bleach to avoid contaminating other plants, and always remove sap and plant residue, too, which dulls the blades.

Watering

How to water wisely

Watering is an important and unavoidable part of gardening, but it's also an area where you can improve efficiency and save time. But remember always to check for any local water restrictions.

▶ The most efficient times to water are early morning and sunset. In warm weather, water in the evening. This will give plants the whole night to benefit from the coolness and you won't have to water so often.

▶ If you have an automatic watering system, set it to work in the evening or overnight, if possible.

TIMELY TIP

Grouping together

Group flowering pot plants together, especially if they're small. Place them on a saucer, or on a tray containing gravel, and keep it moist by watering several times a week – the plants benefit from the moisture resulting from them being so close together. Watering will be easier and faster than with pots spread throughout the whole garden.

▶ No matter what the time of day, if a plant is showing signs of stress due to a lack of water, give it a quick drink (you can conserve water by using a watering can instead of a hose).

▶ Water less often but in greater quantities – often referred to as deep watering. The water soaks into the soil, encouraging plant roots to head down deeper, following the water as it infiltrates the ground. The ground below the surface stays damp for several days, which saves you time and encourages strong, healthy plants.

▶ Install micro-irrigation – a network of hoses fitted with drippers or tiny sprayers that have a small diameter, where water circulates under low pressure. A small control box located between the tap and the main hose regulates the pressure, making it ideal for watering terrace, courtyard, balcony or backyard vegetable gardens.

Automated watering

To free yourself completely from the need to water your garden, and to save even more time, the best solution is automation.

▶ Pre-program start and stop times. More advanced watering systems allow you to program the starting time of all the system outlets in your garden by choosing the day they operate and the duration of the watering time for each one.

▶ Connect the watering system control to a moisture meter, which stops watering when it's raining, and direct the whole thing via a computer or remote-control unit.

▶ Install a double tap. Attach the automatic watering system to one tap head and leave the other one free for ready access to outdoor water so that you can fill a bucket quickly and easily.

TIMELY TIP

Trick to wetting soil

If you're having trouble getting water to soak into large areas of your garden, use a rewetting agent applied via an ordinary garden hose (it's quicker and more efficient than using a bucket or watering can and is easier on your back). This treatment is vital in sandy soils or after extended dry periods.

Working the soil

TIMELY TIP

Break up the soil
Rather than dig by hand, try a U-bar digger or scarifier: the blade is inserted into compact soil, allowing you to aerate without turning the soil over, so you avoid disturbing micro-organisms in the ground. They're easy tools to use, and it's less stressful for your back, so you can work a larger surface area in the one session.

When to wield the spade

Gardening isn't all about endless, time-consuming digging. With good initial preparation, hard digging can be kept to a minimum.

▶ When you're beginning to plant a new part of your garden, spend time digging over the surface to remove weeds and stones, and to break up clods of earth. Dig to at least the depth of your spade, as this is roughly the depth of most root activity of the plants you'll grow. Follow up by spreading manure or compost over the soil, then dig it in well so it blends with the soil. Leave the soil to settle for a few days or weeks before planting.

▶ To dig heavy ground, work in parallel lines using only a spade and a spading fork. Choose light ones that are easy to handle and that are adapted to your body shape (try tools out in the shop before buying).

Mulching and hoeing

Minimise the amount of digging you need to do by mulching and hoeing in between your digging sessions.

▶ Mulch (from your compost heap) decomposes into the soil over time, enriching it and ensuring a good granular structure. For maximum effect, spread compost onto loose, clean soil. Add a generous layer – several centimetres thick – and top it up several times during the year. As a result, you won't need to dig as often.

Power in your hands
Don't automatically reach for a spade – a petrol-powered cultivator makes easy, fast work of digging. If you need to redo the lawn or prepare large vege-table gardens for planting, hire a cultivator. It's well worth the expense if the surface you're digging exceeds 50 square metres.

Take the no-dig approach

If you don't want to dig the soil, simply lay down newspaper or cardboard and build up a garden bed on top. The newspaper or cardboard provides a physical barrier to weeds. To support the raised soil, make an edging with timber, bricks or even straw bales.

▶ Hoeing once is better than watering twice. By breaking up the surface, hoeing allows water to quickly soak in and prevents it from evaporating – a guaranteed saving of both time and water!

▶ If your soil is enriched with organic matter and heavily mulched, occasional hoeing is all that's required. Start hoeing in spring before sowing or planting, then spread out a good layer of mulch on top of the soil. Hoe again in summer, if necessary, if the mulch has broken down into the soil and weeds have developed.

Get the hoe happening

If weeds appear after digging, don't panic, just grab a hoe and chip them out. Most can be left on the soil's surface to dry out and break down.

TIMELY TIP

Feeding and fertilising

Quick homemade compost

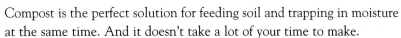

Compost is the perfect solution for feeding soil and trapping in moisture at the same time. And it doesn't take a lot of your time to make.

▶ In a pile, store alternate layers of vegetable peelings, grass clippings, leaves, weeds and finely chopped up prunings or larger biodegradable waste. A layer of soil or sprinkling of manure every now and then keeps the heap damp and adds a culture of micro-organisms.

▶ Facilitate faster decomposition in your compost heap by chopping up kitchen scraps and vegetable waste very finely.

▶ Manage your compost heap well to increase the temperature (to around 80°C), which will break down the vegetable matter, kill parasites and diseases, as well as seeds from the weeds. In a few months – without much effort and at no cost – you'll have good compost, which is ready to be incorporated into your garden beds.

▶ Make a compost heap over a base of around 1 square metre, or tip the waste into a construction made up of small walls, wire mesh or planks.

▶ Accelerate decomposition by adding nitrogen to the compost in the form of cow or horse manure, or commercial blood-and-bone mix. Or water it regularly with slurry from nettles, or simply water it with some diluted activator (available from garden centres).

(*See also* 'Don't forget the compost', on page 375.)

TIMELY TIP

From kitchen to compost

If you make your own compost, sort out reusable waste by putting a second bin in your kitchen. Make sure it has a lid and is easy to clean and transport. Then simply empty fruit and vegetable peelings, coffee grounds and eggshells into the bucket to be carried to the compost heap.

A boost for flowering pot plants

▶ Use liquid fertiliser for flowering window boxes and container plants. To enjoy petunia or geranium blooms all summer long, give them a dose of special flowering fertiliser every two weeks.

▶ Save time on feeding a group of plants at the same time by preparing a large watering can of fertiliser (diluted according to the manufacturer's instructions). Apply it generously to all your flowering plants, after watering, to avoid burning them with a concentration that's too strong.

TIMELY TIP

Fast nutritional watering

Note how many capfuls of fertiliser you need to put into the watering can, how many pots it feeds and how much time it takes to do the watering. Having a set routine helps make the job proceed faster.

Propagating and planting

Guaranteed successful seed sowing

▶ Don't be in too much of a hurry. Seeds sown in soil that's cold or water-logged have little chance of producing vigorous plants. In warmer weather, and with longer hours of sunlight and well-watered soil, you'll have everything on your side: the seeds germinate successfully and quickly.

▶ Allow two or three weeks to pass after the last frosts. If you live in an area that experiences prolonged heavy rains, wait for the soil to dry out sufficiently before you get started.

▶ Sow in soil that has been properly prepared. Work your soil over in autumn or winter, digging in well-decomposed compost.

▶ If you don't get around to preparing in advance, give the area you're going to sow a quick once-over by weeding and loosening the soil. To do this, pull out all the weeds, use a hoe to break up all the large clumps of earth, then even the soil out using a rake.

TIMELY TIP

Easy-sow vegetables

Large seeds – such as those of pumpkins, corn, peas and beans – and seeds that germinate quickly – such as rocket seeds– can be direct-sown, which saves you having to sow them into a container first, then transplanting. Also, direct-sow root vegetables such as carrots and turnips, which do not transplant well.

It's all about timing

▶ Don't use seeds that have passed their use-by date because they often fail to germinate, which is disappointing and a waste of time. The longevity of seeds varies according to the species and how the seed is stored. Some seeds, such as cabbage, can germinate years after they've formed, whereas others, such as peas or beans, lose their viability after two or three years.

Fast sowing

▶ The simplest and fastest way to sow seeds is by scattering them. This is generally the best option if you need to fill in gaps in banks of flowers or in the vegetable garden to sow a plot of radish. Take a handful of seeds and scatter them using a broad sweep of your arm.

▶ Ensure an even scattering of seed by mixing seeds with dry sand: they'll be less dense and spread out better. Scatter a fine layer of soil or rake very gently with your hand to cover the seeds, then water them with a fine spray.

▶ To form clumps of luxurious plantings – for example with beans, nasturtiums or sweet peas – sow in pockets: place four or five seeds in a hole that is a few centimetres wide.

▶ To form a row, space the pockets about 20 cm apart, but only use this technique with larger seeds.

▶ Keep unused seeds in their packets in an airtight container, stored in a cool, dry place.

CAUTION!

Declare war on fungus

When reusing containers such as pots or seed trays, brush off the soil, rinse them, then dip them in a bleach solution to make sure they're sterile. Otherwise, old spores from pathogenic fungi can invade new seedlings or cuttings.

TIMELY TIP

Striking magic

To speed up root formation on cuttings, use powder containing a hormone that encourages the process. Dip the end of the freshly cut cutting into the powder, tap on it to remove the excess, then plant the cutting in soil.

How to take cuttings

Taking cuttings is a simple, quick way to propagate plants so that you can multiply all sorts of species in your garden, and it's cheap!

▶ Take cuttings when new growth has developed to a stage where it's firm (or 'hardened off'). Cuttings at this stage are called semi-hardwood and are readily found on plants in late spring and summer. Roses, buddleias, clematis, camellias, gardenias, fuchsias, lavender and many Australian native plants can all be struck using semi-hardwood cuttings.

▶ Take sections of stem about 10 cm long. Remove the leaves and plant the cuttings in a mixture of sand and peat (or look for pre-prepared propagation mix). If they're kept damp and at the right temperature, the cuttings will have formed roots by autumn and be ready to plant by the following spring. Once a cutting has struck (formed roots), transfer it to its own pot to grow to a size that's ready for transplanting into the garden.

TIMELY TIP

Propagating rhizomes

Propagating plants with rhizomes, such as iris, day lily and bamboo, is incredibly easy – take a portion of rhizome that has roots and simply replant it. With bamboo, if you remove the young shoots that bother you in the spring, dig up the part of the rhizome that has roots, cut it off and put it into a pot immediately.

Water treatment

Some plants can be propagated rapidly simply by putting cuttings in a bottle of water, as is the case with oleander, papyrus and impatiens.

▶ Start your cutting by snipping off a section of stem about 10 cm long, making the cut just below a node (leaf junction). Remove all flower buds, flowers and fruit and all leaves apart from those on the very end (if they're large, cut them back to reduce their size by one-third). Place the stem in the neck of a bottle filled with water. Roots will appear after one to four weeks.

▶ For papyrus, place the stem head down in the water. Roots, followed by a young shoot, will form after a few weeks.

Layering – getting roots ready for use

Layering is a simple method for multiplying shrubs.

▶ Put a branch into contact with the soil, either by keeping part of the branch buried using a U-shaped wire, or simply by letting it lie on the ground in a cool area where there's loose soil.

▶ The easiest plants to layer are climbing plants, such as clematis and wisteria, along with certain shrubs that have very supple low branches, such as azaleas, currant bushes and rhododendrons.

TIMELY TIP

Ready-made pot plants

If you don't have time to do your own planting, buy ready-made pot plants, hanging baskets and window boxes year-round from a garden centre.

Dividing perennial clumps

▶ Dig up perennial plants, such as lady's mantle or perennial geranium, at the end of autumn and divide the clump. After a few years, clumps tend to become bare in the centre and proliferate on the outside, so need to be divided to prevent gaps appearing in your garden design.

▶ Remove the clump from the ground and separate it into two. Make fast work of a dense clump by using two garden forks placed back to back as a lever. Remove the dead parts in the centre and keep the ones on the edge. Replant the divided clumps immediately in a pot or in the ground, then firm down the earth around them and water thoroughly.

Soak before planting

▶ Before preparing your work site, start by immersing seedlings and potted plants in water to make sure their roots are well hydrated. Do this regardless of the type of plant: flowers, vegetables or shrubs all benefit.

▶ Dunk the larger pots of trees and shrubs into a tub or large bucket. Leave them to soak up as much water as they can (air bubbles cease when the root ball is saturated).

▶ While you're soaking the plants, prepare the planting holes so that they're ready for the plants to go straight in.

Refreshing large pots

For very large pots and big plants, replace the process of repotting by surfacing instead. This is a great technique for saving time.

● Remove the first 3–4 cm of the potting mix in the pot using a small garden claw to scratch the soil without damaging the roots.

● Replace this with fresh potting mix for plants and add some slow-release fertiliser pellets. Mix it in gently using the garden claw. As you water, nutrients filter into the root system.

● Add a thin layer of compost or organic mulch over the surface to conserve water and nourish the plant.

TIMELY TIP

Premium quality

Not all potting mixes are the same. In Australia, look for those that meet the Australian Standard. Premium mix costs more, but contains a slow-release fertiliser that can support plant growth for many months.

Water for results

▶ Always water-in after planting, even if it's raining or you've soaked the roots. Pour a generous amount of water directly at the foot of each plant using a hose or long-spouted watering can. Watering helps plants to settle in more quickly and it also removes air pockets. If the soil or potting mix slumps, add more.

▶ Spare your back and put plant containers in their place before you water them – they're much lighter to lift.

▶ If soil runs through the potting mix without saturating the soil, apply a soil-wetting agent to the water – you'll be amazed by how well it works!

Pruning

When a chainsaw is called for ...

▶ Get help to cut a large branch or a dead tree with a chainsaw. To do this job rapidly and safely, it's essential to have two people: while one person is handling the chainsaw, the other person guides the branches as they fall. If you're not experienced, get someone to do the job for you.

▶ If you have to cut down large trees, don't hesitate to call on the professionals. Trying to cut down trees by yourself is time-consuming and can prove to be extremely dangerous, with disappointing results.

Trim hedges fast and well

▶ Trim conifer hedges twice a year, at the end of spring and in autumn, and your hedge of evergreen hardwoods at least once a year. Informal hedges can be left unpruned, save for the occasional removal of old branches or congested growth.

▶ Assemble all the garden tools you'll need before you start, to make the job run smoothly, including a sharpened set of shears or an electric hedge cutter (this tool represents a real time saving if your hedge is more than 10 metres long), protective goggles, leather gloves, brightly coloured rope to serve as a guide and a stepladder or a scaffolding ladder on wheels.

TIMELY TIP

A prune-free zone
Choose shrubs that don't need pruning and you'll save an enormous amount of time in the garden. Examples include witch hazel, camellias and magnolias.

▶ Start by evening out the sides of the hedge, working from bottom to top, then cut the top of the hedge. The shape of the hedge should be trapezoid – in other words, wider at the bottom than at the top – to allow light to reach all parts of the plant.

Get the most out of your roses

Not all roses need to be cut back hard. Many climbing roses and spring-flowering roses need only a simple prune in spring after flowering, so don't make the job more involved than it needs to be.

▶ Prune away any dead, damaged or old branches, to keep a rose bush healthy and aerated. And remove branches that are in an awkward place, or those that grow to become tangled in the centre of the plant (1).

▶ Shrub roses need more rigorous pruning. In winter, shorten all the branches above the buds that are turned towards the outside. Cut on an angle just above a bud (2). In late summer, prune roses again, but not as hard, to encourage a flush of new growth and lots of autumn flowers.

Care for climbing plants

▶ During the first few years, cut back climbing plants to give them more strength and flexibility, and secure branches to train them to grow against the structure they're climbing on.

▶ Save time by attaching climbing branches using plastic fasteners, which are easy to remove or adjust.

▶ Climbers such as clematis and various roses can take some time to settle on their support in the desired shape, but once they have reached adult size, general maintenance is reduced. Each year in autumn, undertake a major clean-up to remove dead branches or branches that are in a bad position, then after flowering, in late spring or summer, simply shorten branches that are too invasive.

▶ For more exuberant plants such as wisteria, honeysuckle and jasmine, repeat this operation two or three times during the summer.

TIMELY TIP

A profusion of roses

To encourage rose bushes to bloom abundantly, cut the spent flowers after the first flowering, just under the flower cluster. At the same time, remove any diseased leaves and destroy the waste. Then you'll be able to make the most of your rose bushes until autumn!

Prevention and treatment

Prevention is better than cure

▷ If plant matter shows signs of disease, bin it immediately. Do the same with rotten fruit, sick plants or diseased branches. These preventive actions will protect your garden from diseases and allow you to save the time spent on treatments.

▷ Remain vigilant. Don't grab your spray gun as soon as you see an aphid, but don't let yourself be surprised by a sudden epidemic either! If you notice a diseased leaf or infected fruit, remove it immediately. Later on, if you find the disease has spread, get your spray gun into action.

Safety before everything

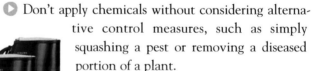

Take a few necessary precautions when gardening and you'll avoid time-wasting complications that occur when you're not adequately protected.

▷ Don't apply chemicals without considering alternative control measures, such as simply squashing a pest or removing a diseased portion of a plant.

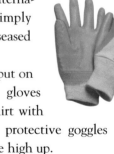

▷ When using chemical controls, put on the necessary protective clothing: gloves and boots along with a mask, a shirt with long sleeves and a hat. Put on protective goggles if you're treating plants that are high up.

▷ After using a chemical treatment, rinse your tools several times, and store poisonous products under lock and key, then carefully wash your hands.

TIMELY TIP

Ready to go

For small problems, buy ready-to-use preparations. These save time and require no special preparation. Always read the safety instructions before using any plant treatment spray.

▶ **CAUTION!**

Remove unhappy plants

The more fragile the plant, the easier prey it becomes for insects, fungus or bacteria, and it will either fail to thrive or require costly treatment, which wastes both time and resources. If a plant is struggling, remove it.

Dealing with pests

▶ Before treating a pest or disease problem in your garden, buy the appropriate materials to enable you to act quickly. And work out whether it's a pest or a disease you're dealing with.

▶ Only prepare as much spray or drench as is needed for one treatment.

▶ Always follow dilution rates, application recommendations and heed safety precautions on the product label.

▶ A spray gun provides better coverage of treatments and is worth the investment if you have large plants, or vegetable or fruit crops that are likely to need regular attention.

TIMELY TIP

Biological weapons

Use natural enemies to combat parasites, or make treatments that are simple and fast to apply as a chemical product your first choice (avoiding those that cause harm to other living organisms). New alternative biological gardening products are coming onto the market all the time, so make enquiries at your local garden centre.

Calendar of interventions

SEASON	TREATMENT	PLANTS
Winter	● Winter treatment, insecticide oils	Fruit trees
	● Copper sulphate (fungicide)	Deciduous trees and shrubs
	● Treatment against peach leaf curl	Peach trees
Late winter	● Selective weeding	Lawn
	● Total weeding	Pathways and terraces
	● Anti-moss treatment	Lawn
Spring	● Treatment against aphids	Fruit trees, roses
	● Combat slugs and snails	Vegetable garden, bulbs, perennials
	● Treatment against fungus	Roses, trees and fruit trees
Summer	● Selective weeding	Lawn if necessary
	● Black-spot treatment (fungicide)	Roses
	● Fruit-fly control	Soft fruits such as peaches and tomatoes
Autumn	● Pick up dead leaves and damaged fruit and destroy them	Trees and fruit trees

Safety and maintenance

TIMELY TIP

Secure window boxes

Take precautions with fastening systems when you buy window boxes or pots for a terrace or balcony. Once planters are filled with potting mix they become heavy and dangerous if they fall. Instead, use an approved fastening system or call in a handyman to do the job for you.

Take care with chemicals and equipment

▶ To dilute any garden chemical – to fill a spray gun or to calculate the right dose – you always need containers, a funnel or a graduated measure. Buy or use special containers for garden-chemical use only. Mark these utensils in a very visible way: a large red cross, for example, to avoid potentially dangerous confusion.

▶ Always rinse containers after use and store them in a toxic products' cupboard so they're always to hand when you need them.

▶ Never use kitchen implements in the garden and never dispense chemicals into recycled food containers – even if you have marked them as poisonous.

▶ Have one spray unit for herbicides only and another for pesticides, to avoid damaging garden plants by using the same container, which may contain poison residues.

CAUTION!

Snake alert

In Australia and South Africa, snakes can slither into gardens – even in suburban areas – usually during summer. To reduce the risk of unwelcome visitors, keep grass areas well mown, block off underfloor access and keep your backyard free of rubbish.

Avoid wasp and bee stings

▶ Don't grow plants and flowers that attract bees and wasps on a terrace or patio (e.g. thyme or lavender). The same goes for eating, swimming and play areas.

▶ Have antihistamine products handy, and if someone is stung by a bee in your garden, make sure you know what to do (see 'Don't wait to treat a bee sting', on page 127). If someone who is allergic to bee or wasp stings gets stung, don't waste time – call an ambulance immediately and administer adrenaline, if appropriate.

▶ Avoid being stung by wearing shoes when you're walking outdoors.

Consult a tree surgeon

If you're worried about a mature tree call a tree surgeon, don't remove it. Most trees are covered by protection orders so you'll need council approval before acting.

TIMELY TIP

Take care with toxic plants

Certain plants have parts that are toxic to humans and animals.

▶ Watch out for plants that can cause poisoning or induce allergic reactions including asthma, swelling and skin rashes. This is the case with yew and lily of the valley berries, digitalis, Scotch broom and datura flowers. Some grevilleas and rhus cause skin allergies, and dogs can be allergic to wandering Jew.

▶ If you have young children, avoid planting toxic plants near play areas. Keep the contact number for your local poison centre near the phone at all times, and don't hesitate to call if you are in any doubt about a toxic plant or reaction to a plant.

▶ If you're unsure of the name of the plant that caused a reaction, save time and potential complications by putting a piece of it in a plastic bag, then take it with you to the hospital.

Keep your gutters clear

▶ Stay one step ahead and cover guttering with leaf guard or mesh to prevent dead leaves from accumulating, especially if you have trees close to your house. Blocked drains often result in water leaks that cause time-wasting complications of varying seriousness.

▶ Blocked gutters are also a fire hazard during bushfire season, so make a habit of cleaning them out regularly throughout summer.

▶ If you have a rainwater tank, keep gutters, downpipes and tank inlets leaf-free to maximise the volume of water you can harvest.

TIMELY TIP

Personal comfort

When you're working outdoors, especially during the summer months, keep in the shade, wear a hat and drink plenty of water to avoid a case of sunstroke, which can put you out of action for some time. Work in the early morning and late afternoon.

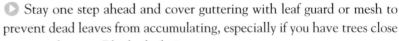

⮕ **CAUTION!**

Safe electricity

Remember to install electrical sockets that correspond to safety requirements for outdoor use. They make using electrical equipment outdoors safer and easier because there's no need for extension cords.

Index

Credits

The pictures in *10,001 Timesaving Ideas* were supplied by the people and agencies listed below. Any images not listed are the copyright of Reader's Digest.

Photographs

Abbreviations: t: top, c: centre, b: bottom, l: left, r: right.

front cover istockphoto.com. **back cover** *tr* istockphoto.com; *cl* CASTORAMA. **end-papers** istockphoto.com. **1** CASTORAMA. **2** istockphoto.com. **4** istockphoto.com. **6** Digital Vision. **10** istockphoto.com. **12** *t* istockphoto.com; *b* photodisc. **15** *tr* istockphoto.com. **16** *b* IKEA France S.N.C/© inter IKEA systems B.V.2004. **17** istockphoto.com. **18** *t* SMEG/ Service Conseil. **18** *b* Michel Gilbert/De Dietrich. **20** *tl* istockphoto.com; *cr* Société THALAS-SOR. **21** *cr* istock-photo.com; *bl* istock-photo.com. **22** *t* IKEA France S.N.C/ © inter IKEA systems B.V.2004; *c* IKEA France S.N.C/© inter IKEA systems B.V.2004; *b* CONFORAMA. **23** *b* CON-FORAMA. **26** *t* Thethirdman/ Dreamstime; *bl* istockphoto.com; *br* Lands' End. **27** *t* istock-photo.com; *b* CONFORAMA. **28** *t* flymeubles.com; *b* istockphoto.com. **29** *c* IKEA France S.N.C/© inter IKEA systems B.V.2004. **30** *tr* istockphoto.com. **32** *tl* Digital Vision at Home; *cr* istock-photo.com. **33** *cr* Digital Vision at Home. **35** *t* Michael Kempf/Dreamstime; *b* Duard Van Der Westhuizen/Dreamstime. **36** *cr* crédit photo HAGER; *bl* istock-photo.com. **37** *b* istockphoto.com. **38** *cl* HORIZON/A. SCHREINER; *br* istock-photo.com. **39** *t* istockphoto.com; *b* istockphoto.com. **40** *cr* Photodisc. **41** *bl* istockphoto.com. **42** *t* Digital vision. **43** *b* Photodisc. **44** *cl* MIELE; *cr* Dyson; *br* istockphoto.com. **46** *tl* Photo JPG.SAS. **51** *t* Digital vision. **52** *t* Corbis. **53** *tr* Photodisc. **53** *cl* istockphoto.com. **55** *cr* Kohler. **58** *c* MIELE. **59** *tr* DOMENA. **61** *cr* istockphoto.com. **62** *tl* Polivac International Pty Ltd. **63** *cr* istock-photo.com. **66** *tr* MIELE. **68** *tr* istock-photo.com. **68** *bl* istockphoto.com. **72** *cl* LA REDOUTE - Catalogue AH 04/05. **73** *cl* Photodisc. **74** *tr* Corbis; *bl* istock-photo.com. **75** *tl* LAGUELLE. **76** *bl* istock-photo.com. **78** *c* Corbis. **82** *tr* Ashley Whitworth/Dreamstime. **83** *c* Corbis. **85** *tl* istockphoto.com; *c* istockphoto.com. **87** *br* Getty Image/Photodisc. **88** *t* istock-photo.com. **89** *tl* istockphoto.com; *cr* istock-

photo.com. **90** *br* Photodisc. **91** *br* istock-photo.com. **92** istockphoto.com. **94** *bl* Kristian Sekulic/ Dreamstime. **95** *tr* istockphoto.com. **96** *tl* istock-photo.com. **97** *tl* istockphoto.com; *br* istock-photo.com. **98** *br* istockphoto.com. **99** *tl* GRACO; *cr* GRACO; *bl* istock-photo.com. **101** *bl* AVENT; *br* istock-photo.com. **102** *cl* istockphoto.com; *cr* istockphoto.com; *br* AVENT. **103** *tl* istockphoto.com; *cr* Société VERT BAUDET/Collection Printemps-été; *br* Société VERT BAUDET/Collection Printemps-été. **104** *cr* istockphoto.com. **105** *tl* Société VERT BAUDET/Collection Printemps-été; *br* Getty Image/Photodisc. **106** *tl* Société VERT BAUDET/Collection Printemps-été. **107** *tr* istockphoto.com; *bl* istockphoto.com. **108** *tr* istockphoto.com; *bl* istockphoto.com. **109** *bl* Photodisc. **110** *tl* istockphoto.com; *cr* istockphoto.com. **111** *tr* istockphoto.com; *b* Lands' End. **112** istockphoto.com. **113** *br* Photodisc. **114** *tr* SOCIETE BIC; *b* istockphoto.com. **115** *tr* istockphoto.com; *b* istockphoto.com. **116** *tr* istockphoto.com; *b* istockphoto.com. **117** *cr* istockphoto.com; *bl* istockphoto.com. **118** *tr* Comstock Pet Vet; *bl* Comstock Pet Vet. **119** *tl* istockphoto.com; *cr* istock-photo.com. **120** *cl* Alexey Stiop/ Dreamstime; *cr* Comstock Pet Vet. **121** Comstock Pet Vet. **122** *tl* armoire-ROSSIGNOL SA-Route de Saint-Cénéré 53150 Monisûr. **124** *cl* istockphoto.com. **125** *bl* istockphoto.com. **126** *bl* Jaimie Duplass/Dreamstime. **127** *bl* istock-photo.com. **128** *cr* istockphoto.com; *bl* istockphoto.com. **129** *t* istockphoto.com. **130** *tr* istockphoto.com. **131** *cr* SUISSES/ DOUBL D. **133** istockphoto.com. **134** Jonathan Kantor/Getty Images. **135** *cl* Matthew Ward/Getty Images; *br* Brinkstock/Dreamstime. **137** *bl* Stockbyte. **138** *tl* Stockbyte; *bl* Photodisc. **139** Stockbyte. **140** *tr* Photodisc; *bl* Stockbyte. **141** *t* istockphoto.com. **142** Photoalto. **144** *tr* Photodisc. **145** *tl* istockphoto.com. *bl* istockphoto.com. **146** *tl* Photodisc. **148** *bl* Stockbyte. **149** *t* Photoalto. **150** *tl* istockphoto.com; *c* istockphoto.com. **152** *tr* istockphoto.com. **153** *tr* istockphoto.com. **154** *tr* istock-photo.com; *bl* Niderlander/Dreamstime. **155** Pioneer. **156** *bl* istockphoto.com.

158 *tl* Alysta/Dreamstime; *bl* stock.photo.com. **159** *tr* Photodisc; *bl* istockphoto.com. **160** istockphoto.com. **161** *tl* Nico Smit/ Dreamstime; *cr* istockphoto.com. **162** *cl* Graça Victoria/Dreamstime; *br* Bartosz Ostrowski/Dreamstime. **163** *bl* Photodisc. **164** Photodisc. **170** istockphoto.com. **173** *bl* CANON Powershot A95. **174** *b* istockphoto.com. **177** Paul Maguire/Dreamstime. **178** *cl* istockphoto.com. **179** *tr* istock-photo.com. **179** *cr* Alexander Paterov/ Dreamstime. **182** istockphoto.com. **183** istockphoto.com. **184** istockphoto.com. **185** istockphoto.com. **186** *tl* istock-photo.com; *br* istockphoto.com. **187** istock-photo.com. **188** istockphoto.com. **189** Getty Images/Photodisc. **190** *tl* istock-photo.com; *br* istockphoto.com. **192** *cr* istockphoto.com; *bl* istockphoto.com. **193** istockphoto.com. **194** *cr* istock-photo.com; *bl* Fotosearch. **196** *tr* istock-photo.com. **197** *tl* istockphoto.com; *br* istockphoto.com. **198** *tl* istockphoto.com. **199** *c* istockphoto.com; *bl* istockphoto.com. **200** *cr* CASTORAMA. **202** *tl* istock-photo.com; *b* istockphoto.com. **203** *cr* istockphoto.com; *bl* istockphoto.com. **205** istockphoto.com. **206** istockphoto.com. **208** istockphoto.com. **209** *tr* istock-photo.com; *bl* istockphoto.com. **210** *tl* istockphoto.com; *br* istockphoto.com. **211** istockphoto.com. **212** istockphoto.com. **213** *tl* istockphoto.com; *c* istockphoto.com. **214** istockphoto.com. **215** istockphoto.com. **219** *cl* La Redoute- Catalogue AH 04/05; *br* La Redoute- Catalogue AH 04/05. **220** Patiwizz com le spécialiste culinaire. **221** *tr* Société Fortunat; *bl* istockphoto.com; *br* istockphoto.com. **222** *tl* GROUPE Seb (Calor, Krups, Moulinex, Rowenta, Seb, Tefal; *tr* GROUPE Seb (Calor, Krups, Moulinex, Rowenta, Seb, Tefal; *b* istock-photo.com. **223** *bl* C Squared Studios/ Getty Images. **226** Photoalto/F. Cirou, I. Rozenbaum. **227** *t* Photoalto/F. Cirou, I. Rozenbaum; *b* 3 SUISSES/SAMSUNG. **232** *br* istockphoto.com. **235** *tl* istock-photo.com. **236** *cr* Photodisc. **238** *bl* istock-photo.com. **240** *cl* Photodisc. **241** istock-photo.com. **242** *tr* BRANDX; *bl* Photoalto/ F. Cirou, I. Rozenbaum. **244** Photoalto/ F. Cirou, I. Rozenbaum. **245** *tr* Photoalto/ F. Cirou, I. Rozenbaum; *bl* Photoalto/Jean-Blaise Hall. **246** *tl* Photoalto/F. Cirou, I. Rozenbaum. **247** *tr* Mindrift/Dreamstime. **248** *tr* Photoalto/F. Cirou, I. Rozenbaum; *c* 3 Suisses. **249** *tl* istockphoto.com. **250** *tr* Photoalto/Jean-Blaise Hall. **251** Photodisc. **253** *cl* Photoalto/ Jean-Blaise Hall. **257** *tl* RESONANCES. **258** *cl* Photoalto/Jean-Blaise Hall. **259** *bl* Photoalto/I. Rozenbaum;

Illustrations

Product code: 041 3592
Concept code: US 4322/IC-FR